Testifyin'

Contemporary African Canadian Drama

Volume II

**edited by
Djanet Sears**

Playwrights Canada Press
Toronto • Canada

Playwrights Canada Press
54 Wolseley Street, 2nd Floor, Toronto, Ontario CANADA M5T 1A5
416-703-0013   fax 416-703-0059
orders@playwrightscanada.com • www.playwrightscanada.com

Playwrights Canada Press acknowledges the support of the taxpayers of Canada
and the province of Ontario through The Canada Council for the Arts and the
Ontario Arts Council.

Cover Design by Allen Booth. Cover Illustration by Lloyd Pollard.
Production Editor: Jodi Armstrong

National Library of Canada Cataloguing in Publication

Testifyin' : contemporary African Canadian drama / edited by Djanet
Sears. -- 1st ed.

Includes bibliographical references.

ISBN 0-88754-597-1 (v. 1).—ISBN 0-88754-664-1 (v. 2)

1. Canadian drama (English)--Black Canadian authors.
2. Canadian drama (English)--20th century. 3. Black Canadians--Drama.
I. Sears, Djanet

PS8307.T47 2000   C812'.5408'0896   C00-930559-9
PR9196.37.A37T47 2000

First edition: April 2003.
Printed and bound by AGMV Marquis at Quebec, Canada.

Dedication

— • —

To my extraodinary family:
Quisbert, Winnie, Rosemarie, Terese, Mark, Celia, Qwyn,
Kyla, VaNessah, Djustice, Ula, Cyrus, Adrien, Melanie, Arienne,
Milton, Sharon, Donald, Donny, Sherie and Danielle.

Without you and your incredible nurturing and support,
none of this would be possible.

ACKNOWLEDGEMENTS

— • — — • — — • —

An enormous thank you to Kate Lushington who took time to help me proofread this massive volume, and to Allen Booth whose graphic design of Lloyd Pollard's illustration so beautifully graces this cover.

Special thanks also go out to: The AfriCanadian Playwrights' Festival, Erica Phillps, Angela Rebeiro, Jodi Armstrong, George Elliott Clarke, Andrea Davis, Ajay Heble, ahdri zhina mandiela, Althea Prince, Natalie Rewa, Leslie Sanders, Rachael Van Fossen, Rinaldo Walcott, Pia Kleber, Don Shipley, Paul Perron, Laura Bennett, Mark Nicholson, Celia Chassels, Suzanne Depoe, Debbie Wood, Lillian Roberts, Lloyd Pollard, University College - University of Toronto, Guelph Jazz Festival, Julie Hastings, Dean Bowman, Yoon Choi, Eastern Front Theatre, Mary McBay, CanStage, Grant Ramsey, trey anthony, Ebony Haines, Cylla Von Tiedemann, John Karastamatis, Wade Gilpin, Rhoma Spencer, Tony Hall, Susan Sandiford, Shawn M. McDowell, Fred Ward, Barbara Barnes Hopkins, Rosanna Carter, S. Colvey, Andrew Moodie, Derwin Jordan, Andrew Jason Wade, Gordon King, Lorena Gale, George Boyd, Jeremiah Sparks, Lucky Campbell, Ken Kam, naila belvett, debbie young, bcurrent, Sandra Alland, Alison Sealy-Smith, Arcadia Housing Co-op, Serge Loubier, AGMV/Marquis.

Table of Contents

—•— —•— —•—

PREFACE

— • — — • — — • —

One evening, towards the end of a question and answer session, after a performance of *Harlem Duet*, a play that I had both written and directed, a woman leaped out of her seat, sending a multitude of superlatives in my direction. As she was about to finish speaking, she added, speaking from her own perspective as a white woman/woman of European descent, "This is not a Black play. This is an extraordinary human play!" The audience, half made up of people of colour, applauded enthusiastically. My response was kind, but immediate. "All Black plays are human plays! What part of the Black experience is not part of the human experience?" Most likely to the discomfort of the woman who spoke, I elaborated further. I wanted her and everyone else to understand that as a society our general perception of humanity is still astonishingly narrow.

The concept that the thoughts, ideas, creations, actions of people of African descent are not human is centuries old, and in this context reflects its unconscious yet powerful remains; certainly unconscious because this woman's heartfelt intent was to pay me an incredible compliment. However, it mirrors one of the intrinsic limitations in Western thought. Preeminent philosopher, Immanuel Kant (1724-1804), is considered one of the Western canons most important thinkers. Credited with formulating the under-pinnings of the Enlightenment, he contributed extensively not only to our thinking on metaphysics, science, and reasoning, but also to our ideas on racial classification:

> The Negroes of Africa have by nature no feeling that rises above the trifling. Mr. Hume challenges anyone to cite a single example in which a Negro has shown talents and asserts that among the hundreds of thousands of Blacks who are transported elsewhere from their countries, although many of them have even been set free, still not a single one was ever found who presented anything great in art or science or any other praiseworthy quality, even though among the whites some continually rise aloft from the lowest rabble, and through superior gifts earn respect in the world. So fundamental is the difference between these two races of man, and it appears to be as great in regard to mental capacities as in color. (Kant, 110-11) [1]

This "reasoning" which defines Blacks as non-human as or less than human is at the heart of the woman's genuine desire to compliment me. Her statement, "This is not a Black play. This is an extraordinary human play," reflects an internalization of Kant's colour codes and its implied hierarchy. Moreover, it covertly promotes me to human [read: white] status, notwithstanding the fact that the central issue of the drama is race, since it tells the story of Othello and his first wife (a Black woman), from her perspective. The woman's statement reflects the contradiction between her unconscious belief system and her experience at the theatre that evening. Furthermore, her words echo an age-old view on the cultural product of people of colour in general and those of us of African descent in particular. As Malaika Mutere so clearly points out:

> Although writing traditions exist on the African continent, Africans are primarily an oral people, and it is from this latter perspective that African cultural agency is best understood even in its Diasporan forms. Early observations made by European missionaries and anthropologists about African cultures had little understanding and much less appreciation of the principles that characterize and inform African life. For instance African dance would be described in pejorative terms such as "lewd ambling" or "imitative fornication," while oral tradition as a whole would be looked upon as "pre-logical" or "pre-rational." Implied in such statements are the related assumptions of a European "high art" or *haute-couture* (such as ballet), and that logic and rationalism belong solely in the domain of a European writing technology. In other words, according to these and later scholars who made their "universal" observations from a specifically European center, Africa doesn't measure up on the evolutionary scale of civilized culture. [2]

That the humanity of my play or the stories of people of African descent can still be called into question by mainstream audiences in this day and age is disturbing enough. However, judging from the initially positive reaction to this statement from the rest of the audience, 50% of whom were people of colour, suggests that there is a desperate need for us to examine our own investment in this prevailing perspective.

I am not attempting to beg for my own humanity here; that is a given. I also do not believe, as some, that I am a theatre practitioner who happens to be Black. One eager feminist (a group amongst whom I count myself) once asked me whether I considered myself "a woman or a Black" first. I was unable to answer the question to her satisfaction since I have always been both. While I do not disparage those who do feel that they just happen to be Black (Blackness is not monolithic and we do not all share the same beliefs), I do insist that my race is an intrinsic and even metaphysical force. I am, however, concerned about the internalization of the idea of whiteness as central and Blackness as periphery in the psyches of Black people. Moreover, what role does the limited selection and the inadequate opportunity for representation in literature and other cultural product, play in this matter?

I can still vividly recall the first time I read a book by a person of African descent (a privilege most people of European descent take for granted). I was seventeen and preparing to audition for the theatre program at York University when my high school drama teacher suggested that I look at a monologue from a play called *A Raisin in the Sun*, by Lorraine Hansberry. The play tells the story of a poor Black family living in a run-down tenement on Chicago's South Side. The patriarch of the family has died, leaving the surviving members of the family a large insurance settlement. Each has dreams of how this money could change their lives and lift them out of the poverty in which they find themselves. Mama, the matriarch of the family, sees that these divergent dreams are likely to tear her family apart. She takes the insurance money and buys a home in a predominantly white middle-class suburb. Her white neighbours fight to keep them out, but Mama struggles against the forces of white supremacy in order to attain her dream of owning her own home and keeping her family together.

I had never been to Chicago. I lived in Oakville, Ontario, a white middle-class suburb, and my family had owned their own home from as far back as I could recall. Nonetheless, in reading this play, I felt that this story spoke about me in a way I had never experienced before.

In a keynote interview at the millennium AfriCanadian Playwrights' Festival, Lloyd Richards, Canadian born, Tony award-winning Broadway director recounted an incident that took place during the pre-Broadway run of *A Raisin in the Sun*, in New Haven, Connecticut, in 1959. Standing outside the theatre watching the hordes of people (mainly white) line-up at box-office for tickets, he spied one woman in particular. She was Black, obviously poor, and stood out amongst the theatre's regular clientele. He approached her and asked her what made her come. She responded, "I heard that there was something going on in this theatre that concerns me."

Nearly two decades later my own experience of *A Raisin in the Sun*, is almost exactly the same as that Black woman's response in New Haven. Hansberry's play set me on a journey from which I hope never to return. It is the catalyst for my insatiable desire for stories by and about people of African descent, and is the motivating force behind my desire to present the dramatic writing of African Canadians in this anthology.

The success of *Testifyin': Contemporary African Canadian Drama: Volume I*, and the continued rise in the number of Black playwrights and Black productions taking place is this country has made the publication of *Volume II* essential. These writers for the stage are modern day griots who are not only engaged in the sacred art of telling their stories, but also span the gamut of dramatic styles, form and language. The extraordinary dramatic writings of each the nine playwrights contained in this volume are accompanied by nine equally remarkable introductions, penned by some of most noted scholars and practitioners in this country. This is a document testament to the cultural explosion taking place in Black drama today, reflecting a diversity of voice, origin, form and tone within Blackness and affirming the vitality of the theatrical arm of what is coming to be known as a Canadian Black Arts Movement.

The dramatic writings contained in this volume are not merely human plays, they are extraordinary Black Canadian plays. Moreover, they actively speak to something going on in the theatres across the country that not only concerns me, but concerns us all.

Djanet Sears
Adjunct Professor
University College
University of Toronto
March, 2003

Works Cited:

[1] Kant, Immanuel. *Observations on the Feeling of the Beautiful and Sublime.* 1764. Trans. John T. Goldstein. Berkeley: U of California P, 1960.

[2] MUTERE, MALAIKA. "African Culture and Aesthetics." http://artsedge.kennedy-center.org/aoi/resources/hg/aesthetics.html

Djanet Sears is an adjunct professor at University College, University of Toronto. She is the driving force behind the AfriCanadian Playwrights' Festival, a celebration and examination of African diasporic writing for the stage in Canada, and a founding member of the Obsidian Theatre Company. She is also the recipient of Canada's highest literary honour for dramatic writing: the Governor General's Literary Award (1998). She is the playwright and director of the multiple Dora Award-winning production of her stage play, *Harlem Duet*. Djanet is also the winner of several other prestigious awards: the Martin Luther King Jr. Achievement Award, the Floyd S. Chalmers Canadian Play Award (1998), the Harry Jerome Award for Excellence in the Cultural Industries, and a Phenomenal Woman of the Arts Award. Her writings for the stage include: *Afrika Solo* (Sister Vision Press, 1990), *Who Killed Katie Ross* (in *Taking the Stage*, Playwrights Canada Press, 1994), *Harlem Duet* (Scirocco Drama, 1997), and *The Adventures of a Black Girl in Search of God*, (Playwrights Canada Press, 2003).

Djanet is the editor of *Testifyin': Contemporary African Canadian Drama: Volume I* (Playwrights Canada Press, 2000), and *Tellin' It Like It Is: A Compendium of African Canadian Monologues for Actors* (Second Scene Editions, 2000), both firsts of their kind in this country. She is a contributing author in several published works including, *Women on the Canadian Stage: The Legacy of Hrotsvit* (Blizzard Publications, 1991), and has recently joined the editorial team of *Canadian Theatre Review*.

Angélique

Lorena Gale

Born in Montreal, Lorena is an award-winning actress, director and writer who has worked in theatres across Canada. *Je me souviens,* her second play, was a finalist for the Governer General's Award (2002), received 3 Jessie Richardson's Award nominations (2000) and was selected by the *Vancouver Sun* as one of The 10 Best Plays of 2000. Her first play *Angélique* had its American premiere at The Detroit Repertory Theatre and in New York, OFF Broadway at Manhattan Class Company Theatre, where it was nominated for 8 Audelco Awards (New York Black Theatre Awards). *Angélique* premiered at Alberta Theatre Projects Pan Canadian playRites Festival 98 and was nominated Outstanding New Play in Calgary's Betty Mitchell Awards. Lorena has published articles in *Canadian Theatre Review, CanPlay,* and her personal essay, "Where Beauty Sits," was published in the anthology *But Where Are You Really From* by Sister Vision Press. *What Colour is Black: Art, Politics and Racial Identity,* premiered in the Halfbred Performance Series at The Grunt Gallery. She is currently finishing her MALS at Simon Fraser University.

Presence out of a Book
Angélique for the Stage

by Natalie Rewa

— • — — • — — • —

They'll raise my name in challenge,
rallying resistance
and incendiary change.

Lorena Gale's powerful words appear in the final monologue as the actor playing Angélique "enacts" taking the noose from the hangman and putting it around her neck. The perspective in this final scene removes it from any historical verisimilitude of 1734 however, as Gale instructs the performer to step up to a microphone to deliver this contemporary elegy by the character for her historical self. Gale has taken as her focus Angélique, a slave imported from Madeira by a Flemish agent and bought by a Montreal ironworks entrepreneur for his wife, and inscribed in the history of Canada as a criminal convicted and hanged in 1734 on charges of arson. She uses her research to create a bracing, dramatic historiography of slavery and racist attitudes in the character of Marie Joseph Angélique, whom she describes in the *dramatis personæ* as: "a slave, in a history book (age 29)." The play emphasizes the difference between historical documentation and the immediacy of performance, insisting, by its *didascalia*, that live performance can resist the historical account by demonstrating the silent complicity between racism and gender politics in historical perspective. Gale maintains a historical Angélique until the penultimate scene when she directs this character to close the book from which other characters, dressed in modern dress, have been reading aloud an account of her torture. Gale's Angélique endures beyond the history book to perform the final monologue as the act of rallying resistance.

In addition to Angélique, Gale employs characters who represent the economic circumstances of slavery – owners, and those who are implicated by the historical account as part of Angélique's personal life – other slaves and an indentured servant from France. Perhaps one of the strongest comments on the representation of "an" Angélique is pointed to by a chorus of eyewitnesses who appear as on-screen *"verité"* documentation of character or testimony of Angélique's culpability. They form a bridge from an earlier reliance on printed historical reports to an analogous contemporary trial by media. This serves as an on-stage intrusion and casts great doubt on the record and thus, along with shifts in language, changes of costume and precise choreography, Gale offers a complex contemporary idiom for remembering.

Gale's play eschews a simple dramatization of Angélique's "life" using documented information. A few simple dates stand in for a biography of an adult woman – but Gale inserts these sparingly. Scenes in which the title figure is given the name of her owner's wife's dead sister, or when her children are named by the owner's wife and their birth and death dates unceremoniously recorded are unembellished by dialogue referring to Angélique's loss. These scenes, an acquiescence to "fact," make the project of recuperation of a figure from documents, transparent in theatricality. Gale sets the action in a theatrical time: "Now/1730s. Then is now. Now is then. Montreal 1700s," and with this consciousness she challenges an absolution from guilt by distance as a tenable position.

Visual and physical disturbances flow silently around the dialogue encouraging the spectator to take up the position of witness, to be conscious of the relationship and responsibility to and for an Other. Gale emphasizes that performance can explore "the concept of witnessing. As servants and slaves are essentially invisible, experiment with who sees what, knows what, etc." In scenes between Angélique and Thérèse, Gale takes up the relationship between the two women in terms of their modes of address: Angélique faces the spectators directly as in "a documentary" while Thérèse provides "a commentary" on naming the new slave after her sister (scene 3) – a moment which records the historical Angélique being created out of the imagination/ memory of her owner. Gale never creates or suggests a name for Angélique other than this inscribed one, thereby emphasizing her own resistance to the historical account pointing to what remains unknown and is thus lost.

Gale adopts a structure which disrupts narrative continuity by a very visible filter. Costume and language telescope the distance between the eighteenth and twenty-first centuries to display an interchangeability in attitudes and practice. Initially the seeming disjunction between periods emerges as if a slippage in language: Thérèse, dressed in an eighteenth century costume outlines Angélique's household duties including schedules for vacuuming and dry cleaning. While such interventions in domestic relations might disturb the clichés of the eighteenth century, Gale introduces an insightful critical feminism when Thérèse's economic status changes upon inheriting her husband's social and economic status. Thérèse is demurely dressed in a "stylish black business suit with the netting pulled over her face" at the funeral, but once she has faced down her husband's business partner and maintains control of her share of the company she wears a red power suit. She replaces her husband also in how she chooses to dispense with Angélique – as is convenient to her. This new businesswoman brokers no alliance with another woman, nor does she seek to create a new role for Angélique, but peremptorily, while sitting at her computer, informs Angélique that she has arranged her sale to Monsieur Cugnet in Quebec. Thérèse's twenty-first century costume is informed by an identifiable contemporary status quo – but Angélique's costume significantly remains throughout this sequence that of the eighteenth century. The empowerment for Thérèse leaves Angélique in an almost three-hundred-year-old void.

Gale's dramatization of the crossroads of power and race bring together for performance the clash of two narratives and the insufficiency of historical "re-enactment." Costumes become silent characters – leaving departures from the eighteenth century to dispense elegantly with physical setting, dialogue and expressions of outrage.

Gale also uses highly choreographed costume sequences within scenes. When François, who was introduced by Gale in a previous scene as having the "cocky confidence of Donald Trump," rapes Angélique, it is to be performed as an on-stage change in costume. François removes Angélique's white uniform to re-costume her in period undergarments using the laces of the corset as reins. Gale sets Angélique's speech dissociating herself from the attack against François's humiliating dehumanization. Similarly, the power dynamics of the servants of the household are captured in their costumes – Claude, the indentured servant, appears in modern clothes, while César and Manon, the Native slave, remain in the costumes of the eighteenth century. This visual imprint of costumes isolates Angélique poignantly in the penultimate scene, the torture scene, when all but Angélique are costumed in modern dress – and she does not respond outside the previously written script.

During the play Gale insists on physical counter-rhythms which have the effect of making the presence of the slave figures distinct. Angélique, César, and Manon are directed to always be working when on stage, while no such silent directions are given for the other figures. This convention enacts precisely the theatrical bind that Angélique's book character evinces. Physical labour by these three figures receives no dialogue in these scenes and serves as a background action integral to the concept of witnessing – watching multiple narratives performed by different means. The growing consciousness of what is and is not referred to in the dialogue disrupts any romanticized view of the past. As Gale indicates, simple household chores of carrying ladders and hauling water become theatrical. Significantly, Angélique's monologue early in the play, when she hopes that this time her situation will be better, is set to a recording of Angie Angel's "Agony," with the "repetitive upbeat tempo like the accelerated drumming of a slave driver" to which Angélique moves in an "abstracted dervish of cleaning." By contrast when it is Thérèse who does something physical—beating the carpet—Angélique is present at this transposition of punishment and acknowledges the blows by a simple refrain of "a growing resolve."

Gale underscores the action with musical rhythms that highlight Angélique's African heritage by drum beats and signal encounters between Angélique and the Native Manon or the French Claude as meetings of cultures of music. During the companionable laundry scene with Manon the potential camaraderie between the two slaves is presented as an African song in response to a mournful Native song. As the two women hang the laundry from either end of the line, they are finally silenced by Thérèse who forbids the "noise" as they meet in the centre and are just about to converse.

Courtship is also handled by song. In contrast to the forced mating of Angélique and César, whose owners observe them voyeuristically through a two-way mirror and comment on them in a "clinical, scientific manner," Claude woos Angélique in private as an exchange of dances. He teaches her the steps to his raucous eighteenth century French folk song and she in her turn beats out the rhythm pumping through her veins that "takes her body anywhere it wants to go."

Lorena Gale's *Angélique* offers a rich recuperation of a figure derived from a historical account and as such points to the way in which this very process negotiates attitudes of several periods. In as much as the reader/ spectator learns about Angélique, one also is shown how stories get imbedded into cultures of performance and risk being re-inscribed by the attitudes which victimize. Period costumes are shown as potential covers for uncritical positions and dialogue, when chosen from the existing accounts, leaves the lacunæ of a personal experience. For actors working on the play, the complexity of the characters—their physical, verbal and racial interactions—points to a theatre that delights its audience by displaying attitudes as operative filters for interpretation and acts of performance.

Natalie Rewa is Associate Professor in the Department of Drama at Queen's University. She was an editor of *Canadian Theatre Review* from 1987 to 1996. Her current research focuses on scenography in Canadian theatre.

Angélique was first produced by Alberta Theatre Projects, D. Michael Dobbin – Producing Director, as part of the Pan Canadian play*Rites* '98 Festival, January 1998, with the following company:

THÉRÈSE	Tracey Ferencz
CLAUDE	Dennis Fitzgerald
FRANÇOIS	Andrew Gillies
IGNACE	Grant Linneberg
ANGÉLIQUE	Karen Robinson
MANON	Alexandra Thomson
CÉSAR	Nigel Shawn Williams

Directed by Sandhano Schultze
Set Design by Scott Reid
Costume Design by Judith Bowden
Lighting by Brian Pincourt
Stage Managed by Colin McCracken
Dramaturgy by Rob Moffatt

—•— —•— —•—

CHARACTERS:

Marie Joseph Angélique: A slave, in a Canadian history book, (29).

François Poulin de Francheville: Montreal merchant, owner of the St. Maurice Ironworks and the slave Angélique, (40).

Thérèse de Couagne: Wife of François. A few years older than Angélique, (35)

Claude Thibault: The Francheville's indentured servant. Angélique's lover, (30's).

Ignace Gamelin: Entrepreneur/Montreal merchant. François' business partner, (40ish).

César: Slave owned by Ignace Gamelin. Lover to Angélique, (30's).

Manon: Indian slave owned by the de Berays, next door neighbours of the Franchevilles, (early 20's).

Reporter, Margeurite, Hypolite, Marie Louise, Marie Josephe, Jean Josephe, and **François de Beray**: These characters are to be played by the members of the main cast.

TIME:

The present and 1730s. Then is now. Now is then.

PLACE:

Montreal, 1700s.

NOTE:

Unless otherwise stated, the slaves are working in every scene in which they appear, either in a modern or historical context. Although the specifics are not written into the text, what can be explored is the concept of witnessing. As servants and slaves are essentially invisible, experiment with who sees what, who knows what.

Painting "Angelique" by Richard Horne.
The Black Studies Centre, Montreal.

Angélique
by Lorena Gale

—•— —•— —•—

ACT I

Scene One

The sound of African drumming. The featureless silhouette of a woman dancing with a book against a backdrop of red, oranges and yellow, suggestive of flames. VOICEOVER – building in a rapid repetitive delivery.

VOICEOVER
And in seventeen thirty-four a Negro slave set fire to the City of Montreal and was hanged.
in seventeen thirty-four a Negro slave set fire to the City of Montreal and was hanged.
seventeen thirty-four a Negro slave set fire to the City of Montreal and was hanged.
a Negro slave set fire to the City of Montreal and was hanged
slave set fire to the City of Montreal and was hanged
set fire to the City of Montreal and was hanged
fire to the City of Montreal and was hanged
to the City of Montreal and was hanged
City of Montreal and was hanged
Montreal and was hanged
and was hanged
was hanged
hanged.

The crackling sound of fire.

Scene Two

FRANÇOIS Poulin de Francheville in a pool of light. He is dressed in full 18th century garb. He talks directly to the audience, with the cocky confidence of a Donald Trump on a roll.

FRANÇOIS
I was hot. I tell you, everything I touched would turn to gold. Or should I say iron. The interest on the loans I paid out was rolling in. And well... there seemed to be no end to the number of furs that could be traded. Something went bing! in my mind. Iron... iron is the wave of the future. So Ignace Gamelin and I laid down the foundations for the Ironworks. Wrote to the Minister of Marine requesting a twenty-year monopoly on the deposits in St. Maurice. And ba-da-bing ba-da-bang!

Request granted from the first day of smelting! Not only that, but the right to exploit cultivated and uncultivated lands next to my own. I felt like a king! Better than Louis! I felt like Midas! With an iron touch. Which is better because iron is stronger and sometimes more valuable than gold.

But do you think I can put a smile on my wife's face?

Our daughter, Marie Angélique, had been dead for two years. Still, Thérèse cried all the time.... Don't get me wrong. I think of Marie and I feel sad. Yes! But hey... life goes on. And we could always have another child. *(beat)* Do you know how hard it is to get close to someone who breaks into tears every time you touch her?

One day I met this really annoying little guy named Bleck. Nicholas Bleck. A Flem. You know what they're like. Just arrived in New France. "With a very rare and special cargo," he says. "Slaves. African slaves. Not those wild things fresh from the jungle. But directly from Portugal. Handsome servants experienced in the ways of Europeans and trained to cater to our every pleasure." A luxury only a fine gentleman like myself could appreciate. And a steal at any price. I wasn't really interested. But the guy was so determined to make a sale, I knew he wouldn't let me go before he displayed his merchandise. So I said I'd take a look. What does it cost to look?

   ANGÉLIQUE in shadows.

The figure of this fine creature could not but attract my particular notice. She was standing off to the side with some others. Perfectly straight... with the most elegant shapes that can be viewed in nature. Her chestnut skin shone with double luster. Her large ebony eyes with their inward gaze. Her proud face... immobile... I don't know...

Do you know what it's like to be flush? To say, "I want that!" And without giving it any more thought, to just reach out and take it. To be able to buy anything or anyone... there is no more powerful feeling in the world! Eight hundred pounds later...

I thought maybe I could give this creature to Thérèse as a special surprise. Make her the envy of female society. Maybe she would be happy.... Want to be close...

What would you pay for your wife's happiness? What would you pay for your own?

Scene Three

Lighting change. ANGÉLIQUE, dressed in a white domestics uniform, in a spot. THÉRÈSE de Couagne dressed in early 18th century in another spot. ANGÉLIQUE directly addresses the audience as documentary, THÉRÈSE as commentary.

ANGÉLIQUE
Angélique… Marie Joseph…

THÉRÈSE
After my sister, Marie Joseph de Couagne.

ANGÉLIQUE
Angélique…

THÉRÈSE
After… *(Unable to speak the name of her dead daughter, she turns away.)*

ANGÉLIQUE
Negro slave born around 1710. Baptized in Montreal June 28, 1730. Hung in Montreal June 21, 1734.

THÉRÈSE
Property of François Poulin de Francheville. 427 rue St. Paul.

The lights come up. THÉRÈSE has been informing ANGÉLIQUE of her duties. She does so lightly and politely, but with the easy authority of one who is in command of her household. FRANÇOIS stands by her.

Beds each morning, change the linen every other day or so. Bathrooms every other morning. Vacuum the main living spaces—bedroom, living room, stairs—daily…. Don't worry. We have a deluxe machine. I hear it makes vacuuming a breeze…. Floors swept and washed every day. Waxing every third week. Are you getting all this?

ANGÉLIQUE
(eager to please) Oui, Madame.

THÉRÈSE
I am very sensitive to dust. You'll have to dust each day. Metal and wood surfaces polished. Mirrors and windows clear. Without streaks…

ANGÉLIQUE
Oui, Madame.

THÉRÈSE
Let's see. What else is there? Laundry, including dry cleaning, is Tuesday and Friday. Hand washing daily. Mending as necessary. Marketing is Saturday.

ANGÉLIQUE
Oui, Madame.

THÉRÈSE
We breakfast at eight, take luncheon at one and dine between six and six-thirty.

> *CLAUDE, the Franchevilles' indentured servant walks across the stage carrying a ladder. He wears modern clothing. THÉRÈSE notices him.*

ANGÉLIQUE
Oui, Madame.

THÉRÈSE
Yours is the little room off the kitchen. Claude will show you where it is. Claude.... This is...

ANGÉLIQUE
Angélique...

THÉRÈSE
Yes.... See that she gets settled down to work.

CLAUDE
Oui, Madame.

THÉRÈSE
There is a place for everything in this house and everything has its place, do you understand?

ANGÉLIQUE
Oh *oui*, Madame. I keep a very clean house. You will not be disappointed.

THÉRÈSE
Good.

> *CLAUDE and ANGÉLIQUE exit.*

FRANÇOIS
So...? What do you think?

THÉRÈSE
Does it matter what I think?

FRANÇOIS
Of course, Thérèse. Your opinions are important to me.

THÉRÈSE
Then I think that we don't need a slave.

FRANÇOIS
I didn't buy her because we needed her.

THÉRÈSE
Why did you buy her?

FRANÇOIS
Because…. Because I thought you would want one.

THÉRÈSE
For me. *(beat)* Thank you. But next time, instead of asking what I think, try asking what I want. *(She exits.)*

FRANÇOIS
(to himself) What do you want, Thérèse? What do you want?

Scene Four

Jungle music on a boom box. "Agony" by Angie Angel. The repetitive upbeat tempo like the accelerated drumming of a slave driver. ANGÉLIQUE with a mop, moving though space in an abstracted dervish of cleaning. CLAUDE and FRANÇOIS witness.

ANGÉLIQUE
This time will be different.

This time everything will work out for me.
This time, I will not just
"live in."
This time, I will
"live with."
I'll make this strange new land – my land!
This house – my home!
These new people,
my people!
This time I will live in reasonable peace.

These people will be different.

These folk will be decent and good.
This mistress will be firm but gentle.
This master will be honest and fair.
There will be no
harsh looks or cruel words,
this time.
This time,
I will be treated with loving kindness and understanding.

I will work hard.
From sun to sun.
Do exactly as I'm told.
I will perform each duty with pride and obedience.
I will maintain their order.
Everything will go smoothly.
I'll know my place.

I will give freely of myself.
Repaying their humanity with loyalty.
Earning their protection and their care.
They'll wonder how they ever lived without me!

Life will be different this time.

There will be holidays…
and happy days…
and good times…
occasional laughter…
and private moments…
and…
and…

It will be good this time.

This time will be different.
This time will be different.
This time will be different.

Scene Five

Light change. Night. FRANÇOIS sits at a small table with a candle and a pitcher of water. CLAUDE and THÉRÈSE witness.

FRANÇOIS
(*whispers*) Angélique… Angélique?

ANGÉLIQUE
Oui, Monsieur?

FRANÇOIS
Viens. Come.

ANGÉLIQUE
Is there something wrong, Monsieur?

FRANÇOIS
(trying to put her at ease) No, no. I just wanted… uh… pour me a glass of water. Please.

ANGÉLIQUE
Oui, Monsieur.

> *He watches intently as she goes to the table, pours him a glass, which she sets beside him. He smiles at her and drinks. There is a moment of awkward silence.*

Will that be all, Monsieur?

FRANÇOIS
Yes… uh… no. *(wanting her to like him)* I have something for you. A present. You like? *Castor.* Beaver. Its worth improves with wear. *Castor gras*… even more valuable. Not to mention warm. It's yours.

ANGÉLIQUE
(perplexed) Thank you, Monsieur.

FRANÇOIS
Don't mention it. *(putting the fur around her shoulders and considering her carefully a moment)* Now come…. Stand over here. I want to take a good look at you. *(There is yearning in his observation.)* Turn around. Slowly. That's it. Nice. Very nice. Yes…. You are a beauty… I wonder… *(with earnest curiosity)* Is it true what they say about African women?

ANGÉLIQUE
(stiffly) I'm sorry, Monsieur. I don't know what they say.

FRANÇOIS
That you're wilder? Freer? Hot like the sun that scorched you? *(She does not reply.)* I would like to know for myself…

ANGÉLIQUE
Please, Monsieur…

FRANÇOIS
No…. Don't fight it. You'll disturb Thérèse. *(She stops resisting.)* See? I'm not so bad. I'm better than sleeping in the snow. If you get my drift. *(beat)* Come on… smile. I will not hurt you. If you obey. I won't hurt you.

Scene Six

CLAUDE in a spot.

CLAUDE
This indenture made the 17th of August, 1729 between me, Claude
Thibault, also known as Claude de la Butanne, aged 29 and François
Poulin de Francheville witnesseth that I do covenant, promise and grant
to François Poulin, from my first arrival at Montreal and after, for the
term of three years, to serve in such service as he François Poulin shall
there employ him.

> *ANGÉLIQUE enters and begins her cleaning dervish in silence. CLAUDE*
> *continues to speak as if he has been doing so for a while.*

Yep. This little piece of pounded wood is all that ties me here. One
day I'm going to wipe my ass with this and stick it to Francheville's
forehead. Take off across the river and not look back till the earth turns
to sand beneath my feet and the sea stretches out unbroken before me!

ANGÉLIQUE
But why, Monsieur? What has Monsieur done to you?

CLAUDE
Nothing, I guess. I just don't plan on shovelling his horseshit for the rest
of my life, that's all. Until then... I guess I'll just have another drink.
(takes a flask out of his shirt and drinks) You want some? It's on the house.

ANGÉLIQUE
No thank you, Monsieur.

CLAUDE
Come on. Just take a swig. I hate to drink alone.

ANGÉLIQUE
But Madame...

CLAUDE
Fuck Madame! Yeesh! That's a scary thought. *(beat)* Just take a sip. It'll
do you some good.

ANGÉLIQUE
If you insist, Monsieur.

CLAUDE
And drop the "Monsieur" bullshit. I'm not one of them. Call me Claude
or call me Thibault as long as you call me, okay?

ANGÉLIQUE
You could be one of them. You look like one of them.

CLAUDE
Yeah, right. I guess to you we all look alike. No, don't confuse me with the rest of my species. I'm just a peon. Like you. Something to pee on. Cheers.

He drinks and hands the flask to her. She drinks.

ANGÉLIQUE
Look...! *(referring to an imaginary window)*

CLAUDE
The first snow is always the best. You see how it melts when it hits the ground. The earth isn't ready. Still too warm. It's not going to stick. Whatever falls will be gone by this afternoon. You see? It's already turning to rain. It will all get washed away. But the next time will be a blizzard and then you'll see.

ANGÉLIQUE
It's beautiful.

CLAUDE
You think so now, but after six or seven months of freezing your ass off you'll change your mind. Snow's a bitch. Let's drink to that.

ANGÉLIQUE
You drink too much.

CLAUDE
And you don't drink enough. *(He drinks.)* Eau de Vie! The spirit of life! Warms the soul, kills the pain! Here.

ANGÉLIQUE
I am not in pain.

CLAUDE
Keep telling yourself that and maybe one day you'll believe it. In the meantime, drink up.

ANGÉLIQUE
(drinks, then gives him back the flask) Claude? Where will you go? When your time is up?

CLAUDE
I don't know. Back to Franche Comte, maybe. Or the Islands. No snow in the Islands. Yeah.... The Islands... that's the place to be. Warm winds,

blue horizons, women running around naked all the time. That's what I hear. Is it true?

ANGÉLIQUE
How should I know?

CLAUDE
Sorry. I guess that's not the kind of question to ask a lady. But you can't blame a man for asking. *(beat)* I don't know. What island are you from?

ANGÉLIQUE
Not the ones you're thinking of. Madiere.... Across from Portugal. A jewel in the Atlantic.

CLAUDE
Sounds good to me. Maybe there. You want to come?

ANGÉLIQUE
Don't make me laugh.

CLAUDE
Why not? You're pretty when you laugh.

Scene Seven

Black. FRANÇOIS with a deer skin and a Bic lighter. He flicks. The light reveals him.

FRANÇOIS
(whispered) Angélique... Angélique?

Black. Beat. FRANÇOIS flicks again. The lights bump up. He is closer.

(whispered) Angélique... Angélique?

Black. FRANÇOIS with a deer skin.

(whispered) Angélique... Angélique?

ANGÉLIQUE in a spot.

ANGÉLIQUE
Angélique became the mistress of Jacques César, a Negro slave owned by Ignace Gamelin, with whom she had a son, Eustache, born in January 1730 and in May, 1732, she gave birth to twins; Louis and Marie Françoise.

Scene Eight

In the darkness we hear...

ANGÉLIQUE
(whispered) Brother? What are we doing here?

CÉSAR
Didn't they tell you?

ANGÉLIQUE
No.

> *Lights come up to reveal IGNACE Gamelin, in full period dress on one side of a two-way mirror. He speaks in a clinical, scientific manner.*

IGNACE
It's very interesting. Notice how they just stand there. It would seem like nothing is going on between them. But look... his eyes... her mouth. Fascinating. See. He is putting some distance between them in order to get a better look. *(beat)* I am surprised he's so contained. I've owned him for years and he hasn't had a woman.

FRANÇOIS
(enters the mirror) That you know of...

IGNACE
Touchée.

> *THÉRÈSE enters. The three are framed as if in portrait.*

THÉRÈSE
Why do they not speak, Ignace?

FRANÇOIS
Perhaps they are shy.

IGNACE
Perhaps they are like dogs. Two males pass on the street and they growl or bark to indicate status and territory. But a bitch in heat struts past and the first thing that happens is they sniff each other out. Circle and sniff. Most animals do that. Hey François, maybe we should make a study of this. The unusual mating practices of the African in captivity. Imagine, we could be scholars as well as merchants.

FRANÇOIS
(guarded jealousy) She won't go for him...

THÉRÈSE
Why not? I would… *(The men turn to her.)* If I were her.

IGNACE
Care to place a little wager? *(takes out his purse)*

FRANÇOIS
I hate to take your money.

THÉRÈSE
Shh…

IGNACE
The sniffing has begun.

> *The lights come up on ANGÉLIQUE and CÉSAR, IGNACE's slave. They whisper.*

CÉSAR
My master says that you are to be with me now.

ANGÉLIQUE
What!

THÉRÈSE
What are they saying?

IGNACE
Look.

CÉSAR
You have been chosen for me.

ANGÉLIQUE
I don't even know you…. And we're supposed to!?

CÉSAR
I guess.

ANGÉLIQUE
What if I refuse?

CÉSAR
I don't know.

ANGÉLIQUE
And you agreed to this?

CÉSAR

It's been a long time, Sister. I don't come into contact with too many of our people. Let alone women. *(pause)* I need… someone.

ANGÉLIQUE

And any one will do?

CÉSAR

Someone…

ANGÉLIQUE

Then you are no better than they are! *(beat)* Come on. Let's get this over with. *(lying down, opening her legs)* This is what it's all about? Well, take it. Here it is. Come on and take it. Just take it. I won't fight you. I've been chosen for you. Well, here I am. Only make it fast. I don't have all day. I have other work I have to do.

IGNACE

Alright César, old boy! The sexual prowess of the African male is legendary. Let this be a lesson to you François. Don't bet with the best 'cause the best only bet on a sure thing. Those two will turn a profit for us in no time. *(FRANÇOIS reaches for his purse.)* Oh…. Put that away. We are, after all, gentlemen.

The two men exit. Lights out on THÉRÈSE who watches with fascination.

ANGÉLIQUE

Well? What are you waiting for?

CÉSAR

Get up off of that floor. You think I want it to be like this?

ANGÉLIQUE

I don't care what you think.

CÉSAR

What am I supposed to do? Just say no? All I did was ask permission to court a woman. I thought he'd just let me find one on my own. There's an Indian girl I see sometimes. I guess my master thought he was doing me a favour.

ANGÉLIQUE

Real generous of him.

CÉSAR

Real generous of your master, for he would have to give permission too. If it makes you feel any better, now that I've seen you up close I'm not much taken by you either. But we've been paired together. And there is no getting away from it.

ANGÉLIQUE
(*pause*) What do we do?

CÉSAR
Make the best of it, I guess. We can start by trying to be friends. Yes? Maybe we can pretend that we are meeting again. In another time, another place. Under more pleasant circumstances. Yes? Sister? (*He pretends.*) Hello. Wonderful woman of the great homeland. I haven't seen you before. I am César. Jacques César.

ANGÉLIQUE
I am... Angélique. Marie Joseph Angélique.

Scene Nine

The painful sounds of childbirth. IGNACE and FRANÇOIS are smoking and waiting. CLAUDE in the shadows. CÉSAR waits expectantly off in a corner. CÉSAR jumps up.

IGNACE
Relax, old man. There is nothing you can do. You will only be in the way. The women have everything under control...

THÉRÈSE
(*off*) It's a boy...!

FRANÇOIS
A boy...

IGNACE
It's a boy! Congratulations, César old man. Or should I say Papa.

CÉSAR
Merci, Monsieur. I am very proud to have a son.

IGNACE
If he is anything like you César, he'll be a strong lad.

FRANÇOIS
And a strong man. He'll fetch a good price when the time comes.

IGNACE
You scoundrel. Don't run off with the profits. I lay claim to half.

THÉRÈSE
(*enters with a bundle*) It's a boy, François.

FRANÇOIS
Beautiful.

He turns away. She addresses CÉSAR.

THÉRÈSE
Would you like to hold him?

CÉSAR
Thank you, Madame.

She delicately hands the baby to CÉSAR. They admire it in silence for a moment.

IGNACE
(looking at the baby) He's awfully fair. *(They all turn to him.)* Which only goes to show that everything is born pure. Perfect! *(beat)* His face all screwed up like that – you know who he reminds me of?

FRANÇOIS
(quickly) Who?

IGNACE
Eustache, the foreman at the Ironworks.

FRANÇOIS
Eustache?

IGNACE
All this baby is missing is his moustache.

FRANÇOIS
(relieved) Yes… *(laughs)* Yes, it does look like Eustache. All red face and hairy. Then that's what we will call it. Eustache.

IGNACE
(to CÉSAR) Well, we better be heading back. Plenty of time to play daddy ahead of you.

FRANÇOIS
Claude. See to Monsieur Gamelin's carriage.

CLAUDE
Oui, Monsieur. *(exits)*

IGNACE
By the way, how is the mother doing?

THÉRÈSE
Fine. She's just fine.

IGNACE
Now hand him back.

CÉSAR hands the baby to THÉRÈSE.

FRANÇOIS
I'll see you to the door.

They exit. THÉRÈSE is left holding the baby. She studies its face.

Scene Ten

ANGÉLIQUE alone with her baby. The sound of a new heart beating. She stands, gently swaying, rocking the child in her arms.

ANGÉLIQUE
In the beginning there was Darkness.
Dense
profound
Darkness.
Like a thick black blanket
stretching
into seamless infinity.
Darkness was all and all was Darkness.
Is.
And would ever be.
And Darkness slumbered,
complete
in her ebony world.

'Til one day there was a movement, a stirring, a rumbling somewhere
deep inside.
An unacknowledged longing to be
more
than everything.
Growing like the sound of distant thunder.
Unsettling her dreams,
but not enough to wake her.

The stirring grew into a churning.
The darkness swirled and eddied.
Rising
and crashing
in

on herself.
She rocked.
She reeled.
Until she woke .
And then she knew
that she would
never
sleep again.

"Something has changed in me. I can no longer bear to be alone."

And with that thought,
Darkness heaved and pushed.
Heaved and pushed.
Forcing
desire from her depths.
Giving birth to
Light.

Light was small.
No bigger than a spark.
But in It,
Darkness could
see
the full extent of herself.

"I am so much more than what I thought I was."

And Light blinked
with the bright eyes of a new born.
Dazzling.
Delighting Darkness.
And a great heat she had never before noticed
spread through Darkness
as she closed
protectively
around Light. Like
mother
cradling
child.

Light,
unlike Darkness,
came into being
complete
with its own self knowledge
which it fed on with a ferocious hunger,
growing fatter,

and pushing back
Darkness in defiance.

Darkness,
being everywhere, still
encompassed Light no matter how she strained
to give It room.

Light,
fueled by it's own existence, grew
hotter
in confinement.

"I am so much more than what I am. At least as much as Darkness,
which is everywhere. Why must I be contained? Without me Darkness
has no Knowledge of itself. Therefore, I am everything! And Darkness is
nothing!

Light burned with greater arrogance.
Growing hotter and denser with a simmering anger,
which bubbled
and popped
beneath its surface of brilliance.
And still
Darkness
closed around it.

"I am more… I am more than… I am more than this," Light seethed.

'Til it was so
full
of itself
It exploded.
Sending shards of its being
hurling through Darkness.
Lighting up
the void.

Light
was now everywhere.
Cutting through darkness with the sharpness of
an axe.
Cruelly
severing
the umbilicus between them.

Darkness
was so blinded by the light

she could no longer
see,
and so retreated
to where she could have some sense of herself.
Though light still pierced her,
as a reminder that It
now
ruled
every
thing.

Light and Darkness.

That is how the two became separate forces.
In constant opposition.
Light in the forefront
and Darkness…
waiting…
on the edge
of everything.

But there is something else we know, my child. That in the end, Darkness reclaims everything. The stars will fall. The sun will cease to shine. Light will collapse in on itself. 'Til once again, it is nothing more than just a little spark. That flickers. Sputters. Pops itself out. Then Darkness will resume her peaceful reign.

That day is a long way off. I will ever see it. Neither will you, my baby…. So light…. So powerfully dark.

VOICEOVER
(whispered) Angélique… Angélique?

> *Puts her hand over the baby's face, smothering it. The heartbeat stops. Silence.*

Fly home and greet the darkness. There are others waiting there. Mama loves you and will join you soon.

> *THÉRÈSE enters. She regards ANGÉLIQUE compassionately and speaks from her own pain.*

THÉRÈSE
Children don't live too long here. Most babies born in the winter don't live to see the spring. I don't know why…. Best it happened early on. That way you don't get too attached. *(looks at the dead baby)* I had a child once…. A girl. Marie Angélique. Eight winters she lasted. Eight sweet years…. And then she caught a fever she was just too young to fight…. So you're lucky it happened sooner.

Scene Eleven

FRANÇOIS looking over a file folder of documents. THÉRÈSE regards him for a tense moment, then begins tentatively.

THÉRÈSE
God forgive me, but I am glad it's dead. *(no response)* At least now we don't have to bear the embarrassment of her bastard running around the streets. *(He pays little attention.)* I find it difficult to believe that César was the father... the baby was so pale.

FRANÇOIS
(still engrossed in his work) What does it matter? It's dead now. It's gone.

THÉRÈSE
Do you know who the father was?

FRANÇOIS
César.

THÉRÈSE
No.

FRANÇOIS
Then how should I know? It could be anyone for all we know. Claude even...

THÉRÈSE
Or you...

> *Pause.*

FRANÇOIS
(laughs) Really, Thérèse. I have more important things to worry about.

THÉRÈSE
(softly) I have wrestled with that possibility since that child was born. *(beat)* I understand how tempting it could be... when it is so readily available. To succumb to temptation...

FRANÇOIS
I don't think I like what you are implying.

THÉRÈSE
(quickly) Did you?

FRANÇOIS
Did I what?

THÉRÈSE
(pause) I think we should get rid of her, François.

FRANÇOIS
And what do you propose I should do with her?

THÉRÈSE
Sell her. Give her away.

FRANÇOIS
Just give her away?

THÉRÈSE
I don't know. Anything. Just get her out of here.

FRANÇOIS
Why?

THÉRÈSE
Because I'm your wife and I am asking you.

FRANÇOIS
(irritated) You're being ridiculous. What's gotten into you, Thérèse? First you accuse me of being an adulterer and now you want me to give up a valuable piece of property just because of some crazy idea you've got?

THÉRÈSE
Please, François.

FRANÇOIS
(after a beat, softer) Listen to me. You are my wife. I love you. Believe me when I tell you that you have nothing to worry about. *(kisses her forehead)* Now, all this nonsense has interrupted my work. I'm going off to collect my thoughts.

THÉRÈSE
François…. Tell me you will consider it? Out of respect for me?

FRANÇOIS
You have nothing to worry about.

Scene Twelve

The sound of one lone drum beating in a slow native rhythm. MANON, a panisse, a young native slave/servant carries a basket of wet clothes. ANGÉLIQUE enters with a basket of wet clothes, notices MANON and halts. She stares. ANGÉLIQUE returns her gaze with similar curiosity.

Another drum beating to a corresponding African rhythm joins with the first. They do not clash. They complement. MANON puts her basket down and starts to shake and hang the clothing at the opposite end of the clothesline to ANGÉLIQUE. As she does so she begins to sing to herself in her native language. It is a mournful song. ANGÉLIQUE starts to hang her wash and once again responds to MANON singing with her own song in an African language. The two songs blend in a call and response style and in rhythm to the beating of the two drums. The women work and sing. All the while getting closer and closer. Freer and freer. Becoming jubilant. They meet in the centre, neither capable of hanging more clothes. They regard each other for a moment. They smile in their song, uncomfortable but friendly. They are about to speak when THÉRÈSE enters.

THÉRÈSE
Stop. Stop that noise immediately. *(tearing the laundry from the line in her anger)* How many times do I have to tell you that it's strictly forbidden. I should have you both whipped. Maybe then you would understand that we are a civilized people and won't tolerate that sort of... savage behaviour. *(to MANON)* Now you get out of here. And don't think I won't mention this to Madame de Beray, because I will.

Scene Thirteen

ANGÉLIQUE drags a carpet or a panel of heavy drapes or a manageable wall tapestry out and hangs it over the line. THÉRÈSE waits silently while ANGÉLIQUE toils. When ANGÉLIQUE is finished, she stands beside the hanging. THÉRÈSE then commences to beat the rug, each blow being a complete and separate beating in itself, meted out over the course of time. ANGÉLIQUE responds as if she herself is being struck — first with pain, then with growing endurance and compressed rage. FRANÇOIS enters and watches from the side and MANON watches from the shadows.

THÉRÈSE
Because you dropped the serving bowl. *(smack)*
Because you were late coming back from the market. *(smack)*
Because you forgot to put oil in the lamps. *(smack)*
Because you were whistling in the kitchen. *(smack)*

ANGÉLIQUE
Each stroke a reminder.

THÉRÈSE
Because the bread didn't rise. *(smack)*
Because he went to you again last night. *(smack)*
Because you burnt the edges of the waffles. *(smack)*
Because he is my husband and I love him. *(smack)*

ANGÉLIQUE
Each stroke a reminder.

THÉRÈSE
Because he stared at you through dinner. *(smack)*
Because I have to pretend this isn't happening. *(smack)*
Because I wish you'd disappear. *(smack)*
Because there is nothing else I can do. *(smack)*

THÉRÈSE crosses to FRANÇOIS and they exit together.

ANGÉLIQUE
Each stroke…

Scene Fourteen

ANGÉLIQUE is drinking Eau de Vie. *CÉSAR is rubbing her back.*

CÉSAR
…eleven times, this slave and his Indian wife. Ten times they ran away.
Ten times they were caught. First time they got caught, the master cut
off one of their feet. Next time a hand. Next time an ear. Next time a
nose. Next time… whatever. These two so cut up makes you wonder
how they were still standing. But the eleventh time… *(He finishes
rubbing her down.)* Hey… slow down. *(He takes the flask from her.)* There.
(He pats her stomach.) This one is mine and I don't want nothing to
happen to it.

ANGÉLIQUE
Well, you just march up there and tell that to Madame. Say, "Madame,
I want you to give my Angélique the day off." She'll laugh in your face.
These people work me harder than they work their horses. *(cautiously)*
Do you remember what it was like before?

CÉSAR
Before what?

ANGÉLIQUE
Before…

CÉSAR
I have no before. I don't remember my mama or my papa. Probably
sold or died off before I could get a good fix on 'em. I got sold to a fur
trader when I was still a boy, and come up north. Been here ever since.

ANGÉLIQUE
I remember. Before this Montreal. This New France. Before this Canada.
I remember Madiere. Picking coffee with my mother and my father. The

coffee beans. Their tender green. Their firmness between my little fingers. We toiled for them. Yes! But it was work. Just work. Hard work is a part of life. And at least we were together.

On the days of rest and celebration we would all descend on the beach. We would build a fire in conjunction to the line of the horizon. As the sun set, the orange and red and yellow of day's transition into night, would blend with the colours in the fire. Everyone would gather round. And to the beating of a drum, they would tell the stories of our ancestors. Our warriors dancing the great battles. Our hunters re-enacting their kills.

The little me would stand on the sandy shore and look out across the inky water. And imagine I could see the land of my ancestors. It was that close. It was that far away. *(pause)* I cannot understand this coldness and this cruelty. I may have always been a slave. But I did not feel like one until I came to this land... *(carefully)* We could run.

CÉSAR

(laughs) Sure. You wait here while I pack my belongings. Hey! I've got everything. Let's go!

ANGÉLIQUE

We could!

CÉSAR

Look Angélique, everywhere we go we're going to be slaves. There's nowhere to hide. And even if there was we can't hide forever. They'll find us. Snap the chains back on or worse. I don't fancy clomping around the rest of my life with one foot. Gamelin isn't too bad a master. And I have you now. And a baby coming. It may not seem like too much. But the one thing I have learned, is to take what happiness I can when I can get it. And everything I have is right here.

ANGÉLIQUE

But don't you want to be your own man? Wake up in the morning and decide what you want to do...

CÉSAR

I am just trying to accept what life has put before me.

ANGÉLIQUE

Accept...

CÉSAR

That's right. Accept. 'Cause there is nothing I can say or do that's going to change my lot in this life. If I am going to have any kind of happiness I have to come to terms with that fact. I suggest you do too. Find some way to live. Something to live for. And life will seem a little easier.

ANGÉLIQUE
But what about those eleven times? Don't they tell you something.

CÉSAR
Yeah. They made it the eleventh time. Into heaven. They were found wrapped in each other's arms. Froze to death. In the snow.

FRANÇOIS
(*whispers off*) Angélique? Angélique?

CÉSAR
Just take what happiness you can – when you can.

Scene Fifteen

Light change.

CÉSAR
Eustache. Natural son of Marie Joseph Angélique and Jacques César. Baptised, January 11, 1731. Buried, Feb. 12. 1731. Age…

ANGÉLIQUE
One month.

CÉSAR
Louis: *fils naturel de la meme negresse* and brother of the previous. Born and baptized May 26, 1732. Buried the next day. Age…

ANGÉLIQUE
Two days.

CÉSAR
Marie Françoise, twin sister of the preceding. Buried October 29,1732. Age…

ANGÉLIQUE
Five months.

CÉSAR
Father – unknown. Though the mother declared it to be Jacques César. (*CÉSAR exits.*)

Scene Sixteen

FRANÇOIS enters and stands behind ANGÉLIQUE. CLAUDE works quietly in the background. Every once in a while he looks in the direction of ANGÉLIQUE. He is aware of what is happening with her but cannot watch openly. From behind, FRANÇOIS reaches around and removes ANGÉLIQUE's uniform, revealing period undergarments beneath her modern clothing. He then commences to dress her up again, only this time, in period clothing. ANGÉLIQUE does not resist.

ANGÉLIQUE
A dog barking.... A baby crying.... Footsteps...
The wind whistling low and breathy...

THÉRÈSE enters and watches in the shadows.

The faint creek of wood giving way to weight...
Someone stepping stealthily on the fourth floorboard
before the doorway to my room.
There is no sneaking in this house where every sound
betrays.
A cat scowling...
Perhaps the dog has caught the cat.
Or maybe,
the cat has caught the dog.

FRANÇOIS places a corset on ANGÉLIQUE.

I could leave here. Right now!

She takes a step away from him. Then another and another which has the effect of tightening the corset.

I am walking towards the door... I am opening it... I am stepping
outside and...

She falls forward. Her arms spread like a bird. She is kept aloft by the laces of the corset which FRANÇOIS holds like reins on a wild horse. But he doesn't notice anything that's happening with her. He pumps her, like he's fucking her from behind.

I'm freeeeeeee! I'm free! I'm free! I'm free! Look at meeee! I'm running
through the gates of the city. I'm racing across the land. I'm floating
across the big river. I am washed up on the shores of my beloved
Madiere...

He pulls her back to him and ties the corset.

But I am not really out there...

She steps into the dress.

I am here.

I see.

The dog has caught the cat. The cat has a mouse in its jaws. The mouse is playing dead.

You think you own me. This body. That complies. That never fights. The heat you feel is white-hot rage scorching the inside of my mind. A blazing fury I bite back. Fire – I would spit into your face. If you would face me you coward, you would know…. One day…

Scene Seventeen

CLAUDE whistles cheerfully to himself, carries two pails of water which we are to believe he has hauled from a well. He carries them to a large black kettle and pours them in. He speaks with great caution, as he works.

CLAUDE
There's a place. Not too far from here. South. Called New England. Ever heard of it? *(She does not respond.)* I went there once with Monsieur Francheville. Not much different from here. Only everyone speaks English. And free Blacks too.

ANGÉLIQUE
(cautiously) How do you know they're free?

She takes up her old clothing and puts it in the kettle.

CLAUDE
We took the horses to the blacksmith. Right next door was a small house. In need of some repair. But it looked safe. Three little African children playing in the yard. I figured they must be his.

ANGÉLIQUE
That doesn't make them free. Makes them children.

Takes a bucket and pours it in the kettle.

CLAUDE
He spoke to Monsieur Francheville directly. Monsieur paid him directly, though he complained about the price. Every man who came into the smithy's shouted at him like he was their slave. But when they left they paid him like a free man.

ANGÉLIQUE
How do you know his master didn't hire him out? Make himself more money?

CLAUDE
I don't. But I'm willing to wager that I'm right and you're wrong.

ANGÉLIQUE
I'm not willing to bet my body parts on your view of the world.

CLAUDE
(*serious*) I'll prove it. It's about two, maybe three weeks journey. Depending on time of year, weather. Weather's great now. Let's go. I know the way.

ANGÉLIQUE
We can't just walk out of here.

CLAUDE
It's that easy. Just put one foot in front of the other. Come on. I'll show you.

ANGÉLIQUE
Why? Why should I trust you?

He takes her hand and kisses it.

FRANÇOIS
(*off*) Angélique! Angélique...

CLAUDE
Any time you want out... I know the way.

FRANÇOIS enters.

FRANÇOIS
Angélique... (*surprised*) Oh, Claude...

ANGÉLIQUE takes a bucket and pours it in the kettle.

CLAUDE
What can I do for you, Monsieur?

FRANÇOIS
Uh.... The Mercedes. I think you should take it in and have it looked at.

CLAUDE
Sure thing.

He lights a fire under the kettle.

You leaving town again?

FRANÇOIS
Soon. Real soon.

He regards CLAUDE with cloaked suspicion. ANGÉLIQUE takes a bucket and pours it into the kettle.

Angélique…. Watching you pour that water has made me real thirsty. Why don't you go and get me a cup.

ANGÉLIQUE
Oui, Monsieur. *(She exits.)*

FRANÇOIS
You're a really useful guy to have around the house.

CLAUDE
That's why you pay me the big bucks.

FRANÇOIS
Yeah, well, maybe you should come out with me to the Ironworks. We could use someone like you out there.

CLAUDE
What about Madame? How will she cope?

FRANÇOIS
Is it Madame you're concerned for? Or Angélique?

ANGÉLIQUE enters. CLAUDE notices but doesn't say anything.

You've been fucking her, haven't you?

CLAUDE
No, Monsieur.

FRANÇOIS
But you want to.

She spits in the water. Stirs it with her finger.

I don't blame you. Everyone should get a taste of brown sugar.

ANGÉLIQUE
Your water, Sir.

FRANÇOIS
(with great show) Why, thank you. *(to CLAUDE)* Salute. *(He drinks.)* Mmmm. That was the coolest, sweetest water I ever tasted. Thanks

again. *(smiles at ANGÉLIQUE and tosses CLAUDE the keys)* I want the car back in two hours. Get moving.

CLAUDE
Excuse me, Sir…

FRANÇOIS
What!

CLAUDE
It might save you some money if you showed me exactly what the problem is. You know. Mechanics.

FRANÇOIS
Don't worry about the money.

CLAUDE
But it might be something I can fix myself.

FRANÇOIS
Jesus, Claude…

CLAUDE
Unless, of course, Monsieur is engaged in more pressing business…

FRANÇOIS regards CLAUDE for a moment. Then ANGÉLIQUE.

FRANÇOIS
Yeah…. Right. *(finishes his water)* Let's go.

They exit. ANGÉLIQUE picks up a long stick and stirs the laundry.

ANGÉLIQUE
Mistah buckra
he get sick
he tak fever
he be die.
he be die

Scene Eighteen

IGNACE Gamelin in a pool of light. Delivers the following as in eulogy.

IGNACE
François Poulin de Francheville. Merchant, fur trader, seigneur and entrepreneur in the Saint Maurice Ironworks. Son of Michel Poulin and Marie Jutras. Brother to Pierre Poulin and loving husband to Thérèse de

Couagne. And, of course, my dearest friend and business partner. Born October 7, 1692. Died November 3, 1733. His early death is a grave loss to this colony.

Light expands to reveal THÉRÈSE in a black business suit and a stylish black hat with the netting pulled over her face.

THÉRÈSE
I loved him, Ignace.

IGNACE
I know, my dear.

THÉRÈSE
From the first moment I saw him. I was taking a bucket of ashes around back to the stables. We'd had a visit by *les Lutins* the night before. And I had heard that the only way to get rid of these mischievous goblins was to put a pail of ashes just inside the stable door. Because *les Lutins* hate ashes. And that would discourage them from ever coming again.

I heard someone coming to the stables. I wasn't expecting visitors. I thought the goblins were back. I didn't want them to catch me. So I hid. *(She laughs at the memory.)* Well, François opened the stable door – ashes went flying everywhere! And François cursed. *Mon Dieu*, I had never heard anything like it before. And then he started to stamp. I didn't realize it but some of the ashes were live and catching in the hay that lined the stable floor. All I could hear was this stamping and cursing and I thought for sure it was the goblins. So I grabbed a pitch fork and went charging out from my cache. Only to find a very strong and handsome young man stamping out the sparks. We were married six months later.

IGNACE
He loved you. He was my best friend and I know. In spite of everything he always loved you dearly.

THÉRÈSE
In spite of everything.

IGNACE
Believe it. He leaves his heart behind with you.

THÉRÈSE
What will I do, Ignace? How will I get by?

IGNACE
He left you well provided for. In addition to this property there is the farm in the parish of Saint Michel. And as his wife you inherit his interests in the St. Maurice Ironworks, which include his own

investments, the seigneury of Saint Maurice, and a small annual income derived from his having contributed to the lands as a capitol asset. Although there isn't much cash, you should never have to worry. You would receive a generous sum should you choose to liquidate any or all of these assets.

THÉRÈSE
I know. I know.

IGNACE
There is someone who would be interested in taking the Ironworks off your hands. His name is Cugnet and he...

THÉRÈSE
I don't want to sell the Ironworks, Ignace.

IGNACE
But it is a tricky business. And the complexities are better managed by those who are knowledgeable in the field.

THÉRÈSE
Then I will learn.

IGNACE
But it would only drain your energy at a time when you should be mourning your husband.

THÉRÈSE
I feel I must carry out his work. I know how important the Ironworks were to François. Perhaps by retaining them, I keep a part of him I never had. By working with you I will get to learn a part of him I never knew. You will advise me, won't you Ignace?

IGNACE
Well, yes, but... Thérèse... I know you're not thinking clearly with François' death so fresh in your heart. Rest. Think it over. I'll call again in a few days or so. I'm sure that in time you will see that unburdening yourself of the Ironworks is the most reasonable decision... *(calls)* Angélique.

ANGÉLIQUE
Oui, Monsieur Gamelin.

IGNACE
Take care of La Dame de Francheville.

He kisses THÉRÈSE on the forehead.

Remember, my dear. He always loved you.

IGNACE exits. The two women are alone. There is a long awkward silence. ANGÉLIQUE, her eyes downcast, stands waiting for some order, as THÉRÈSE regards her with a mixed range of emotions.

THÉRÈSE
(with a genuine desire to know) Tell me something?

ANGÉLIQUE
Oui, Madame.

THÉRÈSE
(with difficulty but without malice) Did you like it? *(beat)* When he came to you at night?

ANGÉLIQUE
No, Madame.

THÉRÈSE
All this time?

ANGÉLIQUE
No, Madame.

THÉRÈSE
Why didn't you come to me?

ANGÉLIQUE
You have punished me for less, Madame.

THÉRÈSE
I have punished you because.... You could have stopped him. You could have tried to stop him.

ANGÉLIQUE
So could you. He was your husband. The master only took from me what you refused to give.

THÉRÈSE
(She advances on ANGÉLIQUE and in her anger, begins to slap her around.)
You ungrateful, jealous, slut. Black bitch. Lying whore. You liked it when he took you. You nigger girls are good for nothing else. You liked it. So don't you lie to me. You liked it.

ANGÉLIQUE
(grabs her hands) And you didn't. You sent him to me. The fault is yours Madame. Not mine. *(letting her go)* I know that you have lost yourself in grief. I know the anger and the rage of loss. How hard it is to contain. How it needs to unleash itself on something. But I'm not going to let you beat it out on me. Do you understand? Do not strike me again.

THÉRÈSE

(*collapses in her grief and tears*) François… François…

ANGÉLIQUE

He's gone, Madame. It's just you now. So you have to be strong. (*ANGÉLIQUE cradles her.*) That's right. Let it out. Let it all out. I know that things haven't been good between us. But that's all going to change now. I'll serve you well. If you will let me. I will serve you.

ACT II

Scene One

MANON in a spot.

MANON
La negresse semble de laisser ce premier amant, César, pour tomber dans les bras d'un blanc, Claude Thibault.

CLAUDE outside in a gentle snow. He speaks as if ANGÉLIQUE is there.

CLAUDE
The thing about snow is that even though together on the ground it all looks the same – each snowflake is different. Each has its own size, shape. Its own tiny crystal pattern. *(trying to catch one)* There. See? Aw, it melted. *(tries again)* Heat is its mortal enemy. So you have to be quick. 'Cause alone, the lifetime of a snowflake is brief. But together, one can last a whole winter. That's why, two, or three, or four or more catch on to each other and fall together. Even snow wants to live… as best as it can.

ANGÉLIQUE enters with her hands behind her back.

ANGÉLIQUE
I like how it makes everything quiet. But what I like most about snow is… snowballs!

She throws one at him.

CLAUDE
Why you…!

He chases her around playfully. She squeals. He catches her. They fall to the ground, laughing. He kisses her briefly. She kisses him passionately. MANON creeps in and watches them from the shadows.

We should be getting back.

ANGÉLIQUE
You go. I want to stay a little while longer.

CLAUDE
I'm not going anywhere without you.

CLAUDE sings a vibrant and raucous French folk song, such as "En Roulant Ma Boule Roulant." He claps and stamps his feet. ANGÉLIQUE laughs. He grabs her and tries to dance with her.

ANGÉLIQUE
Stop! Stop! Stop! Stop!

CLAUDE
You don't like to dance.

ANGÉLIQUE
I can't dance like that. All left feet and straight lines.

CLAUDE
If you just tried a little you would get the hang of it.

ANGÉLIQUE
I have tried. My body refuses to move in that way.

CLAUDE
But I can't dance alone.

ANGÉLIQUE
Why not?

CLAUDE
I don't know. It just doesn't seem right – if there is someone to dance with.

He tries to dance with her again.

ANGÉLIQUE
No.

CLAUDE
Won't you at least try?

ANGÉLIQUE
No.

CLAUDE
Then you show me.

ANGÉLIQUE
What?

CLAUDE
Show me a dance, that you would dance, if you wanted to dance with someone.

ANGÉLIQUE
You would only find it strange.

CLAUDE
No stranger than you find my dancing. Teach me your steps so that I can dance with you.

ANGÉLIQUE
Well, for that we would need a drum, which is forbidden. How can I dance without a drum?

CLAUDE
I can beat out a rhythm for you.

He starts to beat on the ground.

ANGÉLIQUE
No, no, no... not like that. Like this.

She beats out a simple rhythm on her clothing. He tries. She shakes her head.

Imagine that you are a drum. Deep and resonant. And the rhythm is the beating of your heart when your spirit is in flight.

She continues beating on herself. He tries again.

Yes! You catch on quick.

CLAUDE
No flies on me.

ANGÉLIQUE laughs and beats a new rhythm and he follows.

ANGÉLIQUE
First you take off like a startled bird. Fluttering with surprise. But as your wings take you higher into the safety of the sky, they calm... and beat with a certain, steady pace.

As she speaks, she gradually stops beating on herself as her rhythms are taken up by the real drum.

Yes.... Up. Up you fly. Your heart thumps loud. Deliberate. Pumping rhythm through your veins. You soar up to the sun. You spiral down to the ground. You careen on the slightest of air. You move... unfettered... through time and space. There is just the beating of your heart and the beating of the drum taking your body anywhere it wants to go.

She dances, the drums beat, the snow falls around her, and CLAUDE watches with obvious sensual delight. He goes to her and tries to move with her, but he can't keep up. CÉSAR enters he watches. CLAUDE grabs ANGÉLIQUE and kisses her.

ANGÉLIQUE
Look. It stopped snowing.

CÉSAR
Angélique.

ANGÉLIQUE
(stepping back from CLAUDE) César.

CÉSAR
I went looking for you at the house. But your mistress didn't know where you were.

ANGÉLIQUE
I better go see if she needs anything.

CLAUDE
I'll go.

CÉSAR
You wait a minute.

> CLAUDE pauses.

ANGÉLIQUE
César…

CÉSAR
I want you to stay away from her. You understand.

ANGÉLIQUE
César…

CÉSAR
I catch you sniffing around her again…

CLAUDE
You'll what? Eh? What are you going to do? *(after CÉSAR says nothing)* Yeah, that's what I thought.

ANGÉLIQUE
Claude…. Please?

CLAUDE
Sure.

> He kisses her while looking at CÉSAR.

You need anything, just shout. *(exits)*

CÉSAR
He the reason I don't see you any more?

ANGÉLIQUE
César…

CÉSAR
You haven't had enough of one white man you have to have another? *(as he takes out a flask of* Eau de Vie*)* And where are you getting this from? Is he giving it to you? No wonder you're acting like you do.

ANGÉLIQUE
And how am I acting?

CÉSAR
Like a drunken whore.

ANGÉLIQUE
Thank you, Brother.

CÉSAR
Look. It's just…. We're supposed to be together. We have to stick together.

ANGÉLIQUE
Only reason we're together is our masters say so. My master is dead. And I don't plan on replacing him any time soon.

CÉSAR
Your Mistress isn't.

ANGÉLIQUE
She doesn't pay no mind to what I do.

CÉSAR
What about me? What am I supposed to do?

ANGÉLIQUE
I don't care what you do, César.

CÉSAR
We're in this together. You can't choose that white man over me?

ANGÉLIQUE
I don't choose you at all! No more than you chose me! If there were five more to choose from you still wouldn't choose me. I'm just all there is. Better than nothing. Claude has a choice. He chooses me.

CÉSAR
Oh, I see. You think you're special. He loves you…. Dream on. Haven't you been a slave long enough to know that there is only one thing a white man wants from a slave woman.

ANGÉLIQUE
Claude isn't like that. He's different.

CÉSAR
Yeah. Like he's refusing what you're giving out.

ANGÉLIQUE
Yes. I don't give anything. He doesn't take.

CÉSAR
Doesn't mean he don't want.

ANGÉLIQUE
Doesn't mean I won't give. *(beat)* I have been a slave long enough to realize you have to take what happiness you can when you can. Isn't that what you said César?

CÉSAR
Yeah. That's what I said. You're making a big mistake. There's only one thing worse than a rich white master and that's poor white who wants to be one. You think he's on your side right now. But watch out. 'Cause in the end they are all white together.

CÉSAR exits. MANON follows him. He pushes her away.

Scene Two

ANGÉLIQUE in light. CLAUDE in shadow.

CLAUDE
Deep.

ANGÉLIQUE
I want to be close. To feel love. Choose love. Give…

CLAUDE
Rich.

ANGÉLIQUE
Dare I? Trust? Hope?

CLAUDE
Dark.

ANGÉLIQUE
Dare I? Give?

CLAUDE
Ripe.

ANGÉLIQUE
Yes!

CLAUDE
(coming into the light) Mine!

Scene Three

THÉRÈSE, in a red power suit, plays a tug of war with IGNACE Gamelin. They are at the height of their argument.

IGNACE
I tell you Thérèse, productivity at the Ironworks is down! Way down! And the quality of the iron is plummeting with it!

THÉRÈSE
Then perhaps we are trying to accomplish too much in too short a time. If we just focused on producing in smaller volumes we may find that the quality of the iron we do produce is of a higher standard.

IGNACE
It doesn't work like that, Thérèse. We make a little, we make a lot. The problem is the same. Our castings crack!

THÉRÈSE
Maybe it's as simple as too much sand in the mouldings or…

IGNACE
Why do you go on about things you know nothing about and couldn't possibly understand.

THÉRÈSE
Be patient with me, Ignace. I'm just trying to help.

IGNACE
I'm sorry, my dear. But I am running out of patience. And we are running out of time. The bottom line is this. We're losing money. And at the rate we're going, we're not going to make the King's quota. We

default on the quota, we lose the king's patronage. We lose Louis'
patronage, we lose the Ironworks!

THÉRÈSE
What do you want me to do!?

IGNACE
Sell! Sell your shares in the Ironworks to François Etiennes Cugnet.

THÉRÈSE
I can't, Ignace!

IGNACE
We need him, Thérèse.

THÉRÈSE
I can't, Ignace. I just can't. You need him so badly then why don't you
sell.

IGNACE
Because I built this Ironworks! From the ground up! Together with
François! And I have invested more than sentimentality. If you loved
your husband, you would respect what he was trying to achieve with
this enterprise. Instead of trying to destroy it.

THÉRÈSE
I'm not trying to destroy it!

IGNACE
Then sell your shares to Cugnet! And I promise you, you'll be
handsomely rewarded.

THÉRÈSE
I can't! I won't!

THÉRÈSE appears to be winning.

IGNACE
Then you will be the ruin of us all!

He lets go. THÉRÈSE falls back on her behind. ANGÉLIQUE helps her up.

Scene Four

The kitchen.

MANON
I've come for the fish.

ANGÉLIQUE
The fish? What fish?

MANON
The fish you made.

ANGÉLIQUE
I don't make the fish. I just cook it.

MANON
Madame de Francheville promised my mistress some fish.

ANGÉLIQUE
Well, if Madame de Francheville promised…. Here.

She holds up a fish skeleton but with the head and tail still attached.

It's little thin but it's really tasty. As big as ol' Madame de Beray is, she doesn't need much more. *(beat)* Kinda looks like her, doesn't it? Only prettier.

(using the fish head to speak) Eh, Manon. *J'ai faim. Va me chercher un poisson. Je veux manger du poisson. Je suis un poisson. Je vais me manger moi meme! (fish wrestling)* Aghhhhh! *(seeing that MANON is not amused)* Oh, come on. Laugh, Manon. I'm only trying to have some fun. Life is what it is but we can always share a laugh. Yes? *(when MANON doesn't reply)* Well, I guess not.

ANGÉLIQUE gives MANON a Corning casserole dish.

Here. Angélique's famous fish stew. I hope the old bitch doesn't choke on it.

MANON takes it and starts to exit. ANGÉLIQUE stops her.

ANGÉLIQUE
Manon… I am only trying to be your friend. I know I get lonely sometimes. Don't you? So far from home. I wish I had a friend, to make the time go lighter.

MANON
César was my friend! He made me laugh. He spoke my language.

ANGÉLIQUE
I didn't know you felt that way about him.

MANON
He was good to me… until you came. Maybe when you go he will be good again.

ANGÉLIQUE
It was you he.... Oh, Manon. I am so sorry. I didn't know.... Maybe he will make you laugh again. César is free. At least, he's free of me.

MANON
He will never be free of you.

ANGÉLIQUE
But that's not my fault. That wasn't my fault, Manon. You can't blame me...

MANON
When you go... *(exits)*

ANGÉLIQUE
But I'm not going...

Scene Five

THÉRÈSE at her computer.

THÉRÈSE
As of Monday, you'll be staying at the home of my brother-in-law, Alexis Le Moine Moniere.

ANGÉLIQUE
Madame...?

THÉRÈSE
You will stay there until the first canoe leaves for Quebec – where I have made arrangements for you to be sold to Monsieur Cugnet.

ANGÉLIQUE
Sold...

VOICEOVER
(whispered) Angélique... Angélique?

ANGÉLIQUE
Madame.... No.... Madame please... you can't...

THÉRÈSE
I can. And I have.

ANGÉLIQUE
But I belong to Monsieur.

VOICEOVER
(*whispered*) Angélique… Angélique?

THÉRÈSE
You belong to me. Did you think you were freed by his death?

ANGÉLIQUE
But why, Madame? Why? I thought things were better, Madame.
I thought I was serving you better…. No one ever served you better.

THÉRÈSE
(*calmly*) I don't want you. I have never wanted you here. And I welcome
the opportunity to be rid of you. You have brought nothing but
unhappiness and misery into my home. You will lie with anyone.
César. My husband. Now Claude. Gamelin is right. You are like
animals. *Vous êtes trop matinée.* I cannot live with that. I have had no
choice but to endure your presence while François lived. But now
that's over.

ANGÉLIQUE
(*grovelling at THÉRÈSE's feet*) You can't sell me, Madame, Please don't
sell me.

VOICEOVER
(*whispered*) Angélique… Angélique?

ANGÉLIQUE
I can't take another master. I can't. Master after master. Never knowing
which one will be the death of me. I can't go though this all over again.

THÉRÈSE
It is too late. The arrangements have been made.

ANGÉLIQUE
No! Madame. Please. Please…

Thérèse exits.

Scene Six

Fury.

ANGÉLIQUE
YOU BITCH! I WON'T TAKE ANOTHER MASTER! I'LL KILL BEFORE
I HAVE ANOTHER MASTER! I'LL KILL YOU! I'll strangle you in your
sleep! I'll poison your food! You stingy whore! I'll make you rue the day
you sell me! I'll… I'll…

CLAUDE
Calm down…

ANGÉLIQUE
Take me to New England! Now!

CLAUDE
But that's impossible.

ANGÉLIQUE
You promised me, Claude.

CLAUDE
But we can't just pick up and leave like that.

ANGÉLIQUE
Then I will go alone!

CLAUDE
You'll never make it.

ANGÉLIQUE
I don't care!

CLAUDE
Wait. Listen. (*She struggles with him.*) Listen to me. I'll take you. I made a promise and I won't break it. But we can't leave now. I have to plan our escape carefully. Cause we'll only get one stab at it. We get caught we're as good as dead. Until then, just sit tight.

ANGÉLIQUE
How will we know when the is time is right?

CLAUDE
Don't worry. You'll know.

Scene Seven

MANON works outside, singing quietly to herself. ANGÉLIQUE enters and works at her separate tasks. There is some distance between them. There is a large cracking sound.

ANGÉLIQUE
What was that?

MANON
The ice.

CLAUDE
(walking through with a sack of potatoes) It's certainly warming up. *(to ANGÉLIQUE)* Soon. *(He begins to whistle a lively tune.)*

ANGÉLIQUE
(softly, to MANON) When we crossed the great river, some leapt into the water to become froth upon the waves. Some hunkered on their haunches and simply willed themselves to sleep. 'Cause when the spirit leaves the body it flies home to the motherland. What do you see when you look to the river?

> *MANON does not respond.*

What do you hear? *(They look at each other.)* How fast your heart must beat when you look in that direction. Knowing home is close and yet impossible to reach. Does not your spirit yearn to fly this place? Are not your memories still fresh? How do you stop your feet from taking you to where you belong?

MANON
I am where I belong.

> *THÉRÈSE and IGNACE crossing through the scene.*

THÉRÈSE
…six hundred pounds!

IGNACE
For her? *(referring to ANGÉLIQUE)*

THÉRÈSE
Yes. Have I done well in my negotiations?

IGNACE
Not bad.

THÉRÈSE
Perhaps I will be a good entrepreneur after all.

IGNACE
Well, I wouldn't go that far.

THÉRÈSE
(laughing) Oh, Ignace.

> *They exit.*

ANGÉLIQUE
Bitch!

MANON laughs.

You think that's funny? You won't be laughing when the same thing happens to you.

MANON
They say you come from the land of the devil. That the blackness of your skin is the blackness of your soul scorched by the fires of hell.

ANGÉLIQUE
They say that you are bloodthirsty savages. Pagan children, shameless in their nakedness. What does it matter what they say. We are here. Today!

MANON
We are not the same. I serve. I do not slave.

ANGÉLIQUE
A dog and a jackal meet in the forest. "How is it," asks the jackal, that you are so fat and I am so poor and we are both the same animal? The dog says, "I lay around my master's house and let him kick me and he gives me food." "Better then," says the jackal, "that I stay poor."

MANON
Look. Just leave me alone. Okay? Our ways are different. Our stories. Our paths.

ANGÉLIQUE
I'm sorry. I thought I recognized something old and familiar.

MANON
I don't follow you. Do not follow me.

ANGÉLIQUE
I won't. You have forgotten the way.

Scene Eight

All voices in unison: "April 10, 1734."

MANON
(*shovelling hot coals into a bucket*)
My raging heart,
Wey a hey a

Is filled with pain,
Wey a hey a
My César's frost,
Wey a hey a
is searing me,
Wey a hey a.

My blood flows hot,
Wey a hey a
My breath blows cold,
Wey a hey a
Memories of his love,
Wey a hey a
Still burn in me,
Wey a hey.

> *She ululates. CÉSAR enters with a cigar, matches and cigar scissors. He takes the bucket from MANON and prepares the cigar for smoking.*

CÉSAR
I smile. I grin. I keep my eyes averted. I *"Oui,* Monsieur." *"Non,* Monsieur." "Right away, Monsieur." I do whatever I have to do to "just get along." It's survival in the white man's world. And I get by. Why fight what I can't change? But don't think that makes me any less a man.

Don't look at me too closely. You'll see the smile is on my lips not in my eyes which see everything. And though my head is bent, my backbone's strong. My shoulders broad and powerful. And these hands could crush a windpipe just like an autumn leaf. But I don't fight. I'll do whatever I gotta do to "just get along."

Claude thinks that he can beat me with a word. 'Cause in this world where white is might a word is all it takes to silence. But I am a patient man. I'll wait it out. And when the time is right. *(handing the cigar to IGNACE and lighting a match)* I'll strike!

> *He hands the cigar to IGNACE, who takes a light from CÉSAR. He puffs on the cigar a bit, with satisfaction, before speaking. CÉSAR puts the pail beside him.*

IGNACE
Women have no place in business. Their minds can't seem to get around their emotions. And there is no room in business for emotion. I let Thérèse have her way. But she will sell. *(He puffs.)* Eventually, she'll have to sell. *(He flicks his ash into the bucket.)*

THÉRÈSE enters with a candle and slowly makes her way across the stage occasionally stopping and looking behind her, as if she is being pursued by something which isn't there.

THÉRÈSE
(*stopping*) Who's there? Angélique? (*silence*) There are too many noises in this house. Creeks and bumps. Sounds I can't identify. Hear that? (*She stops, listens, whispers.*) Angélique? (*She continues.*) This is my house! I know this house. I love this house. But everything sounds strange to me. Cats cry each night. Dogs howl. Horses stamp their feet. They sense it too. (*She stops.*) Who's there? Angélique? (*pause*) Les Lutins. Yes. Goblins. They're back. I didn't think they could stray so far from farms. But yes! *Les Lutins.* That makes sense. (*She relaxes.*) Yes. Goblins. I can deal with goblins. Goblins and Angélique. Both, I can be rid of.

She takes the bucket and hands it to CLAUDE, who enters with an oil lamp.

CLAUDE
I'm going to be somebody someday. You think I'm going to be hauling buckets and shovelling horseshit all my life? Not me. I'll be as big as Francheville one day. Bigger. You see, I am. I am more than... I am more than this!

In New France, I'll never be more than peasant scum who signed five years of his life away for some new clothes, a few bags of grain and a stony piece of land that may never bear fruit. But in New England or farther south, there's no telling what a man could make of himself! Yes. There's money to be made in the colonies. And, you know what...?

He puts the bucket down and gives ANGÉLIQUE a passionate kiss.

I'm going to make me some.

ANGÉLIQUE
Love. I had almost forgotten it felt like... freedom.

CLAUDE
Soon.

He exits leaving the pail with ANGÉLIQUE.

ANGÉLIQUE
How long can I wait? Each minute brings me closer to a living death. And I'm alive. I am alive!

His touches burn, sear, scorch, igniting fire deep inside where pain and ice had been. And I feel... heat, life, force, power, Black and strong.

She envies that. Cold, passionless bitch! Just like her bastard husband. Both sucking. Sucking life. Denying life.

No! I am not a chair, a sack of grain or a calf to be fattened and sold for slaughter! I am alive. And loved. And I can't wait… any longer.

Smoke begins to fill the stage.

THÉRÈSE
Fire!

ANGÉLIQUE
Fire!

IGNACE
Fire!

CÉSAR
Fire!

Pandemonium breaks out. Church bells ringing, people shouting, panicking. The actors run around and organize themselves into a line in which buckets pass from person to person. ANGÉLIQUE is at the end of the line. Buckets pass swiftly and desperately from person to person. CLAUDE enters picking his teeth. Watches silently for a moment. ANGÉLIQUE turns to grab another bucket, sees CLAUDE and, instead, grabs CLAUDE's hand.

ANGÉLIQUE
Now?

CLAUDE
Now!

They run. The line continues to battle the flames which mount higher and higher. They turn and speak rapidly.

ANGÉLIQUE
The fire was set at the St. Paul Street house of her mistress, in the evening of April 10, 1734.

CLAUDE
The flames travelled quickly from one house to another and, later, to L'Hotel Dieu where the neighbours had started to transport their furniture and belongings.

ANGÉLIQUE
The convent and the church were destroyed.

CLAUDE
This was the third time L'Hotel Dieu had been engulfed by flames.

ANGÉLIQUE
By the time the fire died, 46 homes would be consumed.

Scene Nine

Reporting not unlike "Current Affairs." These scenes are a series of sound bites that play over or are intercut with the ensuing scenes of ANGÉLIQUE and CLAUDE.

REPORTER
It's been determined that yesterday's fire was set by the negress slave of the widow de Francheville, who has escaped with a man named Thibault, also working for de Francheville.

Rumour has it that the negress has often threatened her mistress and the city with the setting of a fire, and that on the same day said that neither her mistress nor many more would sleep in their houses that night. The King's Attorney is calling for the arrest of the negress and the said Thibault.

Scene Ten

ANGÉLIQUE and CLAUDE at a barn near Longueuil. The wind whistles.

CLAUDE
This way... quick... get down.

ANGÉLIQUE
Why are we stopping...?

CLAUDE
Here. Stuff these in your bag...

ANGÉLIQUE
Bread...?

CLAUDE
Six loaves. I hid them two days ago when Madame sent me to Longueuil. It's not much but...

ANGÉLIQUE
Two days ago? Which way now?

CLAUDE
That way. Chemin Chambly.

They run off.

Scene Eleven

THÉRÈSE testifies among the ruins.

THÉRÈSE
Thérèse de Couagne. Age 37. I don't know who set the fire in my house. I did not see the negress go upstairs to the attic unless it was between noon and one o'clock when I went to church for the blessed sacrament. Thibault did come to me the night before and asked to be paid for the time he had worked as my farmer. I told him that I sold the negress and that I didn't want him back in my house either. But I cannot, in all honesty, suspect the negress because there were no fires in my chimneys that day.

Scene Twelve

ANGÉLIQUE and CLAUDE off Chemin de Chambly. They are wrapped in a thick black blanket. Covered by darkness. We hear the thundering sound of horses, wooden wheels turning on a rocky road. Throwing the shadow of its spokes on the mound of the blanket, where we see just the faces of ANGÉLIQUE and CLAUDE frozen with fear, panic, desperation. The sound subsides as it moves into the distance. They remain immobile until there is stillness. Then ANGÉLIQUE and CLAUDE slowly emerge out of the darkness into the dim cast of moonlight.

Scene Thirteen

IGNACE sits comfortably in an arm chair. He is obviously at home and untouched by the fire. CÉSAR stands by him. He testifies.

IGNACE
Ignace Gamelin. And I am old enough to be your father!

Slaves are notoriously inefficient and unwilling. A horse – if it is well treated and cared for, will gladly return all the effort which a well-loved master demands. Some slaves are like horses in this respect (*He smiles at CÉSAR.*) But most are not. Their sense of freedom chafes at restraint. To kindness and forbearance they return insolence and contempt. Nothing awes or governs them but the whip or the dread of sale.

It's fascinating.... While kept in subjugation, they are submissive and easy to control. But let any of them be indulged with the hope of freedom. Then they reject all restraint and become wholly unmanageable: as is the case with this heinous act of arson. It is by the expectation of liberty, and by that alone, that they can be rendered a threat to the population.

Scene Fourteen

The woods. ANGÉLIQUE sits in frustration.

ANGÉLIQUE
The same. Everything looks the same. Those trees, this rock.... Are you sure we're not just running around in circles?

CLAUDE
(angry) Look. I know where I am going! Okay?

ANGÉLIQUE
(surprised) Okay, Claude. *(as he stalks off)* Okay. *(She follows.)*

Scene Fifteen

Testimony.

MANON
Manon, Huron. Age, 19. Just hours before the fire, Angélique came over to me and tried to make me laugh. But I wasn't in the mood. She said, "You really don't want to laugh? You see Madame de Francheville there laughing with Monsieur Gamelin? Well, she won't have a house to sleep in." Angélique thought that was funny.

Scene Sixteen

ANGÉLIQUE and CLAUDE in the woods. Cold, dirty, tired.

ANGÉLIQUE
I don't want to take the chance.

CLAUDE
But we're so far away. They have probably stopped looking for us by now.

ANGÉLIQUE
What if they haven't? If we light a fire the smoke will lead them right to us.

CLAUDE
Angélique. It's been days since we've been indoors. We'll freeze to death.

ANGÉLIQUE
(beat) No we won't. Come here.

He goes to her and she wraps herself around him and kisses him.

We're going to make it.

She starts to make love to him.

Scene Seventeen

The testimonies continue. The following testimonies are doubled by the remaining cast. These are like the specious and ridiculous eyewitnesses often seen on many sensational news programs.

MARGEURITE
Margeurite de Couagne. Age 10. I don't know who set the fire in my aunt's house but just before the fire Angélique was sulking in the kitchen and then I saw her leave by the door on the street and go talk to Mr. de Beray's Indian, Manon. Since then I have heard say that the negress said to the *panisse* that neither she nor her master would sleep in their house. That's all I know, except that two or three times before the fire, the man named Thibault was with the negress in Madame de Franchevilles' kitchen.

HYPOLITE
Hypolite Lebert, esquire. Age 15. I don't know who set the fire in Madame de Francheville's house. But I heard Monsieur de Beray's Indian say to Madame de Francheville that her negress said to her that Mrs. de Francheville would not sleep in her house.

JEANNE
Jeanne Taillandier de la Baume. Age 41. I can't positively say that the fire was started by the negress but when it started I thought for sure it was the negress who started it. I have heard from some children that the negress was threatening to burn her mistress and strangle her and that the negress has said that if she could go back to her country and there were Frenchmen there – she would make them all perish.

The testimonies begin to overlap.

MARIE
Marie Louise Poirier. Age 25. I cannot say anything about the fire but I have heard that the negress said that if she ever returned to her country

and there were white people there she would burn them like dogs. That we were worthless. I also know for a fact that the negress stole three deerskins from Madame de Francheville.

JEAN
Jean Joseph Boudard – 41. All I know are the rumours I've heard that it was the wicked negress of Madame de Francheville who set the fire. But sometimes I would see her drinking *Eau de Vie*...

FRANÇOIS
François de Beray. All I know is what Manon told me. That a short time before the fire, the negress told her that her mistress would not sleep in her house...

The REPORTER cutting though the cacophony.

REPORTER
In dramatic new developments in the O. J.—I mean M. J. Angélique—case, four-year-old Amable Le Moine was brought before the court. Amable, daughter of Alexis Le Moine Moniere and brother-in-law of Madame de Francheville, who swore under oath to tell the truth, testified that on the day of the fire she saw the negress, Marie Joseph Angélique, carrying a coal shuttle up to the attic.

Scene Eighteen

Black. The sound of two wild animals fighting. In the ensuing silence we hear...

CLAUDE
I'm afraid.

Scene Nineteen

CLAUDE and ANGÉLIQUE, wet, ragged, dirty, tired, in the woods.

CLAUDE
If we don't find food, we'll starve to death.

ANGÉLIQUE
We'll be in New England soon. It's been almost two weeks.

CLAUDE
I don't know. I don't know. I was thinking. We passed a cabin a little while back...

ANGÉLIQUE
That was days ago…

CLAUDE
There could be food… warmth…

ANGÉLIQUE
You want to go back?

CLAUDE
Go back…?

ANGÉLIQUE
We can never go back.

CLAUDE
Not after what's happened. Not after…

ANGÉLIQUE
What?

CLAUDE
You know. The fire.

ANGÉLIQUE
What's that got to do with us?

CLAUDE
It doesn't matter now.

ANGÉLIQUE
Claude, you didn't start that fire? Did you?

CLAUDE
(regards her for a long moment) No.

ANGÉLIQUE
Then what do we care! Let's just try to leave it all behind. *(trying to raise his spirits)* It's hard. I know. Sometimes I doubt we're ever going to make it. But we've come this far. We're still alive. And close. New England feels so close. If we can just keep pushing forward…

CLAUDE
Angélique…?

ANGÉLIQUE
Yes…

CLAUDE

...you're right. (*pulling her closer to him*) And when we get to New England, we'll dine on pheasant and roasted potatoes and wash it all down with tankards of beer...

ANGÉLIQUE

Stop. Stop. You're making it worse.

CLAUDE

I know. My stomach is cramping at the thought.

ANGÉLIQUE

Will they have ships there?

CLAUDE

Maybe...

ANGÉLIQUE

Then I will take you home. You will like my land. It's warmer there. And always green. And food hangs from the trees.

CLAUDE

Just like the Garden of Eden.

ANGÉLIQUE

You will see. You'll see.

She curls up against him and sleeps.

Scene Twenty

ANGÉLIQUE sleeps.

CLAUDE

I remember watching my mother's back – always bent, her shirt sleeves rolled above the wrinkles on her elbows. The skin on her arms and hands – rough and red and flaky. She scrubbed laundry for the rich... for pennies. Some days I would beg more than she earned.

And I promised myself that before I left this miserable world, I would become something more than just another hungry peasant or a common petty thief.

So I jumped at the chance to come to this new world. There are opportunities here that I can't even begin to imagine. Just sitting there waiting to be discovered.

I've done everything for you. I've burnt... I've burnt down my dreams for you. But with you, I'll always be running. And I can't run anymore. I can't. I'm sorry. I just can't do it. Please... understand. I can't. I can't. I can't.

He runs off.

Scene Twenty-One

ANGÉLIQUE wakes up alone in the woods to the lonely whistling of the wind through the trees.

ANGÉLIQUE
Claude... Claude...? I had a dream. Claude? We were in New England. But it wasn't New England. It was my village, Claude. Home! I was home. And the sun was setting below the water just as the fire was rising. And you were there. Claude? That's a good sign.... Yes? Claude? *(pause)* Where are you? *(pause)* Claude, are you there? *(silence)* Claaaude!

No response. ANGÉLIQUE listens. Searches for him in all directions with the growing realization that she is alone in the woods. Somewhere, she doesn't know where. Abandoned. No food. No idea of what direction she should follow. She sits, refusing to cry.

It was a good sign. Claude. We could have made it.

Scene Twenty-Two

The lights slowly fall and rise like the setting and the dawning of the sun. ANGÉLIQUE sits in the same place staring out into space. She begins to softly sing a long forgotten song of her home land – accompanied by the muted beating of a drum. Over the course of this speech, two men come and drag her off. She does not resist. The speech continues on an empty stage.

VOICEOVER
Marie Joseph Angélique is declared guilty of setting the fire to Madame de Franchevilles' house, which proceeded to burn down the city. For redress of the damages caused by the fire, and other facts mentioned at the trial, will she make public amends by wearing a shirt only, with a noose around her neck, holding in her hands a burning torch weighing two pounds, in front of the main door and entrance of the parish church of this city, where she will be taken by the executioner of the high court in a tip cart used to pick up garbage and wearing a sign inscribed with the word "arsonist" on her front and back. There, on her knees, will she declare in a loud and clear voice that she wickedly and ill-advisedly set

the fire, for which she repents and asks God, the King, and justice for forgiveness. This done, she will be taken to the public place of the said city of Montreal, to be hanged and strangled to death from the gallows erected for that purpose, her body burned at the stake, the ashes scattered to the wind and her belongings seized in the name of the King. Prior, the accused will be tortured in both the ordinary and extraordinary means to reveal the identity of her accomplices and concerning the said Thibault.

Scene Twenty-Three

FRANÇOIS enters dressed in neutral modern clothes and reads from a book.

FRANÇOIS
Monday, June 21, 1734. 7am. The accused had her shoes taken off and was put on the torture seat by the torturer, and after she'd been strapped in the usual manner with the buskins tied, the accused said...

During this CLAUDE enters dressed in the same fashion, as do all the actors.

CLAUDE
She has no knowledge of anyone and that it's not her. She said "no one helped her because she didn't set the fire."

FRANÇOIS
After the wedge was tightened she said I want to die...

CÉSAR enters.

CÉSAR
At the second blow, she said I'd rather die. No one set, or has helped me set the fire.

MANON enters.

MANON
At the third blow, she said the same.

THÉRÈSE enters.

THÉRÈSE
At the fourth blow she said to hang her, that it was her alone.

IGNACE enters.

IGNACE
After that, for the extraordinary torture, we had a second wedge put in and hit... and hit... and hit... and hit...

FRANÇOIS
She said...

CÉSAR
Kill me.

MANON
It's me alone.

THÉRÈSE
Hang me. It's me.

> *ANGÉLIQUE enters. She is barefoot and naked under a rough raw cotton period shirt.*

THIBAULT
It's me with a hot plate. No one did it with me.

ANGÉLIQUE
No one helped me, nor suggested it. It was my own initiative.

> *She takes the book.*

It's me, Monsieurs. Let me die.

> *She closes the book.*

Scene Twenty-Four

> *ANGÉLIQUE steps up to a microphone.*

ANGÉLIQUE
My name is Marie Josephe Angélique.
I am twenty-nine years old.
I came from Portugal, from the island of Madiere
where I was sold to a Flemish,
who brought me to this New World
and sold me to Monsieur de Francheville.
But before...
before...

Look!
The view is clear...

So clear from here.
In the vista of tomorrow
stretching out before,
I can see this city…
swarming with ebony.
There's me and me and me and me…
My brothers and my sisters!

My brothers and my sisters…
Arrested for their difference.
Their misery
a silent scream,
rising to crescendo
and
falling on deaf ears.

There is nothing I can say to change what you perceive.
I will from twisted history,
be guilty in your eyes.
If thought is sin
then I am guilty.
For I wish that I had fanned the flames that lead to your destruction.
But though I am wretched,
I am not wicked.

Almost ecstatic.

Take my breath.
Burn my body.
Throw my ashes to the wind.
Set my spirit free.
The truth cannot be silenced.
Someday,
someone will hear me
and believe…
I didn't do it.

Until then…

Drums start beating softly and grow.

I am going home.

The hangman goes to put the noose around her neck. She takes it from him.

Can you see the fires rise to greet the sunset?

She puts the noose around her own neck. A male voice calls softly from the crowd.

CLAUDE
(*whispers*) Angélique. Angélique.

The soft sound of drums building.

ANGÉLIQUE
Do you hear it? Drums!

The sound of the platform giving way beneath her. Her silhouetted figure dancing on wall. The overpowering sound of drums. Black.

The end.

A Common Man's Guide to Loving Women

Andrew Moodie

Andrew Moodie has performed in many theatrical, film and television productions including; *Separate Development, The Second Shepherd's Play, Better Living,* and *Our Country's Good* at the Great Canadian Theatre Company. He played MacDuff in *Macbeth* for Grinning Dragon Productions in Vancouver, Minneapolis Dad in *Whale* and the Jabberwocky in *Alice* for Young People's Theatre, Othello in Shakespeare in the Rough's production of *Othello,* Sam in Prairie Theatre Exchange's production of *Master Harold and the Boys,* Dr. Hyde in "Side Effects" for CBC, and Rachel Crawford's evil boyfriend in Clement Virgo's "Rude." His writing credits include a radio play for CBC, an episode of "Drop the Beat" for CBC television, the play *Riot* for which he won a Chalmers award, *Oui* for Factory Theatre, *Wilbur County Blues* for Blythe Festival, and *A Common Man's Guide to Loving Women* for the National Arts Centre and Canadian Stage Company, and *The Lady Smith* for Theatre Passe Muraille. He is currently working on *The Language of the Heart* a play about Harlem Renaissance writer Wallace Thurman.

Post-OJ Black Men?

by Rinaldo Walcott
— • — — • — — • —

I saw the production of *A Common Man's Guide to Loving Women* with another "thirtysomething" Black man in Toronto. The audience was a multi-racial one and we counted more white women than Black women, only a few Black men were in attendance. After the play we hurriedly headed to a bar, ordered a good bottle of red wine and engaged in a debriefing of Andrew Moodie's meditation on the complicated lives of "thirtysomething" Black urban males (Or was it just urban males?). Moodie's play provoked a series of difficult and yet pleasurable responses for both my friend and me. The play is peppered with references to Black urban culture that any clued-in hipster would identify with and respond to (from music to basketball to video games) in a pleasurable affirmative. Thus the play sets in place a structure of feeling for a certain kind of cultural specificity all the while demonstrating how its larger concerns beg a set of strategic universalist questions and concerns. Thus my friend and I found ourselves wondering out loud about the ways in which Black manhood and Black heterosexual masculinity in North America had come to signify the phantasmatic problematic of a more generalized masculinity (usually understood as white) in the late twentieth century and now continuing into the early twenty-first century. We wondered what it meant to be a Black man, especially a heterosexual Black man in a post-OJ Simpson world?

Black masculinity has been in crisis since slavery days, but its contemporary crisis sometimes seems to both distort and overshadow the relation to its (dis)continuous historical crisis. When *A Common Man's Guide* premiered at the National Arts Centre in Ottawa, it was largely lauded for its significant achievement in tackling the racialized and sexualized contexts of Black male urban life. Moodie's comedic rendering of urban Black male life made it easier to sit through the difficult knowledges of the play. Given the context of the play's appearance in post-OJ Simpson North America, which is a significant context within which to view the play, its comedic devises are well warranted. Additionally the comedic impulse of the play cannot be read outside the era of what was then, in the 1990s, at the time of the play's production, the dominance of the Black sitcom on TV (for example Fox Television's shows like "Living Single" and "Martin"). Thus Moodie's brand of comedy had a reference in the wider popular culture and the audience therefore had multiple reference points to enter his play, and through which they could grapple with the difficult material of its performative utterances and still derive pleasure from the performances. The audience at the production I saw clearly enjoyed the humour.

Black masculinities have been in crisis along with a generalized masculinity for quite sometime. But since the era and the gains of second wave feminism, North American masculinities have undergone such a profound crisis that both some men and some women have been working valiantly against what is often perceived as the ill-gotten gains of feminism in an attempt to rescue an uncontaminated masculinity from feminism's allegedly emasculating and "de-male-ing" practices and politics. Moodie's play delves into the territory of how masculinity finds itself in crisis. The play is a commentary on the crisis of identity for four Black male heterosexuals. In this regard Moodie's play can be situated in the ongoing crisis of North American, if not the Western male heterosexual identity. The underlying text of the play is therefore an attempt to come to terms with what the mainstreaming scripts of feminist liberation have meant for the remaking of heterosexual masculinity. The central context of the play concerns accusations of sexual assault; a jilted male lover and cross-racial desire and sex; and revelations of child sexual abuse. These moments of the play's revelation of difficult knowledge of the crisis of heterosexuality for males highlight the play's attempt to intervene in debates that move far beyond Blackness. Thus the partial lives of four Black men are revealed, but something more is at stake in the play's performative rendering of the heterosexual crisis in a post-feminist world.

The difficult knowledge of a potential sexual assault, child sexual abuse and cross-racial desire puts into relief a set of cultural knowledges and debates about how to tackle and resolve difficult events that strike at the heart of who we think we are. In this instance these knowledges strike at the heart of manhood. In Moodie's play, four Black men are forced to rethink much about themselves and their liberal perspectives on life. By so doing each one of them undergoes a certain kind of change in the play. One of the most important moments of the play is the character Chris' advice to Wendle (the accused sexual abuser) to plead guilty. Chris attempts to offer some very good reasons for coming to such a position. His pro-womanist stance is a good example of the mainstreaming of feminism in today's popular and legal discourse. While his advice eventually sparks some very contested conversation among the men, it also opens the way for at least one other character (Robin) to reveal his sexual abuse as a child to his friends. The tensions that these Black men live out among themselves as they try to come to terms with the politics of heteronormativity reveal not only something about Black hetero-masculinity but something about a more general hetero-masculinity.

Thus, what is interesting about Moodie's intervention here is that he seizes the ground of manhood for Black men by not qualifying manhood in the play with the term Black. Thus the play is significantly titled *A Common Man's Guide*. To seize that term, man, without its signifier Black in a post-OJ Simpson world was, and is, to rescue it from some form of contemporary perversity that marks Black manhood out as more damaged and damaging than other forms of heterosexual manhood. In this way the play recentres contemporary debates concerning manhood and masculinity in complex ways, which foreground the ways in which other performances of maleness are deeply racialized. Moodie's *A Common Man's Guide to Loving Women* (note too that women carries no racial signifier) seizes the comedic, political, cultural and social turf for Black manhood in the post-OJ Simpson era and resignifies, and reshapes it from the particular to the universal, all the while revealing through the achingly difficult knowledge, discussion and moments of the play that Black heterosexual manhood is both over-burdened with racialization and simultaneously no different from any other performances of manhood and masculinity in North America or for that matter the western world. In short you simply laugh and simultaneously cry for the troubles and pleasures of heterosexual manhood and masculinity in a world that cannot return to what is often desired as an uncomplicated patriarchy.

Rinaldo Walcott is Canada Research Chair of Social Justice and Cultural Studies at OISE/UT (Ontario Institute for Studies in Education/University of Toronto). He is an Associate Professor in the Department of Sociology and Equity Studies in Education. The second edition of *Black Like Who?: Writing Black Canada*, Insomniac Press, will be published spring 2003.

A Common Man's Guide to Loving Women was first co-produced by National Arts Centre & The Canadian Stage Company, March 1999, with the following company:

WENDLE	Conrad Coates
CHRIS	Derwin Jordan
ROBIN	Andrew Moodie
GREG	Andrew Jason Wade

Directed by Layne Coleman
Set & Costume Design by Victoria Wallace
Lighting Design by Steve Lucas
Sound Design by Marc Desormeaux
Stage Managed by Heather Ann McCallum

— • — — • — — • —

SETTING:
  Wendle's Luxury Warehouse Apartment:
    Front Door
    Wide Balcony overlooking Toronto
    Skylight
    Basketball net
    Kitchen
    Island
    Door leading to bedroom
    Hall leading to bathroom
    Couch
    Television
    Table
    Desk with computer set up

l to r:
Andrew
Moodie,
Derwin
Jordan,
Andrew
Jason
Wade.

Photo by
Gordon
King.

A Common Man's Guide to Loving Women
by Andrew Moodie

—•— —•— —•—

ACT I

Scene One

At rise: GREG is playing Nintendo. CHRIS is in the bedroom on the phone with his fiancée.

GREG
He runs the court, to Carter, for three... brick, brick brick...

ROBIN
Don't start with me.

GREG
You want to make it interesting.

ROBIN
I'm not going to take your money.

GREG
You will not be taking my money.

ROBIN
I don't take sucker bets.

> *WENDLE walks out of the bedroom with a stack of files and goes towards the computer.*

GREG
Come on.

ROBIN
Bite me.

> *WENDLE motions as if he's about to say something. He doesn't.*

GREG
Come on.

ROBIN
Bite me.

GREG
You were going to say something?

WENDLE
No no. No.

GREG
Alright.

WENDLE
You have your cell phone here? Robin?

ROBIN
Yo.

WENDLE
You have your cell phone here?

ROBIN
Naw man, left it at home.

WENDLE goes back into the bedroom.

GREG
Coke, Pepsi, Sprite?

ROBIN
Seven up.

GREG
Yeah. Me too. Thanks.

ROBIN stares at GREG, then goes to the kitchen and grabs two cans of pop.

This game sucks.

ROBIN
Where's Halo?

GREG
You had it last.

ROBIN
I did not.

GREG
You are such a lying bastard.

WENDLE steps out of the bedroom again, looking through files.

Well?

WENDLE
> I think that's it.

GREG
> Oh man.

WENDLE
> You guys gonna stick around right?

ROBIN
> Yeah?

GREG
> Oh uh, Wendle?

WENDLE
> What.

GREG
> Can you get an extra ticket for tonight?

WENDLE
> For who?

GREG
> A friend. Friend of mine. Tabitha. Did you ever meet her?

WENDLE
> Well, I'll have to make a call.

GREG
> If it doesn't happen, I will totally understand.

WENDLE
> No, it shouldn't be a problem. It shouldn't be a problem at all.

ROBIN
> Hockey? Hockey?

GREG
> Uh, sure.

ROBIN
> Have I told you how much I love your new digs.

WENDLE
> What?

ROBIN
This is a great apartment man.

WENDLE
Yeah, yeah.

ROBIN
I wanted to get a place in the Candy Factory, but the muthafucka's charging three hundred thousand dallas for a muthafuckin shoe box.

WENDLE
I need to use a phone.

GREG
Try next door, maybe the neighbours?

WENDLE
You'll be here right?

ROBIN
We're not going anywhere.

WENDLE *leaves.*

GREG
Who're you taking?

ROBIN
Leafs. What?

GREG
I'm taking the Habs.

ROBIN
Fine.

GREG
And I am going to bludgeon you to death.

ROBIN
In your wet dreams you little girlie man.

CHRIS
(off-stage) I am listening to you!!! I am!!!

GREG
You ready?

ROBIN
I gotta set up my lines!

GREG
You think that's going to help?

CHRIS
(off-stage) No no you take a step back! No no, you take a step back!

GREG
I don't care what any of you guys say, even with all this going on, I still want to get married.

ROBIN
You want to get married?

GREG
Oh yeah.

ROBIN
Why?

GREG
Well…

ROBIN
Why?

GREG
I'm thinking it's about that time.

ROBIN
To do what?

GREG
Settle down. You know? And that paternal clock thing is ticking louder and louder.

ROBIN
You want a kid?

GREG
I cannot wait to be a father.

ROBIN
What do you want, boy or a girl?

GREG
Boy. Two boys. That's what I want.

ROBIN
No no give me girls man. Girls are great, they're like Daddy's Little Princess. Boys? Boys are great for about thirteen years, then one day, you open the door to their room and their head's spinning around, eyes rollin' back in their skull going "Must Kill Father. Don't know why. Must Kill Father."

GREG
Not my boys.

ROBIN
No not your boys.

WENDLE returns.

GREG
Not home?

WENDLE
Yeah.

GREG
Is it about the thing?

WENDLE
Yeah.

CHRIS walks out of the bedroom.

CHRIS
The wedding's off.

ROBIN
Get out.

CHRIS
That's it.

WENDLE
Man.

CHRIS
That's it. We're done.

GREG
>What happened?

CHRIS
>She met somebody.

ROBIN
>Aww.

GREG
>Tough break man.

CHRIS
>Yeah.

ROBIN
>Was it another guy or was it a woman?

CHRIS
>What?

ROBIN
>It was a guy right?

CHRIS
>Yeah.

>*ROBIN gives WENDLE and GREG ten bucks each.*

ROBIN
>Fuck me.

CHRIS
>What...

GREG
>So this guy, who is he?

CHRIS
>I don't know, some guy she worked with on tour. You thought it was going to be another woman?

ROBIN
>I was just hoping, that's all.

WENDLE
>So who is this guy, what's his name?

CHRIS
Hughson. Randy Hughson. Some blond-haired, blue-eyed, *GQ*-looking son of a bitch.

GREG
Is he like a big name actor or something?

CHRIS
Yeah. What?

ROBIN
She's star fucking.

GREG
Big time!

ROBIN
Star fucking.

CHRIS
Think so?

GREG
That's the only way she is going to get her no talent ass up to the top.

WENDLE
I'll just be a second.

    WENDLE goes to the bedroom. CHRIS goes to the door.

GREG
What are you doing?

CHRIS
Just going to the store.

ROBIN
What do you need, we got everything here, pop, chips, what do you want.

CHRIS
I just want to go to the store.

GREG
I'll go. What do you need?

CHRIS
It's alright, I'm just going to the store, I'll be back in a second, just get out of my way.

GREG
What do you want to get at the store? Whatever it is I can get it.

ROBIN
What do you want? What.

CHRIS
Just wanted a cigarette.

ROBIN
No no no no!

GREG
No no no no!

CHRIS
Get out of my way.

ROBIN
Come on man, you've been doing so good!

CHRIS
It's just one cigarette, for crying out loud.

GREG
Just stop, sit for a second.

CHRIS
I don't want to.

ROBIN
Just relax, sit down, let's wait for Wendle to come back, then we can go out, have some dinner.

CHRIS
Actually, I think I might just go home.

GREG & ROBIN
What are you crazy! Hey, you can't do that!

CHRIS
I want to go home.

GREG
> Yo G dis here weekend's fa you bra.

CHRIS
> I want to thank you guys but I really can't stay here.

GREG
> Alright sit. I want you to sit.

CHRIS
> Guys.

ROBIN
> Sit ya nigga ass down, aight.

> > *ROBIN makes CHRIS sit down.*

CHRIS
> Alright.

GREG
> We are not going to let you go home.

CHRIS
> Why.

GREG
> This weekend is yours. If you want to chill that's fine, but you are going to have to do it with us.

CHRIS
> Am I on a suicide watch or something?

GREG & ROBIN
> No no no no.

ROBIN
> You don't want to be alone now, come on, think about it.

CHRIS
> Look, I appreciate all the concern, that's great, it's inspiring, but I'm handling it. Okay? It's not a big deal. Now if you'll excuse me, I want to head home.

ROBIN
> But we, we planned a surprise for you.

CHRIS
No strippers guys. Not in the mood.

ROBIN
Okay, then we've got another surprise for you.

CHRIS
What is it?

ROBIN makes a bunting motion to GREG.

GREG
What.

ROBIN whispers in GREG's ear. GREG hesitates. ROBIN slaps him and whispers in his ear.

You remember Tabitha? You know. A month ago, when we met for that movie? She works for this idiot over here.

CHRIS
Oh right, right.

GREG
She's coming to the game, and she wants a post-game beer with you.

CHRIS
Aren't you madly in love with her?

GREG
I'm not in love with her.

ROBIN
She just remembers you from the movie and she wants to get together, have a beer afterwards, that's all.

CHRIS
I find it hard to believe that she would remember who I am.

GREG
How could she forget a man as intelligent, as scintillating…

ROBIN
Scintillating.

GREG
And ebullient as you are.

ROBIN
Yeah.

CHRIS
Look, I know what you guys are trying to do. You're trying to pull a sacrifice bunt...

GREG & ROBIN
No.

CHRIS
You sacrifice the woman you're going after...

GREG & ROBIN
NO!

CHRIS
Thanks for the offer, you guys go out, have fun, I'm going home.

ROBIN
Hey hey hey HEY! Stop. Now just, come here. Come here. We care about you, and I don't think we'd be good friends if we just let you run away off on your own and tear yourself apart. I couldn't do that. Neither of us could. Now, just let us be here for you. Alright? We'll go out, do some stuff together, try and keep your spirits up. Let us do that for you. Alright? Tomorrow night you can do whatever the hell you want to do, but tonight, you belong to us, okay? Alright?

CHRIS
Okay.

ROBIN
What is it?

CHRIS
I'm fine. Back in a second.

CHRIS goes to the washroom.

GREG
He's not fine.

ROBIN
Not at all.

WENDLE enters from the bedroom.

GREG
Good news?

WENDLE uses his body to tell them that he doesn't think things are going well but he doesn't want to give up hope. Noise from the bathroom. WENDLE listens.

WENDLE
How's the kid?

ROBIN
Eeeh.

GREG
Tickets? Did you get the ticket?

WENDLE
Oh for crying out loud.

GREG
If it's a hassle...

WENDLE
No it's not at all, I'm just... let me just call now.

GREG
Seriously, if it's a hassle.

WENDLE
It's not a hassle, don't worry about it.

WENDLE goes back into the bedroom. ROBIN laughs to himself.

GREG
Shut the fuck up.

ROBIN
I didn't say a word.

GREG
You just shut the fuck up.

ROBIN
I did you do not look at me I ain't said shit.

GREG grabs the basketball and takes some shots. ROBIN goes to the liquor cabinet and pours himself a shot of scotch. GREG notices this and continues to play basketball.

GREG
What are you doing?

ROBIN
I'm having a scotch.

GREG
Alright.

ROBIN
I can have one. Okay? It's not a big deal.

GREG
Alright.

ROBIN
We're gonna be eating in like forty minutes alright? So chill. I'll be fine.

GREG
Alright.

       CHRIS comes out of the bathroom.

CHRIS
You know what I just realized?

GREG
What?

CHRIS
I will never have to see another play again.

ROBIN
I thought you loved theatre.

CHRIS
I fucking HATE theatre.

GREG
Then why were you always going?

ROBIN
Because you wanted to be a good boyfriend.

CHRIS
I wanted to be a good boyfriend.

ROBIN
Now you don't have to see a play ever again.

GREG
What was that piece of garbage thing you dragged me to?

ROBIN
You went to see a play?

GREG
Some piece of crap thing…

CHRIS
Chekhov.

GREG
Let me tell you something. Next time I step into a theatre, I want to see something blow up, get swept away in a tornado, I wanna see some dinosaur chomping on some little kid's head, knowhamsayin?

CHRIS
You know what? I am so glad that I am out of this relationship. I am. I am so glad.

GREG
Good.

CHRIS
I was kinda worried there for a second. I thought I was going to feel some kind of like… it's like a weight's gone, you know? It's like this vice has just gone phoomp.

ROBIN
I hear ya.

CHRIS
You know what? Let's get out of here.

ROBIN
Let's have some fun.

CHRIS
I don't… let's… let's get out of here.

GREG
Said and done.

Enter WENDLE.

WENDLE
Got the tickets.

GREG
If it was a hassle.

WENDLE
It wasn't a hassle, I'm just... y'know?

GREG
Tadow.

ROBIN
So what's the plan Stan.

CHRIS
What time does the game start?

WENDLE
Eight. I figure we go to Spinnakers, grab a meal, see the game.

GREG
Sounds good to me.

> *Phone rings.*

WENDLE
Don't answer it.

CHRIS
But it could be...

WENDLE
Well, okay... I'll get it. Just... okay. Hello? Oh, uh, hold on a second.

> *WENDLE grabs a file, goes to his room. GREG smacks ROBIN on the head and points to the Nintendo. As they start playing, CHRIS goes to the kitchen area. On his way he tries to hear what WENDLE is saying.*

GREG
Got your lines?

ROBIN
Got my lines.

GREG
Penalties?

ROBIN
Penalties.

GREG
Welcome to the house of pain.

ROBIN
Welcome ladies and gentlemen to the Air Canada Centre. Tonight's match, it's the Leafs versus the Habs as...

GREG
Just press the damn start button!

ROBIN
Bam!

GREG
Here we go.

CHRIS
Guys.

GREG
Oh you want some of this.

ROBIN
Come here you bastard.

CHRIS
Guys.

ROBIN
Boomshakalak!

GREG
You son of a bitch.

CHRIS
Guys, what's up with Wendle? Guys?

GREG
Damphousse with the wrap around...

ROBIN
He makes the save!

CHRIS
Guys. What's up with Wendle? Come off it guys.

GREG
Tell him.

ROBIN
You tell him.

CHRIS
Tell me what?

GREG
Don't worry about it. Ohhh! That was tripping, right there.

CHRIS
Don't worry about what?

ROBIN
You've got enough on your plate right now. Don't sweat it.

CHRIS
I am going to take that game and beat both of your skulls with it if you don't tell me what the fuck is going on.

GREG & ROBIN
Ohhhh!

GREG
That's gotta hurt.

ROBIN
Sudin on the breakaway...

GREG
No.

ROBIN
Suck it down muthafuckaaaaaaa...

> CHRIS unplugs the game.

Aaaaaargh!

GREG
Aah ah ah ah...

ROBIN
Fuck off Chris!

CHRIS
What's going on with Wendle?

ROBIN
Wendle's been fired.

CHRIS
What!

GREG
He hasn't been fired, he might be fired.

CHRIS
Why?

ROBIN
It's… that's… don't worry about it.

CHRIS
What's going on. Guys?

GREG
You're not supposed to know.

ROBIN pokes GREG with the game controller.

ROBIN
Come on.

GREG
I don't want to play.

ROBIN
Fuck you, you're playing.

CHRIS
Is he going to be okay? Guys…

GREG
Just sit back, relax, don't worry about it, we'll be out of here in no time, just relax.

ROBIN
Ask him about Diane.

CHRIS
Diane? What's going on with Diane?

ROBIN keeps poking GREG with the controller.

GREG
Nothing's going on with Diane, you've got enough stuff to deal with. Sit. Relax. We'll be out of here in a second. I don't want to play!

ROBIN
Where's Halo?

GREG grabs the game with his feet and tosses it at ROBIN.

GREG
So what do you want to do after the game? Go to a club.

CHRIS
Sure. Whatever.

GREG
I know the bouncers at Joker. Tell them that you work with me at CITY and I can get you in. No problem.

CHRIS
Sounds good.

GREG
First off, do you have condoms?

CHRIS
No.

GREG
Here.

He takes some out of his back pocket and gives them to CHRIS.

CHRIS
Extra large?

GREG
That's what I got. Take it or leave it.

ROBIN
I tried those once and they just fit. I hated that. If I'm gonna wear extra large I want it to be tight you know what I mean?

CHRIS
Too much information.

ROBIN
And they're so thick! I couldn't believe it, it was like wearing a shower cap.

GREG
They're not that thick.

ROBIN
Muthufuckin garbage bag, man.

GREG
Not when it's nice and snug.

CHRIS
Alright, enough already.

ROBIN
Is that what you're going to wear?

CHRIS
What's wrong with what I'm wearing?

ROBIN
Do you think he'd fit into one of Wendle's silk shirts?

GREG
Mmmmmm.

ROBIN
What about his leather pants.

CHRIS
I am not wearing leather pants.

ROBIN
Okay, so you're dressed up, you're hanging with us and across the room, a beautiful, 22-year-old starts giving you the eye, you do what.

CHRIS
I, I give up, what.

ROBIN
You ditch us and go talk to her.

CHRIS
Lay off guys.

ROBIN
 I can't work with this.

CHRIS
 I am not in any shape to…

GREG
 Okay, so she walks by the table, she looks right into your eyes, what do you do?

CHRIS
 This is stupid.

GREG
 You talk to her.

CHRIS
 I know you're trying to cheer me up…

ROBIN
 What do you say?

CHRIS
 Hi?

ROBIN
 Hi's good.

GREG
 If she's American? Mmm mm MMM! Get a look at yourself! Girl, you lookin so good right now, I could sop you up with a biscuit!

ROBIN
 Americans love that shit.

GREG
 And say it loud.

ROBIN
 Americans are loud, very loud.

CHRIS
 Guys…

GREG
 Okay, so, you start talking to her. Go for it.

   ROBIN notices CHRIS is staring at his chest.

ROBIN
Hey, watch the eyes buster, up I'm up here, not down here.

CHRIS
Sorry.

GREG
So go ahead, ask her something.

CHRIS
I'm not doing this, it's ridicu...

GREG whispers in his ear.

Did you go to Ryerson?

ROBIN
No. No I didn't.

CHRIS
Okay.

GREG makes buzzer noise.

What!

ROBIN
Right away, you got to get in there right away.

GREG
Next you want to get her name, and when you get her name...

GREG & ROBIN
Remember it.

ROBIN
You can't be waking up the next day trying to figure out how the hell you're going to open up her wallet so you can find her driver's license. That's kinda low class.

CHRIS
Guys...

GREG
So talk about her name for a bit, get to know it. Go for it.

ROBIN
Keeping the eyes on the face.

CHRIS
So what's your name?

ROBIN
Shaniqua.

CHRIS
Isn't that an old Afro-American slave name?

GREG
No no no no…

CHRIS
It's a valid question.

ROBIN
Keep going keep going just keep going.

> *GREG whispers in his ear.*

CHRIS
So Shaniqua, what do you do for a living?

ROBIN
I'm an assistant to the deputy for intergovernmental affairs for the provincial government.

CHRIS
Intergovernmental affairs, wow, what's that?

GREG
There we go!

ROBIN
Well right now I'm an assistant to the deputy but I want to move to the environment portfolio where I can make more of a difference. Besides the deputy is a sexist asshole.

CHRIS
Men are pigs.

> *GREG gives CHRIS an emphatic thumbs up.*

ROBIN
Yeah, I know. What do you do?

CHRIS
I work in a law firm. Corporate law. You know.

ROBIN
Oh really.

CHRIS
Right now my job is to go around to corporations and advise them on employment equity, equal pay for women, stuff like that.

GREG goes nuts, doing a hockey player "goal" move.

ROBIN
Oh really!

CHRIS
If this guy is a sexist pig, I may be able to give you some legal options free of charge.

GREG
Beautiful!

CHRIS
That is, if you could show me your legal options on the dance floor.

GREG
Congratulations Christopher Ewert, you are now officially on base number...

GREG & ROBIN
One!

CHRIS
I just offered free legal advice as a veiled request for sexual favours.

ROBIN
And it was beautiful.

WENDLE
(off-stage) Fuck you fuck you fuck fuck fuck fuck!

The guys want to open the door, but feel they can't.

ROBIN
Eh Wendle. You okay in there? Wendle.

WENDLE
(off-stage) Yeah.

ROBIN
You okay in there?

WENDLE
(*off-stage*) I'll be out in a second.

CHRIS pulls out a twenty.

CHRIS
Guys could you do me a favour and go get some chips and crackers and stuff?

GREG takes the money and heads for the door.

ROBIN
But I want to play Halo.

GREG
Don't make me bitch-slap you.

ROBIN
Imo kick yo ath!

They exit repeating their lines. WENDLE enters with the phone.

WENDLE
Where's Tweedle dumb and Tweedle dumber?

CHRIS
They went out to get some chips and stuff.

WENDLE
Ah. You want to... you want a drink? I've got some Glenlivet here.

CHRIS
No thanks.

WENDLE
Sure?

CHRIS
Yeah.

WENDLE
Do you mind if I...

CHRIS
No, no. Go ahead. So who were you on the phone with earlier?

WENDLE
Nothing. Don't worry about it.

CHRIS
Something about work?

WENDLE
Yeah, yeah. Honestly, don't worry about it. Don't. How're you feeling. You okay?

CHRIS
I'm kinda... I have two extremes; one second I'm fine...

WENDLE
What was she saying?

CHRIS
She's trying to convince me that it's all my fault.

WENDLE
Is it working?

CHRIS
I don't know.

WENDLE
Can I say something?

CHRIS
No. No you can't. No.

WENDLE
I just want to...

CHRIS
I know what you're going to say.

WENDLE
What am I going to say?

CHRIS
There is a direct co-relation between my mother's passive aggressive self abuse and my searching for...

WENDLE
Okay, I'm going to say something.

CHRIS
I attract these women...

WENDLE
Okay.

CHRIS
…who are in crisis as a way of…

WENDLE
Listen…

CHRIS
I don't need a speech right now telling me that I'm a moron, okay?
I don't.

WENDLE
I'll wait.

CHRIS pulls out the ring.

CHRIS
Here.

CHRIS tosses WENDLE the ring.

WENDLE
What's this?

CHRIS
It's yours.

WENDLE
You might need it.

CHRIS
I don't think so.

WENDLE
You might.

Silence.

CHRIS
So Robin tells me I should ask you about Diane.

WENDLE
Did he.

CHRIS
Yes he did.

WENDLE
I wonder why he'd say a thing like that?

WENDLE goes to the kitchen.

CHRIS
Want to tell me about it, or…

WENDLE
I uh… I don't really believe in love at first sight at all. I mean at all.
When you first meet someone, you can project a lot of what you think
you're looking for in a relationship. So I usually take a long time before
I commit any kind of emotion into anything. Just to be sure that you
get to see some of the real content of the person's character. And there
were a few things that kinda… put me off at first. I mean the whole
cheerleader thing…

CHRIS
Right.

WENDLE
I need to be able to command a certain amount of respect in my job,
and… well you start bringing around a cheerleader, people start talking
and they don't necessarily say the nicest things.

CHRIS
Right.

WENDLE
And she's blonde…

CHRIS
And she's younger than you.

WENDLE
Yeah yeah…

CHRIS
Go on.

WENDLE
So we dated and we dated and I took her to restaurants, museums. Get
to know her.

CHRIS
Okay.

WENDLE

Chris... she is... this clever, funny, she's very funny, sweet, caustic, human being. And I kinda...

CHRIS

You fall for her.

WENDLE

I guess you could say that. Yeah.

CHRIS

And...

WENDLE

So we get to the stage where we both think we can... take it to the next step. I suggest making it something special, you know? So one day, when we're both not working, spend the day together, go to the Island, dinner at Grappa, really nice meal. And then come back here. I had the place all decked out with candles, rose petals from the door to the bedroom kinda thing......

CHRIS

You went all out.

WENDLE

Well, I figure... look, if this is going to be it, then let's do it right.

CHRIS

I can see it.

WENDLE

So we get in here, and we start, you know...

CHRIS

Yeah.

WENDLE

So then, she goes, "Do you have a condom?" And uh, I was thinking so much about everything else and uh, you know, I forgot. I did, I forgot...

CHRIS

So you...

WENDLE

Put my clothes back on, went downstairs, got the condoms, come back up here, put one on, and then we start.

CHRIS
Okay.

WENDLE
Okay, so we're going along there for a while, and I start to notice a burning sensation.

CHRIS
Burning?

WENDLE
Yeah, kinda like if you had an infection, only it was sudden, it was like immediate.

CHRIS
And that was when you had the condom on.

WENDLE
Yeah. Now, I didn't know what was happening at the time, but now I think I might be allergic to the spermicide or something.

CHRIS
Oh come on.

WENDLE
No I'm serious. It hurt. Really bad. I'm serious!

CHRIS
Okay, alright, go ahead.

WENDLE
I'm not fucking around with you, it hurt!

CHRIS
Okay, sure, go on.

The front door buzzer goes off. The buzzer has a light that flashes. WENDLE gets it.

WENDLE
Who is it?

ROBIN
(off-stage) Luke, I am your Father Luke…

WENDLE presses the buzzer to let them in.

WENDLE

Anyway, so… so… and this is where things get fucked up, because, okay, what happened was I took the condom off and went to start again, and she was all like, "I don't know." But I told her, Look, you don't have to worry about me, I have only slept with maybe three other woman in my entire life, I don't have any diseases or anything. But she was still like, "I don't know" so we talked for a bit, I think I've convinced her, I start again, and she's just like lying there. I finish and I say look, I'm sorry honey, cause I can tell she's mad right. She goes to the end of the bed, starts putting on her clothes, I tell her I'm sorry again, and she looks at me and says, you know you just raped me. I'm like, what? I try to talk to her, she doesn't want to hear it. She's gone. Next day, I'm calling her from work, calling her and calling her, as I'm sitting at my desk, two police officers come up to me, tell me I am under arrest for rape, handcuff me and take me out of the office and right to the Don Jail.

CHRIS

Whoa.

WENDLE

You know what she told the cops, this is what pissed me off the most. You know what she put in her affidavit? Wait, I got it right here, wait. Where is it. Here. She says that I tore off the condom, and with a look on my face of hatred for all women, I brutally raped her. Here, this is the best part; "Once he was finished, he turned to me and said, 'All you white bitches are the same.' It was then that I knew I didn't want to become another Nicole Simpson."

CHRIS

Let me see this.

WENDLE

By all means.

> *GREG and ROBIN enter. ROBIN jumps on the couch and uses the remote to turn on the TV. Sound off.*

GREG

We have decided that we will go to Insomnia first because… it is a better environment for you and Tabitha to talk and get to know each other.

WENDLE

Why the hell are you trying to set Chris up with the woman you're in love with.

GREG
I'm not in love with her.

The phone rings.

WENDLE
Don't answer it!

CHRIS
But...

WENDLE
Don't.

CHRIS
But it could be...

ROBIN
Get call display for crying out loud!

CHRIS answers the phone.

CHRIS
Hello? Hi. Yeah.

CHRIS takes the phone cord and waves to WENDLE to help him get the phone into the bedroom.

Uhm, no. No it's okay. Yeah. Well I don't know.

CHRIS goes into the bedroom.

WENDLE
Beer?

GREG
7-Up.

WENDLE
Same for you?

ROBIN
I uh... I'll have a beer.

WENDLE
...okay.

GREG saunters over to ROBIN and sits next to him.

GREG
Tell you what.

ROBIN
Yes.

GREG
How about this, alright? Now, you give me the keys to the car, and I can be the Double D tonight? How about that?

ROBIN
Look, I'm fine. Alright.

GREG
Robin...

ROBIN
We're gonna go to dinner, then we're gonna see a game. It's one beer. Leave me alone.

GREG
Things okay between you and Linda?

ROBIN
Yeah yeah.

GREG
Really?

ROBIN
Yes.

GREG
If you give me the keys...

ROBIN
It's one drink. I'm not giving you my fucking keys. Back the fuck off.

WENDLE
You want the beer or what?

ROBIN
Yeah. Yeah.

> *WENDLE hands him the beer. It's an imported beer that doesn't twist off. Gives GREG the 7-Up.*

WENDLE
So tell me about this... you need an opener. *(He gets a bottle opener and offers it to ROBIN.)* So tell me about this Tabitha woman. Greg?

GREG
Yeah?

WENDLE
How did you meet her?

GREG
Uh, through Robin.

ROBIN
She's one of the managers at the store.

WENDLE
I see.

ROBIN
He came in one day, looking for an action flick, she astounded him with her acute knowledge of every Jackie Chan film ever made, and the rest, as they say, is history.

WENDLE
How does it look?

GREG
We're kinda doing the friends thing, but that's cool. I'm not in a rush to do anything right now.

WENDLE
Course not.

GREG
I still get little feelings of... I don't know. There's no time limit on grieving, right?

WENDLE
Well, the funeral was only what...

GREG
Four years.

WENDLE
Wow.

GREG
Four years to the day last Thursday.

WENDLE
Time just…

GREG
She was so sick, for so long. We both invested so much in trying to keep her healthy, around the end, it was just so hard to let go but… you got to move on, right, keep living your life.

ROBIN
Yeah.

WENDLE
This girl you're bringing to the game tonight. What's her name again?

GREG
Tabitha.

WENDLE
Here's to Sheryl who was a beautiful person, who could never be replaced. And here's to Tabitha, and… the future.

ROBIN
Cheers.

GREG
Thanks guys.

WENDLE
I'll tell you something, in all my years of living on this planet, one thing that never ceases to amaze me, is how a woman can be the source of such incredible pleasure, and such great pain. Great pain. It starts off innocently enough; you spend your teens giggling, and laughing at them. Teasing them. Dreaming about them. You spend your twenties chasing them into crouched, dark corners of cheap bars, talking bullshit in some form or another. You bust your ass to get the job, to get the apartment, to get the clothes, to get the car, to build the kind of life that some woman, somewhere, is going to share with you someday. Then, after a while, you start to realize that; hey, it just might not happen for me. This idea that someone is out there for you, that there is someone special out there, just for you, is all a load of bullshit. A deep self-delusion propagated by movies, music, TV ads, your mother, sitcoms, all forms of print media, and something… in some little corner deep inside your own soul. This is not exactly what I saw for myself, not where I thought I would be at this point in my life, but, hey… here I am. Here I am.

GREG puts his hand on WENDLE's shoulder. CHRIS enters.

CHRIS
She'll be here in an hour.

WENDLE
Let's go.

CHRIS
No, I want to stay.

GREG
What are you crazy?

CHRIS
She sent me an e-mail, I want to read the e-mail. I want to stay here and meet her.

GREG
Not a good idea.

ROBIN
Are you sure about this?

CHRIS
Yeah, that's what I want to do.

WENDLE
But we'll miss the first ten minutes of the game.

CHRIS
You guys go, go ahead. You don't have to stay here. It's okay. I mean it.

ROBIN
No it's alright.

CHRIS
Go. Go to the game, I'll meet you there.

GREG
We'll stay until she gets here. Then we'll go to the game, okay?

WENDLE
Fine.

CHRIS
You don't have to do this.

WENDLE
Wanna get your e-mail?

CHRIS
Can I use your computer?

WENDLE
Sure.

> *WENDLE goes to the computer and turns it on.*

ROBIN
Is this new?

WENDLE
Upgrade.

ROBIN
What do ya got?

WENDLE
Pentium IV 2Ghz. Burnable DVD, 160 Gig hard drive, 256 meg DDR RAM, 21" Monitor with an ATI AGP 64 meg Radeon graphics card, ISDN Internet connection.

ROBIN
Can I touch it?

WENDLE
I can have any of the firm's data bases on here and work on it remotely from my laptop anywhere in the world.

GREG
(declares proudly) I've got a Mac.

WENDLE
Chris, you want to enter your e-mail password?

> *CHRIS sits at the computer.*

CHRIS
How do you work the printer?

GREG
Oh my God, Tabitha. Do you have her number?

ROBIN
Where's the phone?

GREG
Let me call her.

ROBIN and GREG go to the bedroom.

ROBIN
She's my employee, and I don't care how much you're in love with her.

GREG
I'm not in love with her!

They enter the bedroom.

WENDLE
If anybody calls while you're on the phone, I'm not here!

CHRIS
Who are you avoiding?

WENDLE
Some bitch from human resources. She's trying to force me out. Thing is, I'm the director of finances. My superior is the VP and he thinks this whole thing is bullshit. He gave me my lawyer and thinks I should fight it.

CHRIS
What is she saying?

WENDLE
She knows that the CEO feels that even though it's a bullshit charge, it could reflect poorly on the firm. The Raptors, they're our biggest client. "Director of finances of Toronto marketing firm rapes cheerleader." If the papers get a hold of this thing, you may as well put a bullet in my head.

CHRIS
So what do they want to do?

WENDLE
They want to suspend me. They don't have a valid reason to suspend me so she's going over all of my shit. Everything. Trying to find some little thing that could give them a reason to suspend the mad rapist.

CHRIS
But... I mean, technically this isn't even called a rape case.

WENDLE
Really?

CHRIS
Well, it's clear that she consented to the original sexual contact, the hospital could not provide any evidence of physical harm, there's no bruises, no evidence of force, and there was already a case very similar to this here in Toronto not too long ago, a precedent has been set. It's not a rape case.

WENDLE
Would you please try my case for me?

CHRIS
What about your lawyer, what does he say?

WENDLE
He thinks I should fight the rape charge.

CHRIS
Really? Has he read this affidavit?

WENDLE
Yeah. What.

CHRIS
What area of law does he practice?

WENDLE
I'm not sure what it's called but he usually does contracts for athletes.

CHRIS
He's way out of his league. He is way out of his element.

WENDLE
Would you try my case for me? Please?

CHRIS
Well, if I were to try your case, I would present the judge with a guilty plea for sexual assault.

WENDLE
You think I raped her.

CHRIS
No.

WENDLE
You think I'm lying.

CHRIS
I think that even with what you told me, an assault occurred.

WENDLE
But I didn't do anything!

CHRIS
In the eyes of the law, you willfully continued intercourse when you knew you had broken the terms of consent.

WENDLE
But we talked about it.

CHRIS
No, you talked about it. If she didn't change the rules of consent, then you committed an offense.

WENDLE
But she did!

CHRIS
What did she say? What did she do? If she did, why would she run to the police.

WENDLE
Fuck you.

CHRIS
Wendle, I feel for your position, I do, but if I were to try this case, I would enter a guilty plea for sexual assault. Hey. I'm just telling you what I would tell any prospective client.

WENDLE
They're going to fire me Chris! If I can't beat this thing, they are going to fire me. That's it. Everything gone. All this, everything. Gone.

CHRIS
Well, but, it's... it's the law. There's nothing I can do about it. Where are you going?

WENDLE
Out.

CHRIS
Come on man, just, Wendle? Wendle...

WENDLE leaves. The printer beeps.

ACT II

Scene One

GREG and CHRIS sitting around, GREG reading Details *magazine, CHRIS skimming over his e-mail. He has already read it. ROBIN taking shots at the net.*

GREG
What is it that you love the most about your wife, her intellect or her body?

ROBIN thinks about it for a while.

ROBIN
Her intellect.

GREG
Yeah, yeah…

ROBIN
I love the fact that we can debate, and argue ideas, from a place of complete mutual respect. There's no way I could live without that. I'm serious. And we have very different tastes. She's always trying to get me to read some damn Toni Morrison novel. And I'm always dragging her to some West African film at the Film Festival. So it's like we're constantly challenging each other. I couldn't live without that. Seriously. I couldn't.

GREG
She's pretty stacked too.

ROBIN
Yes my wife has a great body Greg. Yes. You know what else I love about my wife?

GREG
What?

ROBIN
Her clitoris.

GREG
Okay thank you!

ROBIN
It's so soft, and…

GREG
Thank you very much!

ROBIN
It's not so small that it's not existent...

GREG
When was the last time...

ROBIN
But not so big that...

GREG
When was the last time you told your wife you loved her, a) within the past 24 hours, b) 48 hours, c) why the hell would I do that?

ROBIN
This morning.

GREG
When was the last time you told her she was beautiful, a)...

ROBIN
Yesterday.

GREG
You did not.

CHRIS stands and starts pacing.

ROBIN
Call and ask.

There is a knock on the door across the hall.

CHRIS
Did you guys hear a knock?

GREG
It was across the hall.

CHRIS goes to the door. Looks through the peep hole.

ROBIN
Did he say when he would be back?

CHRIS
No.

ROBIN
Did he say where he was going?

CHRIS
No. No he didn't.

 ROBIN looks at his watch.

GREG
How often do you give your wife the big O? Every time, more often than not, or don't give a damn.

ROBIN
I think I give her an orgasm every time. I think.

CHRIS
You don't know.

ROBIN
I work hard man. I don't know. I hope so.

GREG
Either she has the orgasm, or she doesn't. What will it be?

ROBIN
Hey, look, I'm no genius in the bedroom, but I can mix it up in the corners, I can stick handle pretty good, and every now and then, I get the puck in the net.

GREG
Remember Crystal? She ejaculated.

CHRIS
I'm sorry?

GREG
She ejaculated. When she came, she would ejaculate.

ROBIN
No fuckin way.

CHRIS
Did she have a penis?

GREG
No she didn't have a penis.

ROBIN
You've never heard of that?

CHRIS
I have never heard of that.

ROBIN
You've never heard of that!

CHRIS
I have never heard of that.

ROBIN
Oh fuck off.

CHRIS
I have never ever, ever, heard of a woman ejaculating.

GREG
Okay, this is how it would go. We'd be going along there, everything's fine, then whoomp, she clamps down.

CHRIS
She clamps down?

GREG
And starts to squeeze.

CHRIS
Okay.

GREG
It gets tighter, and tighter, and tighter, then she grabs the bed, tells me to shove it in as far as I can. Which is pretty far. I push push push push, then boom, it contracts, I get shoved out, her eyes roll back into her skull, and she shoots.

CHRIS
Yeah?

GREG
All over the bed.

ROBIN
She's thrashing around?

GREG
She loses her mind. Two minutes. Loses her mind.

ROBIN
What does it look like?

GREG
It's clear, it's kinda filmy…

CHRIS
It's not piss is it?

GREG
No. It's… well, I don't know what it is.

ROBIN
I bet you felt like king of the fucking hill.

GREG
Well, at first it was great, but then…

CHRIS
What?

GREG
Well, after a while, it became all about her orgasm. Know what I'm saying? The tenderness started to disappear. A lot of times she'd finish way before me, and that doesn't bother me, but then, don't just roll over and fall asleep, right? We can talk, we can hold each other…

CHRIS
You sure she wasn't a guy?

ROBIN
Are we done with the…

GREG
Okay you ready?

ROBIN
Give it to me.

GREG
"Those who score between 70 and 85 are what we at the magazine like to call the uber whipped."

ROBIN
I'm not whipped.

GREG

"While the big dogs were getting all the girls, little mister sensitive was sitting in a corner listening to his Smiths albums, whining about why girls don't go out with nice guys like him."

ROBIN

Let me see that.

> *ROBIN tries to grab the magazine. GREG moves away. CHRIS goes to the window.*

GREG

"His wife will have to spend some time training this goomer to not put her up so high on a pedestal, but at least she won't have to worry about him cheating on her. He couldn't even if he tried."

ROBIN

Give me that.

GREG

Does the truth ever hurt.

ROBIN

Give me the damn magazine.

> *GREG tosses the magazine.*

GREG

Bouyaka!

> *ROBIN waves the magazine in the air.*

ROBIN

This is the reason why the women's movement was stopped dead in its tracks. Right here.

> *GREG grabs a newspaper, and starts flipping through the pages as he joins CHRIS at the window.*

GREG

You're not going to see her from this side of the building.

CHRIS

I know.

GREG

Let's get out of here. Get something to eat. Chris?

CHRIS
Ten more minutes.

GREG
Then we go.

CHRIS
Then we go.

ROBIN stands up.

ROBIN
Anybody want a drink?

CHRIS
No it's alright.

GREG
No thank you.

ROBIN
Fine.

ROBIN goes to the kitchen and grabs a beer, opens it, goes to drink and spills some on his shirt. He is a little drunk. GREG nudges CHRIS. CHRIS looks at ROBIN, looks back at GREG, nods.

GREG
What are you having?

ROBIN
I'm having a beer.

GREG
Ah I see.

ROBIN
Would you like one?

GREG
No thank you.

ROBIN
Chris?

ROBIN sits in front of the computer.

CHRIS
No thanks.

ROBIN finds a computer game.

ROBIN
Hey. "Quake." Cool.

He starts playing the computer game.

CHRIS
Could you turn the sound down please.

ROBIN does.

GREG
She's not coming man.

CHRIS
You don't think so?

GREG
She was supposed to be here 45 minutes ago.

CHRIS
Well, let's give it ten more minutes.

GREG
You know what I am going to do for you? I am going to call up Paula. She's my boss. You'll love her. And maybe she can get her friend Andrea to come along…

The door buzzer goes off. CHRIS goes to the buzzer. It is buzzing frantically. CHRIS answers it.

CHRIS
I knew you'd show up.

WENDLE
(off-stage) It's me. I forgot my keys.

CHRIS buzzes him in.

ROBIN
I thought for sure he went to the game·without us.

CHRIS
Maybe he did.

GREG

Naw, it's not over yet. He would have stayed for the whole thing. Come on. We'll go to Insomnia, meet Tabitha. We'll go to Joker, do some dancing, Bob's your uncle.

CHRIS

Tell me more about Tabitha. Who is she, where did you meet her?

GREG

There's nothing to tell man. Come on. Let's go.

CHRIS

Does she know that you're in love with her?

GREG

I'm not... in... go to hell.

CHRIS picks up the Nintendo controller. ROBIN looks at some magazines.

ROBIN

So did you and Wendle talk at all?

CHRIS

Yes we did.

ROBIN

You gonna help him out?

CHRIS

No I don't think so.

ROBIN

Is there a conflict of interest problem or...

CHRIS

No. No no.

ROBIN

It wouldn't affect your job or anything.

CHRIS

No, not at all.

ROBIN

Then what's...

CHRIS

Guys I hate to… this is my job right? And when a close personal friend asks me to do some legal favour for them, I treat that friend with the same professional standards that I treat anyone. My advice to him was; if I took the case, I would ask him to plead guilty to sexual assault.

ROBIN

You think he's guilty?

CHRIS

I know you guys want to help, but you have to let him go out and find other representation.

ROBIN

You want him to say that he raped her?

CHRIS

I don't want anything, a precedent has been set, there is nothing I can do.

GREG

But he talked to her.

CHRIS

Did she say the words; "I give you consent to have sex with me without a condom."

GREG & ROBIN

Awwwww come on.

CHRIS

Did she say the words…

GREG

Okay, so let's say for a second that she said go for it; sex without a condom. But then right before he's about to cum she says; I do not give you consent to cum inside me.

CHRIS

Then you have to pull out.

GREG & ROBIN

Right! Yeah, whatever.

CHRIS

As far as the law is concerned, you have to pull out.

ROBIN

You can't regulate sex Chris! You can't micro-legislate what two people do in bed together, it's impossible.

CHRIS

That's the law.

ROBIN

Okay, let me tell you something: when my wife and I were first, when we started going out, she came with me to visit my dad in Windsor. So, we're in the rec room in the basement, Dad's upstairs, he's gone to bed, I start groping her, she says "I don't want to do it in your dad's house." I say sure fine whatever, I stop. She starts spooning into me. I start again, I get some of her clothes off, she says she's worried that he'll hear us or something, I tell her that the walls are soundproof (they weren't but hey). She says no again, fine, I stop. Then she starts kissing me and... eventually we're naked, we are doing everything but. So I try again. This time, she doesn't say anything. So we're going at it, quietly, she is putting my hand on her mouth to stop her from moaning, we finish, we fall asleep, and that's it. Not once did she ever tell me that I had consent to have sex with her. Not once! She could have gone to a police officer the next day and said, "I told him 'No' twice, but he took my clothes off, forced himself into me, he put his hand over my mouth to stop me from making a sound." and I would have to say "That's exactly what happened."

CHRIS

But she didn't. She didn't go to the police because whatever it was you two were doing, she consented to. Women do not go through the tests and the photographs and the legal hassle and the possible media attention for fun.

ROBIN

Okay, okay, look.

CHRIS

What.

ROBIN

You see that computer over there? You see this couch, that TV? I don't know anything about her situation, but what if? Okay? What if! The credit cards are maxed out, the rent is five months past due, you owe the government, you owe the cable company. I don't know how much those cheerleaders are getting paid, but it ain't this much fucking money, alright?!

CHRIS

I want you to sit down and listen to me for a moment. I never told you guys this, but I had to threaten the firm I'm working for right now with a lawsuit before they would hire me. I had done the interviews, I was told it looked good, I was brought in to see my desk. First day of work I meet the partners. The next day I get a call that I wasn't to come to work, they didn't need me that day. I asked them when they would need me. They told me in about six months. I asked if I was to be paid while I waited for them to need me. They told me no, I wasn't. What do I do? I asked a lawyer to send a little letter informing the firm of Anderson, Johnson and Wade that I would be suing them for a fuck of a lot of money for breach of contract. Well, within two days, I was at my desk. Turns out there was a bit of a power struggle going on. Wade didn't like the idea of someone of my complexion around the office. He, and I quote, "Didn't think I would feel comfortable in that environment." My first day on the job, and they have a whole new department for me. The Department of Equity, that I was to set up and run. It would keep me out of their hair while they did the important business. At first I was real angry, until I realized that I was the one with the most important job in the entire firm. I go around to corporations and give them advice on policies dealing with racial and gender equity. I give seminars. I give one-on-one consultations. I have had a CEO tell me that he will never have a Jew working in his firm. I have had a VP scream at me for two hours that racial equity is a code word for discrimination against the white man. He spent a half an hour trying to convince me that every office tower on Bay street is overrun with Natives and Asians and Blacks. And I have had to explain to a co-worker, a friend of mine, that telling jokes about fucking women until their skulls cave in, is not appropriate for a workplace with a large number of female employees. I know this stuff okay. This is my job. It's what I do. And I am very good at what I do. And I am going to give you something from one of my seminars absolutely free of charge. Now I know this may be hard for you to understand right now, but women have a right to control what happens to their bodies. Period. End of story. I know you guys mean well...

WENDLE enters.

...and I feel for your position, I do, but if Wendle wants my help it's going to have to be on my terms.

WENDLE closes the door.

GREG

Where the hell have you been?!

WENDLE

Looking for a fucking lawyer. Any calls for me?

GREG
No.

WENDLE
Great. Now everybody get the fuck out of my house.

CHRIS
I'm just going to go downstairs for a second.

CHRIS leaves.

WENDLE
Good, now you two, get the fuck out of my house.

GREG
Come here. Come.

WENDLE
I ain't coming any-fuckin-where, you are gonna get the fuck out of my house.

GREG
Okay. Now… I want you to listen to me for a second. Now, you've been straight up with us on this whole situation, right? You haven't left anything out right?

WENDLE
The fuck is that supposed to mean.

GREG
Listen, I am totally on your side, alright? I am. But… okay. What if she's not on the pill, right? Just wait a second, Wendle, listen to me. Maybe she's not looking to have a kid by you, right? And that's not… that's not something that you want right? I know in that situation, things can get kind of… out of control, but… from her perspective, think about it. I've known this guy for what, six months, but I don't know if he… could he possibly give me something that could…

WENDLE
Wait wait wait. Right there, okay? Stop. I want to make this clear to you, as clear as I possibly can. Nowhere, in my soul, did I have the intention of causing her harm. Nowhere. That's the truth. For me to say anything else, I just can't do that. I can't.

GREG
The truth is very important to you isn't it.

WENDLE
You're damn right it's important.

GREG
Alright. So, the people outside the situation are looking at it, trying to figure out what the truth is. The two people that it happened to are trying to figure out what the truth is. And you know what, it doesn't matter.

WENDLE
The truth doesn't matter.

GREG
It doesn't matter. What matters is dealing with the consequences.

WENDLE
What are you saying.

GREG
The first time that a bully called you a name in the schoolyard, and beat you up. What did your mom do?

WENDLE
She called the school, she called the kids parents, called my teacher…

GREG
Right. Now, what did your dad do?

WENDLE
He said the left is for defense, this right one is the one you hit with.

GREG
Exactly! So the next day you went to school and…

WENDLE
I kicked his ass.

GREG
Yes you did. That's right. Now, if you got caught, would your dad want you to scream and cry and say it was all his fault?

WENDLE
No.

GREG
No he wouldn't. He would want you to stand up straight. Admit exactly what you did, everything, and face the consequences.

WENDLE
But… I didn't hit her.

GREG
No you didn't.

WENDLE
You're trying to say that I hit her?

GREG
No no, all I'm saying is that sometimes, we do things that we think are okay, but they're not okay. And when it's not okay, you have to take responsibility for it.

WENDLE goes to his bedroom.

Wendle?

ROBIN
The fuck are your doing telling him he has to plead guilty?

GREG
I'm not saying he has to plead guilty, I just think he's got to say what Chris wants to hear.

ROBIN
Fuck Chris! He's being a fucking asshole.

GREG
Lower your voice.

ROBIN
And all this bullshit about Nicole Simpson. You know why she put that in there. You know why she said that.

GREG
Robin…

ROBIN
I know that women have a right to control what happens to their bodies. I know that fuckhead! This is Wendle we're talking about! Wendle. I mean, he could get fired!

GREG
I just think he has to start saying what Chris wants to hear.

ROBIN
Is he a rapist?

GREG

No, but, I'm thinking that after six months, his body is a little bit ahead of him, if you know what I'm saying.

ROBIN

Did he rape her?!

GREG

No, but I think that it was wrong for him to continue.

ROBIN

Did she try to get up? Did she try to get away? All she had to do was get up. That's it. Get up, put her clothes on.

GREG

Just...

ROBIN

I am so fucking angry right now!

GREG

Lower your voice.

ROBIN

This is his life! This is his fucking life we're talking about!

GREG

Look, this is what we're going to do. I have to make a phone call. When Chris gets here, you talk to him, see if there is any legal way we can protect Wendle's job, listen to me, Robin, if this goes down that he has to plead guilty, we need to know if we can protect Wendle's job.

ROBIN

I don't want to talk to Chris right now.

GREG

Yes you are going to talk to Chris, and yes you are going to find out if we can save his job.

ROBIN

I am telling you, I don't think that it's a good idea that I talk to...

CHRIS enters.

CHRIS

You know what? I don't think she's coming.

GREG
You got something for me?

CHRIS
I beg your pardon?

GREG
You got something for me?

CHRIS
No.

GREG
Alright. Alright.

CHRIS
What?

> GREG encourages CHRIS to lift his arms. He does. GREG frisks CHRIS and pulls out a pack of cigarettes from his back pocket.

Hey, stop, hey.

GREG
What the hell is this?

CHRIS
Alright.

GREG
I... I don't know what to say.

CHRIS
I just had one.

GREG
You had three.

CHRIS
Alright fine. Take them. I don't care. I just wanted one.

GREG
It's the devil's weed man! It's the devil's weed!

CHRIS
Fine fine. Whatever, fine.

GREG
I am going to go downstairs, I am going to make a couple of calls. I am going to the corner store, and I am going to give these back to Mr. Pong. And I am going to tell him, to never sell you a cigarette ever again!!!! I'm not joking!

GREG goes.

CHRIS
So do you think he's got a chance with this Tabitha woman?

ROBIN
She's leaving in two weeks.

CHRIS
Ah.

ROBIN
Going to Korea to teach English. For good. She just wants a meaningless roll in the hay before she goes. She hasn't told him yet.

CHRIS
I see. You going to tell him?

ROBIN
She wants me to tell him.

CHRIS
You gonna tell him?

ROBIN
Well, she wants me to tell him.

CHRIS
That's a tough one.

ROBIN
Yes it is. So you think Wendle's guilty of sexual assault?

CHRIS
It's not about what I think. There was a case like this just a few years ago. A precedent has been set. There's nothing I can do about it.

ROBIN
You read the affidavit.

CHRIS
Yes I did.

ROBIN
Come on.

CHRIS
What.

ROBIN
Come on.

CHRIS
What?

ROBIN
"All you white bitches are the same." The same what? It doesn't make any sense. It sounds like something you would put in someone's mouth to make them sound like a monster!

CHRIS
Well, that's what she said happened.

ROBIN
Women are capable of lying Chris.

In CHRIS' speech, ROBIN echoes "a bit."

CHRIS
Look, it's obvious that she is embellishing the truth a bit, ah ah ah, a bit, to... because she is thinking that she has to plead her case in a justice system run by men.

ROBIN
So we are supposed to allow someone to embellish the truth, because the justice system is run by men?

CHRIS
There are still some judges out there that may not understand that she has a right to control what happens to her own body.

ROBIN
But she had control. She may not have thought she had control but she had control.

CHRIS
But she says that she didn't feel that she did.

ROBIN
Who is responsible for that misunderstanding?

CHRIS
> He is.

ROBIN
> How is he to know that his intentions are being misunderstood?

CHRIS
> He has to check.

ROBIN
> Women are not children Chris!

CHRIS
> I know.

ROBIN
> Sometimes women choose to not say anything and continue because it's just less of a hassle, it's not that she's afraid she'll be brutalized, it's just less of a hassle than to say no and go through having to explain all her contradictory feelings and...

CHRIS
> I can't win a case by saying to a judge that she just didn't want the hassle of saying no! That's not good enough!

ROBIN
> But if you...

CHRIS
> Whoever the judge is, he or she is not going to care who Wendle is, a judge is not going to care that he's your best friend they're not! They are not going to give a fuck. They are going to care about upholding the law!

ROBIN
> Yes but...

CHRIS
> Do you have any idea how many women are assaulted every day? And I'm not just talking about the cases we hear about in the newspapers. Every day...

ROBIN
> Yes I know...

CHRIS
> Women are being raped, beaten, murdered. A judge is going to say do you have any idea...

ROBIN

My wife is more at risk of being attacked by me then anyone else on the planet, I know that!

CHRIS

A judge is going to say you have no idea what that's like!

ROBIN

Yes I do! Yes. Yes I know what it's like for someone to overpower you. To take advantage of you. Yes I know what it's like! And I wasn't a twenty-four-year-old woman, I was a nine-year-old boy. I know what it is like for someone to smash your head against a wall because you're screaming, and you're scared. I know what it's like to reach down into a pile of rotting fetid garbage and place your bloody clothing and hide it at the bottom and pray to God that no-one ever looks there. I know what that's like. I know what it is like for someone to make you feel like if you tell anybody, they will kill you. They'll kill you. I know what that's like! My parents, my mother gets sick suddenly, appendicitis, while my dad is at work. They put me, the couple down the street, they take care of me. Their kid, he's what, 18? Sadistic fuck who, I knew him from... I... it doesn't matter... anyway...

CHRIS

I...

ROBIN

Years later. I'm sixteen right? I'm freaking out a bit, feeling like I want to hurt myself or something. It's late at night, I go to this late-night rape crisis centre that's open till like ten. I go in there and knock on the door and they tell me that they don't have anyone that can council men, they don't. That they don't have any idea where I could go to get counselling, and frankly, they get kinda freaked when some guy comes banging on their door at ten o'clock at night and could I kindly leave. And I understood. I did. It didn't make me angry or anything. I just... didn't have anywhere to go.

He breaks down.

CHRIS

I didn't know.

ROBIN

No of course you didn't know. Nobody fucking knows except my wife and the guy that did it. And you can't tell Wendle or Greg, right? I am not telling this to you because I want sympathy, or healing or anything. I just... I mean, if you're going to...

CHRIS
Hey.

ROBIN
I'm alright. *(CHRIS puts his hand on ROBIN's shoulder. ROBIN jumps in shock.)* Don't touch me. I'm alright.

CHRIS
You sure?

ROBIN
I'm fine about it. I am. Really. I know it doesn't look it, but, I can deal with it.

CHRIS
When did you start drinking again?

ROBIN
Couple of days ago. I stopped in a bar and had a shot.

CHRIS
This is not good.

>   *ROBIN goes to the fridge and grabs a can of cola.*

ROBIN
Everybody's got something. You're going along and life gives you a curve ball and you just have to… deal with it, but uh… I'll be okay.

CHRIS
You sure?

ROBIN
My wife has been a saint. I would not be alive right now if it wasn't for her. I wouldn't be here.

CHRIS
Can I tell you something?

ROBIN
What.

CHRIS
I don't think she's coming.

ROBIN
You don't think so?

CHRIS

I really, really don't think so.

GREG enters.

GREG

Get yourself ready to party tonight. Paula has VIP cards for The Left Bank. She can get us in NO PROBLEM.

WENDLE enters.

ROBIN

What's the Left Bank, what's it like?

GREG

The Left Bank. Very Shi shi. Very shoo shoo. I just have to give Tabitha a call before we head out the door.

WENDLE

I am not going anywhere, you guys go out. I mean it. Have a good time.

ROBIN

If we are going to be entertaining these ladies in this apartment later on this evening, we may need some mix.

GREG

I think we have plenty of... right we have to get some mix.

GREG and ROBIN leave.

WENDLE

Hey.

CHRIS

Hey.

WENDLE

Look, you want to sit for a second? I want to say something.

CHRIS

You say something, then I say something.

WENDLE

Alright. When she was walking out the door, at the elevator, I yelled at her. I said something hurtful. The exact words of what I said was, "You're just like all the other bitches." It was a terrible hurtful thing to say, but.... There were things that happened that night, that I am not proud of. I admit that. Anyway. There you have it.

CHRIS
When you went to the station, they gave you the HIV test right?

WENDLE
Yeah.

CHRIS
Ever been tested for HIV before?

WENDLE
No. Why?

CHRIS
What we are going to do; Monday, we go to your office, we're going to tell them to cease and desist with the witch hunt. You have been charged with a crime, not convicted of one. We are going to see if we can get some time off for you. So that you can chill out a bit. We wait for the results of the test, then we go on from there.

WENDLE
You're saying she may have given me AIDS?

CHRIS
No, no, no. Wendle, it's standard procedure. As your lawyer, these are things I am supposed to tell you. Before I can do anything, there are a whole slew of bits of information that we both have to know so that I can give this case the best that I am capable of.

WENDLE
Right right.

CHRIS
Hey, hey, hey, Wendle… I'm on the case.

GREG and ROBIN come back.

GREG
Guys, come on. Time to go. The girls are going to be there any minute now. And you have to meet my favourite boss, Paula.

CHRIS
Do I?

ROBIN
Paula, CITY TV mogul. Intelligent, opinionated, beautiful body. She may be able to get you in free to the Film Festival shindig later on this year.

GREG
You play your cards right my friend, and you won't even remember that whatserface ever existed.

ROBIN
Designated driver.

ROBIN tosses GREG his keys. GREG offers WENDLE his jacket. WENDLE accepts.

CHRIS
Are you going to bring the car out front?

ROBIN
No! We are leaving through the garage, we are not going by the front door. If we happen to see anything that remotely looks like a former fiancée we are driving right past it, have I made myself clear soldier?

CHRIS
Clear, sir.

GREG
I gotta take a quick whiz!

GREG runs to the bathroom.

WENDLE
Hey.

WENDLE reaches out his hand to CHRIS. CHRIS offers him a hug. They hug.

WENDLE
I'll get the elevator.

WENDLE leaves.

ROBIN
So you two worked things out?

CHRIS
Yeah.

ROBIN
Cool.

CHRIS
Hey.

CHRIS goes to hug ROBIN. ROBIN puts out his hand. CHRIS pulls ROBIN close and hugs him.

ROBIN
Alright. Okay.

CHRIS
I'm just giving you a hug for fuck's sake.

ROBIN
Yo Greg! Hurry up!

A flush. GREG enters, singing a made-up James Brownesque song. The line below is a suggestion of what it could be.

GREG
Hey, good gawd! Sex machine! Heeey! Baby baby baby, baby baby baby!

He leaps out the door.

CHRIS
You got to tell him.

ROBIN
I'm going to tell him.

CHRIS
You got to tell him.

ROBIN
You want to tell him, you tell him.

CHRIS
I don't want to tell him. You tell him.

ROBIN
You can tell him if you want to tell him.

CHRIS
I ain't gonna tell him, so you better tell him.

CHRIS turns off the lights, they leave.

The end.

Jean and Dinah
Who Have Been Locked Away in a World Famous Calypso Since 1956 Speak Their Minds Publicly

Tony Hall
with Rhoma Spencer
& Susan Sandiford

Tony Hall is a playwright and moviemaker and has worked extensively in Western Canada and with Derek Walcott's Trinidad Theatre Workshop. He has also worked with Banyan Limited in developing television for the Caribbean. In 1990 Tony and Errol Fabien launched Lordstreet Theatre Company with the award-winning jouvay masquerade band, A Band on Drugs (1990). His works also include: "And the Dish Ran Away With the Spoon" (1992) – an award winning Banyan Film for a BBC/TVE Series; *Jean and Dinah* (1994); *Red House [Fire! Fire!]* (1999); *Under The Trees Normandie* (2002); and *Twilight Cafe or The Last Breakfast* (2002). Mr. Hall has been Visiting Artist in Residence at Trinity College, Hartford, CT, since 1998 where he teaches playwrighting and moviemaking. Tony is also Academic Director of the Trinity-in-Trinidad Global Learning Site. He divides his time between Hartford and his home island of Tobago in the West Indies.

Rhoma Spencer MFA, (York 2001) is an actor, director, storyteller, play creator and broadcast journalist from Trinidad and Tobago. She has graced stages throughout the Caribbean, Canada and the United States, in such plays as *Mother Courage, The Blacks, The Dragon Can't Dance, Ah Wanna Fall, Fallen Angel and The Devil's Concubine,* and *Jean and Dinah.* Rhoma's directing credits include: *Rum and Coca Cola,* by Mustapha Matura; *Three Kings Darkly,* by Edgar Whyte; *Shango: Tales of the Orishas,* by Spencer and Rawle Gibbons; Lorca's *Blood Wedding* and Zakes Mda's *And the Girls in Their Sunday Dresses.* Her work *Bassman: A Musical Play on Shadow,* Tobago's most distinguished calypsonian, was performed to critical acclaim in Trinidad and Tobago. Miss Spencer is the Resident Director/Manager of the Toronto-based AfriCan Theatre Ensemble, and is presently working on a dramatic adaptation of the late Ugandan poet Okot p'Bitek's *Song of Lawino, Song of Ocol* and Earl Lovelace's *Wine of Astonishment.*

While **Susan Sandiford** is a librarian by profession (20 years), she has also maintained an active role in the performing arts as an actor, director and playwright. Her numerous acting credits include Canboulay Production's *Ten to One,* and *Inward Hunger,* Earl Warner's production of *Water's Bride,* as well, she has performed and directed various projects at the Mausica Folk Theatre. Susan has written and directed several plays for children and has trained children in performance at La Chapelle's Creative Workshop. She has a BA in Literature as well as a Practitioner's Certificate in Theatre Arts from the University of the West Indies. She also holds a Master's degree in Information Studies from the University of Toronto.

Rewriting Calypso as Feminist Discourse: Jean and Dinah "Take Over Now"

by Andrea Davis

— • — — • — — • —

Jean and Dinah Who Have Been Locked Away in a World Famous Calypso Since 1956 Speak Their Minds Publicly is Tony Hall's brilliant retake on the popular calypso that won the 1956 Calypso Crown for the Mighty Sparrow. Tony Hall's play, written almost forty years later, attempts to rearticulate the concerns raised in Sparrow's calypso from the perspective of the two women from which the calypso takes its title. Looking back at the past through their shared memory, the women, now old and dying, speak their lives in a final act of communion and confession. The dialogue is intimate; it reveals the kinds of secrets shared only between friends and yet it is, of necessity, an open script. In speaking their past, the women need to (re)tell their stories to (an)other audience, which they hope this time can listen sensitively and carefully. It is not only the women, but also the community, which needs to heal.

The calypsonian has historically been identified in Trinidad and Tobago and the wider Caribbean as an important social voice that registers the concerns of ordinary Caribbean people. The calypso represents a necessary counter narrative, a resisting cultural form that can challenge oppressive middle-class values or political corruption. Yet, precisely, because calypsonians are not only enormously popular, but have also been reconstituted as the preachers and *griots*, the politicians of the folk, their commentaries can come to represent a kind of unchallenged nationalist discourse – a discourse that is assumed to speak not only on behalf of the national community it represents, but to speak the "truth" about that community. The privileged voice of the calypsonian, with its assumptions of "truth" and public approbation, can therefore come to constitute another kind of oppressive hegemonic discourse.

In addition to being read as part of a nationalist discourse, calypsos are also largely male-centred narratives. Calypso and carnival have historically occupied male-dominated spaces in the Caribbean. Until at least the 1960s, women's participation in carnival was actively discouraged. As Denyse Plummer, a female calypsonian, explains, women who dared to defy the social norms and participate in carnival were labelled "as prostitutes, as whores, people you didn't want your children to associate with" (quoted in Mason 141). But not only was women's participation in carnival discouraged, calypsos often portray women with ridicule, even contempt. According to Merle Hodge, this devalorization of women within calypsos is part of a national ethos that encourages the embarrassment of women (117). In Tony Hall's *Jean and Dinah*, it is the women who respectable Trinidadian society looks down on, the "prostitutes" and "whores," who play mas, who perform their lives. In so doing these brave, bold women not only critically challenge the dominant male discourse of the 1950s, but also re-inhabit the tradition of carnival with a vibrant female sensibility. They rewrite the stories of their lives by breaking out of the silence in which they have been imprisoned in Sparrow's calypso.

Sparrow's calypso, appearing at a significant juncture in the history of Trinidad and Tobago, encapsulates quite clearly the notion of calypso as both nationalist discourse and male-centred narrative. 1956 was the year when the People's National Movement (PNM) came to power under the leadership of Eric Williams, initiating a period of strong nationalist sentiment that would culminate in the gaining of independence in 1962. Sparrow's career in many ways was built on this political platform. His popularity grew enormously during this period as he functioned as a primary supporter of the new government (Regis 4). Before and after independence, Sparrow would explore in many of his calypsos the preoccupation with the question of national identity as Trinidad and Tobago struggled to name itself within a wider region and more powerful world.

"Jean and Dinah" was an important commentary on this quest toward nationhood. The presence of the US military in Trinidad during World War II dramatically increased employment opportunities for Trinidadians, but also sharpened their awareness of the outside world and their position within it, and acerbated class and colour conflicts (van Koningsbruggen 53-56). By 1956 and the coming to power of the PNM, the Americans had come to represent in the political discourse an exploitative foreign interest that, like the British, was inimical to the development of the emerging nation (Rohlehr 527). This opinion would be voiced quite clearly in Sparrow's calypso as he expressed the new emerging national self-confidence. Like other Black nationalist discourses, the reinsertion of the political power of Trinidadian men coincides in the calypso with the reinsertion of their sexual power: "It's the glamour boys again/We are going to rule Port of Spain/no more Yankees to spoil the fete/Dorothy have to take what she get." Sparrow suggests that the new Trinidad had to be reconstituted not only in political, but also in gendered terms. National growth depended on the dismantling of the economic and political power of foreign, white men and the subordination of potentially emancipated Trinidadian women. As sex workers, the women in the calypso are conceived as a threat to the nation's development, although ironically the morality of the men, who now have free access to their labour, is never questioned. The calypso's condemnation of the women in moral terms designates them as standing outside of the new constituted citizenship. They cannot legitimately take part in the project of nation building. In Tony Hall's play, Jean and Dinah reinsert themselves as legitimate citizens by rewriting their histories and asserting their human rights as sex workers, mothers and wives.

Act One, which is framed around a series of questions, repeatedly force the women back into their past. Dinah, who is dying, does not want to jump up on Carnival Monday; she wants to take off the mask, and face for the last time the pain and struggles of the past. In these deeply moving flashbacks, the women examine their life choices, their failed relationships and the anguish of their own friendship. Jean's recurring plea—"You know what day it is!"—establishes the mood of the entire play. It is a day to die, to remember, to make peace with self and the past, but it is also a day to laugh, to dance, however hesitantly, one last time.

Act Two transports the women directly into their memories, by taking them back thirty-five years earlier to another Carnival Monday. In this act, Jean and Dinah perform a series of sketches in traditional masquerade roles, but rewrite those roles from a radical woman-centred perspective. Jean reinvests the Baby Doll character of the traditional masquerade with a new kind of resisting stance. Not only does she indict the community for its complicity in the irresponsible behaviour of its men and the middle-class values that oppress women, but she also rewrites her own history of sexual and emotional abuse by renaming her ancestry through a line of female warriors: "Well, I descend from the seed of Petite Belle Lily and Alice Sugar The Former. I trod the centuries from Na Na Yah come down. I is woman. Watch form. Ebony. From that one seed, I stand up. I grow to these proportions." (203)

Dinah goes even further by taking the traditional male character of the Midnight Robber, "the ultimate bad man" (212), and redefining it as part of a female tradition of warriorhood. Dinah's personal history establishes her as one of the brave early women of carnival, and she retraces the history of carnival through a feminine, rather than masculine line: "I am the mother of the warrior musician, the Pan Man and I prepared for war, the Pan Man prepared for war, I prepare him for war. My son" (204). She names herself, then, as the source of carnival, as the female muse on which male participants rely.

In contesting the roles of carnival and calypso as male-centred discourses, the women also challenge stereotypes about Black women's sexuality. They insist on their own right to make independent choices. Dismissed as "immoral" sex workers and non-citizens in Sparrow's calypso, the women redefine their identities by critically examining the socio-economic realities of 1950s Trinidad and Tobago that severely restricted income-earning opportunities for poor women. They insist on their right to fair wages and define their labour as part of their familial and communal responsibilities. The women, abandoned and abused by the men in their lives, are forced to care for families and children on their own and see sex work as one economically viable option. They argue that their labour as sex workers is intimately connected to their roles as mothers and even wives. This assertion is radical in Caribbean societies where "the discouragement of autonomous expressions of female sexuality as transgressing gender ideals...

results in the maintenance of a discursive distinction between prostitution and family life that denies any correspondence between the two realms" (Red Thread 273). By insisting on their own agency and by reclaiming power over their bodies, Jean and Dinah resist oppressive middle-class and patriarchal values and urge the wider society to critically examine its understanding of family and community.

In giving us access to their lives, the women challenge us to rethink many of our own assumptions. Yet, while they celebrate and justify their choices, this play remains ultimately sad. While Hall strives valiantly to move past the victim/heroine dichotomy, it is difficult not to see how much these women have suffered. Even as we attempt to explore the multiple ways in which women challenge their marginalization in Caribbean societies, we are forced to recognize that the odds against which they struggle are indeed enormous.

Andrea Davis is an Assistant Professor in the Division of Humanities at York University.

WORKS CITED:

Hodge, Merle. "The Shadow of the Whip: A Comment on Male-Female Relationships in the Caribbean." *Is Massa Day Dead?* Ed. Orde Coombs. New York: Anchor Books, 1974. 111-118.

Mason, Peter. *Bacchanal! The Carnival Culture of Trinidad.* Philadelphia: Temple University Press, 1998.

Red Thread Women's Development Programme. "'Givin' Lil' Bit fuh Lil' Bit': Women and Sex Work in Guyana." *Sun, Sex and Gold: Tourism and Sex Work in the Caribbean.* Ed. Kamala Kempadoo. Lanham: Rowman and Littlefield, 1999. 263-290.

Regis, Louis. *The Political Calypso: True Opposition in Trinidad and Tobago 1962-1987.* Barbados: University Press of the West Indies, 1999.

Rohlehr, Gordon. *Calypso and Society in Pre-independence Trinidad.* Port of Spain, Trinidad: Gordon Rohlehr, 1990.

Van Koningsbruggen, Peter. *Trinidad Carnival: A Quest for National Identity.* London: Macmillan Education Ltd., 1997.

Jean & Dinah Who Have Been Locked Away in a World Famous Calypso Since 1956 Speak Their Minds Publicly was first produced at Planteurs Cocktail Lounge & Art Gallery, St. Vincent Street, Port of Spain Trinidad and Tobago, in November 1994, with the following company:

JEAN	Penelope Spencer
DINAH	Rhoma Spencer

Produced & Directed by Tony Hall
Research & Improvisation by Rhoma Spencer and Susan Sandiford
Percussion by Tamba Gwindi
Set Design & Construction by Roger Hicks
Costume Design by Tessa Alexander
Stage Managed by Ken Joseph

The USA premiere was given on April 17, 1998 at the Goodwin Theatre, Austin Arts Center, Trinity College, Hartford, Connecticut.

— • — — • — — • —

CHARACTERS:
Jean
Dinah

SETTING:
PROLOGUE: The 1990s, Port of Spain, Trinidad. A street.
ACT I: The Preparation
  The 1990s, Dinah's apartment, Port of Spain, Trinidad.
ACT II: The Performance
  The 1950s, a street and a hospital in Port of Spain, Trinidad.
EPILOGUE: The 1990s, Dinah's apartment, Port of Spain, Trinidad.

MUSIC:

JEAN AND DINAH
Written by S. Francisco, Published by Ice Music Limited.

STEELBAND CLASH
Written by Carlton Joseph, Published by Ice Music Limited.

MISS MARY
Written by W. Devine & S. Francisco, Published by Ice Music Limited.

DRUNK AND DISORDERLY
Written by S. Francisco, Published by Ice Music Limited.

All P&C vested in Ice Music Limited.

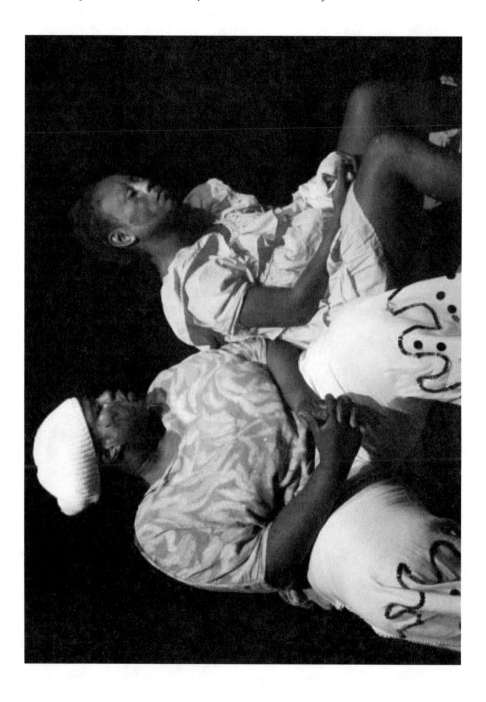

photo by
Shawn M.
Dowdell

Jean and Dinah...
Who Have Been Locked Away In A World Famous Calypso Since 1956 Speak Their Minds Publicly

by Tony Hall with Rhoma Spencer & Susan Sandiford
—•— —•— —•—

"Jean and Dinah..."
Well, the girls in town feeling bad
No more Yankees in Trinidad
They going to close down the base for good
Them girls have to make out how they could
Well is now they park up in town
In for a penny, in for a pound
Yes it's competition for so
Trouble in town when the price drop low.
CHORUS
So when you bounce up Jean and Dinah
Rosita and Clementina
Round the corner posing
Bet your life is something they selling
And if you catch them broken
You can get it all for nothing
Don't make no row
The Yankees gone, Sparrow take over now.

Prologue

"To hell with the clock, I done hear the cock."
—Superblue

Throughout the prologue we hear a "live" recording of The Mighty Sparrow singing the calypso "Jean and Dinah..." at the Dimanche Gras Show, Trinidad Carnival 1956.

JEAN is 56 years old and looks in good health for her years.

She is downstage right, facing the audience (they become her mirror). She is putting on her makeup in an oval shaped mirror of light. She likes bright colours and likes to look bright and alive. We should get the feeling of someone creating a bright and alive mask. Her eyes, cheeks, lips, temples, eyelashes, eyebrows, hair and chin – using one hand she goes over all these parts very delicately. The other hand is crippled. She has a large travelling bag at her side. Once she is prepared she picks up the bag and walks very deliberately across the front of the stage towards stage left into subdued light. This should feel like a stylized jamette performance. It should have plenty of air to it – an inflated performance.

We hear a cock crowing. As the cock crows, JEAN's mirror fades.

DINAH, who is upstage left of centre, gets up to sit on her bed (on a slightly raised platform). She lights a candle.

JEAN stands in the semi-darkness downstage left and lights a cigarette. She draws on it and exhales. A smoke screen.

DINAH coughs a deep guttural cough that puts her candle light out. JEAN puts the cigarette out under her feet. DINAH turns slowly, almost painfully and goes back to sleep on her bed. JEAN turns and walks upstage towards her.

Lights fade.

ACT I

The Preparation

Darkness. There is a sound of steel. The sound comes from the rhythm section (the engine room) of the steel band. The sound is energetic, almost hysterical, as though something is about to happen. This is a sound that will occur throughout the play. The sound of clashing steel. Steel against steel. A cold hard sound and yet it is musical. It is syncopation. We see a shaft of light as if through a door ajar. Daybreak. Inside is dark. JEAN stands by the doorway. DINAH stirs. DINAH is 64 years old and not in good health. Her apartment is in total disarray, clothes everywhere, shoes, etc. Prominently displayed on her wall, there is an aging photograph of the late Honourable Dr. Eric Williams, the first Prime Minister of Trinidad and Tobago. There is a musty smell. The apartment has not been cleaned for some time. The sound of steel dies.

DINAH
Jean?

JEAN
You know what day it is! *(pause)* And you ent wake up yet?

JEAN starts to take things out of her bag. Pieces of costume, a bottle of rum etc.... DINAH starts to cough.

JEAN
You know what day it is? Eh? Eh! *(pause)* You want some coffee?

Holding up the bottle, she goes off-stage to make the coffee. DINAH coughs.

DINAH
What is the time?

JEAN
(off-stage) Time to wake up, high time to get up off your Black arse...

> *JEAN returns and busies herself clearing up DINAH's room. She is laying out pieces of costume, getting ready to change into her own costume. There are many coloured pieces of cloth, etc. on the floor. She sets out a flag. Flag stick.*

DINAH
(She sits up quietly.) Jean you...

JEAN
Dinah, we late you know. *(slight pause)*

DINAH
Give me some coffee.

JEAN
(She steps over some things and goes off to get the coffee.) In the meantime get up and get yourself ready. I put out a few things already. We want to catch the bright noonday sun, remember?

DINAH
Jean, you remember the time when...

> *JEAN appears with a cup of coffee and stands over DINAH.*

JEAN
Dinah, we have no time for that now you know? *(She hands her the coffee.)* Okay? We done late already. It have all kinds of people on the road these days.

> *JEAN starts to undress and then puts on her costume, her hands are in the air. Her face is covered by her bodice.*

DINAH
Jean, remember the time you did come to me inside Lucky Jordan running...?

JEAN
Not now, oh God, not now, Dinah. You know what day it is? *(She gets the bodice off. She is in a bra alone.)* Today is celebration day, Dinah. Celebration time, oh God!

DINAH

Is me, Jean. The man wanted to chop you. And is to me you did come looking to…

JEAN

What? That little poowatee man? He? The problem with he was he wanted a little screw and a little feel up balls for a little five cents.

DINAH

Jean.

JEAN

And, I wasn't paying he no mind, you understand…?

DINAH

Jean.

JEAN

Look at the class of woman I am. That is a little piss'n tail man. Eh? A little piss'n tail man. I didn't want to have nothing to do with he and every time he see me he want to insult me. When I see he, I used to spit on he…

DINAH

And why your hand so? Jean, why…?

JEAN

I used to haawk and sssspit on he.

DINAH

That is why he chop you. *(She turns and goes back to bed.)*

JEAN

And he do time, too. He do plenty time and he get chop back too. Look Dinah, why we talking this today, eh? Oh shit, man, get up nuh. And let us go down the road.

DINAH

And you do plenty time too.

JEAN

What you say? What is that you say? Look he get chop back, he get his arse chop back.

DINAH

(to herself) Wasn't you. Wasn't you.

JEAN
Eh? Was them boys and them in the band. I send them in he tail.

DINAH
(to herself) You too lie.

JEAN
He had to get it in he arse. Because, yes. I stand up just so and talking to them girls in the shop. Ma Popo was behind the counter. And I there talking good, good, good. Eh? And all I hear is, LOOK OUT!

DINAH
Oh God! *(She sits up, pause.)*

JEAN
And as I do so. *(She screams.)*

DINAH
That was it.

JEAN
This is the hand, you know. This is the hand.

DINAH
So tell me something. *(She sips the coffee.)* Whatever become of he now, girl?

JEAN
He arse dead, nah. Dead like a semp. *(pause)* Is six months I nearly dead in that blasted hospital, six months, six blasted months. *(pause)* Dinah, we ent have time for this now, you know. Look how you have me talking. Come, get up, and let us go, nah man. *(She busies herself with a piece of her sailor suit.)*

DINAH
Child, I lie down here thinking how such a big set of man just come to nothing. Ah hear he come out of jail and he was nothing.

JEAN
He must be nothing. He must be nothing. Is a woman energy he take, you know.

DINAH begins to cough. JEAN has to help her to a sip of the coffee.

DINAH
No, bring water. Bring ice-cold water for me.

JEAN hurries out to get the water.

JEAN

What ice-cold water? You have fridge? You see what I mean. We could be down the road long time now. Enjoying we self. Enjoying we self.

She returns with a glass of water and pacifies DINAH who by this time is almost out of breath.

Okay, okay. Let us go now, okay? You taking tablets, right? *(DINAH nods her head.)* Good.

Pause.

DINAH

And he was a real good chantuelle, you hear, you talk about throat.

JEAN

Yes, man, when he hit you. *(She sings and gets more and more frenzied.)*
Out in the road
Come out in the road
Warrior
Remember that…
Out in the road
Come out in the road
Warrior
Ah seeing him and ah remembering the chop
and he taking my energy.
Ah seeing him dancing and is like I can't
dance. Dinah, Dinah, today is my day Dinah, he
arse dead. Eh! Dinah, come Dinah.
Out in the road.

Come out in the road
Warrior
Come out in the road
Warrior
Come out in the road
Dinah
Come out in the road
Dinah

She sings this repeatedly. In the meantime it is as if the song was directed at DINAH. She has miraculously gotten out of bed and begins to dance with JEAN who has taken up a stick and is charging around the room. It becomes energetic as JEAN remembers the particular day and the particular man. DINAH has a stick in her hand and JEAN sees her dancing. They are doing the Calinda dance. JEAN stops. She relaxes.

So you ready to go now. *(pause)* Come take a bath, you will feel better. You want to take a bath? Eh? Come, let us go. *(DINAH goes towards the bed, she stumbles and falls on the bed. JEAN hurries over to her.)* Let us go nah, Dinah. Let us go.

DINAH

(She organizes herself on the bed in a half sitting position.) They take all my energy, girl. They take a woman energy.

JEAN

(sings quietly)
Joe Pringé, lend meh your bois to play
Joe Pringé, lend meh your bois, I say...
Joe Pringé...

DINAH

Jean.

JEAN

(She continues to sing. DINAH sings along with her.)
Joe Pringé, lend meh your bois to play
Joe Pringé, lend meh your bois, I say...

DINAH

Ah could see my father in the ring now. He had a particular crouch as soon as they put a stick in his hand. And coulda move! Faster than lightning.

JEAN

Joe Pringé was your father?

DINAH

Shiffer.

JEAN

Who Shiffer, that?

DINAH

Shiffer Brathwaite, girl.

JEAN

Shiffer Brathwaite, boy.

DINAH

The man was tall and Black. He used to look like he come straight from Africa just to fight stick. He was the champ in Freeport for years. They used to come from all over to Freeport to fight Shiffer. They coulda never touch him. He was too fast. You ever hear about the great Moscobee and Cutaway Rimbeau? Ah hear dem was men who coulda commit delicate surgery in the ring. Shiffer was in that class. *(Pause, she laughs.)*

JEAN

And is how you learn stick?

DINAH

My father used to say Man Man is a warrior who walk from Africa. He used to call himself Man Man. No slave ship for him, he walk for his own self, with his own two foot. And Ma would shout out from the yard, "What stupidness you telling the children? They will get licks in school for telling them stories." *(pause)*

(sings) Mooma, mooma,
Your son in the grave already
Your son in the grave already
Take a towel and band your belly. *(repeat)*

Ever since I was six, or seven, every time I hear the drums, something funny does run through my body. A shiver. A shiver. The first time he take me to the gayelle, well boy. It was like magic. I never see a place like that. It was the same street corner I did know, the same old junction in Freeport. But somehow with the men on the drums under flambeau light in one corner, the fighters with their head ties and stick blazing and chants chanting, I couldn't keep my head on straight. And is like from that day to this… I don't know. I remember once in the darkness on the junction, just before he jump in the ring, my father turn to me and say, "But like you is a warrior too?" That day I feel a heat run through my body. *(pause)* From the time I was ten everybody know me dancing stick, sometimes with man, sometimes with woman. And my mother never say nothing, she always just watch me with them sad eyes. The same sad eyes she kept for Shiffer. She couldn't stop it. *(pause)*

JEAN

(Momentarily she is enthralled by the story, then she gets up.) Dinah, we done late already. *(DINAH sits staring.)*

DINAH

One day he was out in the bush.

JEAN

(stops) Who?

DINAH

Sometimes he went out for days to hunt. That night when he come back he had a limp and only one dog. He looked green and he said a snake bite him. He suck out the poison and fall asleep in the grass. Ma start to say how she dream the night before. She see the sign, a white spider. In her dream she tried to kill it, stamping it with her foot tangled in the web. But it wouldn't die. It just looked at her and laughed with its pink gums and red beaming eyes. Ma, shut up! *(pause)* Pa ent say nothing. He just went and took down his bois and limped out of the house, down the road. The dog running behind him. Ma stay quiet. I jumped up and shouted, No! No! My younger sisters watched and laughed and run out the back door. I was sixteen. I follow him. When I see him in the Rum Shop he was sitting on a stool with his head resting on the counter. Ram behind the counter telling him if he sick he better go home, pushing another petit quart of rum and a clean glass in front of his face. *(pause)*

That night some young boy ride in the port and issue a challenge to all the old batoniers and them. Shiffer couldn't stop himself. He spring in the gayelle. The drummers crack keg, but Shiffer was carrying snake poison and he didn't see where that young bois come from. That was it. It lay him out flat, flat. The men lift him, they take him to the hole and he let out the blood. He never recover. He lie down home in the bed till he dead. We never know if it was from the snake bite or humiliation. He couldn't see the stick from the young boy. After that, things get hard. I had to help out. So I leave Arena, that is our part of Freeport, and come to town to look for work. All it had home was cane field and bush. *(pause)* And now look at me, I have no eyes.

JEAN
Dinah... *(pause)*

DINAH
They say it was Joe Pringé nephew. *(pause)*

JEAN gets up and moves around the room organizing DINAH's costume.

JEAN
Look, the sun hot...

DINAH
Oh God! *(DINAH turns and lies down in her bed.)*

JEAN
(She looks in disgust at DINAH.) Cheups! *(She sucks her teeth.)*

DINAH
(angrily) Let me tell you once and for all. You are a blasted jagabat and will be so all your life. I have my pride and I ent letting you drag my Black, blind arse through the streets of Port-of-Spain on this Carnival Monday for nobody, nobody, no focking body. You understand? I have my dignity.

JEAN

What is your problem? Dinah, what wrong? Today is our day. If we don't play today, we might as well be dead.

DINAH

Listen to me. I played some of the best mas in this place. So you, nor nobody like you, can't tell me about mas. Mas is me and I is mas. And I am telling you that I am staying in my pissing bed, here today. *(She pulls herself under the covers.)*

JEAN

I don't know what wrong with you, nuh. You will let the whole day pass with this stupidness. I dunno...

DINAH

(sitting up) Jean? Where you come from?

JEAN

How you mean, where I come from? Home.

DINAH

(from under the covers) You could go to fock back.

JEAN

Home? Where the fock is home? *(pause, a caged bird)* From the time I was ten, Uncle start to interfere with me. He come just so, early one Sunday morning when Aunty gone to church, and lie down on top of me on the bed. I jump up and push him off. I was always a fighter. My sister and them hear the commotion and they get up too. He say how he was looking for something he thought he leave in the room. Eh? *(pause)*

I used to have a wood dolly, make out of wood, hide up under my bed, since I was small. When I get bigger I didn't used to play with it no more. But it stay below the bed and I used to see it there all the time. All on a sudden, I miss my dolly. Two days later, I find the dolly by the latrine outside in the yard with the left hand break and the head rip off. When I look up so I see Uncle by the kitchen window watching me while he washing his mouth in the sink. I ent pay he no mind. That night he come back again. I tell him I go tell Aunty and he hold me tight, he cover my mouth, he was hurting me. He say if I tell Aunty he will kill me. He say I was a bad girl. I did hate he. I did real hate that man. You know how much time I did feel to stab him, to poison his tea. *(pause)* I didn't tell Aunty. When she came back from church? I didn't tell she nothing. This went on. 'Til one day, when I was thirteen or fourteen it hit me, this have to be done. They had no money. *(pause)* I see my father once. They say he working on the American Base. I have to leave here. I have to leave this place and find him. And find my own way. My own money. These people can't help me. All they could do is fock me up.

DINAH, who has been under the covers for the whole story, uncovers herself and sits up. She starts to cough. JEAN hands her the bottle of rum she brought with her. DINAH takes a swig and hands it back to JEAN who takes a big swig herself.

A year after I leave there, I hear a truck knock him down off his bicycle and kill him. They say he was drunk. God don't sleep. *(She lights a cigarette.)* I used to lime with this dougla girl. Ahm... Elaine. She was from San Juan too. And she used to go to town regular. She was the one who invite me to come to the club in town, that first night, when I went. She was friends with everybody or, in fact, everybody was she friend. Anyway, we went by a table in the corner to have a drink. It was a kind of dark corner. *(pause)* And when she was drinking these two men came in the club. They wasn't Yankee men or anything, they was local, jacket men. And them did know she, what she used to do. *(pause)* So, so they come by the table and we start to talk and thing. And what end up happening was that Elaine went with one of the men and I had it to go with the other of the men. And nobody never say nothing. That is how it start for me, and that is how I remember making my first set of money. Is a little while after I come to know you was in that club and had some weight with Popo and them.

DINAH
Yes.

JEAN
(She takes another swig from the bottle.) That was the first money I ever make. I went and buy a yellow dress with the money, a pretty yellow dress, one with pleats. And I went to a dance. *(She gets up and starts to dance.)* All ah we meet by the abattoir and then we went up the road to the club. That was the first time I meet the Lord.

DINAH
What?

JEAN
Warlord, the calypsonian, nuh.

DINAH
That useless good for nothing. You know if you give them fellas a chance they will give you a bad name. They sing on you, just so. He and Little Sparrow. Next thing you know, people jumping to the tune of you on Carnival day.

JEAN
But you know in the early days he was good to me. As a little girl coming out I didn't know nothing. Is he who show me... but it was later when we was together he start to play the fool. He start to play up in his arse with that red woman. With she two long stringy foot.

DINAH

Is Warlord self who tell me is you.

JEAN

Warlord tell you what? Eh? What Warlord tell you? A day I pass by his house and when I pass by the house he wasn't expecting me. And ah see that bacra-Johnny gyal two red shoes on the step. *(DINAH starts to sing Blakie's "Steelband Clash.")* That bacra-Johnny gyal. Eh? He was lying down on the bed with, eh? With she two foot like two long string of bodi. Eh? Ah went in that house and ah pull out clothes, hear nah man, ah pull out clothes. And ah pull out clothes so and ah throw it in the yard. Eh? Want to play he leaving me for that half-scorched, half-scald, frigging magga head, red ooman, eh? Because she little redder than me. *(DINAH starts to laugh.)* What you laughing at?

DINAH

Red woman cursing red woman. They say she was Syrian.

JEAN

Syrian, my arse. Hear nah man. Ah take out he clothes. And ah throw he arse out in all he drawers. And then you know what ah do next? Eh? Ah take out my blue handle razor and ah stoop down and piss on it, on all he clothes. *(She uses the razor to prevent anybody from coming close to her to try to remove the clothes.)* You think he ever set eyes on a bacra-Johnny woman again? Eh? Not that calypsonian. *(pause)*

DINAH

You know when was the first time I hear about you?

JEAN

When was that?

DINAH

Them fellas, Lance and Leon and Janet gang come down in the club a night and say how police raid a fête up in San Juan. And how some young girl, who now come out, tell the police that she ent going down now, to check she next week. And she walk away like Brook Benton.

JEAN

You know, I don't know where I learn that from. Must be from Warlord and Marabunta and them. But I couldn't see myself in no Black Maria with my nice dress, what? And you know the rest of them just stand up there and watch me walk. *(pause)*

DINAH

They pick you up the next day, though.

JEAN
Yes. But I used to do them that well regular.

DINAH
Jean, why you didn't go back home when I talk to you, eh?

JEAN
Let us go into town nuh. You ent find we waste enough time with this nonsense.

DINAH
Yes, and look at us now. *(pause)* Why you come here? Why you don't go?

JEAN
You feel I can't go by myself? You feel I 'fraid? The road make to walk. I could fock well go and leave your arse right here to rot.

DINAH
Go home, Jean. Go home, it ent have nothing for you here. Go home. *(pause)* And then you go and cut up Rosie. Lord.

JEAN
Dinah, why you bringing up all this today? Today of all days, Dinah? Today is a day to forget. Today is a day when we could be anything we want to be. If we want to feel good Dinah, today we could feel good. Today we could forget and enjoy weself.

DINAH
I can't see my way to forget.

JEAN
(She takes another swig from the bottle which is near empty. She holds it up and looks at the low level.) Shit! *(She hands it to DINAH who smashes it out of her hand to the ground. The bottle breaks.)* What the fock you do that for? Eh? Why you do that? *(She goes for DINAH's throat to choke her. DINAH holds her off. JEAN is on top of DINAH.)* That was my last bottle, you focking old whore you.

DINAH
(DINAH gasps for breath.) I never make a fares yet. You nastiness.

JEAN is scared she may be killing DINAH and releases her.

JEAN
Oh, shit! Shit! Shit! Dinah you all right?

DINAH

How you mean if I alright? You was always a damn criminal. I try my best with you all these years. Now you want to kill me.

JEAN

Dinah, Dinah, this is your fault. All now so we should be down the road playing we mas, happy, happy. Instead…

DINAH

You should be in jail. That is what. I should never let them let you out.

JEAN

It wasn't you. What you talking about? (*pause*) Eh? What you talking about?

    DINAH turns to cover her head once again.

DINAH

For a pair of earrings, Jean?

JEAN

What causing this? What causing this?

DINAH

They never prove that Rosie take your earrings, you know.

JEAN

That was my gold earrings. Fourteen carat gold. They always want what I have. Well, to arse with that. Everybody know that Rosie hand sticky. She always want to go with people man, take other people thing.

DINAH

So you cut her up. (*DINAH gets up.*) She never recovered, Jean. She never recovered up to today.

JEAN

You don't take what is mines. I work hard for that. I have to look good.

DINAH

Rosita never look good again. And she used to look good…

JEAN

She was a old thief! (*She rushes to DINAH again.*)

DINAH

Wait!

DINAH responds as if she can see. She is an old fighter. She gets up and throws JEAN off her. JEAN is thrown to the ground, skating across the room.

You see you! You is a jamette down to your focking heart. Ah not taking that, you know. Ah not taking that a-mother-cunt-all. *(She pulls a white-handle razor from under her pillow.)* I will slice your arse thin, thin, thin, right here and now. Make that the last time you jump me, you hear? *(long pause)* You don't even know how you used to get out of jail. *(pause)* You think is two hot water you put me in? Fock!

JEAN

Look Dinah, I... I... not taking no talk from nobody. You could say what you want. People always jealous me, always. When you see I go into town and buy my nice shoe and my pretty cloth and come out, is so they does jealous me. And if I with a man, you can't be with the man. How you go be with the man? It must have fight. I go cut your arse, eh Dinah? I must cut your arse for that!

She lights a cigarette shakily after the encounter with DINAH. DINAH coughs uncontrollably, JEAN tries to help with water, etc.

Let we go, nah girl. Your body not feeling for it? For the fête, girl. Let us go nah, Dinah.

DINAH

(coughing some more) Too much smoke, girl. Is the smoke I can't take. *(more coughing)* Is the focking smoke I can't take.

JEAN

(Turning reluctantly, she takes a last puff of her cigarette and puts it out. She tries to busy herself with the preparation of costumes.) I don't know why you getting on like this, nuh. You trying to spoil a good, good time yes. Look, Dinah, for the last time...

DINAH

Jean, remember when police used to raid the place. Popo used to get real vex. Because he used to like to pretend that nothing going on in the place. But the first time police come. You remember how you come and hold on to me and you bawl down the place like twenty Tarzan.

JEAN

But I did know that you wouldn't let them carry me down so. So I did try a thing that first time. "She is my mother and I am not in nothing. I just here." And they did believe that before they get wind of me. And then finally they realize I was the little girl, the little red girl from San Juan. Yes, I not taking no talk from nobody, up to today.

DINAH

All you so used to give me real pressure, you hear. All the different girls. All you know the scene and, oh God! I used to want a little rest sometimes. But the police coming with some story. Bodi, that miserable, Syrian bitch, so she thin, so she full up with bacchanal and confusion. And "Bag of Iron," that ugly Bajan, only saying as a police he have he bounded duty. Always looking to lock up somebody. This time is only a little thing he wanted, yes. I remember a time he come up to me with his short pants and his two knock knee and say to me, "I want you to squeeze these."

JEAN

(*in disbelief*) Who is that "Bag a Lion?"

DINAH

Yes, "Bag of Iron" self! So I say, "You want me to squeeze these? You really want me to squeeze those? You better take out your balls and roll it...." He get vex and want to lock up the whole club. (*laughter, pause*) Jean? Jean? Why you choose here? Why you choose here? (*pause*)

JEAN

Dinah, look, ah fed up with you and this shit, you hear.

> *She busies herself as if she is about to leave. DINAH turns and goes under the covers again.*

You know I does vex for you. After all these years of making fares and...

DINAH

(*jumping out from under the covers*) Look, you don't wash your mouth on me. You hear? You of all people. Not one of all you could point your hand in my face and say you see me making fares with any of the men inside here.

JEAN

Oh God, Dinah! Why you so hypocrite? You was to encourage...

DINAH

Me? You was to see me encourage? You make children but you don't make their mind. I was a waitress by trade and inclination. Popo and them entrust me into virtually running the place. Now the men and them has been very kind to me. (*JEAN laughs out loudly, mocking her.*) And for your better information, if you want to know, is only the little striptease I uses to do in the clubs. In my heyday I did like my exotic dancing, a little limbo here, a little limbo there, fire-eating and so on. But you know, as I make child and thing, I get this little belly so I done with that. (*pause*) So, if you know what good for you, you better shut your damn blasted watery mouth. *(JEAN stares at her.)* As there is a God above, *(DINAH makes the sign of the cross and kisses it.)* I never make a fares yet.

JEAN

Awright, awright, nuh. Why you always feel you better than people? What make you better than the rest of us? *(She blows smoke in DINAH's direction.)* You so full of focking shit. After all these years, insisting that you never make a fares yet. Everybody does laugh at you with that shit, Dinah. Everybody know is jackass talk, focking jackass talk. Everybody know that between you, "Winnie," "I Is A Whore Too," "Alice Sugar" and even "Big Six," all you probably make the most money out of all of us from the Yankees. Is true you must be give some money away, but all you lie down flat and make it. *(laughs)* Stand up too. I know that for sure.

DINAH

You know that for sure?

JEAN

Yes! For fock sure.

DINAH

Get to fock out. Leave my place now. Out! Out in the road!

JEAN

(surprised) Awright, awright. You don't have to say it twice. I gone. Long time now I planning to leave you in this nasty hell-hole you living in. This nasty arse place here. When I gone, see who the arse will come and visit you in this rat hole.

DINAH

But Jean? Why you does come? Eh, tell me why? Why you come this time?

JEAN

To......... for we to play mas, you arse!

DINAH

Well, from now on stay to fock away. I don't want to see you here again. You hear me?

JEAN

You ent have to say that twice you know, I gone.

She readies herself, packs things up quickly. With a cigarette in her mouth, she can only use one hand in her hurried action.

DINAH

Jean *(pause)* Why you pelt the bottle?

JEAN

(She stops at the door.) Look, Dinah, let we go down the road and enjoy we self. You mean you go let Monday pass and we go still be here like two fools carrying on with this shit. *(JEAN stands with the bundle in her hand not wanting to leave just so.)*

DINAH

Why you pelt the bottle, Jean?

JEAN

Dinah, me ent pelt no bottle, Dinah.

DINAH

We coming up Charlotte Street. As I say, Desperadoes coming up Charlotte Street, beating really sweet. San Juan All Stars coming down so, beating rather slow. Outside the Colonial Hospital, somebody say, "Look out!" Now, I didn't see who pelt the bottle eh, because they say, "Look out!" And you know what it is. When you hear "Look Out!" is to focking duck. Defend yourself.

JEAN

I ent pelt no bottle.

DINAH

Jean, Jean, everybody. Everybody saying is you. Ah don't know why after all these years that you wouldn't say that is you is the cause...

JEAN

Dinah, Dinah.

DINAH

...the cause why my eyesight...

JEAN

Dinah! Dinah!! I go watch you and pelt you and burst out your eye? Just so, Dinah?

DINAH

Jean, maybe you didn't mean to pelt focking me. But it hit focking me.

JEAN

Just so Dinah? Dinah, Dinah.

DINAH

Jean, everybody see you. Warlord.

JEAN

Dinah, fock Warlord. Dinah, Dinah. You not hearing me. Dinah, you are not hearing me. Dinah, I go watch you, you who I know so long...

DINAH

Awright, why you pelt? Everybody say...

JEAN

Who get house for you? Who get man for you? Who get work for you?

DINAH

Don't! You didn't get no man for me. I is a married ooman, you know. Don't bring me into your commess. I have five girl children in wedlock, in wed-lock.

JEAN

Oh God! You gone again. Where them, Dinah? Where the children? Why you so? I go watch you just so you who I know so long and pelt you with a bottle and burst your eye, eh?

DINAH

Awright, Jean. You didn't pelt me with the bottle. You didn't pelt and burst my eye. But why you pelt the bottle, Jean? *(pause)* Jean, why you pelt the bottle? *(pause)* You can't answer me. You pelt a bottle, awright, it hit me...

JEAN

Dinah.

DINAH

You didn't mean to pelt a bottle to burst my eye. But you pelt a bottle. Why you pelt a bottle?

JEAN

I was holding on to my man in San Juan All Stars good, good. And you see me pelt bottle? What kind of bottle it was? Eh? Since you see so good, eh? What kind of focking bottle it was? Eh? Tell me that.

DINAH

A focking Eclipse bottle.

JEAN

I don't drink that, girl.

DINAH

And how you could be holding on to your man and waving flag? You trying to mamaguy me or what?

JEAN

I never drink that, girl.

DINAH

Is the same man you did holding on to. Is the same man bottle you pelt. Is he bottle of rum.

JEAN

I don't drink Eclipse.

DINAH

I don't consult with what you was drinking. The man you was holding on to, he was drinking Mount Gay Eclipse. That is the rum everybody was drinking that time.

JEAN

So how I was waving the flag?

DINAH

Is you who tell me you was holding on to the man, you know, awright. And if it is so, then is he bottle you had. Is he bottle you pelt. And we didn't do all you nothing.

JEAN

(*pause*) Dinah, all you was playing NOAH's ARK, right? And in the Ark had endless cutlash. What that was for, Dinah? Eh? To plant garden? Eh?

DINAH

You pelt a bottle and it hit my eye. (*pause*) I spend my time in that hospital fighting to save my eye. You never come to visit me. Not once, Jean, not once. (*pause*) Jean, why? Why Jean?

JEAN

Dinah, I didn't pelt no bottle, Dinah. Look at me in my eye, Dinah, I pelt any bottle?

DINAH

Jean, I can't see you. How I looking at you? How I going to see you?

JEAN

Look me in my eye and tell me I pelt a bottle. (*pleading*)

DINAH

(*pause*) Jean, what happen? You sorry, now. Eh? Jean, you is the reason and I don't know why after all these years you wouldn't own up. Jean, if you miss this one, that is it, you know. That is it.

JEAN
You know what day this is? What day it is?

DINAH
But let God be the judge.

JEAN
Dinah, you know what day it is?

DINAH
I don't want to know what day it is!

JEAN
You know what day it is?

DINAH
This day doesn't mean anything to me.

JEAN
You lie down there, Dinah.

DINAH
Jean look, I can't go on no more. My heart ain't good. Bubalups gone, I couldn't even go to the funeral. Ah hear nobody went. Now Mayfield up and gone. *(pause)* Where my five girls? Eh? Tell me this thing! *(pause)* If James was alive, God rest his soul. He was a good man. He had a good work. He worked in the Colonial Hospital and then when the People's National government come in, he had a party card and get a good work with Ministry of Works.

JEAN
Dinah, all you was always behind this politics thing. Where it get you? This party thing and this Doctor Williams, eh?

DINAH
Don't talk thing you don't know about, child. When James hear it have meeting in the Square, he gone! He march in the rain when that same Doctor Eric Williams make the call to take back the Chaguaramas base from the Americans. Freedom for one and all! He even drag me and all along. They needed a flag woman. *(pause)* James was a good man.

JEAN
I did never like them People's Nationals peoples. They come up by me plenty times. We went with them... by the bus load. The calypsonians sing. We get rum. I never trust them.

DINAH
I try my best with them children. I don't know what went wrong. Everybody always know what is your problem and could tell you

about your problem. But I know I tried my best. I had one boy I adopt, that make it six children really. He working mechanic with Forde on the Eastern Main Road. But the girls and them, oh God! Jean you see them sometimes? Them children ent please my heart at all.

JEAN

I does see Katherine…

DINAH

(*JEAN lights a cigarette.*) I don't want to talk about it. I don't want to talk. (*pause, cough*) And imagine we had a good, good house and that and all I lose… oh God… eh? (*pause, steel rhythm*) What is that? You hearing something?

JEAN

No! What happening, Dinah?

DINAH

Like if ah hearing and seeing a steel band coming closer to me. It coming, Jean. It coming straight for me. Jean, it bursting my head. Jean do something. Do something. Jean, Jean…

JEAN

Dinah, Dinah. (*rhythm gets louder*) Dinah, I can't hear anything. Dinah, it is alright, is okay. Shit, Dinah, what happening? What happening?

DINAH covers her ears in the bed. JEAN hugs her and tries to pacify her. The sound of pounding steel subsides. It cools down to a soothing rhythm before it dies completely. Long pause.

Dinah, you awright? (*pause*)

DINAH sobs uncontrollably as JEAN hugs her tightly. Long pause.

Dinah, what is…?

DINAH

Jean?

JEAN

Yes…

DINAH

What you was doing in San Juan All Stars?

JEAN moves away from DINAH.

You shoulda be with us, Marabuntas, Desperadoes. All the boys that we know on Duke Street by Lucky Jordan was in them band.

JEAN

Dinah, why you...?

DINAH

Jean, is that what cause the fight you know. *(pause)*

JEAN

Dinah, that is my business. My... *(pause)* ...focking business.

DINAH

You will never see. *(She turns and goes under the covers.)*

JEAN

(She continues to pack her things and goes towards the door.) You don't know how Harry used to beat me. And tell me all kinda things. He used to beat me bad, bad, bad. And he was with Elaine when he was with me. When the big girl died, he come around. I don't know for what. All these marks you see on my skin here, he is responsible. But I did real like the man. I did real like that man. *(pause)* When he drink he rum he used to tell me all kinda things, about how I having this man and that man. *(pause)* I couldn't complain to nobody, I didn't have nobody to complain to...

DINAH

Jean.

JEAN

Look, the Yankee I was to marry, Leroy father, did give me a slave band – gold, expensive. He always used to bring expensive thing every time he come. Harry take the thing and gone. You know I never get back that slave band my Yankee man give me. I never get back that slave band. I tell him keep it. It just right for him. It go blight he. One day he even plan-arse me. He beat me up with a three canal cutlash and tell me if I would only shut my cunt we would be better off. *(pause)*

He used to feel I was his property. But I was to get my freedom some-how and Carnival time was a time when I used to go on my own. Nobody could own me. Nobody could tie my foot that time.

DINAH

And that is when you went looking for Ramon. That slippery Bound Coolie, his hair dripping with tallow grease.

JEAN

Ramon? Ramon wasn't no Indian. He was a Creole. He used to like to slick his hair like the Warlord.

DINAH
Ramon wasn't an Indian?

JEAN
He had you fooled too. *(pause)* People used to take he for Indian or Spanish. He was a good, good, man, you hear.

DINAH
They say he had a stick like Mastifé.

JEAN
Hush, nuh. With him I used to feel I could do anything, anything, anything. Me and that man struggle together. I do work till I get the house down south. *(pause)* But the children was nothing like Ramon. The big girl, Dolores...

DINAH
(from under the covers) But she wasn't Ramon child.

JEAN
No, that was Harry own. Worthless, just like he. She eventually went to the States and become a nurse. All my money. She was up there in New York nursing. She never send for me. And then she come and dead just so in a motor car accident up there. The car didn't see the lights. Same time Harry turn up by me asking if she ent leave nothing for he. Ah say: "Like what?" He say: "Well, you never know." Ah say: "Damn right, you never know." He did never know nothing. I used to hate to hear him say that. He used to say it all the time: "You never know." Ah feel he thought that was a joke. "You never know." And then he open his mouth wide, wide and laugh, a kinda horse laugh, *(slight pause)* arse hole, jackass. *(She starts to throw her clothes around the room.)*

DINAH
Jean.

JEAN
Arse holes. *(She starts to weep, pause.)* They let my baby bleed to death.

She slips to the floor in a sitting position and clutches herself tightly. She starts to rock.

She didn't have to die. *(pause)* She was the first child with Ramon, a sweet angel. He did real like she. She was always quiet. Nice, nice child. Growing up good, good. She was only nineteen. Still young. She gone and pick up with these faith healers. Me ent know what it was. Some people say it was Witness. But if it was Witness, I woulda know it was Witness. I know a Witness when I see a Witness. *(pause)* Why she didn't go and have the operation? Ramon did know a good doctor fella in

Brighton, who was willing to help out. Oh God! Oh God! Oh God! My baby bleed to death. She bleed to death, Dinah. Dinah, all I see is red. Red. Red! Dinah is that what kill Ramon, you know. He couldn't take it, Dinah. I had to be strong. I had to hold on for both of them. I had to hold on. *(pause)* After that, Ramon get small. All the energy went out of him. The spirit get weak. He take to going for long walks by himself. Then one day he disappear.

DINAH

And that was it.

JEAN

That was it. *(pause)* Then it was just me and small boy Toto alone, left in the house. And you know Toto does look just like Ramon. Ramon in print. So Toto get everything. They say I spoil the child. But Dinah, he was all I had. With Ramon gone what ah go do? Eh? Tell meh nah, eh? *(pause)* All of a sudden, he start calling me jamette to my face. He and he little Junior Secondary hangman friends. I try with him and give him everything. By that time ah had was to go back to work. Next thing I know, I see he pick up with some white men, strange looking white people. They always just passing through.

DINAH

(She sits up in disbelief.) Toto is a macomé man? *(pause)* I never realize...

JEAN

Well, me and he used to get away bad, bad... ah mean in we heyday we used to do we thing.

DINAH

We?

JEAN

But not like this. Oh God. No, not like this. *(pause)* We used to have some serious fight and on this day in particular he get vex... he went and get a big can of pitch oil... *(pause)* and burn down my house... I lose meh house... *(pause)* I had nowhere to rest meh head... nowhere to rest meh head because of Toto. After all them years, Dinah, I had nobody... *(pause)* I never feel like if I ever love anybody.

DINAH

Eh, heh? *(pause)*

JEAN

Dis town have no love in it. Dis town never know what love is. And if Jean "In Town" say so, is so. Nobody know like I know. I did always want what I want. *(pause)* And look at me now, I old. I can't fix my teeth, the arthritis. And Cyril home there, he real miserable too, you know. He does help out, but he old in he arse… *(pause)* Dinah this is shit, man. I never carry on like this. This is real shit that going on here today. Dinah, like you put a spell on me or what? *(JEAN jumps to her feet, energized.)* Dinah, you know what day it is, eh? Dinah, look I bring a sailor suit. You could play fancy sailor.

DINAH
Jean… let me.

JEAN
It have two piece of thing in the bag here. It have some sequins. It have some nice feathers. We could put it on it. And ah bring a socks. If you see socks, girl. Spit bring it from New York, is a New York socks. We go put it on. And you know what too, we go hold your cane. You see that cane you have there? Oh God! We go pretty that up. And ah have some spray paint. We go put pink and yellow and blue and it go look like a rainbow. Oh God, Dinah!

DINAH
Ah hearing it.

JEAN
Dinah, this year we go play a mas. We coming out with real fire. And when you hear you put that stick and you putting that thing on your head.

DINAH
Jean.

JEAN
Eh, Dinah?

DINAH
Jean, ah hearing, ah hearing… it…

JEAN
A teka, teka, teka, teka, teka, teka……

DINAH
Ah seeing them coming down the road…

JEAN
A teka, teka, teka, teka.

DINAH
Ah hearing the music… yes.

JEAN
A teka, teka, teka, teka.

DINAH
What was the music? The road march? What was it? Ah hearing it.

JEAN
(*dancing and singing*) Drunk and Disorderly, meh friends and meh family...

DINAH
It wasn't that nah, nah.

JEAN
What it was? What it was?

DINAH
You know what it was, Jean! (*pause*)

JEAN
Dinah?

DINAH
Jean!

JEAN
You know what day it is? You know what day this is?

DINAH
Ah not hearing this day. Ah not hearing the day... that bitch, is he that tell me is you.

JEAN
The Warlord, nuh? Ever since the time with Bodi. And he did never like Ramon.

DINAH
(*starts to sing Blakie's "Steelband Clash"*) Is a bacchanal, fifties' carnival, fête for so...

JEAN
You ent know what today is?

DINAH
Hush, husshhh (*continues "Steelband Clash"*)

JEAN
Today is mas day. Come, come, let we try it on nuh, right?

DINAH sits up. She is spaced out.

You hearing the music? Dinah, oui, Dinah...

She starts to dance and sing "Drunk and Disorderly." She drowns out DINAH's "Steelband Clash."

DINAH
Oh God, Jean, that smoke, that smoke. *(She starts to cough.)*

JEAN
What you talking about? Dinah, come on!

DINAH
(as if far away) Eh?

JEAN
What happen you can't hear or what? Dinah! You deaf now?

DINAH
Eh, heh.

JEAN
Dinah.

DINAH
(as if in a trance) What we playing?

JEAN
We playing sailor. Ah tell you sailor already. And we go have a pretty kinda rainbow stick. Where your stick?

DINAH
What kinda sailor? Fancy Sailor?

JEAN
Rainbow sailor. *(DINAH gets up out of the bed.)* And we go drop so and drop so and drop so. Where yuh stick? We go seek revenge on dem glamour boys again. *(DINAH is up starting to dance by this time. JEAN is in full flight.)* All Hands on Deck! Remember that band, Dinah? Where your stick? Bring your stick. Bring your stick, girl. *(JEAN puts a stick into Dinah's hand.)* Get a stick. Get a flag. Get a man. Eh? A stick...

They are both dancing and laughing and having a good time.

And we gone. Look at we... heh, heh, heh, heh, heh.

A delicate, energetic sailor heel and toe dance ensues.

Remember when we used to move with Marabuntas, eh? With Desperadoes, eh? *(DINAH laughs. She stops dancing.)* You get up? You get up then?

DINAH
Yes.

JEAN
We going and play, right? Let me get the bag and thing. Come. *(pause)* You going and bathe first?

DINAH
Cheups. *(She sucks her teeth.)*

JEAN
You bathing first?

DINAH
Nah.

JEAN
Dinah? What happen now? *(childish, as if to her mother)* You don't want to play sailor or what? *(near to tears)*

DINAH
(stumbles back to bed) Them days done, girl.

JEAN
You want to play Princess Anne? What happen?

DINAH
Them days done! Done! *(pause)*

JEAN
How you mean them days done?

DINAH
Is only de Lima and de Verteuil and them who...

JEAN
But now we could play that. We could play them.

DINAH
(confused) Why? How? How?

JEAN
How you mean how? We will play them!

DINAH
(like a little child) We go play Queen?

> JEAN *puts on a cape and a tiara on DINAH. She hands her the rainbow stick.*

JEAN
(*continues like a child*) Yes, and I have my tiara and all kind of Queen thing from when I used to be Queen. We could use that and we go make you look pretty, pretty, pretty.

DINAH
Oh God, Jean. (*DINAH becomes a queen.*)

JEAN
(*She struts like a queen, trying to keep DINAH up.*) We could play Queen. Hear it now. Presenting Queen Dinah... (*Laughter, DINAH gets into it.*) ...of Lucky Jordan.

DINAH
Them French Creoles ent want nothing with we.

JEAN
(*high accent*) Nothing. Most definitely. They do not want anything to do with us. Most definitely.... And now, sponsored by Ma and Pa Popo. Presenting, Miss Dinah!!!!!!!

> DINAH stands and starts to move forward. She stumbles into a piece of furniture and is guided by JEAN. They both sing, "Valerie Valera."

And there she goes, Ladies and Gentlemen. Doesn't she look splendid? A lusty round of applause for Princess Di...

DINAH
(*She tries to speak properly.*) My name is Dinah Jordan Brathwaite, Braithwaithe, Jordon. (*clears her throat*) I am originally from Freeport. I am a Freeportian... ah... (*laughter*)

JEAN
Another lusty round of applause for this busty Freeport Queen. (*JEAN starts to sing the calypso, "Jean and Dinah."*)

DINAH
(*dancing forward, she sings*) The Yankees gone and Dinah take over now...

JEAN
Come on... let's hear it for the Princess of Freeport... (*applause*)

Fade.

ACT II

The Performance

Bright sunshine. JEAN and DINAH are thirty-five years younger, before JEAN got her hand wound and DINAH lost her eye. They are dressed in white, worn sailor suits. The suits are not clean. They have been playing mas in them all day. Most of Act II is played off-stage, close to the audience. It is performed as if on the street on Carnival day with an impromptu audience.

This opening sequence is a clown routine based on the movements and characteristics of the badly behaved sailor masquerade of the street. JEAN holds a large shoebox in one hand and has a baby bottle, with rum and a nipple attached, hung around her neck. DINAH carries a stick (the rainbow stick prepared in Act I) and a huge tin of talcum powder. She throws powder (as is the tradition) at the audience liberally from time to time to punctuate her speech. They have been drinking.

JEAN
(*They enter singing.*) You see Miss Mary.

DINAH
One pound.

JEAN
She big and hairy.

DINAH
One pound.

JEAN
You see she mother.

DINAH
One pound.

JEAN
You see she father.

DINAH
One pound.

JEAN
For Carnival this year
I have Miss Mary here
Miss Mary weighing.

DINAH
One pound.

JEAN
So come and see she.

Pointing to the shoebox, she gives a few audience members a peek in the box. In the box is the broken wooden dolly.

DINAH
One pound.

They end the song with a scandalous laugh.

JEAN
You ent see him? How he peeping?

DINAH
Yes. You ain't make out that... woman from...?

JEAN
Is she? That is the one who does be up by Lucky Jordan there? Is she? Is she? No.

DINAH
Heh? You know me? She look like she...

JEAN & DINAH laugh with each other.

JEAN
It well look like she. Ah did burst she arse.

DINAH
Madam, sorry.

JEAN
Ah did burst she arse.

DINAH
I am very sorry.

JEAN
Is not she? The same woman arse who we burst.

DINAH
Oh gosh, hush, nah. *(JEAN laughs.)* Good evening, *(to another member of the audience)* enjoying the show...? *(pause)* ...Ah like your hair cut.... You ever see a bald head with a part? *(pause)* ...Check your bumsee. *(laughter)* You remember me?

JEAN

We play sailor. You can't remember? You play sailor with Jean and Dinah...

DINAH

What you playing? He playing he can't remember we...

JEAN

Last year.

DINAH

You can't remember? A big old...

JEAN

Last year we play sailor, we playing sailor again this year. What happen, you don't want to play with we or what?

DINAH

Aye, aye, I will embarrass you here tonight. Don't play you don't know me, you know.

JEAN

You ent want to play sailor again?

DINAH

You accustom coming and make your fares on the Gaza Strip, you know... *(They laugh.)*

JEAN

Come, come, give we a little sailor, a little sailor thing.

They dance some heel and toe and invite an audience member to dance with them. They encourage a white man to get up from the audience and dance with them.

You know the thing. You know the thing.

They dance for a while. DINAH throws powder on him. Laughter. He returns to his seat as they get the audience to give him a round of applause.

(They sing.) You see Miss Mary.

DINAH

One pound. *(She uses her waist to good advantage.)*

JEAN

She fat and juicy. *(She gives an audience member a peek in the box.)*

DINAH
> One pound.

JEAN
> For Carnival this year, I have it right here.

JEAN & DINAH
> Miss Mary weighing, one pound.

JEAN
> So come and see she.

> *She gives another person a little peek. Laughter as they stop singing.*

DINAH
> But listen, I remember he you know.

JEAN
> You remember he?

DINAH
> Yeah.

JEAN
> Which part? *(laughter)*

DINAH
> It could be he. But it ent have to be he.

JEAN
> Oh ho, Cyril.

DINAH
> You resemble the man.

JEAN
> Cyril who does come by me all the time. He look little bit like Cyril, you know.

DINAH
> Your name is Cyril? You not Cyril? You is Cecil? *(laughter)*

JEAN
> It must be Cyril brother…. You is Cyril brother then?… is Cyril brother?… *(DINAH looks at JEAN, pause.)* Is Cyril brother in truth… but what the arse? *(much laughter)*

DINAH
Listen, no offense meant to Cecil but I go tell all you something about Cyril brother. Is Cyril brother or Cecil? Is Cyril?

JEAN
Me ent know girl. Is one of them. Let me tell them. We bounce up this same Cyril. Cyril come up by the club. We liming there a Friday night. Things was a little hard. It didn't have no ship so we wasn't down on the strip. We up the road looking to make a little change with some of the locals. And this one. He is not a regular. So we say we go hit on he. He new and looking easy to pick. He look like he have money because most of them boys round here so cheap. So I went up to him and...

DINAH
(to the audience member dubbed Cecil) Business today? Let we go upstairs, nuh.

JEAN
(to another audience member) You see how good she doing it?

DINAH
Come. *(to the rest of the audience)* Hello, he playing shy tonight.

JEAN
You see, you see?

DINAH
(to JEAN) You trying to set me up or what? You do it. You do it.

JEAN
(to an audience member) Sweetness.

DINAH
You know you could do it well.

JEAN
Sweetness, you looking for some action or what? You looking reeeaal good.

DINAH
You see, she know she thing. She know she onions.

JEAN
We ent even going upstairs. You could come by me and sleep. Not so?

DINAH
She brave. She inviting man home to spend the night with she and she have man home waiting on she, you know.

JEAN
Anyway, he went home by me.

DINAH
Don't trust him. Ask him where he was on Saturday night exactly quarter to eleven in the PM...

JEAN
He spend the whole night...

DINAH
By she...

JEAN
You hear what I telling you...?

DINAH
By she...

JEAN
He went round the world and come back again.

DINAH
Eh, heh?

JEAN
He give me a blank focking cheque.

DINAH
A blank cheque, oh shit. Let we beat his arse. And Jean, you self too, ah tell you only take Yankee dollar. Ah shame for you.

JEAN
You have to live. But that was because I did done pick his pocket. *(She demonstrates how she did it.)* While he was snoring dead to this side of the world. He tell me I coulda put in on the cheque any amount I want.

DINAH
Yeah? So how much...?

JEAN
Fifty...

DINAH
Dollars...

JEAN
Thousand!

DINAH
Oh God, Jean, you does always overdo. Is greedy you greedy so...?

JEAN
But it had a catch to it. The bitch.

DINAH
You is an arse or what? It must have a catch.

JEAN
The focking account had no money in it and them half-white girls in the bank watching me a kinda way...

DINAH
So you see, Mrs. Cecil, the kind of confusion your husband putting whores in town in.

JEAN
Ah want my money!
(*She sings.*) You see Miss Mary.
One pound.
Big and hairy.
One pound.
You see she mother.
One pound.
You see she father.
One pound... of flesh.

> *They are both very drunk by this time.*

DINAH
(*sings*) Brown skin gyal, stay home and mind baby...

JEAN
Dinah, shut up...

DINAH
(*She continues to sing and gets the audience involved. They sing a verse or two with her*) Brown skin gyal, stay home and mind baby...

JEAN
Dinah, ah warning you. Dinah!

DINAH
What Leroy father name again? The Yankee. What you used to call him? Jack on top the box.

JEAN
Jack...

DINAH
(*mocking JEAN*) Jack...

> *Pause. She sings plaintively, slowly, as if it is an old Negro Spiritual.*

Brown skin gyal, stay home and mind baby.
Brown skin gyal, stay home and mind baby.
Ah going away in a sailing boat
And if I don't come back,
Stay home and mind baby. (*repeat*)

> *While singing this song, as the lights go to a delicate pink, DINAH dresses JEAN as a pink Baby Doll masquerade character and takes her into her arms as if she was a little baby. She rocks her in her arms. During this transaction DINAH moves as if in a slow ritual.*

JEAN
Mammy? Where Daddy is? Who is Daddy?

DINAH
Child, Daddy in America. Your daddy is a big man in the Navy.

JEAN
When Daddy coming to see us, Mammy?

DINAH
He going to send for us soon. Any day now, he will send for us.

> *She sings another verse of "Brown Skin Gyal."*

And if I don't come back, throw away the damn baby. (*silence*) Leroy, today I have to carry you by some people who...

JEAN
What people, Mammy?

DINAH
Some nice people, people who will take care...

JEAN
(*She hugs DINAH tightly.*) Mammy, Mammy. No Mammy, no! (*She starts to cry and breaks from DINAH, becomes adult and walks downstage.*) Why you tell Leroy all that?

DINAH
But you must tell the child what happening. You can't just lie about the Yankee and fool up the child all the time. It was your child.

JEAN
Dinah, I couldn't mind no child that time. You know that.

DINAH
Leroy was still your responsibility. Not the responsibility of the Yankee man. Regardless to what, not the responsibility of the Yankee.

JEAN sobs. DINAH takes JEAN in her arms.

Come child, come.

JEAN
(through her tears, she screams) Daddy! Daddy! Daddy!

She gets louder and louder. DINAH tries to hold her and then lets her fall to the ground. DINAH exits.

Fade.

The Hospital

JEAN rips off the headdress that was part of the Baby Doll outfit DINAH put on her earlier. She sits and wraps a piece of cloth around her left arm. JEAN is in a solitary pool of light. DINAH enters, approaching her.

DINAH
(rubbing JEAN's head) Jean, you could have avoided this, you know.

JEAN
What is that? My life...?

DINAH
Jean, I understand, I understand. *(attempting to calm her)* You remember the very first time you reach by the club on Prince Street?

JEAN
You see me, I don't want to talk...

DINAH
Watch me. Hush, listen to me.... If, as I did tell you to go home, you did go home, today you wouldn't be in this position.

JEAN

I is a big woman. I know when to go home and when not to go home. I don't want to talk about it.

DINAH

I want to talk about it, right?

JEAN

Just leave me alone. *(pause)*

DINAH

Jean, you, you… you don't know…. All of us in the life together.

JEAN

Don't play no mother for me. I ain't looking for none. I too big for that.

DINAH

You don't have to…. Try and be constructive with yourself, nah man.

JEAN

My whole life people beating up on me. Beating me up. If is not some woman, is some man or somebody who want something from me.

DINAH

I ever beat you?

JEAN

I could take care of myself.

DINAH

Look at me Jean, watch me. Watch me!

JEAN

What happen? What happen?

DINAH

Why you so? Eh? Everybody in the hospital watching. What is it Jean? Is me.

JEAN

Enough people say they care. Enough. And what?

DINAH

When you get chop on the street there, and you start bawling for your life, anybody come, eh?

JEAN

Who appoint you Queen? I don't want to hear…

DINAH
Who you run to? Who? *(pause)* If it wasn't for me, you would be dead. Is me. Is me!

JEAN
Better you did leave me to dead.

DINAH
What?

JEAN
Because I can't work again. I can't work again. *(pause)* I used to be a pretty, gorgeous woman in the town, beautiful, sexy woman, eh. Now look at me. *(pause)* Disfigured.

DINAH
You does pray?

JEAN
(dry smile) That gone out, girl. For people like me and you. You ent know that? God gone out. *(pause)*

DINAH
You know you could make a change with that... hand, you know.

JEAN
I not talking about that. When I call nobody don't hear. No God, no nothing.

DINAH
Watch me, watch me, Jean.

JEAN
What? Why?

DINAH
Watch me. When you come out of this place you going live with me. I don't want to see you back on the road. It ent have nothing on the road girl, I know. Nothing for nobody. Nobody.

JEAN
And who go mind me? You could mind me how I accustom living? You could mind me? You know I like pretty things and expensive clothes.

DINAH
Jean...

JEAN

Nobody never mind me yet. Not even a man. All of them promise but none of them ever mind me. You can't mind me.

DINAH

So you going back out on the road? Who want you with your hand... so?

JEAN

What wrong with my hand? You see anything wrong with my hand? Somebody tell you something the matter with my hand? Cheups! *(pause)*

DINAH

(She reaches out to touch JEAN's hand, wanting to help.) Look at your state.

JEAN

What you touch that for? You put something there to touch? What the fock you touch that for?

DINAH

Jean, shut up. Shut your blasted mouth.

JEAN

What you touch it for?

DINAH

What you going to do? What you going to do? You will beat me?

JEAN

Leave it alone. Just leave it alone. *(pause)*

DINAH

Look, you is a whore. Everybody know that. The man come to you. He offering money. What is the big thing? Go with the man. That is your work out there.

JEAN

I might be a whore...

DINAH

Listen to me, you just listen to me. Hush.... If what you accustom doing is taking man, then take your man. What you making style for? You feel you will get Yankee man all the days of your life. You think they will always be around to let go money in Trinidad?

JEAN

You supposed to be my friend. Now, you hear what I have to say. You feel because I is a whore, I must go with any and everybody. That little pissin' tail man who want to pay me a little $2 and a little $3. I don't go with them kind of man. That little half a man from behind the bridge. He can't give me stick. Cave man come to town. I don't want to see he. And every time he see me, he only ridiculing me, that now the Yankees gone I have to take what I get. That good for Dorothy so. Not me. You mad or what? You crazy? For what? Eh? For what? I is Jean you know. Oh, ho. *(pause)* I will do for his Black arse.

DINAH

What you will do? What you will do?

JEAN

My spiritual mother coming here and we going and organize something. When we done with he, he will want to know if corbeaux piss on him. Bird brain, like he. He will find out.

DINAH

Jean, I didn't come here to argue.

JEAN

Cheups! What you come for?

DINAH

You so ungrateful...

JEAN

All right, all right. Next time I get cut, leave me, let me dead. Just leave me.

DINAH

Sh! Look how everybody watching you, sssh!!

JEAN

Leave me, let me dead.

DINAH

No! I wouldn't leave you for you to dead. Not a arse of that. Ah know that is what you want. But you damn lie, you hear me. You lie! *(pause)* I love you like my own daughter, like my own flesh and blood. Yuh understand? And if as I did tell you, you did go home the first day I set eyes on you, this would never happen. Is a kind of love that come out for you, girl. A young bit of a girl that come inside the club. A next young girl on the road! I watch at you, Jean. And I say, "Girl, what you doing here? Go home!" And the only thing you didn't tell me was to kiss my Black arse... eh? *(pause)*

JEAN

So, you wasn't taking man too?

DINAH

How long you know me in the club? Eh? I is a dancer.

JEAN

Cheups!

DINAH

I is a waitress of trade. You does see me whoring with you and them dirty little almirantes it have around the town?

JEAN

I hear enough talk. You take enough. *(pause)*

DINAH

Well, if I take enough then I have the authority to come here and sit down and talk to you. Because I know what it have out there. *(pause)* I know out there.

JEAN

I have children to mind. I have to put food in mouth and clothes on back. I have children to mind.

DINAH

I didn't come here to argue. I didn't come here to fight with you, Jean. And I didn't bound to come here. *(pause)*

JEAN

You have cigarette? You bring any cigarette with you?

DINAH

Yes! *(gives her a cigarette and lights it for her)* How are you?

JEAN

I there. *(pause)* Same old Jean. Same Jean. *(pause)*

DINAH

When you leave here, you don't want to work in the bar? Serving drinks. Eh? If it is survival you looking for...

JEAN

Cheups!!

DINAH

Listen to me. Just listen. If it is survival you looking for out here, you don't want to just work in the bar, serving drinks? I running that bar.

Popo know what happening with you. He wouldn't mind. *(JEAN starts to cough.)* Cough it out, come on, cough it out. Give me the cigarette.

JEAN
(takes it back) My damn cigarette. *(pause)*

DINAH
Answer me. *(pause)* Eh?

JEAN
I look like any waitress to you?

DINAH
I know you don't look like a focking waitress. But... they out for you. Jean. Jean come and work by me. Jean, just serve drinks alone. That is all. *(pause)*

JEAN
You see, for me, it is always about money. I never had money yet in my life... in my life. No waitress work can't pay me. It will always be about money for me.

DINAH
How waitress work can't pay? I don't understand...

JEAN
Can't pay me. Can't live...

DINAH
You can't live off of being a waitress?

JEAN
No, can't live, can't mind. Money is the only way out. You hear me? Since I small so. We never had nothing. They always want money. Looking for money. Looking for money. For books. For school, clothes...

DINAH
Jean, Jean, I living off that work, Jean. And I minding the children with that...

JEAN
Well, that is you. Where I come from you can't mind nobody with that money and expect to live.

DINAH
So you settle. You going back out on the road?

JEAN

That is where the money is… where the money is… I will always have a price. *(pause)*

DINAH

You think you still have a price? *(pause)* Jean?

JEAN

Still have a price.

DINAH

Watch yourself good. You think you have a price? *(pause)* Well, what cost of a price?

JEAN

Dinah…

DINAH

Jean. I want you to stand up…

JEAN

Listen to me, Dinah. You could be a waiter, that is your business. The road I walk had nothing. It didn't have no money, no food. I didn't have no mother. I didn't have no father. All I ever wanted in my life was money and that is the only way I know how to do it. And that is how I going down. You hear me? So for me is plenty money and waitress work don't do that. You hear? It just don't do it.

DINAH exits.

Fade.

Baby Doll (The Pink Side)

JEAN puts on her pink Baby Doll headgear very slowly and painstakingly. She turns to the audience and takes up her shoebox. She moves in to the audience and uncovers the shoebox. She rests the cover down and takes the broken, wooden dolly out of the box. This scene is done as if an audience has gathered on the pavement to hear her.

JEAN

You know this child? This child is six months old. You never pass to see the child. Since it born, you never bring nothing for the child. He? Wait, that is your wife? Madam, this is your husband? Well this child belong to you too, you know. This is your husband's child. Yes, your husband Mr. X from Bayshore. This child resemble you, you know. Look at the eye, nose, look at the lip. But, why you wouldn't support the child? You know what I going through to mind this child? You breed me and you leave me. The child is yours, paternity test or no paternity test. Ah don't want to hear. He find he self in my yard, night after night. Now, tell me? What Mercedes doing in my yard? Eh?

I is a woman like my sleep. I clean out people house in the day and wash their clothes. When night come, I may go by the club a little but after that I home. Mr. Benz find he self outside my window. Mr. Cecil Brown Skin Blank Cheque Esquire climb up my board house to find his ecstasy. He come by me quick, quick, quick and gone. He ent know how child stand up, how child navel string drop. Ent know nothing, nothing at all. But you don't know who I is? Look at me well, look at me. Well, I descend from the seed of Petite Belle Lily and Alice Sugar The Former. I trod the centuries from Na Na Yah come down. I is woman. Watch form. Ebony. From that one seed, I stand up. I grow to these proportions. I see, it is this same boy who break in your house and tie up you and your wife and your little daughter and hold gun to your mouth, between your teeth. He is your son. But you don't know him. Because you never take care of him. You never come to see him. Now he grow like a man, he doesn't listen to me. So is jail and courthouse for him. Listen, he will terrorize you till you own up. He ent fraid the hangman cemetery, he is my son. He ent need no human rights. You hang him now you need human rights. He is my son, he is your son, and you will have more and more sons to hang, necks to pop. You ask me? Mark what I tell you. Watch me good!! Watch me good!! Madam talk to him and if he know what good for him he will get to know his children, support the children. I come now, you watching me simple, simple just so. I could turn you round you know. I could put your foot before, behind, you know. I could take away what God give you, you know. And even what he didn't give you. So hear me! Hear me! Listen to me well! Listen to my prophecy! It will come to pass. I is Jean. "Jean In Town" and if "Jean In Town" say so, is so! And if you don't want to heed I will go down deep in the bowels of hell and throw some devil shit on you. So watch it! Watch it!

JEAN exits.

Danse Macabre (Black Baby Doll)

Enter DINAH. She is dressed in black robes reminiscent of the Midnight Robber masquerade. She has been in the underworld. She carries a coffin, the size of a shoebox in her hand. Inside the shoebox is a skeleton. This scene is done to the same pavement audience. She blows her whistle.

DINAH
Stop! Drop your keys and bow your knees and call me the Princess of the Dead. I is a woman who deliver my own self out of my mother

womb. And I come down Blap! Just so. I get up and slap my own bottom and I gone. I fight man with stick, gun, bomb, hatchet, even saw. Any kinda weapon that good for war. My battle scars does heal before I get them. Young fella, you ent make me out. You ent make me out, you know. I will torment you and destroy you boy, yeah! With wine. (*She gyrates her waistline.*) Watch me good! Watch me good! Bacchanal!!! Look! On my way down, I Ruby Rab had a confrontation with Lucy, the great Luciphobia. Flag woman at the gate. And when Lucy see me, Ruby Rab, Dinah the Dancer in a past life, the Grand Jamette, she say, "pass." She didn't want nothing to do with me. That was Lucifix! Lucifer wife. Yes! I pass Gan Gan Sarah. When she see me so she fly out she grave. First time in years. She free a lot of people if you don't know. She and Matron from Tobago, by the Silk Cotton Tree. She and Soucouyant Jane. That bloodsucker. All of them so bow to me, since I up there and that is why they send me on this mission. That if any of all you feel all you bad and could face the Grand Jamette, Princess of the Dead, all you could come now. Right now before me. Step right up! Step right up! I am the mother of the warrior musician, the Pan Man and I prepared for war, the Pan Man prepared for war, I prepare him for war. My son. Before I depart the world you have to pay up. You have to pay up! You got to pay up!! You see me, I fight stickman from the free port to this port of Spain and then down to the main and I still fighting. Across the borders of Uropa and Merica my dragon straddle-dance the water, the agony, all the pain, and the brain drain. I never fraid any kinda stick yet. No bois could deceive these eyes. No bois could dislocate these sockets because is a long line of us you know. From Bodecia who come back now as Bodi in San Fernando. Bodecia is a woman who tear plenty man arse loose. She never fraid Hannibal, nor the grave. Then it had my god-daughter, gas station Jean. She did travel miles to stamp out corruption. All you wreak havoc with she. All you send she mad. She tell me the story up there. But she have a plan for all you, boy! I sorry for all you when that woman come back on this highway. In fact I think she here already. All who feel they is Silver Fox and could do what they want, better watch their arse. Listen to your music box. You better listen to your chutney box. You better listen, good. Who'll see, will see!! Because I is Ruby Rab, Princess of the Dead, music maker of Pan and the Pan Man and if you don't want to feel the full wrath of my tongue you better pay up! You got to pay up! Because I will embarrass from cock to cockatoo. I will peel your balls like is fig self. Yeah! I will peel your balls like a gizzard here tonight if you feel is joke we joking. Watch me good! Watch me good! Look upon me, man. Know me better!!

DINAH exits.

Steelband Clash (A Pas de Deux of the Street)

JEAN and DINAH are on different streets and cannot see each other. They encounter each other only at the time of the steel band clash.

JEAN
(*with a San Juan All Stars flag in hand*) Where Dinah? Look All Stars waiting for me by the Croiseé. I going. She go find me. I gone. (*She moves from stage left to right.*)

DINAH
(*She appears on the other end of the stage, stage left, with a Desperadoes flag in hand.*) Well, you see your girl, swansdown coming down the side. Medal on my chest. Fancy Sailor hat on my head.

JEAN
Ramon waiting for me. I have to find he today, today in the band. Ah looking pretty?

Music. They both dance the Flag Woman dance.

DINAH
The band beating sweet. We leave on time in the yard. We leave on the hill and we coming down Piccadilly Street at about quarter to one in the afternoon.

JEAN
Coming down the road I see Jocelyn with Janet and her gang by the corner in some sailor suit. They ent even put anything new on it. They looking bad. But I looking good. My suit up to date. When Dinah see me so, she go bawl!

DINAH
Wait! (*music stops*) Something missing. Where Jean? She say she was going to be with us this year. She must be late.

JEAN
All you where banjo? This band can't move? Where the rhythm man? What, nobody ready? They ent even have no coffee to drink, no nothing. I need a mirror to see my costume, to fix my costume. Ramon! Come on, let us go. This is the uniform? Ramon? I thought all you say all you had uniform. We arrange this white jersey with this black pants. Eh? Nobody wearing it. This band. Oh God! Anyhow, is only because of you I here, you know. Let we go in town. I tired wait. Let us go, nah man. I find I fretting too much, sweating up myself. Where the mirror? Now is Ramon, the band, the uniform and it have man with no stick come to beat pan. Man who ent pay no dues. They know they supposed to pay me their dues. Look, all you, this band must leave San Juan for

town now. Is Port of Spain! (*Music. She does a Flag Woman dance.*) Where Dinah? Ramon, you see Dinah? Once we hit Henry Street we go meet she. You can't miss she on Charlotte Street.

DINAH

Stop! Wait! All you wait! (*music stops*) Hold some strain, we waiting for Jean. She supposed to come with us. To meet anywhere around here. Give me some rum there. Oh God! Yes! Good! Where you get this? Country thing? Babash, eh? (*She screws up her face.*) Good! That nice.... Where this woman is? You know, when I ready to move I don't want nobody to keep me back. Where the arse is Jean? Where she is? I don't trust her, you know. Wait a minute, I ent see Ramon last night. Listen to me, fellas, my blood hot and that sun coming up, so let us move. "Iron Man!" (*music*) We moving. All right nuh. "Talkative," we moving. "Ocean," "Five Rivers," "Neighbour?" I go see you later, down in town, all right. (*She moves her flag and dances a vigorous Flag Woman dance, for a while. Pause.*) Let we take a rest here. Good. Jean go meet us here, outside home headquarters. (*to audience*) This music sweet, too sweet. (*pause*) Something must be wrong. (*pause*) So we moving. Up Henry. Across Oxford and we hitting Charlotte. (*music gets louder, more vigorous flag dancing*) Aye! Come, you making out that band coming down the road. That ent San Jaun All Stars? Is San Juan? Well, well, what they doing on this side? They brave. What the arse they doing on this route?

JEAN

Rhythm man! Banjo! Aye! You falling back. Keep the pace, nah man. (*music increases in tempo*) Look, but that is Piggy. Oh God! Is Desperadoes? Why we band beating so slow? (*music, more tempo*) Look Dinah, out front. Ramon! Look! This...

DINAH

Listen, you know he? That is not a San Juan man? Aye, what you doing here? Get to fock out this band.... (*more dancing*) Get to fock out! Out, I say! (*more dancing*) Aye! Get to.... Fight! Fight! Throw cutlash, fight! Throw cut arse... (*pace of music increases*)

JEAN

All you, look out! Aye! Watch the ark. Ramon, Noah's Ark full up with ammunition.... Oh... (*JEAN throws a bottle.*) Mother arse...

DINAH holds her eye.

Blackout.

DINAH

Is Jean? Oh Shit! Jean, Jean, you traitor!!!

JEAN tries to run and hide when she sees DINAH holding her eye and doubling up on the ground. They exit.

Epilogue

"It is an indication, the Carnival is over."
—Lord Kitchener

In the blackout, DINAH, dressed in her Sailor Suit, moves back to the bed in her apartment. In this scene JEAN and DINAH both appear in the apartment as though they have been there all along.

DINAH
Oh God! Is you Jean. Is you.

JEAN
Is time to go, Dinah. Now is not the time to.... Oh shit man.... Dinah, we still have time to play. Let's go. Let us go now! What is that? You forget me?

DINAH
You pelt that bottle, Jean, *(She is losing strength.)* you, you... *(JEAN hurries over.)*

JEAN
Dinah, you take your pills? *(JEAN is confused.)* I going and get help. Where everybody? *(She runs back into the road.)*

DINAH
Jean, Jean!! It over, it will take too long. They can't hear you. They are somewhere else, girl. In another place. They won't hear you. *(JEAN hurries back to DINAH.)* I lie down in that hospital, weeks on end and Jean you never come and see me. *(She weeps.)* Jean, weeks, Jean...

JEAN
I was coming... but... work... and them children.

DINAH
It was more than seven weeks. Oh God, Jean, seven weeks. The pain...

JEAN
Dinah, you vex with me for that?

DINAH
I vex with you since then. Since then, Jean. Jean, why you don't come out and say it, eh? The bottle that pelt... the fight.... Jean, you was even looking for somewhere to hide. I see you with my one eye trying to

hide from me. So you ent come to see me in the hospital because you can't face the fact that you burst my eye. Not dropsy Clementina or one of them so, you know. But is my eye you burst. Eh? *(pause)*

JEAN

Cyphus was the one who...

DINAH

Look, Jean! Hush!! And what is this every year coming by me? Your conscience bothering you or what?

JEAN

I could watch you. I could face you in your eye and tell you that I, Jean, didn't pelt no focking bottle. And that is that. And what is all this? Is only one eye you lose.

DINAH

I can't play no mas, child. I can't play no mas. I will be no part of your conscience, you hear me.

JEAN

Come, Dinah, let us go. We can talk all this tomorrow.

DINAH

Tomorrow and tomorrow and tomorrow. Your conscience creeping up on you or what? Petty Jamette! *(pause)* Now, let me sleep. I tired...

JEAN

What? Come on...

DINAH

Them days done...

JEAN

What you saying? The day still here.... This is Carnival Tuesday. Let us go...

DINAH

This is Tuesday?

JEAN

Yeah...

DINAH

This day don't exist for me, Jean. It done, long time. Is midnight mass. I want to lie down. Let me lie down, nah.

JEAN

You can't lie down. We going up the road, up the road. *(She tries to pick up DINAH. She gets her to stand.)* We going up the road and we will dance. *(She tries to make her dance, she tries to dance with her.)* We must dance Dinah. *(They fall down on the floor. JEAN is on top of DINAH. She tries to sit up and put DINAH's head on her lap.)* Dinah? Dinah?

DINAH

Oh God! Jean, bring one of them tablets and some water. *(JEAN hurries out and rummages around for the tablets.)* I want to sleep. I have to take a rest.... The pain, the pain.... Look at us, eh? Like two old whore in one of them fellas calypso. Oh! Oh! *(pause, silence)*

JEAN

Dinah, Dinah, Dinah!!! Oh shit! *(She shouts. She is agitated, scared.)* Neighbour, neighbour, neighbour! Dinah, Dinah? Get up! Neighbour! Neighbour! Everybody gone.... *(pause)* After Ramon leave and I lose my house, you is the only one who used to take care of me, Dinah. That is why I used to come. That is why.... *(She weeps with DINAH in her lap.)* Dinah, you can't dead. You know that, you can't dead. *(pause)* I go bury you, right? What dress you want? You ent even tell me what dress you want. We will buy a new dress. I will bury you, right? I go bury you. Me and Cyril go bury you. Right next to James. And Stallion and Marabunta and all of us will be there. And we go dance and wave flag, yes. *(She sobs uncontrollably. Pause.)* You know, Dinah, is I who burst your eye. Dinah, oh God man, get up nah man. Get up! Is I... *(pause)* ...I who... Dinah.... *(pause)* Oh God, Dinah, what I go do? Who I go play mas with? Who will go with me to buy cloth? When I have no food, no money, who I going by? Eh? You gone and dead. *(music)* You sure you don't want to get up? Look Renegades steel band passing. You don't want to go and hear them beat? *(pause)* You... you don't want to... dance?

Fade.

The end.

Glossary

—•— —•— —•—

ALMIRANTES: A young prostitute whose fare is cheap.

BACCHANAL: A good time, confusion.

BACRA-JOHNNY: A local white person of low economic status.

BAJAN: Another name for a person who comes from Barbados.

BATONIER: Stickfighter.

BODI: A long string bean.

BOIS: The stick used in the calinda or stickfight.

BUBALUPS, MAYFIELD, STALLION, MARABUNTA: Famous flag women.

CALINDA: Another word for a stickfight or stickplay.

CHANTUELLE: Lead singer in the calinda band.

COMMESS: Confusion (adjective - commessive) one who likes confusion.

CROISIE [QUASAY]: A famous junction leading to the town of San Juan.

DESPERADOES: The famous steel orchestra which started as the street gang "Dead End Kids."

FRENCH CREOLE: A member of the French Caribbean planter and land-owning class who came to Trinidad from Haiti, St. Lucia and Martinique in the 18th century under a Spanish administration.

GAN GAN SARAH: African slave who tried to fly back to Africa from Tobago but was unable to do so because she ate salt.

GAS STATION JEAN: Jean Miles, a famous Trinidadian public servant who tried to fight government corruption in a gas station scandal. She died in the struggle.

GLAMOUR BOYS: A street gang.

HANNABAL: A famous calpysonian and stickfighter.

I IS A WHORE TOO, BIG SIX: Names of famous prostitutes.

JAGABAT: Low class prostitute.

JAMETTE: The Trinidad patois for the French diametre. This is the diametre or line below which most of post-emancipation Trinidad lived. Jamette became the word to describe the ordinary people of the street, the carnival reveller, the members of the calinda and stickfight bands, etc. Later, the word was used to mean prostitute, or bad woman.

MACOMÉ MAN: Homosexual.

MAMAGUY: To trick or fool.

MARABUNTAS: Another street gang which later became Tokyo Steel Band.

MAS: Masquerade.

MASTIFE: A famous badjohn who it is reported was heavily endowed.

MATRON: High priestess of traditional African religion in Tobago. She is also a traditional midwife. In 1994, she was 94 years old.

NA NA YAH: Female African slave liberator.

PAN: The main instrument of the steel band. Pannist – one who plays the pan.

PETIT BELLE LILY, ALICE SUGAR, RUBY RAB, BOADICEA: Famous jamettes.

POOWATEE: Insignificant.

RENEGADES: A famous steel band or steel orchestra.
ROSITA and CLEMENTINA: Street women, prostitutes, made famous by Sparrow's calypso.
SAN JUAN ALL STARS: A famous steel band or steel orchestra.
SEMP: A small yellow bird, which lives on bananas.
SOUCOUYANT: A female folk character who gets out of her skin and flies around at night in the form of a ball of fire. A bloodsucker.
SOUCOUYANT JANE: A famous soucouyant.

Carnival Traditions

—•— —•— —•—

BABY DOLL: The stickplay of the calinda or stickfight define a concept of warriorhood. This is a warriorhood which, in the history of Trinidad Carnival, is not restricted to the male. This attitude can be traced to women of the post-emancipation Jamette Carnival and to the Baby Doll character of the Traditional masquerade in particular. The Baby Doll, a character that was popular in the thirties and forties, was a woman masquerader usually decked in a frilly dress carrying a large doll (sometimes in a box). Her action included stopping, on Carnival day, any respectably dressed gentleman and by the way of a long speech about renegade fathers she insisted that he help her mind the child, represented by the doll. It is implied in this drama of instant theatre that the gentleman, who may be on the street with his family, is the father of the child. Some researchers say that there were times when men played Baby Doll as well.

MIDNIGHT ROBBER: The Midnight Robber is one of the most beloved characters of the traditional masquerade in the Trinidad Carnival. It is believed that this character appeared sometime around the 1920s. It was usually played by men in a fancy costume which comprised a kind of cowboy trousers with breeches enhanced with beads, braid and other adornments. On his head, he carried a huge exaggerated hat (sometimes in the form of a tombstone) with fringe around the brim, making the hat crown-like. His shoes were a wire structure of some animal, which moved as he walked with his characteristic long steps. This rather intriguing costume was completed with a long flowing cape on which were painted or embroidered skulls and crossbones and other signs of death and destruction. In his hands, he carried a gun and a wooden cash box. Around his waist he stuck more guns in a cartridge belt and he blew an ever-present whistle which hung from around his neck. On Carnival days, when he accosted bystanders on the street, the speech that emanated from his mouth like shots from an automatic pistol was no less extravagant than his costume and rhythmic dance movements. You had to give him a few coins to get this fearsome character to move on down the street. For he is the ultimate bad man, full of empty threats and the wildest implausible boasting possible. There is nothing he has not done. He is the one who "at the age of two, drowned my grandmother in a spoonful of water." Over the years, this character had almost disappeared from the Carnival but within recent time he is enjoying a welcomed revival.

SAILOR/FANCY SAILOR: Just as the Baby Doll character is about keeping the truth, the Sailor/Fancy Sailor is about Yankee Imperialism. In the 1930s, steel drums were brought to the island by Americans who went there to refine oil, a natural resource found on the island. The pan, the musical instrument created from these, is the main instrument of the steel band. However, what began at this time, among the ordinary people, was a fascination with things American. By the 1940s, World War II had broken out and Trinidad became a place for American military bases. There was a Jungle Warfare School set up on the island. The locals responded to this development through the calypso and the carnival. The sailor is a mas portrayal, popularized mainly by the steel bands. Called "bad behaviour sailors," these characters came out in the hundreds, in their simple white costumes year after year and displayed the freedom and "gay abandon" which they observed the "drunken" yankee sailors enjoyed on the streets of Port of Spain. The yankees, of course, had US dollars to spend on wine, women and song. This attitude of free expression so captivated the imagination of the masqueraders that pretty soon the plain sailor suit was not enough to capture the spirit of celebration and emancipation that is the carnival. They began to decorate the basic white costume and developed many appropriate dances. So today we have the Fancy Sailor and King Sailor, which can explore Japanese, African, even environmental and other themes through designs built on to a sailor suit. The Fancy Sailor, created by the ordinary people of Trinidad and Tobago, has added a new dimension to surrealist art.

Québécité
A Jazz Libretto in
Three Cantos
(Third Draft)

George Elliott Clarke

George Elliott Clarke is the 2001 recipient of the Governor General's Award for Poetry for *Execution Poems* (Gaspereau Press). A seventh-generation African Canadian, he has published five books of poetry. His dramatic works include two verse dramas, *Whylah Falls* and *Beatrice Chancy*; an opera libretto of *Beatrice Chancy*, and an award-winning feature-film screenplay, "One Heart Broken into Song" (CBC Television, 1999). Clarke has also edited anthologies of African-Canadian writing. In 2002, University of Toronto Press released his critical study, *Odysseys Home: Mapping African-Canadian Literature*. Next year HarperCollins will release his first novel, *George and Rue*. Honoured as a poet and as an activist scholar, Clarke has received several awards, including the Archibald Lampman Award for Poetry, the Portia White Prize, and a Rockefeller Foundation Bellagio Residency. He won a National Magazine Award for the best poems published in a magazine in 2000. He was nominated for the Pearson Canada Reader's Choice Award for his latest poetry collection, *Blue* (Polestar Press).

You Break No Laws by Dreaming: George Elliott Clarke's *Québécité*

by Ajay Heble

— • — — • — — • —

Jazz opera: not a well-documented genre, to be sure, but *that*, I suspect, may well be part of its allure. Alert with the snap of the new and untried, and unfettered by settled habits of convention, this hybrid genre compels us to imagine an alternative vision of human possibility. It's a grand objective, I admit, but let's recall that opera has almost always been about grand-scale gestures, about excess, about staging the spectacular. Throw jazz into the mix, and what you get, as George Elliott Clarke's libretto for *Québécité* so eloquently, so resiliently, demonstrates, is a gumbo concoction: one where hope and imagination rainbow over orthodoxy, where improvisation and the capacity to dream reinvigorate our commitment to new understandings of identity, belonging, and collective social responsibility.

The libretto's title, *Québécité*, is itself deliberately and playfully provocative, especially considering the mixed-race couples at the centre of the plot, and in light, too, of the fraught role that ethnicity and race have played in struggles for Quebec nationalism. Eschewing the exclusivist, monolithic, and anti-ethnic sentiments that too often attach themselves to expressions of national or cultural identity—think, for example, of Jacques Parizeau's now infamous remarks in October 1995 about how the "ethnic vote" defeated his attempts to win sovereignty for Quebec—Clarke's emphasis on "*le Quebec de couleur*" represents a bold attempt to counter the demonization of the "other" in attempts to fashion homogeneous national communities. Indeed, as cultural theorist George Lipsitz writes, "During times of economic decline and social disintegration, it is tempting for people to blame their problems on others, and to seek succor and certainty from racist and nationalist myths. But the desire to seek certainty and stability by depicting the world solely as one story told from one point of view," Lipsitz argues, "is more dangerous than ever before" (132). With *Québécité*, George Elliott Clarke seeks to break free from these dangerously monolithic ways of knowing the world, and instead engages in an explicit broadening of the cultural scope of (and subject matter for) new Canadian opera. And this, of course, is in keeping not only with our nation's stated multicultural objectives, but also with the democratizing impulses that, in its most provocative instances, have shaped so much of the history of jazz and improvised music.

Set in modern day Quebec City, Clarke's libretto tells the story of two inter-racial couples whose respective and developing romances expose the inherent minefield of establishing relationships that cross racial and cultural boundaries. Now if, as Linda Hutcheon and Michael Hutcheon have argued, "the history of opera as a European art form suggests that it has always been intimately linked with issues of national identity" (5), then *Québécité*, as a Canadian jazz opera set in Quebec and written by one of Canada's most celebrated African-Canadian poets, is an exemplary *post-national*, transcultural text. It traffics in the dialogue between cultures, and it insists on the necessity of seeing the world from perspectives other than those fostered by institutionally-determined epistemic orders.

Clarke's efforts to work towards a more inclusive understanding of issues such as belonging, identity, and citizenship is, moreover, worth thinking about in relation to comments he himself has made on the Canada-Quebec schism. In the introduction to his 1997 anthology of African Canadian writing, *Eyeing the North Star: Directions in African Canadian Literature*, a text whose own *raison d'être* Clarke explicitly articulates in terms of an insistence on "new, more inclusive definitions of Canadianness" (xxiii), he writes, "The primacy assigned the Canada-Quebec schism marginalizes *all* other ethnic-racial-linguistic questions" (xvii). In this context, Clarke "references the pandemonium that then-Parti Québecois MNA Jean Alfred, a Haitian Canadian, aroused at a National Black Coalition of Canada meeting in Toronto in May 1979, when he declared, before a hundred delegates at the King Edward Hotel, that Quebec's 'liberation' was more important than Black national unity" (xvii). Clarke's point in recalling this episode is that "language dynamics drive some Black francophone intellectuals to prioritize linguistic issues ahead of racial matters" (xvii). Now *Québécité*, clearly, isn't making a statement about Black national unity, and it isn't—as anyone who reckons with the richness, the playfulness, and the extraordinary musicality of Clarke's poetry will immediately recognize—about to pay short shrift to the vitality of language; it does, however, exert a necessary challenge to mainstream assumptions about Quebec as white. And in this context, its non-compliance with dominant knowledge-producing elites in Canada seems to me to carry a salutary—indeed an urgent—political force.

That force, I'd like to suggest, is perhaps most profoundly registered in the text's insistence on the power to dream. "You break no laws by dreaming," announces one of the opera's characters, Colette Chan, as the libretto draws us towards its finale. Colette's remark hastens us to reflect on the fact that the capacity to dream (as Martin Luther King's famous "I have a dream" speech so eloquently and so brilliantly made clear) remains an absolute necessity in face of the degradations that threaten to beset aggrieved peoples. It is a force registered not only in the opera's dedication to Clarke's mother and to composer D.D. Jackson's mother—"two dreamers of beauty"—but also in the vision at the opera's end of a better, more inclusive world, one where "Our children will be / every colour eyes can know," a world, furthermore, where "states, parents, gods / must have no say." It's there, too, in Clarke's use of architecture as a metaphor for building new models of cultural trust and social obligation. The emphasis here on dream puts me in mind of African-American historian Robin Kelley's recent book, *Freedom Dreams: The Black Radical Imagination*. Addressing "anyone bold enough still to dream" (7), Kelley explains how, from very early in his life, he was taught to "see life as possibility," to imagine "a world where gender and sexual relations could be restructured," or where we could learn to recognize "the poetic and the prophetic in the richness of our daily lives" and "to visualize a more expansive, fluid, 'cosmos-politan' definition of Blackness" (2). In like fashion, George Elliott Clarke's libretto, it seems to me, is calling on all dreamers to work towards a more inclusive vision of valued social practices.

Indeed, just as, in Clarke's words, African-Canadian literature is "heteroglossic, a callaloo of languages... a medley of accents," so too, he reminds us, "*Québécité* is an Absinthe-Champagne-Chartreuse-Chicoutai-Grappa-Palm Wine-Pastis-Rum-Saki-Sangria-Scotch-Tequila-Vodka opera, one coloured intensely with notes of ebony, dark-cherry, India indigo-ink, and bronze-beige the shade of papyrus or bamboo." Furthermore, Clarke adds, "If possible, your eyes must smell lilies here – lilies and licorice; your ears must sense African strings, Asian brass, European percussion, First Nations song." In a world inflected with legacies of prejudice, misunderstanding, and injustice, the resources for hope opened up by such dreams of diversity are of vital importance. Lipsitz, again, is forthright on this point:

> nation states may be best served by those who refuse to believe in... unified narratives, and who insist instead on cultural and political practices that delight in difference, diversity, and dialogue. These do not need to be conjured up by political theorists, or wished into existence by mystics and visionaries. They already exist (albeit in embryonic form) in the communities called into existence by... many... unauthorized and unexpected forms that people have for understanding and changing the world in which they live. (132)

Clarke's libretto delights in envisioning new forms of social mobilization that accent diversity and difference. When one of the text's main characters, an African-Canadian saxophonist named Malcolm States, sings "Quebecois claim they're white niggers of America, / *Peut-être*, but I'm the Black *nègre* of Quebec, Quebec!" or when another character, a Quebec-born woman of East Indian descent named Laxmi, tells us about her brown skin but quebecois heart ("*La peau brune, mais le coeur quebecois*"), the text makes clear its explicit challenge to settled understandings of cultural belonging. Worth noting in this regard is how the music—at least as it is articulated here through Clarke's telling stage directions—itself captures something of the transformative impact of dialogue and diversity. The opening scene, where the sound of a bass commixes "in bluesy discord" with the chiming of church bells, and the closing sequence, with its celebratory commingling of sonorities from a diverse range of world traditions, remind us of music's power to shake us out of orthodoxies of response and judgement.

Offering an alternative to the doggedly Eurological operatic tradition, *Québécité*, in short, marks an unprecedented opportunity on the Canadian operatic stage to generate bold new stagings of identity. Music, like dream, *this* jazz opera tells us, can empower us not only (to borrow again from Kelley) to hear "life as possibility," but also to foster (and to sustain) vibrant artistic and critical initiatives dedicated to sounding a more inclusive vision of community-building and intellectual stock-taking for the new millennium. And in an era when demands for tighter controls on immigration and border-crossing threaten to put the dreams of aggrieved peoples at risk of being abandoned, the structures of hope, possibility and momentum embodied sonically and analytically in Clarke's rainbow quartet of lovers seem particularly pertinent.

Ajay Heble is Professor of English at the University of Guelph, and Artistic Director of The Guelph Jazz Festival. He commissioned George Elliott Clarke and composer D.D. Jackson to write *Québécité* to be premiered at the 10th anniversary edition of the Guelph Jazz Festival in September 2003.

Works Cited:

Clarke, George Elliott. "Introduction." *Eyeing The North Star: Directions in African Canadian Literature*. Ed. George Elliott Clarke. Toronto: McClelland and Stewart, 1997. xi-xxviii.

Hutcheon, Linda, and Michael Hutcheon. "Opera and National Identity: New Canadian Opera." *Canadian Theatre Review* 96 (Fall 1998): 5-8.

Kelley, Robin D.G. *Freedom Dreams: The Black Radical Imagination*. Boston: Beacon Press, 2002.

Lipsitz, George. *Dangerous Crossroads: Popular Music, Postmodernism and the Poetics of Place*. London: Verso, 1994.

Québécité: A Jazz Libretto in Three Cantos premiered at the 10th anniversary edition of the Guelph Jazz Festival, Guelph, Ontario, September 2003.

Written by George Elliott Clarke
Composed by D.D. Jackson
Commissioned by Ajay Heble, Artistic Director, The Guelph Jazz Festival

—•— —•— —•—

DRAMATIS PERSONÆ:
Laxmi Bharati: A Université Laval student architect, 21. Also, a Hindu, of Indian descent, born and raised in Montréal.
Colette Chan: A Université Laval law student, 21. Of Chinese origin, she escaped the 1989 "Goddess of Democracy" *pogrom*.
Ovide Rimbaud: A Haitian of Black-white ancestry, brought to Québec by his parents in 1989. Also a Ville de Québec-based architect, 25.
Malcolm States: A Montréalais jazz saxophonist of African-American and Mi'kmaq Nova Scotian heritage, reared in Halifax. He's 25.
Musicians: A-J, piano; Sans Souci, bass; Blue, drums; Sept-Îsles, trumpet. (Other personnel may be drafted as required.)

SETTING: Fin de xxe siècle Ville de Québec, Vieux-Québec.
NOTE: The First Draft of *Québécité* appeared in *Canadian Theatre Review*, 112 (Fall 2002): 27-46.

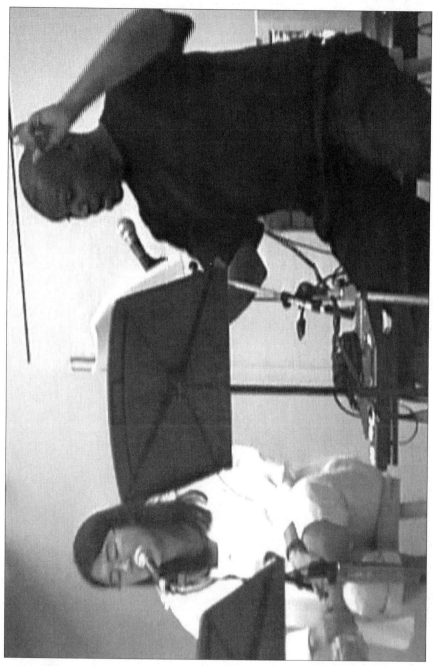

l to r:
Yoon Choi,
Dean
Bowman

video still by
Hilary Martin.

Québécité
A Jazz Libretto in Three Cantos
(Third Draft)
by George Elliott Clarke

— • —   — • —   — • —

CANTO I

The Production IS the beloved.
—Pound, Canto CIV

Scene i: Devant Le Château Frontenac

In a blue-lilac dusk lit with light petals of rain, the pollen of cream-blossomed April, OVIDE holds a black, velvety umbrella. He is natty in a pink shirt, mauve jacket, and black pants. Wearing a gold and turquoise sari, and holding a turquoise and gold umbrella, LAXMI faces her wanna-be amadou. They stand before a silhouette of the Gothic-styled Château Frontenac. Gargoyles jut from a low roof, but blossoms arc upwards to meet them – as if in love. The sound of a bass commixes with church bells chiming in bluesy discord. OVIDE gestures at a tree.

OVIDE
Laxmi, when apple blossoms blaze,
call them beautiful,
feel the tender warmth of *Love*
that flames eternal.
Will you fulfill my meaning?
Am I meaningful?

LAXMI
You've invited me to savour jazz–
Lightning born alive as chocolate....

Why taint it with saccharine hints,
Or cadence of decadence?

Is there some fault in your feelings?
Are your plans purely floors and ceilings?

OVIDE
I speak only as an architect
speaking to a Laval student architect.
I've my own firm; I'm stable, mature.
My designs are pure.

LAXMI

Only my blueprints, Ovide, should be blue.
I'll build gilded shrines to golden *Virtue*.
Virtue is the steely mettle I trust:
My husband will be iron, not rust.

OVIDE

Virtue should not buckle to *Vice*.
(Québec's no Puritan paradise.)
But, your eyes could set fire to ice.

LAXMI

To breathe Occidental oxygen,
say my parents, is to go rotten.

So I hex all wrecks and vexations of men.
Oh, what is wrong with women is men!

OVIDE

Laxmi, you'll always be beautiful.
You are going to always be beautiful.

LAXMI

Ovide, you're as magnetic as a collision;
But kisses are prefaces to perdition.

OVIDE

I could scat sing my ballad valentine!

LAXMI

Just serve me *verres* of very fine wine.

OVIDE

Je suis Haïtien, with pure, sugar love to advance.
We'll sip chilled Haitian rum, distilled in France.

LAXMI

Non, I just don't trust,
don't trust *Romance*:
too much is lust,
too much is chance.

OVIDE

The bed decides
who is competent to wed.
The bed decides
what grooms wed which brides.

LAXMI
Seduction is a satisfaction sated with pain.

OVIDE
Such gargoyle words could scare off rain–
Québéc City's April-freshening rain...

LAXMI
I prefer Puccini with cappuccino
or Picasso with espresso
to vain talk that's all in vain.

So let's go hear the Malcolm States Quartet
at La Révolution Tranquille, *mon bon architecte.*

OVIDE
Oui, let's scat!

Their umbrellas set and poised, the pair strolls to the jazz club.

Scene ii: À La Révolution Tranquille

In this scene, it is seen that MALCOLM hoists a saxophone to his lips.
A suave man in a black suit and crisp white shirt (offset by a skinny black
tie), he stands in a corner of the bar/nightclub that a crimson fluorescent
sign proclaims to be "La Révolution Tranquille." *A poster features*
MALCOLM in a dour, Miles Davis pose, scowling, pouting, sporting dark
sunglasses, standing before the equally surly "The Malcolm States
Quartet," featuring A.J. on piano, Sans Souci on bass, Blue on drums, and
Sept-Îsles on trumpet. The bar itself is tones of warm maple and silky grey
stone, soft-lit. In one corner, a small shrine to Chinese ancestors and
deities glows red, to summon good luck. On one wall, 1960s-era posters of
Pierre Elliott Trudeau, Martin Luther King, Jr., Ho Chi Minh, René
Levesque, Oscar Peterson, John Coltrane, Miles Davis, Chet Baker, Juliet
Gréco, Ella Fitzgerald, Jean Lesage, Charles De Gaulle, Adrienne
Clarkson, and Jawaharlal Nehru appear. The bar is retro in style.
MALCOLM blows scales that are really piano glissades. Then, he sets
down the saxophone and sings.

MALCOLM
If I was not your lover, who was?
Those days, hungry in the grass,
Your skirt, spread like an hourglass,
Butterflies mobbing us at dusk:
Baby, we are close enough to know
We are no longer close now.

COLETTE enters the bar. Beautiful, she wears a white silk blouse, set off by a thin black tie, a short, white, pleated skirt, low-heeled shoes, and her two black braids fall across her breasts. She carries a heavy law book and a bag of clementines. When COLETTE sets these items on a table, MALCOLM motions his quartet to cease playing.

Take a break. See y'all in an hour. A'-'ight?

The band exits (apparently). COLETTE sits and begins to peel a clementine.

(to COLETTE) Don't judge these sounds too harshly.
The notes echo a man who loved too archly.

COLETTE
I'm just a Laval law student.
I don't try to judge music,
though I courted piano as a girl.
But the law states, Mr. States,
nothing can be done about lost love:
but no one's free who isn't free to love.

MALCOLM
You speak so deliciously,
and with such cadenced balances.
You parley so judiciously,
like spectres at séances.
If I may say so, Ms Chan, I presume.
Please, please call me Malcolm.

COLETTE
My Anglo-Québécoise name's Colette.

MALCOLM
Its accent's perfume, scented, in a novelette.

COLETTE
If only English weren't so English!
If only French were not so *gauche!*

MALCOLM
That's the anomalous calamity of Canada:
Anglos muck up the Queen's English;
Francophones fuck up French.

COLETTE
Canada is as lovely as fine china,
but no place is as lovely as China.

MALCOLM
> Why did you leave that place you love?
> Was it fear—or love—that drove your move?

COLETTE
> Bullets blasted away ballads and ballots,
> and bodies were "miscounted" everywhere:
> only "nobodies" numbered as the dead,
> when China drove us out in '89,
> when I was nine.
> A Communist comrade warned us
> worshipping "freedom" could be fatal,
> so my Lincoln-minded parents,
> two profs adoring forbidden Ellington,
> fled with all their hidden Ellington:
> our total worldly goods were music.
> Then, they opened this jazz club – café,
> dreaming of a liberal, free Cathay.
>
> How did you, Malcolm, come to the sax?
> Why are you, Malcolm, ex of Halifax?

MALCOLM
> Halifax is a Hell of Haligonians–
> Amid an abyss of Nova Scotians.
>
> To forget my regrets, I picked up piano,
> but sax was lighter to pick up than piano.

COLETTE
> Do you mind if I listen in tonight?
> I used to study piano and… I like your sax.

MALCOLM
> *(impishly)* It's not just biology; I'm practiced.

COLETTE
> *(laughing)* I said *sax*, not *sex*.

MALCOLM
> I'd love to hear your fingers dancing, Colette.
> Sit beside me and debut a duet.

> *MALCOLM sets his saxophone on top of the piano and slides onto the piano bench. COLETTE wipes her clementine-wet fingers on a wet napkin, then rises to join MALCOLM, sitting at the piano.*

COLETTE
Look! My legs are so short,
my feet can hardly touch the ground.

MALCOLM
I'll sit close by, close, to feel each sound.

> *COLETTE's feet dangle while she plays the piano.*

COLETTE
Lushly, a dewed light falls,
blushing branches.
It clears what doubts had pressed down leaves
and lets kissed lips–
lilacs, lilies, tulips–
flourish
and more flourish.

MALCOLM
The new spring, with fresh blossoms, comes.
Lovers purr, purl, pour themselves like balm
Or ointment on each other, then, comely, calm.
Let the sun heap light in their eyes – and poems.

COLETTE
(*smiling*) I must shout, sing–
Loud, liberal–
To have sweet lungs:
Plus, it's April.

MALCOLM
You may be *une étudiante en droit*,
but you *are* a pianist – *si vous désiriez l'emploi*.

COLETTE
No, it's your music that resembles
Beautiful, fragrant apple blossoms.

> *Song continues anew. A duet commences, repeating verses sung above.*

COLETTE
A dewed light falls…

MALCOLM
A dewed light falls…

COLETTE/MALCOLM
Lushly.

A burst of thunder, then shouting rain. COLETTE smiles at MALCOLM, leaps up, grabs her law book, and swirls out of the bar. MALCOLM holds up two clementines.

MALCOLM

Ah, clementines like fine china,
lovely like fine-boned, delicate china,
these choice clementines, finely, from China.

Scene iii: Blues de Malcolm

LAXMI and OVIDE sit at a table in La Révolution Tranquille. Gigantic, olive-garnished, martini glasses sit swimmingly before the pair. Sound of the Malcolm States Quartet tuning up. Wearing a lime-green skirt and an aquamarine blouse, COLETTE sits at another table. Holding his saxophone and standing at a microphone, MALCOLM begins to sing.

MALCOLM

Ici à Québec City, *voici "Blues de Malcolm."*

If you're down and out,
Good and evil don't matter.
If you're down, dirty, and out,
Vice and virtue don't matter.
But if you're up and coming,
Your innocence will shatter.

Now I go from drink to drink,
And I've gone from gal to gal.
Yes, I slip from bad to worse,
And I've fallen from gal to gal:
The ones I want promise Paradise,
The ones I get just give me hell.

I ain't blue: the rain still works;
The wind hasn't broken down.
I ain't blue: the rain, it still works,
The wind ain't all busted down.
And the sun, it still burns, it burns,
It burns right down to the ground.

The audience applauds. MALCOLM signals for a break. The band members exit (apparently). COLETTE rises and approaches LAXMI and OVIDE.

COLETTE

How erect's the architecture?

LAXMI
How prospers the law?

COLETTE
The law prospers the few – as usual.

LAXMI
And we architects bulldoze flowers.

Les jeunes filles *laugh.*

Colette Chan, do you know Ovide Rimbaud?

COLETTE
(to OVIDE) You designed La Révolution Tranquille, I know.

OVIDE
C'est un plaisir encore, Ms Chan. I'll buy us rum.

OVIDE rises and goes to the bar.

COLETTE
Laxmi, *est-ce qu'* Ovide *serait ton chum*?

LAXMI
Pas du tout, Colette!

COLETTE
Pas encore, peut-être!

*MALCOLM approaches the table. OVIDE returns with three glasses and
a bottle of rum.*

COLETTE
May I introduce Malcolm States?
Malcolm, this is Laxmi Bharati,
an architecture student at Université Laval…

MALCOLM
Je suis charmé par votre élégance.

COLETTE
And the architect, Ovide Rimbaud, is her…

LAXMI
Acquaintance.

COLETTE
Laxmi, his name is handsome with romance.

OVIDE
Ovide—like the poet; Rimbaud—like the poet.

MALCOLM
Poets never sound like anything but poets.

LAXMI
The word *love* is cheap in their sonnets.

OVIDE
Yet, Petrarchan sonnets premiere with Sade–
Because Petrarch loved an ancestress of Sade.

LAXMI
Poets are eyes looking for eyes
To look into, eyes to inspire fresh lies.

COLETTE
You're both quite talkative.

LAXMI
It's recitative.

OVIDE
Your style, Malcolm, recalls dd Jackson;
No, it's more like, *oui*, J.J. Jackson,
His 1960s hit, "But It's Alright."

MALCOLM
Oscar Peterson is my idol.
De temps en temps, I dream I'm his rival.
But I also worship Portia White.

LAXMI
It's late, the rain is strong, and so, good night.

COLETTE
The rain and the streetlights compose a poem.

LAXMI
Au revoir, Colette; *à bientôt*, Malcolm.

OVIDE
O! Laxmi, to win your sunshine, I will sing.

LAXMI
If you don't sing well, you'll just get rain.

OVIDE

Then I'll love the rain as if it were sunshine.

LAXMI

Never mistake ginger-ale for champagne.

> *LAXMI and OVIDE take their leave, leaving COLETTE and MALCOLM alone together.*

Scene iv: Clémentines

> *MALCOLM and COLETTE sit side-by-side in the darkened La Révolution Tranquille. The saxophone rests atop the piano. MALCOLM clasps COLETTE's hands in his own.*

MALCOLM

Like late Lear, I'm lighthearted,
finally humbling to love.

COLETTE

It's too early to speak of love.
It's too easy to speak of love.

> *MALCOLM begins to play "Clémentines" on the piano.*

MALCOLM

Your hair unclasps like wine,
your fingers blush to orange.

I taste your flurried moans,
sugar Aprilling lips.

Il neige sur tous les toits
after two clementines,

clement, Laurentian wine,
plush, orange-cinnamon tea....

On ne vit pas d'amour
et d'eau fraîche.

Sino-Québécoise,
imago of Beijing,

stitch together aubades,
monostich by monostich,

til a sudden poem whips,
thrashes, frothing your book.

COLETTE
It is so beautiful, Malcolm, I can't move.
But words, oh words, contaminate love!

COLETTE begins to cry and turns away. MALCOLM turns her to face him and he hugs her.

MALCOLM
Why? Why? Why?

COLETTE
Words have an annoying tendency
to turn into lies.

MALCOLM kisses COLETTE. She responds, tentatively, then voluptuously.

MALCOLM
We'll cleave as one, then, in past tense, clove.

COLETTE
Malcolm, you could prove you love a stove!

Again, kisses.

I wish love were simple. I wish many things.
But my heart is a song your love now sings.

Scene v: Au centre-ville, sous la pluie

In this scene is seen LAXMI and OVIDE, umbrellas unfurled, running through a Pluviôse downpour and down a cobblestoned, twisting street. They shelter in a Gothic, gargoyle-headed archway. OVIDE kisses LAXMI and she pushes him away.

LAXMI
You're as sophisticated as Mephistopheles,
Ovide, but any hypocrite can give out kisses.

OVIDE
Why can't we be enlightened?
Laxmi means *light*. Perhaps you're frightened?

LAXMI
Am I to be coupled like a boxcar?
Is that what all your words are for?

OVIDE
Our love will erect a cathedral...

LAXMI
Or do you mean a *Kama Sutra* brothel?
Le Moulin Rouge is more your moral style,
Ovide, not the immaculate Taj Mahal...

> *OVIDE shakes his head "no" and then kneels before LAXMI. He touches her feet.*

OVIDE
As you pass, yellow
    marigolds bow down in awe
        at your auburn feet.

> *LAXMI turns away.*

LAXMI
Love is always, always, a risk.
Ah, who can I ask? Oh, who can I ask?
What is true in a kiss or embrace?
What a lover reveals is always less.

> *OVIDE stands and embraces LAXMI.*

LAXMI/OVIDE
Oh, these vexations will go on like hexes
for nothing's as vexatious as the sexes
when it comes to sex.

LAXMI
Ovide, I'm no tabloid starlet–
Half Girl Guide and half coquette.

OVIDE
Laxmi, your purity is a treasure,
Not plunder to loot–

LAXMI
Or pollute–

OVIDE
At leisure.

> *LAXMI lets OVIDE kiss her—tentatively—in the rain. Sound of a foghorn.*

CANTO II

Sacrum, sacrum, inluminatio coitu.
—Pound, Canto XXXVI

Scene i: Au Château Frontenac

In a pink-and-gold wallpapered hotel room in Le Château Frontenac, overlooking the Saint Lawrence River, MALCOLM and COLETTE, wearing bathrobes, sit on the king-size bed. COLETTE's feet don't touch the floor; MALCOLM's saxophone rests on the bed. It is night.

MALCOLM
Your daddy's A-1, a real jazz aficionado,
to castle a saxman like he's Quasimodo.
The Château Frontenac is swank civility.
Does he know you're here with me?

COLETTE
If he knew, he'd be in Hell – hellishly.

MALCOLM
There's no Hell like the Christian one.
Let's sip cognac – and scotch all sin.

MALCOLM opens a mini-bar, pulls out two small bottles of cognac, pours them into two glasses, and hands one glass to COLETTE. They sip, then recline on the bed and kiss. MALCOLM removes the saxophone from the bed. He gulps his cognac. MALCOLM and COLETTE climb into bed. They cover themselves and doff their bathrobes. MALCOLM looks softly at COLETTE and then extinguishes the light.

Your beauty's as natural as honey.

COLETTE
When I was a girl, about twelve,
Mama ushered us to a Liberal Party *fête*–
all those Grit Québécois kvetching,
and I wore a white dress she bought me
that was totally, utterly, see-through,
showing my panties and bra-less t-shirt!
Imagine....

MALCOLM
To picture you thus is no sin....

Rain showers pizzicato, *petulant, upon the window.*

COLETTE

> Perhaps you are a Casanova, callow,
> and I'm a morsel you'll swallow
> and forget… in an ellipse–
> like a satisfied gourmet wiping his lips.

MALCOLM

> Of flesh, and blood, and bone,
> We are made alone.
> With these same things,
> We are made lonely:
> The white moon only
> Seems to own wings.
>
> When that dawn sun blasts forth light,
> I'm gonna ring a tambourine.
> Oh, I'll love you 'til forever–
> And each day that falls between.

> *The lovers kiss. Darkness, an erection of flutes, then a triumph of Tijuana-*
> *flavoured trumpet braying Olé!*

Scene ii: Trop d'amour

> *Church bells chime as dawn commences. While MALCOLM slumbers still*
> *in the hotel room bed, COLETTE, wearing tangerine-coloured underwear,*
> *dons a short, crimson skirt and a gold shirt, then pulls on orange, knee-*
> *high stockings, and then, standing before a full-length mirror, fits on a red*
> *beret. She steps into red shoes and dons a red backpack, then leans over*
> *and kisses MALCOLM. He awakes and sits up, bare-chested, in bed.*

COLETTE

> Law school awaits my anarchy, *mon chéri.*

MALCOLM

> Careful: lawyers go to legislatures–
> or the hoosegow, just like whores.

COLETTE

> And musicians? Don't they go to asylums
> or end up waxed, shellacked, in museums?

> *MALCOLM pulls COLETTE onto the bed and kisses her.*

> When first to Québec I came,
> > I stood once in this endless forest
> > > with endless snow tumbling around.

MALCOLM
I remember fields snowy with clover
saluting the wild Nova Scotian Ocean,
its blue-grey circumflexes of waves,
and I see my mother's golden face,
smiling, as my rum-coloured father,
brought me a toy piano, black and silver,
echoing a baroque Bosendorfer.

COLETTE
Je t'aime, Malcolm.

MALCOLM
I love you, too, Colette, my balm.

COLETTE
Je t'aime beaucoup, beaucoup. À ce soir.

MALCOLM
Oui, à ce soir,
    that hour just before
        indigo melts azure to *noir*.

    COLETTE jumps up, blows MALCOLM a kiss, and leaves.

Scene iii: Récit d'Ovide

Wearing a black beret, a pink shirt and a black suit, MALCOLM stands at the bar of La Révolution Tranquille. He pours green-yellow absinthe into a glass. OVIDE, dressed in a white suit and mauve shirt, downs it. A vase jets dazzling sunflowers in sunlight.

OVIDE
Absinthe maketh the heart grow fonder, eh?

MALCOLM
If not that, it cuts it asunder.

    MALCOLM drinks. OVIDE looks out the window. He wolf whistles.

OVIDE
Is it their sheer nylons, that shimmering,
Polyhexamethyleneudiapide, simmering,
that sets girls' legs chicly glimmering?

MALCOLM
Uh huh, Québec *Cité's panochitas*
Say "*Buona notte*" with *aqua vitae*.

OVIDE

I adore cosmo mosaics—rainbows—of women:
Their plum-copper hair, their tangerine skin....

MALCOLM

This mania you mention, so manic and mad,
seems like something straight out of Sade.

OVIDE

There was a woman. *Il y avait une femme.*
Her cigarette smoke glinted silvery posh–
as if haloing a fresh Coco Chanel. Gosh!

There was a woman. *Il y avait une femme*–
all silky black blouses and carousing curls
and inky black skirts, milky, slinky pearls.

How hot it was, that summer, didn't matter:
Her scalding kisses were even hotter.

MALCOLM

A rich, white gal crowning a Black man's sex:
She was Desdemona, you was Oedipus Rex.

OVIDE

There was a woman. *Il y avait une femme.*
Even weather was not as hot as she! Damn!
Our dalliance, *mésalliance*, had a blues blueprint:
We founded love that crumbled like poor cement.

MALCOLM

But Laxmi?

OVIDE

A *femme fatale* Salomé, pure silk and teak,
Her carriage Georgian, her columns Greek.

The curvature of space?
Who cares?
Her curves erase
All fears.

The beauty of time?
So what?
Her thinness is what time
Has not.

MALCOLM
You sound like you're teetering at a cliff.

OVIDE
I could find love, a way to be loved, if....

MALCOLM
(*shrugging*) Just seduce disingenuous, sinuous ingénues.

OVIDE
Oh, what's the use? What's the use?

> *MALCOLM puts away the absinthe. OVIDE goes absent.*

Scene iv: Sur le pont

> *On Le Pont-Pierre-Laporte, a suspension bridge, OVIDE stands at the pedestrian railing as vehicles pass behind him. Sounds of traffic. In the murky night, the Saint Lawrence River seems invisible. Tipsily, OVIDE pulls a photograph from his jacket pocket.*

OVIDE
See April water swarming in channels
under the dark-blue, April atmosphere;
see white foam churning black, abysmal,
in cataracts as catastrophic as tears.

> *OVIDE pitches the photograph into the wind.*

Our essence is need:
To be born is to crave–
To gasp for air,
To grasp for love.

Farewell, Maria. *Oui, adieu.*
Only the sky should be blue.

> *OVIDE begins to leave the bridge.*

Scene v: Au magasin de confection

> *At a dress shop tattooed with a neon sign promising, "La Nouvelle Vague," COLETTE, wearing a blue and gold tartan sari, examines a rack of white blouses. LAXMI enters. She wears a blazing pink sarong. COLETTE smiles broadly at LAXMI.*

LAXMI

Ah, Colette! Is this shop where you work?

COLETTE

No. In the firm Étienne Agnant, I'm a clerk.

LAXMI

I'm at Hydro-Québec – as an assistant
To a Chief Deputy Adjunct Assistant.

I see saris are in vogue, and you're in love.
Am I right? I am right. Rightly, I approve.

COLETTE

Laxmi Bharati, I admit I adore
the blue-black in his skin and hair;
that black indigo in Malcolm's hair....
Blackness blacker than black, I adore.

LAXMI

Beware: Men have sex, but women have babies.
Men make love, but women make mistakes.

Why must we be comic *hymenoptera*,
our mandibles and incisors and feelers
clutching and biting and gnawing
in sex acts that dissect insect opera?

COLETTE

All women should, I'm sure you could prove,
Give love and have love and make love.

LAXMI

Men's desire is to deflower,
devour, and depart.
They annex your sex and, after,
snort, and ask, "Who's next?"

COLETTE

Men's morals are desolate, detritus.
But should women be acidic, citrus?
What about you and your avid Ovide?

LAXMI

I'm myself, pure, still, and he is – Ovide....
Have you told your parents about Malcolm?

COLETTE
I can't! I can't! I can't bring him home!

LAXMI
So you see him secretly, sneak out and back?
Because he's Black. Right? Because he's Black.

If you are so lyrically in love, law clerk girl,
Brave your parents, face, anew, our true world.

LAXMI leaves. COLETTE weeps.

COLETTE
Everything about our pairing is in despair.
Everything about our pairing is in despair.

Scene vi: Devant l'Assemblée Nationale

Before the National Assembly, the parliament of Québec, that silver-grey, rococo edifice (law and architecture married), LAXMI, in black knee-highs, a black skirt, a white blouse, a black beret, and black, low-heeled shoes, strolls with OVIDE. He wears a beige suit, a white shirt, and a black tie. Red, yellow, white tulips offset the grey legislature.

OVIDE
Over there, across the valley, beyond Sillery,
Pines sprout, dark as rains, but silvery.

LAXMI
Black pines gather – like crowds of mourners
Around *Love*, that disease, coronary....

OVIDE
Love is human: even a haughty aristocrat
Can kowtow to a slut from the proletariat.

LAXMI
Ask me, "What does a woman want? What and which?"
My answer is, "To be young, single, and rich."

OVIDE
Must we spat outside Québec's parliament?
Ici nous sommes — tous — Québécois, suprêmement.

LAXMI
"*La peau brune, mais le coeur québécois*"?
Tell that to the "*pure laine* Québécois"!

Everybody here asks me if I'm *Indienne*,
If I answer "Canadian," they ask, "Since when?"

OVIDE

When my parents fled here, thus dodging Duvalier,
le Parti Québécois disait, "Bienvenue, restez."

LAXMI

My Brahmin parents flew from Mumbai.
A doctor and a teacher, once of Bombay,
they crossed that sea, that cerulean sea,
to build fortunes and a haven for me.
Now, I'll erect temples, raise cathedrals–
to satisfy, harmonize, all religious souls.

OVIDE

If you were to die right now, you'd regret,
not having loved, not having been fit.

LAXMI

Why would I regret
    not being lied to?

> *OVIDE strides away. LAXMI chases after him and grabs hold of his arm.*
> *OVIDE turns, angry, and pulls LAXMI roughly to him. He kisses her*
> *callously. She slaps his face.*

OVIDE

Now I regret....
I love you.

LAXMI

How can three words stand for as much as that?

OVIDE

Your *Virtue* is only an old-fashioned, Bollywood
Cliché that's fake both in real life and in Hollywood!
It's surrealism more unreal than a Dali–
All your clinical cynicism about sex!

LAXMI

Beware: my household goddess is seven-armed Kali,
Who swings seven swords and severs seven necks!

> *OVIDE exits in a fury.*

Scene vii: À l'extérieur de la boîte de nuit

In a dark dusk, glowering outside La Révolution Tranquille, MALCOLM, wearing a beige suite, milk-white shirt, and sable tie, faces a regretful, tearful COLETTE. She is dressed in a Nova Scotian tartan kilt, a white blouse, and a tartan beret.

MALCOLM

So your parents denounce me as a "nigger"?
Now, ain't that some shit? Sugar!

COLETTE

That's not what they meant.
That's not what they mean.

MALCOLM

I know what they mean–
"a brutal physiognomy,
ignoble, igneous ignominy."
Oh, I know what they mean!

Québécois claim they're white niggers of America,
Peut-être, but I'm the Black *nègre* of Québec, Québec!

COLETTE

We can still love. Don't be so mean!

MALCOLM

I want to love meaningfully,
not meanly, not mean.

COLETTE

I thought I was hallucinating
when Mama swore she'd suicide.
She pointed a steak knife at her heart,
but she was really aiming it at my heart,
and I felt it go in.
Next, Papa grabbed her wrist,
arrested the blade,
but told me I was banished.
I stumbled, dizzy, out these doors,
tears replacing my eyes.

MALCOLM

Loving you is like, like, Heaven and a lynching!
Pops abandoned Tennessee to escape such flinching!
To get good love, he motorcycled to Nova Scotia,
And met and married a Black-Mi'kmaq madonna.

COLETTE

Should I just destroy my parents' hearts?
They dreamt of golden, Chinese grandchildren,
Can I coldly stab their dreaming hearts?

MALCOLM

It's theirs—or mine—or ours.
It's theirs—or mine—or ours.

COLETTE

Would our children be black or gold?
Would they be free or free to be sold?

MALCOLM

Do you think our kids'd be striped like zebras?
Or look like Neapolitan ice cream? Or ameobas?

> *COLETTE begins to cry.*

COLETTE

My folks said you can't play here,
Unless we separate, clean and clear.

MALCOLM

Well, hell, no, my quartet won't play!
We'll put our silver instruments
And put our Black music away. Away!
This ain't no time for innocence.

> *MALCOLM walks into the nightclub, rips down his band's poster, and storms out and away.*

CANTO III

And the old voice lifts itself
weaving an endless sentence.
—Pound, Canto VII

Scene i: Malcolm à l'extérieur de l'hôtel

MALCOLM paces before Le Château Frontenac. He wears a yellow shirt,
black pants, a red silk jacket, and a black overcoat. His suitcase and
instrument case occupy a hotel luggage cart. It is night. MALCOLM
unlocks his horn case. He holds up his saxophone.

MALCOLM
Oh Colette,
I can't forget.

I cry
the smell of good-bye
in the way you vanished,
ma jolie Chinoise-Québécoise,
how you folded yourself like a map
of a mysterious geography
I can never know,
and packed yourself away.

Crying, MALCOLM again packs up his saxophone.

I'll not be a decomposing composer,
with an asphyxiated sax.
To Hell with a keep-quiet "revolution"!
I'll holler *Love* maximally max!

MALCOLM beckons for a taxi.

I am a star; Colette's a galaxy.
Taxi! Taxi! My music for a taxi!

Scene ii: Colette au bar

Inside the dark La Révolution Tranquille, COLETTE, in a white dress
patterned with black bars of music, sits at the bar. She opens a bottle of
absinthe. She pours the boiling verdancy into a martini glass. She daubs
at her eyes with a napkin.

COLETTE

(*ironically*) Finally, I'm called to the bar–
the bar of prosecution,
the bar of ripped-up bars of music,
the bar of persecution…

Yes, Africa is far from China,
    but their histories are close:
On so-called yellow niggers,
    Canada a head tax imposed,
and bid my slaving ancestors
    lay down its railroads.
But China isn't pure Eden:
    The first art Mao damned
was jazz. He called it "decadent,"
    declared it banned.

But jazz is a black market, black magic music:
Its voodoo fuses Malcolm X and Confucius.

Now I lust for the look of leaves, leaves in fresh wind,
Blown startlingly green against Malcolm's sable skin!

Why can't we have May rains in April?
Why can't *Joy* flower just like maples?

Scene iii: Ovide sur le pont

With the wind whipping his black cape, OVIDE, dressed in a black suit,
stands again upon Le Pont-Pierre-Laporte. Traffic crisscrosses the bridge.
OVIDE stares into the distant void of the Saint Lawrence River.

OVIDE

My heart, still beating, is a tragedy.
I've exchanged bliss for obscenity.

O! Her beauty could topple Plato
and give eyeless statues eyes too.

OVIDE climbs over the bridge railing and prepares to jump.

Before her eyes, I, a poem, changed to fire,
    And she backed away.
Now her looks suffocate me, like this wind.
    I'm moral decay.

My heart seethes as furiously as the river:
But what if, Laxmi, her love, I do recover?

Scene iv: Laxmi sur le quai

In the fog-white night, LAXMI, sporting a long black overcoat, walks along the ferry terminal dock. A sign indicates Le Traversier *for Lévis. Sound of a foghorn.*

LAXMI
This foggy, tubercular chill makes April hurt!
When will the ferry deliver me from this murk?

I try to see reality uncut, uncensored:
Ovide has acted like the lowest class of dirt.

He thought me *"une pute exotique–
une lascivité proprement asiatique."*

*Mais, je ne suis pas une débutante lubrique,
avec "une chatte gluante, pimentée, impudique."*

No, a true love must be honourable and pure.
My husband must also be our children's father.

He who'd love me—inviolate—must love
Eros immaculate, *His* golden trove.

Scene v: Dans le brouillard

COLETTE and OVIDE wander separately in fog. Their songs interlock.

COLETTE
This riverscape is one from Li Po–
Just mist, mist and water everywhere....
But where is Malcolm, where are his eyes?

OVIDE
This sky coffining us, oh I deserve!
Clouds are sinking down in mire.
My heart's a dire abyss of bias.

COLETTE
I should go naked in the fur of snow,
Sprawl in its soft chill and weight,
Feel cold corset my breasts, my thighs.

OVIDE

Laxmi is Belle Époque India,
Exquisite sepia, lavish, precise.
But I've spouted fog – opaque, white lies.

COLETTE/OVIDE

Malcolm, Laxmi, do not let our romance end:
I miss you as hurtingly as a kite misses wind.

The wanderers continue off on their separate searches.

Scene vi: Sur le quai

*MALCOLM arrives in a taxi at the ferry terminal. He sees LAXMI,
pacing. He steps out and removes his suitcase and his saxophone case.
Then, MALCOLM approaches LAXMI.*

LAXMI

Malcolm, aren't you playing tonight?
Why wander in this chill, dull light?

MALCOLM

Colette's parents have parted me from their daughter,
so I'm departing, Laxmi, across this parting water.

LAXMI

I'm sorry for this news about your love.

MALCOLM

What of Ovide and your project of love?

LAXMI begins to weep silently.

LAXMI

My *chateaux* are ruins of romance–
    and even your rupture with Colette
is my fault. I nagged Colette
    to tell her folks of your romance.

MALCOLM

Soon or late, they'd find out, I knew, about us.

LAXMI

And Ovide was pushy, pushy like Priapus.

*MALCOLM opens his suitcase and removes a bottle of absinthe. He offers
it to LAXMI.*

I really shouldn't; perhaps it's impure.

MALCOLM

Sorrow improves with a good liqueur.

LAXMI accepts the bottle, tips it carefully, and sips.

So Ovide's a *papier-mâché* playboy, *un poseur,*
a masher, *pas un gentilhomme de couleur*?

LAXMI

Oh, why must men be born immoral?

MALCOLM

True: our high notes are only musical....
But Ovide's no more egotistical
Than any man who's got testicles.

LAXMI

Rapacity is the only male capacity,
Violating *Virtue* in every vicinity.

MALCOLM

Such icy iciness could frost June flowers!

LAXMI

Why should I dignify *Vice* that devours?

MALCOLM

Ovide is Prufrockian, defrocked, "fucked up."
But, Laxmi, you need humility to love.

LAXMI

Marriage can't be left to amateurs:
Amours must be lived as a *tour de force.*

MALCOLM

Happiness takes work; *Pleasure* is exacting.
Joy requires exercise; it's not play-acting.
You detest *Vice*, but Ovide's not so vicious:
Why is *Desire* deplorable malpractice?

LAXMI

When I was twelve, I accidentally saw
Father kissing some blonde Québécoise:
She was viscous, a creamy *vichyssoise.*
He didn't know I saw, such viciousness saw.

MALCOLM
Put aside your father's betrayal,
Laxmi, if you love Ovide at all.

LAXMI
I love Ovide because I shouldn't
(because he so enrages me,
because he does so outrageously,
things I wouldn't or couldn't)...

If my father forbids us to marry,
I may "live in sin" and not be sorry.

Your advice, Malcolm, should you abet.
So how will you recollect Colette?

MALCOLM
She tried to reason with me; *Love* was reason.
But, oh, instead I committed tragic treason.

> *MALCOLM takes the absinthe, drinks, and weeps.*

LAXMI
It's not too late. Confront her parents.

MALCOLM
I hadn't thought I should, but now I must.

LAXMI
A woman has only her trust.
A man has his calculated indifference.

> *The night fog is punctured by footsteps. COLETTE appears. LAXMI fades into shadows.*

COLETTE
Malcolm, I looked everywhere! Please come home,
to whatever home we can make *ensemble*.

> *MALCOLM and COLETTE embrace and kiss. A foghorn sounds.*

MALCOLM
I must go and face—face down—your parents.

COLETTE
I'll stay with you; I don't need their clearance.

You and I have been through much
and should not surrender touch.
Grant me the love that our parents found.

MALCOLM

Like this rain mumblin, bumblin, round,
Like this rain grumblin, rumblin round,
Without you, I got no solid ground.

COLETTE

Africans and Chinese both adore
watermelons and watercolours.
We are too alike not to be *ours*.

MALCOLM

Let's start our own *révolution tranquille*,
with a wrecking ruckus, gay with glee–
an unquiet riot–
half in bed and half out.

LAXMI coughs to announce her presence. She emerges, gleaming, from the shadows.

COLETTE

(to LAXMI) You are unpleasant, plus unwanted.

MALCOLM

Truth may be unpleasant, but is always wanted.

LAXMI

Still, I regret, Colette, any doubts I planted.

MALCOLM

(to COLETTE) Laxmi and I were mourning you and Ovide:
We resolved that *Love* must be plucked from the void.

A foghorn sounds. The Lévis ferry arrives.

LAXMI

Voici le traversier. I'll say *"Bonsoir,"* Malcolm, Colette.

COLETTE

Laxmi, stay with us awhile, stay awhile yet.

Through the mist, looking haggard, the black-caped OVIDE appears. LAXMI and OVIDE see each other, pause, then run to each other, embrace, and kiss.

OVIDE

    I heard Malcolm's saxophone from the boat.
    I decided to follow—like *Fate*—each note.

       MALCOLM and COLETTE approach the other pair.

MALCOLM/COLETTE

    Believers, lovers,
       you must begin again.

OVIDE

    (to LAXMI) Your eyes are eloquent, luculent obsidian,
    But I have been insidious, seditious, simian....

LAXMI

    Ovide, I'll bring you enlightenment yet.
    You'll be my *Kabir*, my *ghazal*-poet.

OVIDE

    I'll write a whole opera on love.

LAXMI

    Please omit jealousy, deceit, and hate.

OVIDE

    This time, Laxmi, virtuous I'll prove.

COLETTE

    Let's waltz in styles cinematic, up-to-date.

       The two couples dance together a contemporary, Québec quadrille.

LAXMI

    We'll love without skill, but without scheming.

MALCOLM

    Oh, if I were King of Nouvelle-Écosse....

COLETTE

    (You break no laws by dreaming!)

MALCOLM

    All lovers would be *bel*, never bellicose.

       The ferry moans.

    Let's sip Chicoutai and gulp sugar pie.

COLETTE
And thus we may celebrate "you" and "I."

OVIDE
Laxmi, I'm prodigal, my mouth full of songs;
My eyes seek lush light; rum sweetens my lungs.
I like baroque structures, those especially soft.
Please, *acushla*, accept this tender gift.

OVIDE withdraws a roll of papers from his inner coat pocket.

These are my blueprints for a stained-glass cathedral–
To be dedicated to Laxmi, Kali, and *avril*.

LAXMI embraces OVIDE. They kiss. COLETTE and MALCOLM applaud.

LAXMI
I'd like a temple, *mera pyar*, not a cathedral…
But I'll help you shape it – as your equal.

MALCOLM removes a small box from his coat pocket and hands it to COLETTE. He kneels.

MALCOLM
(to COLETTE) I will still ask your parents for your hand,
But it's essential I ask *you* for your hand.

MALCOLM opens the box to reveal a diamond, engagement ring. As MALCOLM slides the ring onto COLETTE's finger, she kisses him. LAXMI and OVIDE applaud.

I propose we marry on May the First.
Those who oppose *Love* must stand accursed.

COLETTE
I love you! O! The delicious jazz we'll make!

LAXMI/OVIDE
Put away tears; *au revoir*, heartbreak.

COLETTE reaches into her pocket and hands MALCOLM a clementine.

MALCOLM
Mine clement, clement clementine.

The couples kiss.

ALL

> *Love* is air that all things must have.
> Without *Love*, it is impossible to live.

Scene vii: Le finale

> *Under a banner proclaiming, "1 mai, Fête des travailleurs, Fête du*
> *printemps," COLETTE, wearing a white silk Mao suit, plus a white,*
> *diaphanous veil, and carrying red roses, stands with the black-suited*
> *MALCOLM. They are joined by the sable-suited OVIDE and by LAXMI,*
> *who is dressed in a scarlet sari, gold jewellery, and carrying white lotus.*
> *The couples stand before Le Château Frontenac.*

MALCOLM/OVIDE

> She is sea-smoked beach.
> I am the province's poem.
> She is wild apple, russet.
> I am dark and pungent rum.

COLETTE/LAXMI

> Apple blossoms, rain-wet,
> Froth and foam in our groves.
> Our destiny's delicious, lush:
> April sows perennial loves.

ALL

> May ushers in with lilac–
> sweet apple blossoms too–
> cutting in buttery,
> fluttering,
> suave colours of cream plum
> and honey *pluviôse*
> and perfumes fuming
> musky lemon,
> and smells of cedar in fresh rain.
>
> We are not only
>   philosophies and religions,
> languages and races,
>   but also skin and breath,
> thought and blood,
>   and on that basis,
> that axis,
>   yes, *oui*, may amalgamate
> and mate and propagate
>   just as we wish.

Our children will be
    every colour eyes can know,
and free:
    and states, parents, gods,
must have no say:
    Love is a tyrannical democracy.

Vive le Québec.
Vive le Québec.
Vive le Québec libéré.

Vive aussi le Québec de couleur–
Toutes les couleurs.
Vive notre québécité.

    The lovers exit as couples. Then, church bells, horns, sitar, Chinese violin
    (p'i-p'a), harmonium, harp, and thumb piano commix. The Québec flag is
    lowered from the rafters, but its four panels are, here, beige, pink, gold, and
    indigo.

    Fin.

'da Kink in my hair
voices of black womyn

Trey Anthony

Trey Anthony is the Artistic Director of Plaitform Theatre. Her work has been staged at the Harbourfront Centre and Second City. She is the playwright of *'da Kink in my hair: voices of black womyn.* *'da Kink* has toured and received critical acclaim in the Toronto Fringe, The Atlantic Fringe, and has recently been showcased in the New York Fringe and PSNBC, NBC's studio theatre. Trey is a former television producer for Women's Television Network (WTN), and a writer for the Comedy Network and CTV. She is also the producer of Canada's Urban Womyn's Comedy Festival. She is currently the Creative Program Director for Y-Arts?, an arts centre for urban youth. She is a 2002 Canadian Comedy nominee.

If you want to know a Black woman, touch her hair

by Althea Prince

— • — — • — — • —

After a writer has spent some time exploring "the finding of voice," there is a moment when "the laying claim to voice" is more than what she is engaged in writing. Things are taken up a notch as the writer embraces the playing field of her voice. That is how I hear Trey Anthony. For I have read her non-fiction writing on African women, on African women writers, and on *the doing* of life by African women. I have also seen Anthony perform comedic monologues.

Trey Anthony's work focuses like that of other Canadian women playwrights on cultural identities informed by gender, ethnicity, class, race, and sexuality. She has a gift for using Jamaican language and Standard English with powerful effectiveness in discussing these things. Her work naturally conjures up for me a continuum with two other African writers living in Canada: Louise Bennett and Ricardo Keens-Douglas. The same orality of the tradition of telling Story that is present in Bennett's comedic poetry, and in Ricardo Keens-Douglas' comedic monologues, is the basis of Anthony's work.

Performed in Fringe Festivals in Toronto, Halifax and New York, and at Toronto Harbourfront's Kuumba Festival, the play explores seven African women's experience in *the doing* of life. The writer uses her skill as a comedian to pull laughs out of the pain (and sometimes, out of the agony) that the women discuss. They are all African women of Caribbean origins.

'da Kink in my hair is a welcome addition to Canadian theatrical composition. Its focus on hair as a metaphor for *the doing* of life is the first play in Toronto that focuses on the complexities of African women's hair. The play also affirms an important event that takes place every day in hairdressing salons, and wherever there are African women touching hands to hair: African women talking about hair, revealing feelings about race, gender, sexuality, beauty, and power.

Given the proliferation of panels, films, books, comedians' skits, fiction works and poetry that are available on this topic (mostly created in the US), it is time, is it not, for a play set in a hairdressing salon in Toronto, dealing with African women's hair while the women speak about *the doing* of life?

The most recent documentary about hair and African women in Canada was written and produced by Jennifer Kawaja and Julia Sereny in 1999 (*Black, Bold and Beautiful: Black Women's Hair*). Like Anthony's play, it focuses on race, culture, class, politics, pain, joy and celebration… it includes scenes in a hair salon… with the touch of hands to hair… with African women talking about their lives.

'da Kink in my hair is a very timely play. So convinced am I of its timeliness that I anticipate an enterprising film-maker will move it swiftly onto the large screen. It will be spoken of as a kind of surprise-out-of-the-blue kind of happening… like "My Big Fat Greek Wedding." I envision the same kind of *eye-view* slice of *the doing* of life as that film… a way of being that no one outside of these particular people knows about.

Anthony instinctively moves from the style of her own more frenetic, staccato, poetic performances to prose-length dialogue. This is an effective tool; for in some shorter lines in the play, her voice feels restrained. She straddles two forms of writing, and this is obvious to the reader; especially if one has seen her perform comedic monologues. She thus relies on long pieces of storytelling (a chorus) to bring her characters to light, while creating powerful images of how life has been for them.

She hints at the latent spirituality in hair, having one character declare: "If you want to know about a Black woman, touch her hair." It is an area that I believe warrants full exploration in more artistic and dramatic creations. I suspect there is more focus in general by African women on the politics of hair than there is on the spirituality of hair. Perhaps Anthony's acknowledgement of the opening that comes with the touch of hands to hair will bring more work from her that includes spirituality and/or magic realism, as she claims the richness of the imaginary in this power centre. There are many possibilities that this mechanism can provide a playwright.

"Fried, dyed and laid to the side" was the first comment I recall hearing about African women's (and African men's) hair when I moved to Toronto nearly forty years ago. The process has changed to be much less physically painful than Madame Walker's hot iron-comb. The social life in the salon remains much the same: the women tell much, release much, cry and emote; heal, laugh, and vent on many areas of their lives.

Some of the telling is painful (a child dealing with sexual abuse); much of it is full of joy, humour and compassion. The narratives—true to what happens in some hairdressing salons—focus on predictable themes: betrayal, abuse, pain, joy, love. I see it as no coincidence that those were the topics in my experience of the salons in my days of "fried, dyed and laid to the side."

There will be a time when the movies, plays, and panel discussions on African women's hair transcend *what is* and inject some of what lurks in Anthony's work: an accepted understanding of the spirit-basis of the experience of hands touching hair. The hair salon scene in these productions may then move to be the rightful centre of a film that includes the spiritual basis of African women touching hands to hair.

It is satisfying to me that I found a more than ephemeral resonance with the monologues of the women in 'da Kink in my hair with the release of my novel, Loving This Man, (Insomniac Press, 2001). This is not shameless self-promotion: the lived experiences of the characters were different, but it was the use of the space to release Story that resonated with me.

In my novel, a mother and daughter talk of things that are not usually expressed, while the mother combs and plaits the daughter's hair. Like Anthony's women, the touch of hands to hair creates a space for the release of deep emotional issues in the mother and daughter. In the space created by the closeness and the touch of hands to hair, the mother talks of the beloved and missed husband and father; of how his face learned to smile differently when his daughter was born; and of his critique of the politics that keeps the country in a stranglehold. It is also the first time that the mother allows herself to speak to her daughter of the romantic and sensual love between herself and her husband.

What strikes me as remarkable is the similarity of the use of the space created by the touch of hands to hair, as well as the difference in the issues brought to the surface by Anthony's women and the women in my novel. The narratives reflect the differing objective realities of the women's lived experiences.

The lived experience of the characters in Trey Anthony's play is what I will carry as a melody with me. The politics is a background song, given foreground treatment. And so the Story does not end. The voices of women touching hands to hair continue to resonate with the doing of life of African women. As they continue the ritual touching of hands to hair, they will vent, they will commiserate, they will vilify, they will heal, and thus continue to do life. For this is a space for these things to take place. It is a space where narratives have freedom of voice.

Anthony has succeeded in her objective of using æsthetic sensitivity to give voice to Story; and Story has no end. So we can expect more works from this writer in this eye-view that she has plunged into.

And my last words? A vivid-in-a-nutshell phrase from the Hip Hop nation comes to mind: "That's what I'm talking about!"

Althea Prince's essays have appeared in several academic texts as well as magazines and journals. She is the author of a short story collection, Ladies of the Night and Other Stories, and two books for young people, How the Star Fish Got the Sea and How the East Pond Got Its Flowers. Prince has a doctorate in sociology and has taught at York University and the University of Toronto.

'da Kink in my hair: voices of black womyn was first produced by Plaitform Theatre, with the assistance of 'da Kink Collective, as part of the Toronto Fringe Festival, July 2001, with the following company:

NOVELETTE	Trey Anthony
SHAWNETTE	Keda
LADY ONE	Zena Brown
PATSY	Ordena Stephens
SHERELLE	Miranda Edwards
NIA	Ngozi Paul
STACEY ANNE	debbie young
CARRIE ANNE	Renee Brady
CHARMAINE	Rachael-lea Rickards

Directed by Weyni Mengesha
Production design by Trey Anthony & Weyni Mengesha
Set Design by Janet Romero
Lighting by Weyni Mengesha
Stage Managed by Annamie Paul

— • — — • — — • —

TIME:
    The present.
PLACE:
    Hair Salon on Eglinton Avenue.

Graphic Logo design by Janet Romero.
Photo of the backs of the cast by Ebony Haines.

'da Kink in my hair
voices of black womyn

by Trey Anthony

— • — — • — — • —

ACT I

Scene One

Dark stage. A hairdressing shop. Alone on the stage is a hairdressing chair; at the edge of the stage is a tight coil, representing the hair. As the actors walk in, the stage is washed with a red light. Each actor sings the verse "Walking around and no one knows my name." The actors walk in a circular motion around stage and sing, but never connect with each other. "Could you give me shelter from the pain. Cause I'm walking around and no one knows my name. Hurts so deep, it's burning in my soul. Cause I'm walking around and no one knows my name. Can't put a colour on my pain." Two actors go to front of stage and start pulling the coil apart as the other actors re-enact the daily frying, sizzling, and straightening which Black hair is subjected to; cries of pain can be heard. Lights go down, and NOVELETTE enters. Actors freeze in tableau.

NOVELETTE
(addresses the audience) My work is never done. You want me to talk to you, explain what's going on in this play well forget it! Pick up a paper because I have no time to talk to you today! I'm a busy busy career woman. Being a hairdresser is not an easy ting. People rushing in talking about oh I want this style, that cut, this washed, this coloured, Don't they see I'm busy–

LADY ONE interrupts her.

LADY ONE
Excuse me I have a 7:30 appointment and it's now 11:30 and you haven't started my hair.

NOVELETTE
(She looks her up and down with distaste.) See what I mean. Listen here Lady I said come for 7:30 I did not state anywhere or at any time I would start you at 7:30 because, you booked an appointment you never book a guarantee. Now sit down and when I'm ready for you I will let you know.

LADY ONE sheepishly returns to seat. NOVELETTE addresses the audience again.

Out of order! I'm telling you if it's not one thing it's the other. Womyn rushing in here, looking like they got ran over by a Mac truck, then expecting me to mek look like Janet Jackson. I said lady I'm a hairdresser not a magician and I tell you as a hairdresser you know everybody's business. Not that I'm a nosy person. I just know everything. Because if they don't tell you the hair will. Don't believe me? Well let me tell you my mother was a hairdresser, my mother's mother was a hairdresser, and my granny granny, granny, granny used to be a hairdresser. It's been a long time since the Browns have been doing hair. We are very entrepreneurish. And my granny granny, granny, granny, granny, granny, granny, used to say, if you want to know about a woman, a Black woman that is. Touch her hair. 'Cause that's where we store all our hurt, our pain, our hopes, our dreams, every disappointment all in our hair. *(two beats)* Why do you think it's kinky? We got all our sexual fantasies in there too!

Calls LADY ONE over.

Come I'm ready for you.

LADY ONE sits down in chair and NOVELETTE starts to touch and comb her hair. As her fingers are going through the hair she knows exactly what's going on. NOVELETTE closes her eyes and inhales and laughs softly to herself.

She's cheating on her husband. He's lousy in bed. Viagra didn't help him. And not only is she cheating she's cheating with her best friend's husband. Dirty little hussy!

LADY ONE
Excuse me?

NOVELETTE
I said I hope you're not too fussy!

LADY ONE
Well could you hurry up I got places to go, and people to screw, I mean do, and see.

NOVELETTE
I'm sure you do. Well Claudette will finish you off. Give her a B-12 finish and a Kera-silk rinse conditioning. *(Two beats and she talks again to the audience.)* I'm telling you the hair sends me a message. Some of the things it tells me makes me want to laugh, makes me want to cry. And sometimes I get to know thing I don't even want to know. Cause some of us are really hurting really bad. And you know Black womyn we cry, cry a lot on the inside too proud to cry on the outside. And things, which the hair tells me, make me want to cry. But I don't, I keep it up

here. Right in mi head. In mi hair. Tings me hear is in mi hair. Come Shawnette I'm ready for you. *(She sits her in chair.)* What a way this locks is growing long and pretty.

SHAWNETTE
Yes, I've been twisting it myself.

> *NOVELETTE looks at her, and starts to touch her hair, and SHAWNETTE gets up. Lights change, SHAWNETTE steps into spotlight.*

I got a kink in my hair. You used to love to play with that kink in my hair when it was all sweaty and damp. Kinky hair matted to my face. Sweat and your love dripping between my thighs. My love and me imprinted on your ebony skin, and you tracing my nose with your tongue. You just loving the roundness of my butt, grabbing chocolate brown skin between your fingers. Kneading me like dough, kneading chocolate dough. *(beat)* Needing me? *(SHAWNETTE looks into audience.)* And we sat in that match-box apartment dreaming about the house on the hills, the Benz in the driveway, the maid getting the door, our kids running around. I said my girl would have a pony and you said my little man gonna take golf lessons or something. *(laughs softly)* And let me tell you I would go to the beauty parlour all day. Get my nails done and do my hair. And you would say do those nails and even them bad feet, but don't get rid of that kink in your hair. And I believed you. *(shakes her head in disbelief)* I believed. I believed you when we didn't have money for the rent. As I swept and scrubbed white women's floors I still believed… I believed in you even when a can of tuna was an appetizer, a three-course meal and a late night snack I still believed. And you used to say "Baby, pretend it's caviar." And I tasted the caviar. Tasted your hunger. Tasted your thirst. Tasted your need to fill me up. And I became full on your hopes, dreams, full with your desires. *(beat)* Satisfied with just you I became full. Unbuckled my belt buckle as my stomach overflowed with you and your wishful food of dreams. And we laughed and we dreamed. And we dreamed and we laughed. And you played with that kink in my hair. *(beat)* So I got another job so you could go to med school. *(beat)* Left you studying at night as I caught the 5 Downtown train of Faith, connecting to the #23 Bus of Hope. I cleaned those offices and I dreamed. *(beat)* I ate caviar sandwiches on my ten-minute break. And when I came home all tired and torn you played with that kink in my hair. Sweat and your love dripping between my thighs. *(beat)* Filling me up again with you…. So forgive me if I feel to choke now! I got a burning desire to spit you the Fuck out! *(beat)* Because I paid my dues! I did my time! I made you! I loved you! I believed you! *(softer tone and in disbelief)* So I just don't get how she's there and I'm here. *(begins to cry)* I don't get how you got a house-full of beige kids and not my kids! I don't think she remembers tuna/ caviar! *(beat)* I don't think she mended your spirit and patched up your soul! *(beat)* She met you! But she never dreamed you! Believed you! *(softly)* She could never dream you... *(Two beats, then Shawnette looks into the distance and delivers last line with strength.)* And I know there ain't no kink to play with in her blonde hair. *(beat)* You used to love to play with that kink in my hair.

> SHAWNETTE *returns to chair and looks up at* NOVELETTE. NOVELETTE *pats her shoulder tenderly.*

NOVELETTE
You'll be okay girl.

SHAWNETTE
Yes, I know. *(sighs)* See you next week.

> SHAWNETTE *exits and* SHARMAINE *enters.* NOVELETTE *greets* SHARMAINE *and she notices* PATSY. *She speaks to* PATSY.

NOVELETTE
How you doing darling? I've been meaning to come over and have a little tea or a strong drink of rum with you.

PATSY
Oh no Novelette, you know I'm a Christian.

NOVELETTE
Well drink some rum on a Saturday and go to church on Sunday, God can't be mad at that.

PATSY
Oh Novelette, I going to pray for you on Sunday chile.

NOVELETTE
Tanks I need it. And while you're at it ask him about the Lottario number, cause I need to win some money. But really how you doing?

PATSY
My faith is seeing me through, ain't no burden God gives you too heavy to carry, but Lord knows my faith been tested with this one.

> NOVELETTE *nods her head, seats* PATSY *in the chair and touches her hair. Transition into monologue.* PATSY *remains seated.*

Romey used to say Mom you worry too much. Ain't nothing ever gonna happen to me. And then he would smile that easy slow smile that crept across his beautiful face. And those eyes, eyes full of mischief. Eyes which always let me know that chile was up to something. *(beat)* Like taking four cookies instead of two. Changing that C-minus on his report card to some messed up looking A, or sneaking in here at 2am when he knew his behind was supposed to be home by 12:30. That chile had me fooled for awhile, turning back all the clocks in the house, and me not even knowing he was late! Until I turned up at church Sunday morning and found out that I had missed an entire hour and a half of Sunday Service. And Pastor Thomas ain't looking too impress with me, rolling up late for church. Sister Rosemary huffing and a puffing because I had missed my choir solo and Sister April had to sing it. And everybody know that woman is stone deaf. Only reason she in the choir because she and Pastor Thomas got a little thing going on. *(laughs to herself and shakes her head)* Oh the flesh is weak chile! And me missing my solo because of that boy was I ever mad. I tell you that day I prayed to the Lord to give me strength to deal with that boy. And when I got home, some divine intervention got into me, and I torn his ass up. *(sings to herself)* God bless the chile. *(laughs to herself)* Six-three, real tall you know, but I still wasn't afraid to give him something. *(beat)* But nothing could stop Romey. Oh with that boy there was never a dull moment. But he was a good kid. Yeah he was. *(beat)* I would say Jerome. I would call him Jerome when I get serious or I got something important to say. Otherwise he was just Romey, my Romey. And I remember that night, I said, Jerome I ain't got a good feeling about this. Why don't you and Damion rent some movies and I'll fix you some Kool-Aid, order some pizza and you boys just can stay in. The streets ain't safe for young boys. *(beat)* And Romey rolled his eyes and smiled that easy slow smile and kissed me right here. *(points to the area on her forehead)* Right here on my forehead. And he said Mom, you worry too much ain't nothing gonna happen to me. And besides Mom, we ain't on the streets it's a school dance. Ain't nothing gonna happen at a school dance. And Mom you know Denna Stewart going to be there, and you know I got a thang fo' Denna Stewart. I'm gonna show her my moves on the dance hall and she's gonna be all mine. *(She laughs.)* Po' Denna Stewart having that boy step all over her feet. And we laughed. Romey's, he got this real deep happy laugh. *(beat)* But I guess everyone is happy when they laugh right? And before I know it Damion's at the door, honking the horn. And Romey is racing down the front step. And I said *(very urgent)* Jerome! Be careful. And he smiled that easy slow smile. And he said I'll be home by 12:30 and I said you better be in here by 12am and he took off running. And we both knew he wouldn't be home till 12:45. That's Romey always trying to get away with something. But he was a good kid, my boy was good.

And that's all I said be home by 12. And he was gone. *(beat, emotions begins to build, voice wavers)* And I'm real mad with myself. Cause I thought I should have told him wear your brown cause it's a real warm coat. But I let him leave wearing the blue one and that ain't a real warm coat. And I should have told him I loved him *(yells out)* I love you! And I should have just listened to that rotting feeling in my gut and begged him to stay. *(yells out)* Stay home Romey! But I didn't. I should have just said (yells) wear your brown coat Romey, it's a warmer coat! Because he was lying on the ground you know, on the cold hard ground. Bleeding to death. And maybe if he was just wearing his brown coat – maybe the coat would have kept him – maybe...

But brown coats don't protect little Black boys from eight bullets do they? Cause Damion said he was driving really fast. It was 12:40 and Romey was watching the clock. Never knowing he wasn't going to be late, he weren't ever coming home. They killed him! They can do that! Kill little Black boys coming home from a school dance! White men in blue uniforms, hunting them, stalking them, killing them! How come we protect animals in this country better than we protect Black children? You need a license to shoot a damn bird! You go to jail for leaving your dog outside! But you can leave my baby, lying on the ground for 25 minutes before anybody calls an ambulance! (beat) Cause there ain't no sign posted "warning Black boys are in danger of becoming extinct." How come they can't grow up to be Black men?

He was just reaching for his ID and they shot him! Eight times! Eight times and my baby's gone. (begins to cry) And I know as a mother, you're supposed to love them, teach them, keep their butt in line, tell them to wear brown coats instead of blue – but you're not supposed to bury them! (beat) A mother isn't supposed to bury her son... (three beats, gets up from chair and rubs her stomach) I took my ultrasound yesterday. And it's a boy. Me a Mom again? And I thought about you Romey. Maybe he'll have your slow moving easy smile. Or maybe he'll have your eyes. Eyes full of mischief. And I cried. Cried for my baby. Right there in the waiting room I bawled, nose running and everything, a real ugly kinna cry. I cried for my sons. Cried for our sons. (two beats) And all the other mothers in the waiting room, they just looked away. Just looked away. Cause they understood. (beat) No they understand.

Lights change.

NOVELETTE
So when are you due?

PATSY
Miss Novelette, what are you saying to me?

NOVELETTE
You a breed right? There's a bun in the oven!

PATSY
How did you know? I ain't told no one but my husband and God.

NOVELETTE
I know.

PATSY
(*looks up at her*) Novelette you don't think I'm too old do you?

NOVELETTE
As long as you can put your foot on your husband's shoulder, and your ankle around his neck – you're never too old. And I'm no Christian or anything, but I believe God knew you had a lot more love to give. I knew Romey and that boy was a good kid, and good kids don't raise themselves. That kid had manners, well-spoken beautiful young man. You were a good mother. And you, now you're going to be the best baby mother around. You know there is a reggae song, called, (*singing*) "you are de best baby mother."

> *NOVELETTE starts to do a little reggae dance. Her and PATSY begin to laugh.*

PATSY
Oh Miss Novelette. You know I'm married I ain't trying to be nobody's baby's mother.

NOVELETTE
No but you're going to be the best.

> *NOVELETTE hands her the mirror to look at her hair. PATSY nods her approval and gets up to leave. She attempts to pay NOVELETTE, but is refused. PATSY heads towards the shop door.*

PATSY
Can I look for you in church on Sunday?

NOVELETTE
Look very hard!

PATSY
I'm going to pray for you chile. (*She exits stage.*)

> *NOVELETTE notices SHARMAINE.*

NOVELETTE
Come Sharmaine. What you having today?

> *As SHARMAINE is seated SHERELLE rushes in. SHERELLE eyes the chair hungrily. SHARMAINE gives her a bad look.*

SHERELLE
Novelette, I need to be in your chair and out of here in an hour. I got a lunch date at 12 and I got a dinner at 6 and I'm meeting my sister at 9 and somewhere in between all that I got to take a power nap. So let's do this!

NOVELETTE
Well. Let me tell you Sherelle, I have just put Sharmaine in the chair, and I still have to finish Miss Jenkins hair. And I have at least two more womyn coming in and Miss Brown is sending her two bad pickneys over here, and there's two more womyn before you. And somewhere in between there, I need to take a power nap. By the way what is a power nap?

SHERELLE
Novelette! Could you not just squeeze me in please.

NOVELETTE
Next week. I'll put you down for my first appointment.

SHERELLE
(looking disappointed) But Novelette I need–

NOVELETTE
(not looking up at her) Not now Sherelle I'm busy. See you next week, be here for 7am. Just because you have some big fancy job and a little education dat doesn't mean you can come in here and tell me how to run my shop. I'm a career woman too. I couldn't walk into your office downtown and demand Sherelle, see me now. You run me! I don't have time for you now, I'll see you next week okay?

> SHERELLE *walks away looking dejected, the spotlight follows her into her apartment. Her phone rings she answers it.*

SHERELLE
Hello? Don't worry Angie, I can lend you the money. No don't worry about paying me back it's okay. Well I couldn't stand by and watch you lose your house. Okay. I'll deposit the money in your account tomorrow. All right kiss the boys. Yep I'm fine, just tired. Umm kiss the boys for me, tell them I love them. *(She hangs up the phone, and it rings again.)* Hey Donna I wanted to talk to you. Oh Davey's in the hospital again. Don't worry that kid is a trooper. Give him some wheaties and a plate of mom's cornmeal dumplings and that kid will be fine. *(pause)* Well when you have some time we can get together. Hang on the other line, okay? I'll let you go. *(She answers the other line.)* Hello? Yes, Mr. Walters I closed the deal. I'll have the report on your desk Monday morning. *(pause)* No it's not a problem, I'll come in. You'll have it on your desk by noon tomorrow. You have a good night sir. *(She hangs up the phone looking defeated.)* Bastard! Oh, do I mind working on a Saturday? Well if you have just worked 74 hours for the week hey what's another 10! *(She sighs.)* It's not easy being at the so-called top. Constantly explaining how I got here. Why I need to be here. Try walking into a room of stuffy white men in outdated expensive suits. You know the old boys network, and trying to explain to them,

e-commerce, stocks, shares, bonds. *(beat)* And then come the looks and the unspoken questions and the polite question. Where did you study? Just checking to make sure the Black girl's got a high school diploma. Then when I tell them I got a PhD in economics from Yale, either it shuts them the fuck up or gets them hard. All of a sudden I'm not the hired help, but a good exotic lay. And naturally I'm supposed to jump at the chance, because of course I slept my way to the top, or I must be some lucky recipient of affirmative action, employment equity or some old white man's guilt. An old little man who maybe thought he needed some colour in his office when getting his morning coffee. But not too much colour just enough. Don't be acting too Black because then they have to deal with my Blackness every morning. So I put my Blackness or lack of Blackness in some womyn of colour box to make you more comfortable. And I'm tired of dealing with them and them not wanting to see me! Trying to always prove myself. Pulling 16-hour days, skipping lunches, not knowing it was actually okay for me to leave the office and go home. Because I had to prove to them that I could do this! I could do this! I could do my job! Sherelle can do it! Of course Sherelle can! I do everything else! *(beat)* And if not my job, it's Mom, Donna, and Angie. You know the family shit. Everyone needs something from Sherelle. Cause she's got it all. The great job. No kids. Single by choice. The great house. The fancy car. Everyone wants to be me except me. So if your husband leaves you, call Sherelle, she'll know what to do. Your kid is sick or skipping school, call Sherelle, she'll know what to do. You out of money call Sherelle, Mom needs a drive to No Frills call Sherelle! You want a friggin report on your desk Saturday not Monday morning call Sherelle! *(She breaks down crying.)* And I'm tired of looking after everyone. Being the responsible one. The good one. The one with all the answers, the level headed one. *(two beats)* Mom calls me the glue. She said I'm the one who keeps this family together. *(beat)* So would it be okay for me to just fall apart sometime? How would you handle it if I told you that I get scared sometimes? Lonely. Empty. If I was weak, could you hold me up, glue me together, patch me up, so I could deal with my shit and your shit! Cause I'm falling apart. I'm disappearing. I can't believe I'm still standing. *(beat)* My legs fell off three months ago you know. My arm just disappeared last week. I reached for my coffee yesterday and my fingers dropped off one by one and nobody noticed. Nobody noticed I was gone. Just gone. And today I spoke and I couldn't hear me! I couldn't hear my voice! I couldn't hear me! So you see I'm not really here. *(two beats)* I was tired! I couldn't do this! I couldn't be everything! And it's not really that I wanted to die, I just wanted to take a rest. A long-needed rest. But nobody would let me. They wouldn't let me! *(two beats)* I wouldn't let me…

She reaches for the pill bottle, stuffs the pills into her mouth and swallows some water. She slumps over as the pill bottle drops to the ground.
The womyn enter and hum the heartbeat melody. Lights go down on
SHERELLE, *and raise up on* NOVELETTE *and* SHARMAINE *in shop.*

SHARMAINE

(*already in chair*) Novelette, I was thinking maybe a auburn this week or maybe I should go back to my natural colour.

NOVELETTE

Well if you can remember what your natural colour is, please let me know. I don't understand you, you know. Always doing your hair, doing your nails. Such a pretty woman and you na have nobody. You mean to tell me Sharmaine, you can't find one person you like, you is too picky. But I'm going to help you out. (*two beats*) Well mi have a friend name Bunny who is quite nice. A handsome guy. Tall dark and handsome. Six-two and strapping – a decent job. Nothing is wrong with Bunny. (*pauses*) The only ting… is he has two teeth missing at the front, but nothing a good dental plan couldn't fix. You have a dental plan Sharmaine, maybe you can help poor Bunny out.

SHARMAINE

You're not serious.

NOVELETTE

Well you want a good man you help him out!

SHARMAINE

I think I'll be okay Novelette.

NOVELETTE

(*starts to do her hair, while mumbling*) Every good woman needs a good man – ain't nothing wrong with Bunny and his teeth.

SHARMAINE

My girl Miriam just got engaged. Four years and Marlon finally popped the question. Right after she said a breathless yes, they had mind-blowing sex. It's something about commitment, she said, that makes the sex better. Maybe it's knowing that this is the penis you're going to spend the rest of your life with. (*beat*) So what about you, when are you getting married? Dating anyone? Well…. My girl Dana 8 months pregnant. And we all pitched in and got her the cutest gift basket. We all ohh and ahhh, and patted her stomach and shared delightful baby stories. And that's when everyone felt a need to focus on my unused, uninterrupted, childless, womb. So when are you going to have one Sharmaine? Well of course she's going to need a husband or at least a man! Sharmaine you're so pretty how come you haven't got a man? Well…. So when is it okay to drop into intimate sista talk that you're a lesbian? Should it be when everyone says how gross why do they, "they" being gay and lesbian, need to get married and throw it in everyone's face. Yet I won't mention how your heterosexuality chokes me every day. How it's okay for you to walk down the street holding your man's hand. How it's even okay for you to slip him a little tongue when he picks you up from the GO Station. But me, I can get stared at, beaten or even killed for holding my girl's hand. But really maybe I need to be honest and just say "hey girls I'm a Lesbian!" after all my friends have offered to hook me up with their grandfather, the postman, men with no teeth, and let's not forget the efficient plumber in the baggy blue jeans. And please let me know when it's okay for me to come to you for support. Yeah you! Cause we are Sista's in the struggle right? Late night talks about racism, oppression, and the pervert in your office that you can't stand. And of course we talk about your man. Your man, your man, your man, your man, your man, your man, your man, your man, your man. But why does it make you so uncomfortable when I take a second to talk about my girl. *(two beats)* Or let's get real deep, Sista. Let's talk about me being a Black Lesbian. All of a sudden we ain't down no more! I ain't Black no more! *(beat)* Because of course that's something only white girls do. Now you can't drink from my pop or share a glass, because everybody knows what those lesbians do. But it's okay for you to talk to me about how you finally convinced your man to go down. Town. So let's get this sisterhood thing straight. Real straight. I'm one of you as long as I'm not one of them. So in order for me to come to you and be a part of your struggle, our struggle? Be your sista. I have to leave my sexual identity at the door and stop being such a lesbian. *(beat)* Well do me a favour girl, the next time you come to chill at my place could you leave your vagina at the door and not be such a womyn. And while you're at it could you leave your Blackness at the door and not be so damn Black! Impossible? Yeah, tell me about it.

As SHARMAINE goes to her seat, STACEY ANNE and CARRIE ANNE run into the store playing a game of tag.

NOVELETTE

Hey Miss Stacey Anne and little Miss Carrie Anne a bruk, you want to bruk down mi shop. This is a place of business, not a playground. I'm not your mother but I will beat you right here in mi shop. Where is my belt?

CARRIE ANNE

Hi Miss Novelette, I have two Juicy Fruit gum leave, and I save one for you, so you can always have fresh breath Miss Novelette.

NOVELETTE

I beg your pardon little miss. Come here and give me a kiss. How you doing Stacey Anne?

STACEY ANNE

Fine Miss Novelette. Carrie never means to insult you about your breath Miss Novelette. Sometimes she say tings she na mean. But she never mean to cause no trouble and we never mean to come in here and bruk down you place.

NOVELETTE

Mi know darling. Cause if you bruk it up I will bruk you up! *(She smiles.)* Come here and give Miss Novelette a kiss, a long time mi no see you. How is your mother?

CARRIE ANNE

She's at work again. And Mr. Brown a look after we, him give Stacey money to come do her hair. Miss Novelette you can perm my hair today please, please–

STACEY ANNE

Yes Mr. Brown sey mi can perm mi hair, but Carrie can't. I want tall hair like mi teacher at school.

NOVELETTE

You want tall hair today. *(She looks at STACEY ANNE's bald head in surprise.)* Today? *(She seats STACEY ANNE in chair.)* And Stacey Anne take off your coat, it's summertime now in Canada you don't need the winter coat.

STACEY ANNE

(sits in chair and laughs) Mi know Miss Novelette, but mi still find it cold sometimes.

> NOVELETTE touches her hair. Transition into her monologue.

Mi excited mi come a foreign but lawd it cold! Mi love de feel a snow pun mi lip and mi luv to lick it but lawd it cold! And no matter how much jacket, coat and sweater you wear it still cold! Mi wear three pair a long john, mi na know why dem call it long john because it catch mi right here. Mi wear three pair and mi still cold! *(points midway to her knee)* Bwoy Canada cold! But mi know sey mi lucky fi come a foreign because nuff people back a yard mad fi come a foreign. And when Granny hear sey Mommy did marry Mr. Brown im a mi stepfadda now. Granny sey you lucky you madda marry Mr. Brown so now she can send fi onnu. A Granny a she luv Mr. Brown. One time Mr. Brown send Granny two hundred Canadian dollar one time! When Granny get de money, she jump and dance, and grab up me and Carrie. Dat a mi likkle sister and dance round de place. It was di funniest ting mi did ever see, every time mi tink about it mi have to laff. And Granny sey Mr. Brown a di best ting which ever happen to dis ya family. And she tell mi nuff times, mi beg yu Stacey Anne when yu go a foreign, do na do nothing which mek Mr. Brown mad cause im send fi onnu and im can send onnu right back. And when she drop we a de airport she sey again, unno respect and mind Mr. Brown, listen to him cause im is a good man. And Mommy and Mr. Brown pick we up a de airport wid Gary who is mi likkle bradda who mi never did see before. And Mommy cry and hug up me and Carrie and she start bawl and sey what a way unno grow big. Lawd a six years now mi never see unnu. And Carrie grab up pun mi cause she never did remember Mommy. Cause she did one likkle baby when Mommy did leave and mi did six. But mi still remember Mommy. Mi remember she did wear one daisy-smelling perfume, and when she hug mi a de airport mi did remember. And Mommy did feel bad sey Carrie na look like she remember her. And she ask Carrie if she did get di dress and di clip fi wi hair, and de socks and de soap powder, and de tin of bullybeef. And Carrie sey yes but she still wouldn't go to Mommy, and she put down one piece of bawling fi granny, and she wouldn't let go a mi hand. And Mr. Brown him did look like im a get mad. And im sey to Mommy mi hope sey yu na badda bring na spoil spoil pickney inna mi house and try talk to dem inna a de car because mi a pay fi parking. And im did look so vex mi did tink im would a send we right back pun de plane we did come. So mi whisper to Carrie try na badda do nothing which mek Mr. Brown mad. And Carrie mussey stop bawl fi one minute and 62 seconds and den she pun down one next piece a cow bawling. But now Carrie git used to Mommy, but she still stick pun mi some time. And she na talk bout Granny much. And she luv her school, cause her teacher have yellow hair, mi mean blonde hair. And Carrie like her cause she remind her a woman pun Gilligan island. We used to walk mussey two hundred and fifty-two mile fi watch pink people wid yellow hair pun tv, cause we never did have no tv awe yard. And mi like foreign now cause mi have a tv inna mi room. And mi na have to wear uniform go a school. And mi learn to talk properly and correctly. And mi have nuff nuff clothes, nuff nuff long john, and mi eat nuff nuff McDonald's and yam peanut butter sandwich every day with jam. And mi did tell yu sey mi have mi own room. My own room. Cause in Jamaica mi and Carrie and Granny used to sleep pun one bed, in one room! But now in foreign mi have mi own room. My own room for mi and mi alone. *(She becomes quiet and looks down on the floor.)*

But sometimes Mr. Brown come inna mi room. When Mommy gawn a work a night time im come inna mi room. And im touch mi. And do things which Granny sey yu shouldn't mek bwoy do but Mr. Brown im do it. And first time mi did sey no Mr. Brown but im did look like im a go get mad. And mi know sey Granny na want mi fi get im mad. And mi na want im fi send wi back, and mi na want im to stop send Granny de money. And Carrie she just a get used to Mommy and she woulda really bawl if wi have fi go back now, cause Mr. Brown just buy her three new Barbie and im sey im a go buy wi a dream house dolly house, big so! *(widens her arms to express the length)* And mi na want fi go back now! And mi na want fi mek im mad. So Mr. Brown happy when mi mek im touch and im want to touch mi... and when im inside a mi it hurt... but mi na sey nothing which will mek im mad. *(begins to beat her leg, mimicking the rhythm of sex)* So when im inside a mi, mi just tink bout Carrie three new Barbie, Carrie teacher wid her yellow hair, mi and Carrie laughing when we a eat McDonald's french fries, and mi

licking snow offa mi lip. (*Two beats, and she hits her leg for the last time.*)
And my favourite one to tink about, is Granny dancing with mi and
Carrie when Mr. Brown send her di money. By the time Mr. Brown
finish. (*beat*) Granny still a dance innna mi head...

*STACEY ANNE begins to hum and GRANNY enters dancing, very
dreamlike, the other womyn enter and surround STACEY, giving her
energy and love. And they begin the dance of "healing." After the dance,
they exit the stage.*

*NOVELETTE takes a seat in chair, removes her red wig and addresses the
audience.*

NOVELETTE
What, did you think I was a natural redhead?

NIA enters into the salon.

NIA
Where is everyone?

NOVELETTE
Don't ask that question. The shop is closed. Day is finished. Shop lock
up and time for everyone to go home and that includes you.

NIA
Please Novelette, just a wash and set. I got a funeral I'm going to
tomorrow.

NOVELETTE
I'm sorry. Your sister told me. How are you doing?

NIA
Oh I'm doing okay, but I guess Sandy's taking it hard, her and Mom
were close.

NOVELETTE
Well come. But please just a simple wash and set, because God knows
I am tired. And I have no time for fancy hairstyles, pictures in a
magazine, and you wanting me to give you false hopes and promises,
because I am a hairdresser–

NIA
Yes Novelette, we know, a hairdresser, not a magician.

*They both laugh and NOVELETTE touches her hair. Lights change, and
NIA steps into her spotlight.*

Sandy held her breath, when you pulled back the blanket. Pity the bitch didn't pass out, while you were looking it all over. I'll always remember how you smiled when you looked at his ears, then laughed out loud when you saw his pale fingers. Sandy knew the shit was good, and she had passed again. *(beat)* I couldn't do it. Couldn't believe the bitch was back on her pedestal. *(laughs bitterly to herself)* Yeah you knew she had skipped more classes than she had ever gone to. Hung out with the wrong crowd. Dropped out of high school because she was pregnant. But you conveniently forgot all of this because she had given birth to a bundle of brown joy. *(two beats)* Her kid's hair was so wavy, I thought you would jump right in for a swim. You were such a proud grandmother. Quickly calling all the family and telling them how the baby could easily pass for white. *(shakes her head in disbelief)* And I just wanted to go over there and smack you in your damn Black ugly face, and ask you, what about me! What about Tasha? Did you know that Tasha's birthday was last week? Did you know that her kindergarten teacher said she's reading at a grade two level, and today she tied her shoelaces all by herself? But you wouldn't give a fuck would you because you can't find a wave in Tasha's hair. No good hair, no mistaking my baby for white. Her skin is black coffee, black coffee without the milk. And I know it's all my fault cause I chose to lay down with a man that if he closed his eyes and didn't smile you would have thought he left the room. *(break)* Quarter past midnight you called him, but personally I think he looks more like 12:30am. And when Tasha was born you marched over to the hospital, hoping for the best but expecting the worst. And you got that didn't you? You didn't laugh when you looked at Tasha's dark fingers and even darker ears. And your face said it all. No need to speak Mom, because I had heard it all before. *(imitating her mother)* "How many times do I have to tell you girls, pick the men you lie with, anything too Black is never good." *(pause)* Anything too Black is never good. Anything too Black is never good! I should have known that because I was never good enough for you was I! You hated my Blackness. Ranted and raved every Sunday afternoon as you heated up the pressing comb to press my bad hair. While Sandy ran outside, the good hair one. The light one. The right one. We stayed in the hot kitchen and I pinned my ears back holding my breath, not daring to move because I didn't want to get burnt again. And as you fried and cooked my bad hair, you cursed my Blackness. Cursed my father, hating to see him in me, you in me, hating to see the Black in me. *(two beats)*

And you know I'm 32 years old and I still cry when I see little Black girls in red ribbons. You wouldn't buy me them, you said I was too Black to wear red. No little red dresses, or red socks. Cause I was too Black for red. *(getting emotional)* Too Black to wear red? And you know last week I bought Tasha 14 red ribbons and put all of them in her hair, yep all 14 of them in her hair. *(laughs to herself)* And Tasha looked in the mirror and laughed and said Mommy I think I got too many ribbons in my hair, and I said no baby Mommy just like to see you in red. It's my favourite colour. *(two beats)*

And I want to believe that you tried to love me, but I just couldn't feel it. I couldn't compete with Sandy. Because I lost that race before I even started. And I've been trying all my life to win it, just to get you to love me not as much as you loved Sandy but just a little bit.

And now you're dead. *(beat)* And I know I'm supposed to feel something. Maybe cry, maybe mourn. I want to feel something. And for God's sake you're my mother and you're dead and I want to cry and I can't. *(two beats)*

(tries to convince herself) Maybe at the funeral I'll cry. Because I'm wearing a black dress, a black hat, black shoes, black stocking all black. All black. Mom I'm wearing all black! Mom look at me I'm wearing all black! Please will you just look at me…? I'm wearing black. *(three beats)* I've been wearing black all my life.

> *All the womyn enter individually and state proudly "I've been wearing black all my life." NIA looks at them. They touch her stomach and begin to hum and heal her. Offering to NIA, healing affirmation and the celebration of Blackness. They begin an African dance which celebrates life, healing, pride and self-identity. NIA joins in and then leads the dance. The play ends with the womyn inhaling and then exhaling as they release the ribbons, symbolically releasing themselves.*
>
> *The end.*

Somebody Somebody's Returning

Frederick Ward

Poet, novelist, playwright. Born: June 7, 1937 at Kansas, Missouri. Parents: Samuel and Grace (Douglas) Ward. Education: University of Missouri Conservatory of Music at Kansas City (1957); Dalhousie University (1969). Occupation: Teacher, Dawson College; composer. Awards: Canada Council for the Arts grants (1974, 1976, 1983, 1987, 1993). Honorary degree: Dalhousie University (LL.D.). Anthologies: *Fire on the Water* (1972); *Present Tense* (1972); *Canadian Childhoods* (1989); *Voices: 16 Canadian Writers of African Descent* (1992); *Crystallizations: 20 Works by Baha'i Artists* (1996); *Eying the North Star* (1997). See also: Kimber, S. "Halifax's Hot, But Unknown, Author" in *Halifax* (November 1981); Diamond, A. "Life at Full Tilt" in *Books in Canada* (December 1992). Writer-in-Residence, Centaur Theatre (1983, 1986) Unpublished work includes: *Do Blind Men See Ghosts* (1982) drama; *Juka* (1984) drama; *P.A., A Fugue in Multiple Personalities* (1986) drama; *Pleasing Father, A Permanent Performance* (1988) drama; *Gospel Women & One Night Stands* (1994) drama; *My Name is Istaban, Conga at the Algonquin Hotel* (1995) drama; *Oliver Jones in Africa* (1990) film; *The Road Taken* (1997) film; *Crossroads: Three Jazz Pianists* (1998) film. Home: Montreal, Quebec. Publications: *Poems* (Duende Press, 1964); *Riverlisp* (Tundra Books, 1974); *Nobody Called Me Mine* (Tundra Books, 1977); *A Room Full of Balloons* (Tundra Books, 1981); *The Curing Berry* (Williams-Wallace, 1984).

Feeling the Blues Inside the Spirituals: Frederick Ward's *Somebody Somebody's Returning*

by George Elliott Clarke

— • — — • — — • —

Playwright, poet, novelist, screenwriter, editor, and teacher, Frederick E. Ward is to be read, is to be acted, is to be sung, is to be understood – *one day*. He is not of our time, but for all time. He is, most likely, the greatest practitioner of the sound, music, rhythms, of "Black" speech in print that you, we, will ever know, and he weds the jazzy sensibility of his language to the vivacious humanity of his faith. He is, has been for decades now, a Baha'i, thus practicing a religion that has no time for racism or sexism or homophobia because it insists we truly are all one – under one God. With this inspiration for his æsthetic, Ward treats ideas and tales as melodies to elaborate and examine, to accentuate and attenuate, to revisit and veer away from as he wishes, just as the jazz artist may depart from a known melody, pursuing its *impression* instead. Ward's *musicalization* of language renders his writing—at times—obscure, but it is the obscurity of a Jean Toomer or a James Joyce or a Toni Morrison and it demands our most bodacious perspicacity. *Can you get to this?*

Employing only slightly the virtuoso, surrealistic, stream-of-consciousness "scorings" of his three novels – *Riverlisp* (1974), *Nobody Called Me Mine* (1977), *A Room Full of Balloons* (1981), and his book of poems, *The Curing Berry* (1983), this play, *Somebody Somebody's Returning* (1987), is, thus, a deeply accessible treatment of familial tension regarding love betrayed, love strayed, and love mislaid. The play is part-Shakespearean comedy—the restoration of disrupted relationships—and part-Grecian tragedy – witness the slaying of a brother by his adult sister, her subsequent incarceration, and, therefore, the endangerment of her daughter's love. Layers upon layers of *angst* and desire, regret and hope, and realism and fantasy seethe within Ward's characters. A turn of a phrase reveals one facet, while the turn of a head reveals some contradictory, ramifying other. Protagonists' rich, interior lives—memories and dreams—colour and shadow the reality they *think* they inhabit.

Ward has come to his excellent, poetic, compositional style, not primordially through Canada, but through his special past, flamboyantly African-American and flagrantly "artsy." Born in Kansas City, Missouri, in 1937, Ward was the son of a tailor and a mother who had him playing piano when he was wee. As a youth, Ward quit the piano and studied art on a scholarship at the University of Kansas. Then, he returned to music, trying out composing at the University of Missouri. Following a stint in Hollywood as a songwriter, Ward picked up jazz piano with Oscar Peterson in Toronto. Next, he journeyed to Arizona, where he published his first book in 1964. His next book, *Six Baha'i Poets*, appeared in 1966. This edited anthology included his own verse, but also that of his fellow African-American, the splendid poet, Robert Hayden, whose work—with its gorgeous imagery, ecstatic, symphonic lyricism, and homage to Black culture—Ward's own poetry resembles. Landed in Detroit in 1968, Ward, after seeing the city burn in a race riot, left for Quebec City, staying for two years. In 1970, *en route*, by ship, to Denmark to scrutinize piano, Ward was stranded by a dockworker's strike in Halifax, Nova Scotia. Here he met exiles from the recently assassinated village of Africville. (This experience inspired his writing of *Riverlisp*.) Bonding with this atomized community, Ward stayed in Halifax, writing and teaching, into the 1980s, and then relocated to Montreal, where he now lives and teaches, though he also maintains a home in rural Nova Scotia. His odysseys among art, music, and poetry, along with his steadfast adherence to the pacifism and the universalism of the Baha'i belief, inform Ward's *synesthesiac* æsthetic and his cosmopolitan attitude. Even so, his humanitarian vision is evinced squarely within a Black—really, African-American—cultural matrix as well as within a Black—usually, African-American—milieu. So, Ward's characters speak, sing, and think in a "Black" lingo that is soul food, soul music, and *spiritualistic*.

Ward's *arts* are displayed to advantage in *Somebody Somebody's Returning*. In this one-act, thirteen-scene, tragicomedy – or blues-spiritual, a girl, two women, and the spectre of a cross-dressing man must resolve the chaos and sorrows wrought by homophobia, anti-transvestitism, and philistinism. At base, its three female principals are beset by self-induced guilt that cancels their ability to love – and love fearlessly. This sin is, for Ward, the worst: the corruption of love by jealousies that interfere with people on the basis of gender, race, sexual orientation, and faith.

So, the play opens with Bertha Beatrice Little and her great niece, Najean, feeling estranged from Najean's mother, Roena Watts. In prison for the past seven years, Roena, having missed much of Najean's childhood, feels alienated from her daughter, but also fears that her Aunt Beatrice may have hijacked Najean's affections. True: Najean *has* rejected her absent mother; she has invented a friend in the phantom—or "figment of [her] imagination"—of Odell, her cross-dressing uncle, whom her mother stabbed to death during a fight. Too, Beatrice loves Najean as her own daughter, and she rues Roena's imminent return. While in prison, Roena loved another woman, Rita, and Roena feels guilty about it – just as she does for the death of Odell and her "distance" from her daughter. Najean also feels guilt, however, for her uncle's demise, a point that sparks her rage at Roena and her conjuring up of the playmate-spook, Odell. As Roena and Najean slough off their fears and reveal their true affections for each other, the invisible presence of Odell loses, writes Ward in his Notes to the play, "his clothing (a piece at a time) until near the end of the play, we find him "a man" and standing on the window ledge nearly nude with no facial features…. He then disappears." This play is pure, psychological complexity.

An allegory serves to establish the crises. In Scene One, Beatrice tells of having seen "Two sparrows... squat and squabbling in the cold, pecking the hell out of every spot come up available on the other till their blood directed their beaks – they bloodied the snow." The sparrows, of the "Same family," represent the truth that "Everything fights." So, the women here—especially Roena and her daughter—behave like the birds. Indeed, in Scene Four, Roena informs Najean, "It's so hard to talk to you... it's fighting of sorts." But Najean replies, "You know what I mean, it runs in the family – like confinement": Like "jailbirds," then, aunt, mother, and daughter are all imprisoned – by guilt and fear. Thus, the killing of Odell occurs, in part, because he is a "transvestite" who dressed up in front of Najean, thus angering Roena; but it also occurs because Najean enjoyed viewing Odell as her mother, a pleasure Roena felt threatened her maternity. If Roena had accepted Odell as a secondary mother to Najean, his death could have been avoided. Similarly, if Roena had dismissed social criticism of her "lesbian" affair with Rita – she would have let Najean visit her while she was in jail, thereby reducing—or eliminating—their mutual feelings of rejection.

One way out of such spiritual quandaries is to ask questions, even those punctuated with Ward's mysterious exclamation "!?!". But another way is to *listen* to inner voices, to *hear* the truths whispering and humming within, and then to give them utterance. Beatrice comments, in Scene Three, "the truth forces everything to come uncovered." To not speak out is, as Odell warns in Scene Eleven, "to send [one] to hell with... silence." Thus, Beatrice, Najean, and Roena must question, listen, hear, and, ultimately, forgive. This act requires the rejection of nihilism, of deeming anyone "nothing." (Significantly, these terms—*hear*, *listen*, and *nothing*—recur across this text.) Although the price of familial healing is his disappearance, it is Odell who asks the fundamental question: "Why do mothers teach their children to love so deeply... to become so attached, then punish them with misplaced rage and expect them to learn trust[?]" (Scene Twelve). The play illustrates this precept: To frustrate love is to create homicidal—or suicidal— "Disillusionment" (Scene Ten).

In *The Spirituals and the Blues* (1972), African-American theologian James H. Cone proclaims that slave spirituals record "The authentic community of saints... bound up with the encounter of God in the midst of a broken existence, struggling to be free." The blues are, in contrast, "existential," facing the nitty gritty of the here-and-now. In *Somebody Somebody's Returning*, Frederick Ward feels the blues—the pain and self-doubt—inside the spiritual – that struggle to be liberated by faith and love. Of course, he does it beautifully. Critics may continue to ignore such marvellous work, but that is no failure of Ward's. Rather, some of us need to address our own failures of vision and failures of nerve.

George Elliott Clarke is the author of *Odysseys Home: Mapping African-Canadian Literature* (2002), a critically acclaimed study of the literature.

Somebody Somebody's Returning premiered at the Centaur Theatre, Montreal, in February, 1988 with the following company:

ROENA   Barbara Barnes-Hopkins
NAJEAN   Cree Summer
BEATRICE   Rosanna Carter
ODELL   Graham Greene

Directed by Clarke Rogers
Setting by Andrew Lue Shue
Lighting by Alexander Gazale

— • — — • — — • —

CHARACTERS:
Beatrice: (58) Aunt to Roena, Najean and Odell; stout.
Roena: (38) The mother of Najean.
Najean: (15) The daughter of Roena.*
Odell: (25) The uncle of Najean; a transvestite; he was the brother of Roena; he is a figment of Najean's mind.
*Because Najean's father is not known, Najean may be ethnically different from the rest of the family.

TIME: The present.
PLACE: A large Victorian home.
NOTE: To be presented without intermission.
NOTE ON PUNCTUATION: Unitalicized dialogue in brackets means that the character is debating audibly with herself.

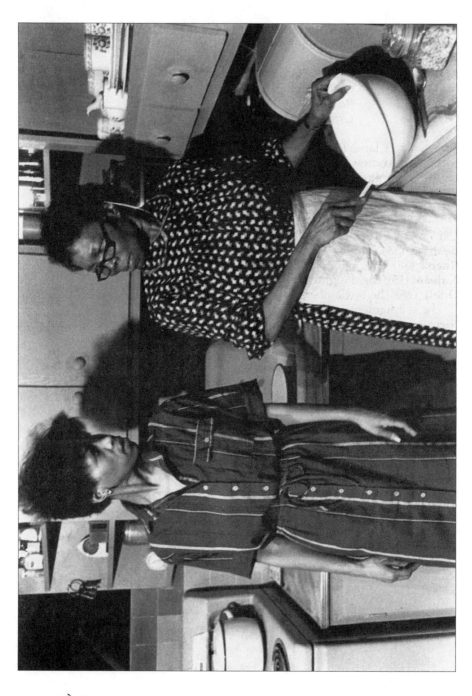

l to r:
Barbara
Barnes-
Hopkins,
Rosanna
Carter.

Photo by S. Colvey.

Somebody Somebody's Returning

by Frederick Ward

— • — — • — — • —

Scene One
THE PARLOUR. MORNING.

An upstairs room turned into a parlour with a prominent bay window. The walls border around an old flowery carpet on which is placed a wing chair, a lamp table with old lamp, a hassock, a hide-a-bed. Everything is covered with white sheets. BEATRICE enters the parlour to tidy it up for the arrival of ROENA. BEATRICE is dressed in a pink faded dress; scoots along in run-over slippers; she carries a bucket of water and some rags, and goes directly to the window; places the bucket on the floor before it. NAJEAN enters, sleepy and hesitant; she wears an out of style man's (Odell's) black and white checkered shirt opened down to the waist button and hanging out over her jeans; she wears dirty white tennis shoes; her hair is in a rag, yet she is still very beautiful; she carries some plastic garbage bags; crosses and places the bags on the floor.

BEATRICE
(*sighs*) This window… it will take three washings stead of one. (*She prepares by dusting the window frame.*) When I first moved into this old house (so many rooms) I was poor enough, with nothing but my husband James… him most always off on a speculation. (*She moves away from the window.*) I'd walk into an empty room (well, you know, it was like running round in a big backyard)—and I'd stop—and listen. (*silence*) Just listen.

NAJEAN
I am, Aunt Bea.

BEATRICE
No, not you! I'm not talking to you…. Well, where's the rest of the garbage bags, child?

NAJEAN
What you mad about/warn me when you're mad, will you!?! (*NAJEAN exits.*)

BEATRICE
(*shouts after NAJEAN*) Warn you… (*to herself*) Nobody warned me – Nobody.

(*She continues dusting the window.*) The first snow come'd, come'd-whoosh! (Nobody warned me)…. It swirled round the house…. All the circlings… *(an echo from inside her)* "All the circlings…" *(She shouts after NAJEAN.)* ALL THE CIRCLINGS, NAJEAN! drifts up over the windows downstairs – and the WIND! Oh, my to God, Najean! Curious…. You listening, girl? (My to God.) *(Pause; she shivers; waves it off; brightens, continues dusting the window; agitated, she moves away.)* I wandered through all these old rooms just listening to it… the wind pushing and sucking at the place… *(She moves to the window, looks out and memory startles her.)* OH! *(She leans, looks out the window; pulls back from it.)* Twenty years I was in this house before your mother came – brought you here. *(Pause; she moves away from the window; wraps herself in her arms.)* Two days I was in this room before she come'd (weren't insulation then, everything blowed through the room like the Union Station) I was cheered to recognize the chatter of birds and I went to the window to see.

My to God!
My to God

Two sparrows… squat and squabbling in the cold, pecking the hell out of every spot come up available on the other till their blood directed their beaks – they bloodied the snow. *(pause)*

Two sparrows! Same family.

Everything fights
Mymymy!
(Everything fights)

(shouting after NAJEAN) EVERYTHING FIGHTS, NAJEAN! I banged the window, "get-on way from here, hear?" *(resigned)* Who'd ever hear me? *(She reflects; returns.)* I ran downstairs, tried my door but the snow… *(Pause; she folds into herself, holds her shoulders, hums.)* It took a day and a half to dig me out… they had to shovel up to my door… the sparrows (so close to each other) I watched them freeze in their own blood, and… *(She swallows into a hum; NAJEAN enters carrying rags and a can of spray polish; BEATRICE mumbles aloud to herself; she regards the wing chair; shudders.)* Roena brought this on my house. *(She finishes dusting window; NAJEAN stands off from the wing chair staring at it; BEATRICE coming to herself and noticing.)* Well?

NAJEAN places everything she is carrying on the floor, yawns; BEATRICE yawns.

Oh, stop-it, girl – it's contagious. *(BEATRICE begins to uncover the lamp table, NAJEAN uncovers the hassock, sneezes, dropping the sheet to the floor.)* A good cleaner learns how not to sneeze…. You bring garbage bags for them dirty sheets?

NAJEAN finds a garbage bag, puts sheets into it; BEATRICE continues dusting table.

There's not too much dust. *(pause)* I'm up here ever so often.... Seven years – I dust... didn't want to lose your mother's spirit for tidy traits. *(She nearly breaks.)* Precious soul! *(a command to NAJEAN)* Thank God, she's coming home, girl.

NAJEAN's eyes are fixed on the wing chair; BEATRICE moves the chair, pulls the sheet away from it; underneath the sheet and seated is ODELL, dressed in drag – ROENA's clothes. (Note: He is an illusion; NAJEAN's projection of ODELL as she remembers him on the day he was killed by her mother.) BEATRICE does not see ODELL, nor will she. ODELL is primping himself.

Funny, this chair never takes on much dust... *(She dusts about it anyway; dust over ODELL; he hates it.)*

ODELL sits as if he were the only one in the room; he wears a brown wig of ringlets in the style of seven years past, a necklace of pearls over a knit sweater; acrylic-and-nylon warm weather white, elbow length dolman sleeved patchwork patterned pullover, a pull-on lined skirt in white, and a woman's casual pair of shoes also in white; he smiles at NAJEAN, she acknowledges his smile; BEATRICE notices NAJEAN's smile.

BEATRICE
You always did like this chair... your mother loved this room. She was proud of what she done with it. *(no response)* She worked so hard upholstering this old chair... stripping it – nights.

BEATRICE finishes the chair, moves away to the window, reflects out of it a moment; NAJEAN goes like a little girl and sits in ODELL's lap; they tickle each other's nose, kiss—a mother and child kiss—and hug; BEATRICE turns to the chair from the window.

BEATRICE
What a strange way to sit in a chair... maybe you'd better get off the chair. *(no response)* I mean it, Najean!

NAJEAN
(reciting, as a child, a poem about ODELL)
Flower will not fight
She is a spitter
The crest-moons in her fingernails
Rise into painted claws
But she only spits

It is her friend who will kill you
She has a cage around Flower
Flower thinks for her though
She sometimes spits with Flower
She kills
Flower carries flags:
Is a flag

ODELL throws his hands up waving them broadly and giggling along with NAJEAN.

BEATRICE
My goodness, child, what was that you saying?

NAJEAN
A poem...

BEATRICE
One you'll keep to yourself...

NAJEAN
...about a kitten – Flower was its name. *(ODELL purrs.)*

BEATRICE
(feeling guilty) I know I know, come on, help me... get off the chair (like that).

NAJEAN leaves ODELL's lap, helps to tidy up.

ODELL
(to NAJEAN) Tell her.

NAJEAN
(to BEATRICE) I don't want her back.

BEATRICE
What!?!...

NAJEAN
...I – I'm scared of her...

BEATRICE
You're afraid of her? Why? *(beat)* Roena's been keeping herself alive on the love she's got for you... a mother's love... a real mother's love you need.

NAJEAN
She ain't my mother! (She killed her.) *(ODELL laughs.)*

BEATRICE
You-so-full-of-hell-child. I could go to jail, myself, if it weren't for the Lord, Himself! *(She moves on NAJEAN.)*

ODELL
(to NAJEAN) Don't back off, go with it... see what'll happen!

NAJEAN
(to BEATRICE) Go on... I dare you.

BEATRICE
(measured) You-what...

ODELL's laughter becomes a roar.

ODELL
My! Girl! We can do some living together! Dare her again.

NAJEAN
I dare you!

BEATRICE
SHUT UP! *(pause)* You got a mouth on you worth slapping off. *(pause)* Why didn't you say these things a few days ago – I'd have hit you then and you'd have recovered by now. *(NAJEAN starts to speak.)* Uh-uh! Don't you say a word.

ODELL
You can't win this one, baby... back off. *(silence)*

NAJEAN eases off, picks up spray can, sprays the hassock and dusts it; BEATRICE begins a hum in herself which crescendos and is punctuated by her jerky dusting strokes as she continues; ODELL sits dormant in the wing chair.

NAJEAN
You know how I feel about that woman... *(BEATRICE exaggerates her humming louder.)* She never wanted me.... Never! Never let me come to the prison... never to come and see her...

BEATRICE
She never wanted you to set foot in that place/see her in there like that.... Affix that in your thinking about your mother... and, I kept my word to her... I didn't let you go. Blame me for some of it! (Kept my promise.)

NAJEAN
I still know she was there!

BEATRICE
Do you. *(beat)* Maybe it's just a figment of your imagination.

NAJEAN
Is she alive!

BEATRICE
What the hell are you talking about?

ODELL begins to primp himself again.

NAJEAN
She never sent me a letter.

BEATRICE
You've reduced her on that? *(pause)* I told you.

NAJEAN
Messages – from you. You might have made it all up.

BEATRICE
I'm a lie!?!

NAJEAN
...No. *(pause)* How come she never sent nothing?

BEATRICE
(cautioning) You asking me? *(They stare at each other; look away; continue cleaning.)*

> *NAJEAN follows BEATRICE, spraying and polishing after her; NAJEAN catches up to BEATRICE and hugs her around her waist from behind.*

NAJEAN
Womp-womp! *(They giggle; BEATRICE prouds-up into a hum; NAJEAN with the hum.)* You're me mama, Aunt Bea. *(BEATRICE wheels on her: a relentless wall of stare.)* ...My play mother... *(chagrin)* ...more or less.

BEATRICE
LESS!... a lot less... I ain't that much to you. *(pause)*

NAJEAN
Why are you staring at me like that? *(pause)*

BEATRICE
It's about the future. You?

NAJEAN
I'm staring at the adults.

BEATRICE
You a smart-ass child, Najean. Just like your Uncle Odell was.

ODELL
Well!

NAJEAN
Roena ain't no good!

ODELL
Good!

BEATRICE
Roena? Good! Good then.... Good... good.

NAJEAN
She ain't nothing.

BEATRICE
Then what are you!?! *(pause)* Get it out... get it all out.

NAJEAN
Unnecessary!

ODELL
Good – again!

BEATRICE
NAJEAN! *(silence)* Before God! you gathered a plenty to yourself. *(pause)* You want Roena perfect. *(pause)* You think a mother don't need you, child? *(pause)*

God-put-the-*lights*-in-your-breast for a mother who wanted you. Lord! they ain't the lungs of a slaughtered animal.... He ain't put life into nothing woke up hurt! And... *(BEATRICE moves away; from a closet she takes a carpet sweeper and begins to sweep the rug, humming through her next speech.)* I raised better than that... I ain't no mother to nothing like that...

NAJEAN
Don't cut me out, Aunt Bea.

BEATRICE
I ain't... I'm humming to brighten up the aspects of the spirit around us.

ODELL

I'm so pleased. *(pause)*

NAJEAN

She won't like me.

BEATRICE

Is that a hope?

NAJEAN

I don't care.

BEATRICE

Nonsense. Your mother loves you so... she's been improving herself in that place. I told her how much you've grown, how you study hard, and she's keeping up to you... learning new words, language, history and such, so she can have lots to talk over with you – impress you.

NAJEAN

What if I can't impress her?

BEATRICE

Hush, Najean. You sure got a lot of moves, girl. When the Lord gets you back, He's gonna study you. Come on, finish up here.

NAJEAN

How can I face her?

ODELL

You don't have to face her.

BEATRICE

Don't face her... just be beautiful before her. *(pause)* Najean... I won't ask you for too much... I would have hoped you'd have gotten some forgiveness in you over the years... but, it's too late to ask for an improvement of an impurity of heart... so, I just ask of you, that you be respectful of your mother while you're in my house. *(pause)* Come cuddle me, come cuddle me. *(They embrace; ODELL disappears.)* Just wait till Roena sees you... sees what a lovely child I've raised. She'll be hoppin happy honey!... Oh my God, the time. We ain't going to get to that window before Roena comes... *(They start to pick up things.)* No, you put the sweeper away, then help me gather up these things... we still got the kitchen to do.... She'll be hoppin' happy, honey! *(BEATRICE exits; calls back to NAJEAN off-stage.)* Come on, girl... your mother'll be here.

NAJEAN lingers, staring at the wing chair.

Scene Two
ODELL.

NAJEAN is alone in the parlour; she is having a flashback; she is twisting her hair into ringlets; ODELL appears, dressed as described but with no blood stain on his blouse; they begin to giggle together about ODELL's new outfit and the way he is modelling it; ROENA appears – she too is an apparition; ROENA is dressed in a hat and coat of a style seven years back; there is a tense pause and ROENA goes into a rage.

ROENA

(to ODELL) I told you not to dress up!... You swore! I held your hand on it... you didn't flinch but your skin scurried about, screwed up around underneath my fingernails just at the slightest touch (but you promised!). Your eyes did not move from my stare (but I knew it, and damn you). You promised not to dress up before my daughter! *(NAJEAN giggles.)* Why do you stand there giggling... those damned ringlets! *(no response)* I think you'd better leave the room awhile... go on... I want to talk to your uncle. *(ODELL bows, clowning; NAJEAN giggles again.)* Najean! I'm talking to you – leave this room. You're excused! *(ODELL folds his arms against ROENA.)*

NAJEAN

(folding her arms) No, I'm not. You can't make me. You can't excuse me for nothing I did.

ROENA

(to NAJEAN) Why you coming up against me like this? *(ODELL laughs; NAJEAN giggles.)* I mean it! *(to ODELL)* You've done this. *(to NAJEAN)* LEAVE-THIS-ROOM-NOW!

NAJEAN

I won't, cause you ain't my mama. *(She points to ODELL.)* If my mama says for me to leave, I'll do it.

Quick pause; ROENA looking from ODELL to NAJEAN.

ROENA

Oh-My-God! Dammit! I told you not to dress up... told you not to do it... *I'm* your mother, Najean!

NAJEAN

No, you're not! *(to ODELL)* Mama, Mama!!!

ROENA

Get over there! Get out of here, get out of here! *(no response)* You little bitch! *(She raises her hand to NAJEAN; ODELL grabs ROENA; she pounds him.)* You ain't fucking taking my child away from me like this!

ODELL hits ROENA very hard; she falls; charges back into him; he gets the upper hand; hurts her; she defends herself with a pair of scissors; stabs ODELL and they fall together into the wing chair before NAJEAN; they stare at each other as ODELL dies.

NAJEAN
(from quiet inner screams) Mama... Ma...?

ROENA
ODELL!?!... NOOOoooo... Odell, Odell... Odell... Najean, Najean, Najean, Najean. *(silence)*

ROENA rises off of ODELL; pulls the scissors from his chest; NAJEAN cannot swallow, she mouths a cry that will not come.

You go stand behind the door, Najean... and don't you sing none, neither... I don't want to be reminded of your sweetness while I'm mad at you – if you cry I'll tie you to your bed.

ROENA disappears.

NAJEAN
Mama... Mama... Mama... Mmmmmmmm.

Scene Three
THE PARLOUR. 10:30AM.

ROENA stands on the threshold of the parlour momentarily paralyzed; she is carrying a small suitcase and a raincoat draped over her right arm; she is wearing a sun splashed spring dress—early for the season—and low cut shoes to match; her hair is covered by a scarf; she is bearing up under fear, apprehension and the awkwardness of returning home. She takes a deep sigh, lowers her eyes; BEATRICE enters the kitchen quietly; takes a wrapped pot of flowers from a cupboard and places it on the table; she prayerfully gazes at the kitchen ceiling, listening for movement in the parlour.

ROENA
I hoped you'd let me in... room. *(pause; takes two steps in)* Please don't keep me walking along the edges of your carpet... room.

She takes two steps sideways, then steps further into the room; gathers her confidence; BEATRICE quietly unwraps the plant; she exits the kitchen, carrying the plant to the parlour.

Seven years... *(beat)* I wondered what you'd be like, room... *(She slowly raises her eyes, scans the room becoming alarmed.)* Oh, Beatrice – why?... Even the chair!

BEATRICE

(entering, cheery) Well… you are the centre of it. This room's missed you… needed your spirit. *(beat)* What you think?

ROENA

(beat) The neighbourhood looks the same. *(pause)* In the taxi over here, I wondered if the telephone numbers in my old book still worked. The driver said, "We're still the same around here. Nothing changes much…" except, the Jones family? *(beat)* He said they were gone – evicted.

BEATRICE

No better for them. Mean minded they were (no better for them). I believed all my life that's the way them people was like that. No better for them, Roena!

ROENA

I wonder if people will remember me with "No better…?"

BEATRICE

I expects…. Sorry, you'll get used to it – I have.

ROENA

I told myself, it would be like opening an old chest of drawers. I know what's in them…

BEATRICE

(simultaneously with "them") What's the matter, Roena? *(No response; she offers the plant.)* For you… *(ROENA does not take it.)*

ROENA

For all the living heart, Beatrice! Everything is the same!

BEATRICE

Why, yes. Walk around in the room – try yourself out in it.

ROENA

No wonder Najean wasn't here when I arrived, Beatrice, the memories it must keep for her.

BEATRICE

(simultaneously with "her") Honey, I wanted only to keep the memory of you for her. *(She takes the plant to her bosom.)* Keep your memory alive. *(She places the plant on the window sill.)* These'll get some sun here. *(pause)* Don't you like it?

ROENA

I'll have to change everything… the walls, a new table… everything – a new chair – yes.

BEATRICE

What's wrong with that chair... I washed it... I'm sorry. I – I truly am sorry, Roena, I didn't mean it. *(pause)* It's Najean's favourite piece up here...

ROENA

She comes up here?

BEATRICE

...It will be strange for her if you change it now...

ROENA

Does she often come up here?

BEATRICE

...She sit in it just this morning... cuddled in it... we were cleaning up here for you...

ROENA

DOES SHE COME UP HERE OFTEN!?!

BEATRICE

...It won't do for you to turn on me!

ROENA

What is it you been doing to me! *(BEATRICE hums, pause.)* Forgive me, won't you.... It's just that I meant to come back... not step back.... Do you understand? *(beat)* Won't you? *(pause)*

BEATRICE

You lost two that day, Roena.

ROENA

Yes. Odell... and my daughter?

BEATRICE

No...

> *The two women stare each other off; BEATRICE is disinclined to answer more; she continues to hum, and will hum a wall between them after each of her speeches.*

ROENA

For a moment Odell wasn't my brother... he was bad company for my child...

BEATRICE

Worryworryworry in my house...

ROENA
Please, Beatrice...

BEATRICE
A child in bad company, a mother will still pray. Bad company will make a good child go astray...

ROENA
You taunting me?

BEATRICE
...no matter what that child will do, mother will be grateful day and night...

ROENA
Beatrice, don't taunt me...

BEATRICE
...mother will say, "that child is mine..."

ROENA
You saying I disowned my child!?!

BEATRICE
...her eyes raised to the heavens, mother'll have her eye upon her child.

ROENA
Does she come up here often! *(pause)*

BEATRICE
There's something up here for her.

ROENA
WHAT! *(No response; BEATRICE continues to hum.)* Beatrice!?!

BEATRICE
I don't know – her cat got lost up here once. *(pause)* ...Even if she does, it's to be nearer to you – your spirit, in the room she done so much living in. She cuddled up in that chair this morning, I thought I seen you in it a moment... Najean sitting on your knee. *(beat)* It will be terribly strange for her if you change the room now – change anything in here. You'll see.

> *Silence.*

ROENA
What will I say to her... I had things... I've forgotten everything.

BEATRICE
(cheering) Just stare at her…

ROENA
Oh, Bea…

BEATRICE
Really. Be cheery. She wants to see that in you. Smell her… taste her.
(ROENA laughs.) I've seen people get happy over the *prospect* because
the taste was in their hearts. Oh, yes. The heart can taste things – it can.
Make you awfully happy…. Eat her up with your eyes, Roena. I have…
and tell her the truth… the truth forces everything to come uncovered.
(pause) Don't you feel a little silly?

> ROENA looks at BEATRICE questioningly.

You can put your wall down…. You been clutching that valise and your
raincoat ever since you came here…

ROENA
Oh. (She timidly places the bag on the floor.)

BEATRICE
Hang your coat in the closet, and change that dress. It ain't spring yet.

ROENA
Does she like me, Beatrice? I need her so much… I want to take my
place as her mother.

BEATRICE
Like I said, right this morning, she cuddled about you right there…
hugging and blowing kisses at you.

ROENA
Why didn't she stay, come up with us?

BEATRICE
She went to get you a present.

Scene Four
THE PARLOUR. MIDMORNING.

> ROENA stands looking out the window; she is dressed in an old dress
> from the closet. In the kitchen, NAJEAN holds a wrapped present;
> BEATRICE encourages her, in mime, to enter the parlour; NAJEAN
> resists.

ROENA
(in her thoughts) …Rita. (beat) Rita.

BEATRICE stares NAJEAN down; NAJEAN exits.

ROENA
...Rita...

NAJEAN hesitates at the doorway of the parlour before entering; hides the present behind her.

ROENA
...Rita. *(beat)* Oh, Rita...

NAJEAN enters. BEATRICE listens in the kitchen.

NAJEAN
Hi? *(beat)* We never started the windows.

ROENA shocked, turns quickly, swells with emotion, swallows wrong and begins to cough uncontrollably; NAJEAN looks at the floor until ROENA's coughing subsides.

ROENA
It's okay.... Forgive me... *(clearing)* Najean? *(She coughs again.)*

NAJEAN
I thought it would make you sick to see me.

ROENA
No, no, I'm fine... fine, dear. You could never make me sick.

ROENA reaches out to embrace NAJEAN who holds her off by giving her the present.

NAJEAN
It's for you. *(She looks at the floor.)*

ROENA
Oh!... I have nothing for you. *(They stare at each other; ROENA opens the gift.)* A scarf. *(miraculously)* ...A scarf!... It – it... it's so... nice! *(She models the scarf.)* I'll have to get me a new dress... one that's in style... and a present for you, too... tomorrow. *(No response; ROENA reaches out to touch NAJEAN's shirt; she pulls away; pause.)* I used to wear checkered shirts like that when I was younger. Your grandmother made checkered skirts and blouses for me. I remember the feeling... I used to feel checkered – checked. The checks used to jump up off my blouse at me when I looked down. *(She reaches for NAJEAN's chin; she moves away.)*

NAJEAN
Grandmother had a piano... I used to go with Flower over there to play it...

ROENA

Flower? *(no response)* What a pretty name...

NAJEAN

Grandmother liked horses and I like horses...

ROENA

She had pictures of horses.

NAJEAN

I adored my Grandmother. I wouldn't show off in front of her.

ROENA

You were never a show off... I remember your sweet little singing... little tunes with handkerchiefs after them.

    Silence. ODELL appears.

Your cat... Beatrice told me you have a cat.

NAJEAN

I was allowed a cat when I was twelve... because I loved cats so much.

    ODELL mimics the conversation.

ROENA

Your own cat... nice for you, eh?

NAJEAN

No one else was interested. *(to ODELL)* There was no talk at the table about it.

ROENA

Sometimes.... Yes – maybe?

NAJEAN

No. Never.

ROENA

But something of your very own... to keep you company... *(She looks around for the cat; calls for it.)* Kittykittykitty? Here kitty. What's its name?

NAJEAN

The cat died.

ROENA

Aw, girl, don't tell me that. What happened? *(pause)*

NAJEAN
(to ODELL) Flower? *(ODELL mimics a cat; prowls around.)*

ROENA
The cat's name?

NAJEAN
Yes. Flower. *(beat)* I didn't know what she had, so I got her to the vet, and he wouldn't take her…. He said she had some kind of infectious disease…. He gave me some pills for her. *(pause)* He should have put her to sleep, but he left her to die on me. *(pause)* She wasn't allowed in my room. Aunt Bea wouldn't have it for one minute.

ROENA
Why? My God, child… your little Flower… *(ODELL hisses at ROENA.)*

NAJEAN
Because Flower was sick and clogged up inside. *(accusing ODELL)* But *somebody* opened the cellar door and Flower dragged herself up to my room to die… I cried… and… and Aunt Bea got very annoyed with me. She said it was just a test…

ROENA
A test?

NAJEAN
…and I had better get over it quickly because I was going to get another one. *(imitating BEATRICE)* "Every capitulation…" *(ROENA joins in with her imitating BEATRICE.)* "…brings the next one nearer." *(NAJEAN continues.)* What does it mean?

ROENA
Trouble… through suffering. *(pause)* Your aunt believes in some strange form of purification.

NAJEAN
I talked about Flower so often…

ROENA
You kept its memory alive… that's normal… made up stories about it, I bet – with Beatrice, hum? *(no response)* You still like stories? *(no response)* You read a lot?

NAJEAN
I think Aunt Bea told me I like stories. She would read to me.

ROENA
I brought you your first real book… a lovely story… you loved it so much. I would read to you… uh-ah…

NAJEAN

I loved it? *(pause)* I remember I loved to read. I had a little flashlight and I'd read under my covers, or else, I'd... something... stuff! – a rug under the door so you couldn't see the light. Yes. I loved to read. *(pause)* It would bother you to read to me.

ROENA

You bothered the hell out of me to read it to you... bothered the hell out of me – till I did something wrong.

NAJEAN

I *liked* ringlets!

ROENA

Oh, those damned ringlets...

NAJEAN

I wasn't allowed my ringlets.

ROENA

You went and carefully tore out every page I read to you from that book.

NAJEAN

All I can remember is your voice... always comparing me to other children as inferior... I'd get discouraged, you'd get discouraged...

ROENA

I only wanted to make you aware of how nice you'd look in other styles...

NAJEAN

(taking the rag off her head) You haven't really looked at me.

ROENA

It may have been a mistake – the ringlets.

NAJEAN

No... I learned... I learned there was a certain way to act... that was drummed into me.

ROENA

LET'S... not talk about it.

NAJEAN

I know. One shouldn't find fault with one's parent.

ROENA

There's other things to learn, like… love… loving. *(silence)* I took a course in cosmetology. *(beat)* Maybe you'd find that interesting…

NAJEAN

You're still finding fault with me!

ROENA

No… no… *(an echo)* …no. *(She goes to the window, stares out.)* Come here…. Please. *(no response, pause)* You used to come up behind me and rub my stomach… you'd rub my stomach and you'd say, "How do you get this?" And I'd say, "This is called a plump lump," and you'd say, "Womp-wump?" …or something like that… and you'd try it again. You'd wobble about the room with your hands making a big stomach, and shouting, "womp-wump!" Then you'd run to me, you'd say, "Let me rub the womp-wump!" and you'd hug me, do all kinds of things… all to take my attention away from what I was doing – till I'd hush you.

NAJEAN

Really!?! I did those things?

ROENA

Then you'd cry. *(pause; stretches her arms towards NAJEAN)* I love you, Najean. *(NAJEAN avoids her; moves away.)* What does love mean to you!

NAJEAN

So many different things these days! Including – nothing! *(pause)*

ROENA

Is that it? Nothing?

NAJEAN

It costs you nothing.

ROENA

(lovingly) Najean. *(pause)*

NAJEAN

I think you *think* you love me…

ROENA

That was the substance of life for me in prison.

NAJEAN

You forgot me!

ROENA
I DIDN'T! I thought of you... but you are not what I imagined. *(Pause; she softens.)* I look at you.... Such strength.... You're beautiful... and you smell nice, too.

NAJEAN
Did you lose your sense of cleanliness while you were away?

ROENA
What?

NAJEAN
...It's not a ritual for me.

ROENA
What do you mean? *(pause)* I had a head full of notions this morning... a little talk... to get to know you – again. *(pause)* It's so hard to talk to you... it's fighting of sorts.

NAJEAN
You want me to fight you... so you'll have something to hang on to – not take care of... *(pause)* My love wouldn't suit you.

ROENA
Why would you say that? I want to take care of you.

NAJEAN
You found no one in prison to take care of?

ROENA
(measured) What are you saying?

NAJEAN
You know what I mean, it runs in the family – like confinement. *(ROENA slaps NAJEAN; she cries to ODELL.)* MAMA! *(NAJEAN breaks; ODELL comforts her; BEATRICE exits kitchen for parlour.)*

ROENA
You don't know nothing about me! *(She opposes herself.)* Nothing about me. *(pause)*

A week after I got into prison, I was so confused I forgot what you looked like. Beatrice brought me your baby photograph... I never had another picture of you.... That was my confinement. Beatrice said you were nervous after I left... your face, your hands were swollen... I dreamt it... I woke up shivering in my cell... and screaming, "I don't know what she looks like any more!" *(beat)* Beatrice said you got very quiet... I asked her what she meant... *(pause)*

The next time she visited me, she was quiet. Then she asked me, "What is it like to be separated from your daughter?" She asked it like she didn't know you... like she were interviewing me... "I don't know what my daughter's doing!" I told her. *(pause)*

That was my confinement. *(She drifts.)* I just want a chance to show my daughter that I love her and I want her – I said that to myself every day, late into the evening, the shadow of the cell bars lying on my lips, "I want her" before I could sleep, I said it a hundred times – To God, at first... *(She breaks.)* ...but He didn't believe me... for years!... and then I lost faith. After a while, *(to NAJEAN)* I had to train myself to trust that I could believe I loved you. You became everything I could hold in the cell – the bars! *(beat)* I kissed your face off the baby picture.

Had to make it up from then.... Made it up out of mine in a mirror... and I'd talk to you. *(beat)* While I sat on my bed. I'd take my chair, pull it with its seat pointing away from me... pulled the chair close up between my knees, and I'd fold my arms around its back, hug it, and talk over the back of it... "Oh Najean, Najean, sweet (sweet, sweet) Najean" ...I asked for your forgiveness. *(pause)* I played like every little privilege that they gave me in prison was a gift from you... I got stronger... and then I realized that God did believe me. He forgave me.... He made me stronger so I could suffer waiting...

Scene Five
THE PARLOUR: PREOCCUPIED.

BEATRICE enters.

BEATRICE
What's going on in here?

NAJEAN
(to ROENA) Who are you!? I don't know you!

BEATRICE
Najean! I begged you. *(to ROENA)* Roena?

ROENA
What does she know, Beatrice? She's fifteen, Beatrice! What does she know!?!

BEATRICE
What do you mean?

ROENA
She called you mama, you tell me. *(beat)* She hates me?

BEATRICE
I don't believe so. *(beat)* I've raised... *(apologetically)* She's been respectfully raised.

ROENA
Does she hate me? *(to NAJEAN)* Do you?

BEATRICE
She's preoccupied...

ROENA
Preoccupied?

BEATRICE
Preoccupied, Roena.... It's preoccupied, she is...

ROENA
With what? *(pause)*

BEATRICE
With death. *(ODELL sits in the wing chair; he is primping himself.)*

NAJEAN
Aunt Bea!

BEATRICE
I believe so.

ROENA
Odell's?

BEATRICE
No... not that poor child's. Lord! He was so self-absorbed he wouldn't notice his own death.

ROENA moves to the wing chair; grips the chair and pushes it out of position; ODELL does not respond to the push.

ROENA
DAMN YOU, BEATRICE! It's your keeping this room the same as when.... Why you keeping this room like this!

NAJEAN
(with BEATRICE) NOoooooooo!

BEATRICE
(with NAJEAN) I don't want to walk around in no empty room...

ROENA
(to NAJEAN) What the hell you yelling for!?!

BEATRICE
...can't afford to buy no new furniture for this room. (silence)

NAJEAN
(to ODELL) Flower!

ROENA
Flower?

ODELL
(primping his hat) It wasn't much – on sale.

NAJEAN
(to ODELL) It's ugly!

ODELL
Ain't nothing wrong with this hat.

BEATRICE
(grabbing her breasts; grunting) MMM! Mmm. Mm-mmm!...

ROENA
Flower?

BEATRICE
...mmmMmm... Mmm/mmm/mmm.

ROENA
Flower, Beatrice?

BEATRICE
Everything she loves that dies, she calls Flower... for a while, you were Flower.

ROENA
Me.... She thought I was dead?

BEATRICE
After you left, she'd invite me up here, say, "Come and see Flower." I'd come up and she had little piles of your clothes surrounding the wing chair. She'd say, "Mama's a flower, now."

ROENA
Oh, God... (pause) I always told you how I was... told you to tell Najean I loved her. You should have told her that... you were supposed to...

BEATRICE
Supposed to? *(beat)* I did.

ROENA
Well, then?

BEATRICE
(to NAJEAN, coldly) Your mother "is fine" ...your mother "loves you."
Seven years!

ROENA
I didn't say it like that!

BEATRICE
How was I to interpret it?

ROENA
I was fine! *(beat)* I thought Najean was happy. You told me she always
waited at the door for you to return (you to return)...

NAJEAN
(denying it) Aunt Bea!

ROENA
...always eager to hear from me, about me... asking you things.
(accusingly) What did you tell her, Beatrice?

BEATRICE
She heard things, Roena...

ROENA
What things?

BEATRICE
...things about women in prison...

NAJEAN
(fearful) Aunt Bea!

BEATRICE
...I was supposed to interpret that, too?

ROENA
(to NAJEAN) I never did nothing wrong! *(to BEATRICE)* You know how
much I love her.

BEATRICE

Her? *(Pause; ROENA and BEATRICE glare at each other.)* Najean needed much more. Not just a somebody somebody's returning. Something specific.

ROENA

Specific?!

BEATRICE

Yes... a letter, a note! You sent nothing specific – sometimes, nothing. It was left up to me... I'm the one that made *(beat)* that made a mother out of you, with cheery messages that would get me through my own front door and past *your* child.

ROENA

Nobody asked you to go that far.

BEATRICE

(measured) I told myself that it's what God would have me do.

ROENA

How did you interpret what she heard?

BEATRICE

With love.

ROENA

You blaming something on me, Beatrice?

BEATRICE

(to NAJEAN) Najean never sent you much, either.

NAJEAN

Oh, Aunt Bea.

BEATRICE

(to ROENA) The child's scared, Roena. *(pause)* I guess I mustn't blame it all on you. My sister...

ROENA

Mama?

BEATRICE

Your mother had something to do with it before she died. Scared the child.

ROENA

Don't you remember nothing on my mama for my daughter!

BEATRICE

Ask Najean… she remembers. Your mama told her something before she died – scared the child.

ROENA

What did your grandmother say to you, Najean?

NAJEAN does not respond; ODELL withers into an imitation of his mother.

BEATRICE

Something she didn't do what she was told. *(to NAJEAN)* Ain't you described that to me, Najean? *(no response)* Ain't it?

ROENA

Beatrice? *(no response)* What did my mama say, Najean? *(no response)*

ODELL

It's alright, girl… answer.

ROENA

Najean…

NAJEAN

If you hear me… *(mouths)* If you hear me… *(Her mouthing continues as ODELL takes over her speech.)*

ODELL

(imitating his mother) Najean, darlin, if you hear me crying in my room, come stand next of my bed all the time whilst I'm lying here… stay with me, even under the penalty of tight-red-gummed-round-the-necks-of-their-teeth hounds dragging you off… stay with me!

ROENA

Answer me, Najean!

NAJEAN

(taking over from ODELL) Don't want Beatrice's hands hesitating over my face, scooting air and brushing breath back into my mouth – checking to see if I'm dead or not… brushing breath what tickles the lips around your grandmother's mouth. You hear?

ROENA

Oh, my God.

BEATRICE grabs her own shoulders and rubs them rhythmically; hums.

NAJEAN
Flower?

ODELL
(as himself) It's okay… tell them.

NAJEAN
I never heard her crying.

ROENA
What is my baby talking about, Beatrice?

BEATRICE
She heard me crying (in your mother's bedroom) come stood in the doorway… *(to NAJEAN)* Over at your Grandmother's house. *(to ROENA)* She seen your mother touch me at my elbow and laugh up clots of blood onto my wedding band whilst wiggling her finger at the child. *(to NAJEAN)* Didn't she. *(no response)*

ROENA
Beatrice!

NAJEAN
I watched Aunt Bea polishing her own shoulders…

BEATRICE
Until dry dirt-wigglings lift up my fingertips. *(pause)* Then Najean rushed to a window, stuck her hands… cover-cupped held, out of the window like she had a bird in them… made a bobbin-up up movement and let loose… her palms spring-happy-spread as wings do, and pressed full-open up – gainst the window's frame, come to fists – burst-stretched into waving. I tell you, it was a *"taking leave…"* Something to it!

ROENA
Ridiculous!

BEATRICE
Ridiculous?

ROENA
Like the voices of old women.

BEATRICE
Ridiculous.

ROENA
Beatrice, my daughter's hurting and you talking about…

BEATRICE
(simultaneously with "about") Your daughter? (your daughter)...

ROENA
Yes. My daughter.

BEATRICE
...you don't know nothing. *(beat)* I'm talking about death, Roena, and that child hugging up to it.

ROENA
Najean?

> *NAJEAN runs from the room; ODELL disappears.*

Scene Six
APPLESAUCE CAKE.

BEATRICE is in the kitchen; she is preparing an applesauce cake; she has already put two cans of applesauce, 1 cup of oil and 2 cups of brown sugar into a sauce pan on the stove over heat; she turns on the oven to 350°; on the table is the following: a cup, baking soda, salt, two eggs, cinnamon, cloves, nutmeg, walnuts and raisins. She discards the empty applesauce cans in the garbage as ROENA enters; they exchange glances. BEATRICE takes a large bowl from the cupboard and sets it on the table; ROENA moves around the room but does not meddle with BEATRICE's cooking. BEATRICE gets two spoons from a drawer: one a teaspoon, the other, a large wooden spoon.

BEATRICE
(distracted) Well...

ROENA
Mmmm? *(pause)* Najean's sleeping.

BEATRICE
Almost very.

ROENA
What?

BEATRICE
You seem almost very occupied. "Very" if I weren't around and "almost" ceptin, you want to talk.

> *BEATRICE gets a large jar of flour, opens it, measures out four cups into the bowl, replaces jar.*

ROENA
Not necessarily… I was just thinking – private.

BEATRICE
Privately.

ROENA
Whatever.

BEATRICE
No. Get it right. *(She measures four teaspoons baking soda into bowl, puts soda away.)* What are you privately thinking about?

ROENA
…Odell.

BEATRICE
(putting a dash of salt into bowl) That could go on and on, couldn't it? *(She puts the salt away.)* Puts me in mind of a man in his car once… drove circles of tire ruts in the mud around the telephone pole across the street. *(no response)* Why you thinking so much about Odell? *(She measures out a teaspoon of cinnamon into bowl.)* Lord knows it's a trouble to you.

ROENA
Since I came back, I can't get him out of my mind.

BEATRICE
(puts away cinnamon) Tire ruts… same as the man in the car.

ROENA
I'm thinking of Najean, too! *(Pause; BEATRICE measures one teaspoon nutmeg into bowl.)* What's wrong with that girl… there's not much I believe in her.

BEATRICE
(puts nutmeg away) You questioning what I done bringing her up?

ROENA
No, it's not that. It's just something I can't touch in her. It's…

BEATRICE
(measures 1/4 teaspoon cloves into bowl) It's a sort of fraudulence which happens to be her mind's habit, otherwise, she'll have to face something.

ROENA
(agitated) What are you saying?

BEATRICE
(puts cloves away) She's like you.

ROENA
(through nervous laughter) You bitch.

> *BEATRICE stirs up bowl with wooden spoon; passes a dirty look at ROENA.*

BEATRICE
That language...

ROENA
I'm sorry. *(Pause; she seats herself; stares at floor.)* I just want a chance to show my baby that I love her.

> *BEATRICE cracks two eggs into a cup and beats them; sits the cup on the table and turns off the applesauce mixture on the stove; lets it cool a moment.*

BEATRICE
I can see that in you. *(pause)* I been standing in your shoes so long, I know you as myself.

ROENA
I appreciate what you've done. *(pause)* I can see you've taught Najean so much.

BEATRICE
Well, I didn't start out to... I didn't think of being a... teacher or anything. When I got Najean *(beat)* I started to reading more, writing more, and learning everything I could – developing myself. I tried to pass that on to her.

ROENA
I appreciate it. *(pause)*

BEATRICE
When you and Odell were little – four and five or so, your mother stood off from you, in the spring winds, and watched you play. She told me this: You were both playing with the wind – a near stormy day. You held your hands out in the wind *(imitating)*, grabbed at it, licked it off your palms and giggled at each other. You, Roena, held your hand out and patted the wind, then stood back and told it what to do. Odell'd *(imitates a bird in flight with her hands)* let his hand lean on the wind, lolling there as a bird does careening.

ROENA
(*amused*) Oh, Beatrice.

BEATRICE
Your mother say, that this sight of the two of you "set the character" of her children.

> One would be a flower,
> Prey to wind
> The other would tell the wind
> Where to blow the pebbles

You might think on that for the rest of your life, but let me tell you.... She seen that Odell, honey, was going to move throughout his life sleeping in the eye of a storm... and you were going to be the one to take care of him.

ROENA
What a hell-of-a-thing to say to me now.

BEATRICE
Well, you're being so occupied with him. (*beat*) When you're blocked and yet try to have your own autonomy and you take the initiative, it's very challenging. Ain't it?... I read that and memorized it. (*BEATRICE pours the applesauce mixture into the bowl; puts pan in the sink; stirs the mixture.*) It's a selfish thing occupying you, though.

ROENA
You making some mighty bad vibes for that cake.

> *BEATRICE adds eggs to mixture; stirs; adds walnuts and raisins; stirs.*

BEATRICE
That's off the subject. Ain't nothing wrong with this cake. But you might tell me what it is you think you lost. You been looking for it on the floor ever since you came in here.

ROENA
Me and my lady friend.

BEATRICE
(*moving the bowl away from ROENA as to protect the cake from a bad vibration*) So it was true.

ROENA
Come off it. You know nothing happened. Rita was close—real close—we made believe things. (*beat*) We started this morning arguing... the guards let her walk me to the door of the cell wing for sentimental

reasons... she come with me from our cell carrying my things. We passed the cell of a new woman inmate, and Rita leans my way, staring over me into the cell at the woman. She was standing in a... corner and looking down but Rita waves at her anyway... then we walked on. Rita starts telling me all the particulars about the woman. *(imitating Rita)* "Oh, that's Psittacine. Cute, ain't she." and all that personal shit about somebody... everything about the wallpaper in the bitch's cell, and I ask her, "Why you trying to fuck with me this morning – trying to fuck with my mind..." She kissed me hard then, then took me to the door in a mean silence. *(pause)*

  BEATRICE looks at ROENA questioningly.

She kissed me... I didn't have nothing to do with it. *(pause)* I can't tell my daughter I ain't been touched by another woman.

BEATRICE
Why you telling me this?

ROENA
This woman really fell in love with me, but I put her off – for years!

BEATRICE
It was selfish of you, wasn't it.

ROENA
Cause I had this strong love for my daughter? I wanted to come home pure to her.

BEATRICE
Seven years. *(beat)* Mmh! *(BEATRICE reaches for a 9 x 12 cake pan but ROENA gets it; gives it to her; pause; BEATRICE pours the cake batter into the pan; puts the bowl into the sink; she shakes the pan.)* Now, we have to be quiet in here... tip around, because the cake will fall otherwise.

ROENA
Oh, really.

BEATRICE
Yeah. *(beat)* You don't have to tip around... just don't make too much noise. *(She puts the cake into the oven.)* At nine we'll have cake. *(pause)*

ROENA
How do I get my daughter back? Can you help me? I did wrong. I've served my time – I've paid! I've got to get her back. How Beatrice? Shit!

BEATRICE
You mustn't discourage the child – that kind of language...

ROENA
My language is what I been living.

BEATRICE
Up to now.

ROENA
I ain't no scholar... I noticed you been talking over my head at times.

BEATRICE
You blaming me for something?

ROENA
You knew about them and never told me.

BEATRICE
Hush it! Najean and Odell – listen. The Lord took Odell. However it was done, it's done. I give you that, but you got to know something. *(pause)* You filled that child's head with so much trouble about a father she never knew, you scared her off from any man she maybe ever going to meet. From the moment Odell come into this house, the girl was terrified of him, and you closed your eyes to it – never acted like you seen it once. *(ROENA protests.)* Hear me out! I think that Odell, when he came to this house and you told him not to dress up like a woman, meant not to do it. He might have done it, but I think he would have taken it outside. What happened was, when he saw that Najean loved him one day when he was dressed up – it was an accident she caught him... went right into his room without letting him know she was coming... ran right up to him, hugged his legs... and from that day on.... Well, when he seen that... when he seen that that can happen... well... that's a great excuse for him to dress up.... She really loved him, Roena.

ROENA
I'm going upstairs.

BEATRICE
Go on... that might help.

ROENA exits; lights fade on the kitchen.

Scene Seven
THE PARLOUR. AFTERNOON.

NAJEAN and ODELL are sitting in the wing chair playing; it is the play of two friends – not mother daughter but that of a deep friendship – there is remembrance in their playing, familiarity and an enjoyment of each other: they chew on each other.

NAJEAN
Flower? Stop / stop – snuggle! *(They giggle.)*

ODELL
Oh, no, no, no…

NAJEAN
I love you… you're my only friend…

ODELL
To chew on…

ROENA comes, stands in the doorway to the parlour observing NAJEAN giggling and enjoying herself; ROENA enters.

ROENA
It sure is nice to see you laughing. *(A wall of fear confronts her; NAJEAN moves away from the chair.)* Oh, don't be scared…. *(pause)* You looked so happy – so wonderfully happy, I just wanted to… *(She moves to touch NAJEAN, who avoids her. Silence.)*

BEATRICE clears off the kitchen table for dinner and begins the preparations; listening for anything coming from the parlour.

ROENA
Don't cut me out… I need your love.

NAJEAN
You can't demand it.

ROENA
I considered it – honestly. *(pause)* I thought you'd want to hear that – know that.

NAJEAN
It's all or nothing with you.

ROENA
What is it you think I want that you ain't willing to give me? *(silence)* Say something won't you? *(no response)* I came back here with some fun

in me for you… *(pause)* I ain't got a thing to ask of you if you don't want it… I won't demand… but say something before my heart give out. *(silence)*

Is that demanding something of you! *(pause)* ANSWER ME GIRL!?!

Lights up on kitchen, BEATRICE has finished setting the table and is ready to serve dinner.

BEATRICE
Roena!?! Najean? Come eat… Najean, come eat.

NAJEAN rushes from the parlour; ROENA follows; lights out on ODELL and the parlour.

Scene Eight
THE KITCHEN.

BEATRICE stands at one end of the table to display her spread; NAJEAN rushes in and falls into a chair at the table; ROENA enters.

ROENA
It's a nice place-setting, Beatrice. Where do I sit?

BEATRICE
Here. *(to NAJEAN)* Now. Get up and let Roena sit there. *(beat)* Move it! And you wait till I tell you where to sit. *(ROENA sits; BEATRICE indicates an opposite chair to NAJEAN.)* Be seated here. *(NAJEAN flops.)* Afore God, you sit up straight to my table, girl. I made the table pretty for you too. You don't come in here and just flop yourself down. There's manners and a proper way to observe them. Did you wash? *(NAJEAN snaps her hands up; shows them, palms and backs.)* Washed? Huh!

ROENA
(to NAJEAN) Well, neither have I, Beatrice.

BEATRICE
You know better. Najean has to practice.

NAJEAN
You didn't do this before.

BEATRICE
Hush! *(silence)*

One of you say grace. *(They all bow their heads.)* Well? *(silence)*

ROENA
We never had to say nothing like that – all these years.

BEATRICE
(to Najean) I taught you something lovely to say – you remember it, Najean. *(No response; BEATRICE moves around to NAJEAN, puts a hand on NAJEAN's shoulder; prompts her.)* You remember. We used to say it together at first. *(no response)* Najean, quit fooling around, girl. *(no response)*

ROENA
You the mama now, eh?

BEATRICE
(measured) In my kitchen, at my table, in my presence... seven years... *(to NAJEAN)* You – say – it. *(pause)*

NAJEAN
Oh God... Oh God... this is a recording/this is a recording...

BEATRICE
(with ROENA) Child!?!

ROENA
(with BEATRICE) Najean!

> *NAJEAN runs from kitchen.*

BEATRICE
What's *wrong* with that girl?

ROENA
You tell me.

Scene Nine
THE PARLOUR, LATER.

> *ROENA enters; NAJEAN sits in the wing chair; the sun on her eyes; she moves to leave the room.*

ROENA
Najean... don't go just yet.

NAJEAN
I – I'm hungry... I think I'll... get me a sandwich... I...

ROENA
I want to tell you something.

NAJEAN
Is it something bad?

ROENA
No... I don't want to ever tell you something bad. *(pause)* You don't mind? *(pause)*

It's about your Uncle Odell. *(No response; NAJEAN appears not to know who she is talking about; ODELL appears.)* I think it's something we have to talk about... clear up... I mean... to get a new start, we need to be able to talk about this. *(pause)*

He was a nice person. I know you never heard me say much nice about him – about any man, but he was nice and I miss him...

ODELL
The closest I got to playing house was with her and a neighbourhood girl.

ROENA
I hope you believe that. *(no response)*

ODELL
They dressed up in our mama's clothes... decided to "take the baby for a stroll in the baby buggy..." I was the baby...

ROENA
He was always a homebody...

ODELL
No I wasn't! *(beat)* I didn't get out much.

ROENA
Well, he for sure didn't get out much. *(She contemplates.)*

ODELL
I was the baby. They stripped me down to my underwear, picked me up by my head and feet (hammock-style which tilted over the buggy) and pushed me/stuffed me into the thing while it lay on its side. Then they turned the buggy upright. They covered me with some old damp-dust smelling curtains and "strolled" me up three blocks of steep hill (which 21st Street was known for – big women would stop halfway up it). When they got me to the top of the hill, they turned the baby buggy around and pointed it downhill (in them high heel shoes, the "ladies" lost their footing and control of the buggy) and let it (me!) go.

ROENA
(*contemplating*) My God...

ODELL
Now, you got to remember that the cross streets – Wabash and Olive, had possibilities: car traffic coming opposite ways at any time. I was screaming and hollering, and as my mouth was in the wind, the hollering didn't come out right... sounded like I was (*imitating*) gagging... I was trying to twist-guide the baby buggy off the street. I got past Wabash and Olive streets safe enough... near the foot of the hill my twist-guiding paid off... I got just the right tilt on the buggy and it slid over on its side to the curb, hit it and stopped short/I come out flying... least ways, that was the flash I remembered... it left a slide-scar on my right wrist. One of them instances of luck, if you take my point.

ROENA
When Mama went out, he'd have to wait around, then go find her.

ODELL
Mama'd say, "Going shopping." Don't ask nobody (old woman!). Don't ask nobody. She usually end up in – about the park somewhere – mostly around the pigeons.

ROENA
Your grandmother liked gazing – called it shopping.... Odell was a very sensitive person. He worried every time Mama left the house.... He'd stay near the phone in case of trouble.... He feared she'd get lost or something.... Do you understand what I'm saying? (*no response*) Mama left the house everyday.... Odell was afraid to leave it. He got used to not leaving it.

NAJEAN
Was Grandmama a strict woman?

ODELL
Severe.

ROENA
Yes. She kicked both of us out of her house – but Odell had more to do with her than I did.

ODELL
(*rapidly*) I try to help her, she always want to go alone. I say, "Mama?" She always want to go alone.... It dampened my soul.

ROENA
Mama had him tensed up all the time – expectant. She'd get lost. (*She drifts.*)

ODELL
I look at my watch... I think: Mama, where's Mama? *(beat)* The park! *(pause)* She was so old the pigeons'd grab her cane... refuse to let her leave the park... I'd have to go get her... she standing there in hesitations... then hit at me when I try to take her elbow and lead her away – the damned pigeons up over us – I never liked parks.

NAJEAN
(to ROENA) Didn't you ever go find her?

ROENA
Once. *(pause)* Mama accused me of the most horrible treatment of her...

ODELL
(imitating his mother) "You given me a dry heart... ought to leave me-lone with my nature."

ROENA
...Right there in the park before... *(She drifts.)*

ODELL
(himself) Before whoever! *(imitating his mother)* "Spider-webs covers cracked ice here where there once was a river for you!"

ROENA
...EVERYONE! She accused me... before everyone.

ODELL
She accused me! She did!... did that to me! I talked back to her.

ROENA
Mama said, I'd carry everything I'd done in this world into the grave with me for my back talk.

ODELL
She said that to me... it was my back talk.... She'd say *(imitating his mother)* "Celestial Opportunity! That's what you gonna pay for your oppressive opinions – your dwell-in-a-rock commentary!"

ROENA
We walked along (walked along) walked alone... wasn't any pride in my walk... a few steps and I looked as old as she. I'd reach out to take her elbow and she'd shout...

ODELL
(imitating his mother) "Listen!"

ROENA
Listen!

ODELL
(imitating his mother) "Do you hear me?!"

ROENA
The whole damned neighbourhood wants to hear!

ODELL
(imitating his mother) "Give me my elbow! Give me my elbow!"

ROENA
(breaking) She'd shout...

ODELL
(imitating his mother) "Do-you-hear-me!?!"

NAJEAN
Yes, Flower!

ROENA
What?

NAJEAN
Oh! Nothing – what?

ROENA
She'd shout, give me my elbow...

ODELL
(imitating his mother) "I'm so pleased." *(He hums a gospel.)*

ROENA
...and she'd walk on ahead of me.... Mama would hum a homemade gospel. *(She wanders into humming gospel to herself.)*

ODELL
I'd hum along once I knew where she was going with it. *(He hums.)*

ROENA
By the time we would reach our front porch step, she'd softened. *(She hums.)*

ODELL
(imitating his mother) "There ain't all hell in you, is there. Here, take my elbow and assist me into my house." *(As himself, he shouts to the heavens.)* YET LIFT ME UP!

ROENA
(a bitter echo) Yet lift me! *(pause)*

Scene Ten
THE PARLOUR, A MOMENT LATER.

ROENA
Mama had a wonderful way with a word. She knew how to use it.

ODELL
(imitating his mother; will say word throughout ROENA's speech)
"Disillusionment. Disillusionment. Disillusionment."

ROENA
She'd say it as a mask up to you... dressed herself in it... and me...
she'd accuse me with it/of it... try it out on me to see if I'd fit it—am
it—cared about it, and she'd say it as one of her own: a testimony to
survival...

ODELL
(seating himself) Never wanted nobody to come and take that word
down from her. *(imitating his mother)* "Look at the way you dressed,
enough to bring disillusionment on the Lord."

ROENA
She'd put power into any old word like...

NAJEAN
(simultaneously with "like") Disillusionment?

ROENA
Yes. *(beat)* Strange you'd come up with that word. Mama held that
one up against Odell the day she caught him dressed up in one of her
dresses – said it the same as she'd say the Saviour's name...

ODELL
(holy) Oh, Disillusionment!

ROENA
...with a halo about it.

ODELL
(agitated) Her plants would shudder after she'd pass. And she'd give
you nothing to talk on. *(imitating his mother)* "Sorry to come after you
you know... if you don't jiggle the toilet stool handle, the darned
thing'll let the water running all day." *(as himself)* She know I know
this... but think about it: standing in that bathroom, holding my breath

among the vapours, waiting for the right moment to jiggle the toilet handle, when all she had to do was get it fixed. *(imitating his mother)* "HELP ME!" *(as himself)* Got her finger in my face. *(imitating his mother)* "Help me! to keep a house so you can have some place I live in." *(as himself)* Oh, I can't stand it! I fix something, she say, "I don't like that that way" I say, you will when you get used to it – she change it. Take away any power I have – it hurt!

ROENA

(simultaneously with "hurt!" while addressing the wing chair where ODELL died) Why did you dress up?!

ODELL

(beat) TO BE WITH MAMA! *(pause)*

ROENA

She took a lot away from him – what she did to him. *(pause)* Mama would have trouble getting buried if he owned the earth.

ODELL

I wouldn't give her dirt.

ROENA

Oh, Mama.

Scene Eleven
A LONG SILENCE.

ROENA

Najean, we got to leave here.

NAJEAN

(to ODELL) I don't want to leave…

ODELL

You don't have to. Stick up to her. Do it yourself. *(ODELL disappears.)*

NAJEAN

(to ROENA) I don't have to…

ROENA

We got to…

NAJEAN

I don't got to do nothing. *(beat)* Don't you tell me what I have to do. You come here bringing *mother* to me like you somebody!

ROENA
Najean, I-am-somebody… and don't you forget it! *(beat)* I know my leaving was like a jumping off the bridge for you…

NAJEAN
(bitterly) No it wasn't!

ROENA
What are you saying? *(pause)* So it wasn't. *(silence)*

NAJEAN
(needling) Where did you really go – where where where where?

ROENA
You know where I was!

NAJEAN
I was told.

ROENA
Don't do this, Najean.

NAJEAN
Don't do what?

ROENA
Don't put a wedge between us.

NAJEAN
Like my father?

ROENA
Your father?

NAJEAN
Where did my father go?

ROENA
He was as much a mystery to me…

NAJEAN
You knew him well…

ROENA
No, Darlin…

NAJEAN
(simultaneously with "no") In the beginning he was here.

ROENA
He was never here...

NAJEAN
He was silent...

ROENA
You're the only way I have of knowing he was real...

NAJEAN
You had so much bad to say about him...

ROENA
I made it up! *(pause)*

NAJEAN
I remember sitting at the kitchen table...

ROENA
(relieved) You were so tiny then.

NAJEAN
...and I had propped my head up so that my eyes and chin rested on my fists where they gripped the table top...

ROENA
...Everything, so tiny.

NAJEAN
...and asking you, who the man was sitting at the other end of the table.

ROENA
Oh, Darlin...

NAJEAN
It might have been a figment of my imagination...

ROENA
NO!

NAJEAN
He *was* here. He was silent... and I was afraid of him.

ROENA
That was Odell, Baby.

NAJEAN
Who is Odell?

ROENA
(*shook*) Odell? – Odell, your uncle, my brother – your Uncle Odell. When he first came here to live with us... you were afraid of him.

NAJEAN
He was here! Did my father rape you?

ROENA
NAJEAN!

NAJEAN
Is that how I got here?

ROENA
(*weakly*) Who the hell are you asking?

NAJEAN
(*demanding*) Is that how?!

ROENA
STOP IT! STOP IT!

NAJEAN
He did rape you.

ROENA
(*breaking*) NOOOooooo, NO!ooooo...

NAJEAN
(*simultaneously with "No!ooooo"*) He did he did he did!

ROENA
...oooo.... No, no he didn't, Najean! Your father was never here.... Who told you this.... Are you making this up.... Why are you doing this?

NAJEAN
How am I to know you didn't kill him! (*pause*)

ROENA
GET OUT! GET OUT OF HERE! (*She turns away; NAJEAN rushes and hides behind the door; pause.*) I never knew who he was.... He was like many men who come to the party – looking... all dressed the same, all with the same face... their tongues matched their eyes – only he held a mask before his. (*She goes to a closet; takes an old dress out of it; smells the dress; hugs it to herself and stands rocking herself.*) I never knew if you a working man... cause you dressed so nice on Saturday, on Saturday you dressed so nice.... A preacher maybe... or what my mama warned me of: one of them men that takes care of women that pass them their

money... I never knew cause you dressed so nice.... Is you a student?
I asked myself that cause Saturday you off, ain't you?... Dressed so
nice.... How were I to know?...

BEATRICE enters.

BEATRICE
(whispering) Roena... what's the matter, child.... What's all this noise?

ROENA
(not responding to her) I couldn't form more than the thought: "You
touched me...." The whole week it repeated itself in me... and rubbing
my stomach is as close as I come to where I was stirred. *(BEATRICE
moves about her.)* My dress have the cleaner's smell in it off your suit
where you pressed me – it caused me to stop crying – middle of the
week. *(ROENA sits on the hassock; BEATRICE reaches to touch her but does
not; ODELL appears.)* I noticed it when I were sniffing up.... Never knew
the cleaner's smell to be so pretty... so nice, on Saturday it were so nice.
(pause)

Mama caught me gazing through the week... I put some vinegar on my
dress but she smelt you in it anyway.... Mama grabbed me to her
bosom and rocked me, say... *(She mouths ODELL's speech with him.)*

ODELL
(imitating his mother) Do he dress nice?

ROENA
Oh, yes Mam, he do...

BEATRICE
What, child... Roena?

ODELL
(imitating his mother) And what he do? *(silence)* Don't you try to send me
to hell with your silence!

ROENA
OHhhhh...

BEATRICE
Oh, Roena... Lord, bless this swollen soul.

ROENA
I sit between Mama's knees and whilst she braided my hair, she sneak
a play whiff of you off my dress for us to share in a giggle together...
I stop... and she stop... she join in in my gazing... *(BEATRICE hums.)*

ODELL
(*imitating his mother*) I raised better.

ROENA
(*gazing*) I dreamt a postcard from you... show it to my mama... it pictured a tall tendrilled passiflora, and say on the back: You seen it – thought of me.... It's enough – when you're far away, where you are – seen it, thought of me. Mymymy. And I thought of you, where you seen it – Mexico, I imagines...

ODELL
(*imitating his mother*) You're no good – no good...

ROENA
I had the baby... but I ain't named her at first. Mama seen her – thought of you...

ODELL
(*imitating his mother*) What kind is it?

ROENA
Fixed it in her Bible, say... (*mouths ODELL's speech thinking of NAJEAN*)

ODELL
(*imitating his mother*) I should have watched you more closely.

ROENA
...she like her...

ODELL
(*imitating his mother*) I don't care no more/you ain't no daughter of mine/and I want you out of my house.

ROENA
...say, she don't care no more... so, when you come home, she won't mind you visiting. (*beat*) I tell the baby, every day, a name for you – but I forgot your face, ceptin, for her first smile: I seen it – thought of you. (*beat*) Mama and I, both bothered, trying to figure: "maybe he a preacher...?"

BEATRICE
(*mouths: a preacher?*) A preacher maybe, Honey.

ROENA
(*not responding to her*) He dress too nice.

BEATRICE
You sure?

ROENA
Yes, Mam.

BEATRICE
You never know.

ROENA
No'M...

> *BEATRICE embraces ROENA bringing her back to herself in a slight start.*

BEATRICE
Don't put a worry with it no more. The hurt will pass.... Oh Roena, you had so much trouble with a man you never know'd.

ROENA
You never knew Uncle James all that well.

BEATRICE
(a reproach) Bertha-Beatrice-Little is *my* name.

ROENA
I have a name, too!

BEATRICE
Whose? *(pause)*

ROENA
I'm sorry... I don't want to be cruel...

BEATRICE
DON'T BE! *(beat)* I was loyal to James Little – I was! *(pause)* He was 40 – I was 22. *(pause)*

My husband wanted to be important... invited important people for dinner... preachers, lawyers, *in and out of business* men... hustlers of all types – even pimps! He argued with none of them – believed none of them. *(pause)*

I had to make dinner... I'd never cooked for more than two. *(pause)* The first night *important* people came to dinner, I was... terrified. Dinner was to be *arranged*. He requested that of me. I phoned "Madam Dulcinea's Oven" for a delivery... she suggested, and I purchased snails for dinner... they came pre-prepared, all in shells, with garlic – and buttered, in open egg cartons covered with cellophane... I pre-warmed my oven and set the snails on top of the stove... went, and sat dutifully by as the men talked. They rooted about for conversation to begin with, but as the wine twisted their heads, their talk turned from posturings to bold strokes and words of prey—*this* business deal and that deal—great laughter forced the room… iced the eyes and mouthed the mouths in the portraits I'd hung on the walls – I looked away from them… onto arrested smirks (muh!) the *important*. My husband summoned dinner, "Is it ready, Darlin?" …I went to the kitchen–

> MY TO GOD! (My to God)
> Holyholyholy!

The snails were loose! Oozing up my walls – I know'd nothing about them being alive! I panicked… but then I thought, "What the hell," and I invited the *important* into the kitchen, "Gentlemen, your dinner is on the walls. Help yourselves!" Well, that broke the ice… we laughed for real… those men danced around their own laughter, picked the snails off the walls – and I had a great idea – we tripped out the back and off the porch, through our yard to next door and danced – spread the snails in the neighbour's garden – what a night! *(pause)*

For twenty years I *arranged* dinner – our home was always filled. Then, when my husband was 62, he said I wasn't important and left… I was 44.

ROENA
Beatrice.

> *BEATRICE and ROENA embrace; NAJEAN comes from behind the door; stares at the two women.*

NAJEAN
(a whisper) Mama?

> *There is no response; BEATRICE and ROENA hold their embrace; ODELL moves to NAJEAN; his facial features are nearly gone.*

ODELL
Most likely, it's *(hissing)* Miss.

> *NAJEAN backs back behind the door; BEATRICE leads ROENA and seats her in the wing chair; comforts her; gestures to her to rest; she covers her with the raincoat ROENA has brought home with her; BEATRICE exits; ROENA sleeps; ODELL takes the raincoat off ROENA and puts it on; he moves to the closet, gets and puts on a pair of high heel shoes, and primps.*

Scene Twelve
SUNSET.

ROENA sleeps in the wing chair; NAJEAN comes from behind the door; ODELL's facial features are gone; underneath the coat he wears only undershorts.

NAJEAN

(*whisper*) Miss? (*no response*) Miss? (*She takes a step into the room.*) Miss? (*no response*)

ODELL

(*primping*) You know how I love to sit before the window in the afternoon sun...

NAJEAN

Miss? (*no response*)

ODELL

...and feel my clothes heat up around my body...

NAJEAN

Miss? (*no response*)

ODELL

(*a gesture in ROENA's direction*) Well... we're out of place here. I didn't want to sit there anyway.

NAJEAN

Miss? (*no response*)

ODELL

Besides, there's things on the window panes – tiny patina things...

NAJEAN

Please, Miss...? (*no response*)

ODELL

There's screams on those window panes... fear confusion implication admission guilt...

NAJEAN

(*struggling*) Mam... (*No response; she reaches to touch ROENA; does not.*)

ODELL

I don't want to sit in the window any more – not alone.

NAJEAN

Ma…. Ma… *(no response)*

ODELL

We're taught to love by our mothers…. Mama taught me love…. I got so attached to it…. Papa… hated me. Mama hated Papa for it, hated him so much he ran off… one day, she punished me.

NAJEAN

Miss, don't punish me…. Mmm… mmmmm…. Miss.

ODELL

(imitating his mother) …Going to teach you! What have I given birth to? *(himself as a man)* Why do mothers teach their children to love so deeply… to become so attached, then punish them with misplaced rage and expect them to learn trust – She was caught there pinned to the floor with emotion, raging and trying to send me "beyond this land!" *(beat)* I was six!…

NAJEAN

I was eight.

ODELL

…and she'd caught me wearing her best dress… she'd never wear it! *(imitating his mother)* Never-had-the-opportunity-to-wear my own dress! *(pause; himself)* She wrenched herself free from the spot, grabbed, tied and gagged me to a chair… tipped it backwards and dragged me into the closet…

NAJEAN

Miss? *(Beat; ROENA stirs but does not awaken.)* Miss, the happiest moment in my life was when I'd go to bed and you would tuck me in – then I'd feel safe.

ODELL

…closed and locked the door on me…

NAJEAN

I didn't kill him…. It wasn't my fault. You said you'd tie me to the bed for the rest of my life!

ODELL

…A thing like that breaks you with the world.

NAJEAN

It was my fault? *(no response)*

ODELL
I never felt loved again.

NAJEAN
(*resigned*) It was my fault.

>   *ODELL removes his shoes; climbs onto the window shelf; opens the*
>   *window and looks down; stretches and takes off the coat in a mood of*
>   *celebration; folds the coat over his arm.*

ODELL
Come on... you're better off with me... me and you, girl... (*NAJEAN*
hesitates then goes to the window.) Come on! Look down there... the earth
so flat, and the sky so flat against it.... It's all sky.... So close you can
spit on it – and it will drip back on you before you can duck. (*They*
giggle together; it eases off.) Bullshit! COME ON!... With you I want to
mirror love – all I can remember... can you remember?

NAJEAN
(*lovingly*) Flower.

ODELL
(*extending a hand*) Come on, it's alright... it's like... standing on a
precipice, wind-dizzy-dared and prickly, eh? – knowing you can fly!...
for a second... for a second.... Girl, you can walk out of this world...

NAJEAN
On a second? (*They giggle.*)

ODELL
Yeeeessss, a second called...

NAJEAN
Love?

ODELL
Un-uh.... Trust. (*pause*)

NAJEAN
Wait.

>   *ODELL further extends his hand to NAJEAN; she half takes his hand*
>   *and grabs the coat off his arm; is half pulled up onto the window shelf but*
>   *slips backwards from ODELL's grip, and keeping the coat in her hand,*
>   *accidentally kicks over the potted plant on the shelf waking ROENA up;*
>   *ODELL disappears.*

ROENA
Najean! What are you doing, girl?

NAJEAN
I – I wanted... I'm cold. *(pause)*

ROENA
You have my coat... *(She closes the window, pause.)*

NAJEAN
I'm sorry.

ROENA
Should you be? *(pause)*

NAJEAN
I wasn't doing anything with it...

ROENA
Put it on. *(pause)*

NAJEAN
I don't need it. *(She puts the coat down.)*

ROENA
You said you wanted my arms about you.

NAJEAN
I did?

> *ROENA opens her arms and bids NAJEAN to come to her.*

ROENA
I did... *(pause)*

> *NAJEAN avoids ROENA; puts on the coat; models it like ODELL would have.*

ROENA & NAJEAN
It doesn't fit. *(pause)*

NAJEAN
(with ROENA) Aunt Bea...

ROENA
(with NAJEAN) It's not...

A great burst of nervous laughter from both; ROENA slides out of the laughter.

ROENA

It didn't fit me none neither... it ain't mine.

NAJEAN

Oh? *(pause)* Whose is it?

ROENA

Give it here. *(NAJEAN hesitates; takes the coat off; hands it to ROENA; she puts it on.)* It's Rita's coat.

NAJEAN

Rita?

ROENA

...In jail, Rita. *(She adjusts the coat.)* Muh. You really don't know about it, eh? *(No response; ROENA hugs herself in the coat.)* She gave it to me.... You see, it doesn't fit. *(spreads the coat like bird's wings)* I'm free of her. *(She takes the coat off; puts it down.)* Rita's hair hung about her ears like dead leaves that hang on throughout the winter (she didn't care). *(beat)* "What colour is your hair, Rita?" I'd say that and she'd say, "It don't have no colour in here," and I'd try helping her to keep it up... combing it... I'd say, "It looks to be blond to me." "Once," she said. "You ought to know the colour of your own hair, Rita. What colour your eyes" ...and she'd take my hand off her hair, pull it down about her brow and say, *(sensuously)* "In darkness, I'm dark-eyed, Mama..." *(beat)* "I have a daughter at home, Rita Faye Wright!" ...and I'd go get you in my memory, Najean.... It's like, if I got into church, Dracula wouldn't come in. *(pause)*

You sucked a lot off me today, girl. *(pause)* You want me to comb your hair? *(no response)* Rita? See, Rita!

NAJEAN

It's so...

ROENA

Rita, I can't even comb my own daughter's hair!

NAJEAN

It's so hard...

ROENA

Then, it's not a good time to visit me!

NAJEAN

You're not in prison!

ROENA

How would I know!?! *(beat)* It's the same doing without. *(pause)* You're still here, Najean.... Why? What do you want with me?

NAJEAN

Nothing!

ROENA

Then fuck it, Najean! *(beat)* Maybe you think I've come to visit! See you high on top of it! *(pause)* It seems to me you're the type that climbs the high dive to show how independent you are, struts out to the tip of the diving board and vomits off it!

NAJEAN

VOMITS?

ROENA

Yes, vomits!... You fuck the pool up for everybody. Then you turn and ask everyone on the ladder behind you to step down while you descend... *(pause)*

NAJEAN

I – I'm sorry...

ROENA

Then you say, *I'm sorry. (pause)* I knew a woman in prison like you... sorry... loved loneliness, sit with her chin in a palm.... She had one fish... referred to it as *Him*.... You'd go to her cell to see her, you'd visit the fish... the damned thing lay on the rocks at the bottom of the bowl, and she'd spit at it – chin-in-her-palm-spit at it. Laugh every time she'd hit the bowl. Are you laughing at me, Najean? *(no response)* I ain't no fish bowl for you, girl! *(no response)* You laughing at me! *(no response)* ANSWER ME! *(no response, silence)*

Must I go on paying? *(beat)* Answer me! *(no response)* If I knew your lousy, f'n father, I betcha I'd know your answer.... It's him you take after.

NAJEAN

How would you know! You don't even know him.

ROENA

He might have come back if you hadn't come. *(beat)* I – I'm sorry.... Please forgive me. *(pause)*

NAJEAN
You blame me for that.

> *ROENA looks at her questioningly.*

Blame me, blame me!... same as for Flower. You blamed me for
murdering Uncle Odell!

ROENA
Oh no.... Nooo... *(beat)* God, no.... Baby?

NAJEAN
DON'T TOUCH ME!

ROENA
You been carrying that around with you all this time?

NAJEAN
You sent me behind the door.

ROENA
I – yes – I did – but...

NAJEAN
It was my fault!

ROENA
NO! I told you...

NAJEAN
You said, "You go stand behind the door, Najean, and don't you sing
none neither... I don't want to be reminded of your sweetness while I'm
mad at you... if you cry, I'll tie you to your bed."

ROENA
I never meant to blame you... why did you think I meant to blame you?

NAJEAN
Whenever I did something wrong, you'd send me behind the door. You
said long-suffering guilt was better than a beating.

ROENA
THAT WAS TO TEACH YOU SOMETHING!... It's not what I meant
then.

NAJEAN
It ain't true!

ROENA

Well, for a moment, maybe I did… but not for always… I sent you behind the door to spare you the sight of Odell's dying.

NAJEAN

After I'd seen it?

ROENA

I was ashamed of what I'd done!

NAJEAN

Ashamed!?!

ROENA

Yes…

NAJEAN

IT WAS MY FAULT!

ROENA

What / wait…

NAJEAN

It was my fault.

ROENA

I did it… I did it… Najean? *(pause)*

NAJEAN

It was my fault… I didn't want you to be mad at me… I didn't want you to be hurt… I don't know why, but it was my fault.

ROENA

STOP-IT, GIRL! STOP-IT, NAJEAN! *(pause)* It wasn't your fault. *(pause)* Not you… ME. *(pause)*

You were stolen into my life by a man we'll never know… I filled that blank with a dream of what I was going to make of you – a pretty little thing – and PRIVATE! *(beat)* to keep you a mystery to men. *(pause)*

Then Odell was going to steal you away from me… steal my dream, and I liked him, Najean… as I thought he was a thief, I – killed – Odell. *(pause)*

Beatrice said I lost two things that day… I thought it was Odell and you she meant… but, I've realized that I lost myself… I lost confidence. *(pause)*

It ain't your fault, baby... Najean, I swear it—God, surround us and make us sweet again!—it ain't your fault. I became a thief... I stole time from you.

NAJEAN
Oh, Mama... Mama... *(They embrace.)*

ROENA
I wish I had lived with more confidence... taken more chances... had less pride... you'd have had a father... I was pretty enough. *(pause)*

I tried to have you thinking of me while I was gone... I'd tighten my eyes and think hard on your name... Najean, Najean, Najean...

NAJEAN
I felt it... but it didn't last.

ROENA stands NAJEAN back from her; stares at her as if this were the first time she'd seen her; NAJEAN is embarrassed.

ROENA
Beatrice says I should just look at you... taste you... eat you up with my eyes... *(pause)* Oh, Darlin. I need time, Najean.... We need time... we need time. *(pause)* Thank you, Najean. *(pause)* Thank you, God... thank You.

Scene Thirteen
THE PARLOUR, 9PM.

BEATRICE enters the parlour carrying a tray containing three plates and three forks; a piece of applesauce cake on each plate; ROENA and NAJEAN are still in an embrace.

BEATRICE
It's nine o'clock.

ROENA
Oh, Beatrice...

BEATRICE ignores them; goes to the window and puts the tray on the window shelf; she notices the flower pot mess on the floor; ROENA and NAJEAN wipe their eyes and otherwise straighten themselves up; BEATRICE picks up the pot pieces and flower, putting the flower back into the pot; places it on the window shelf again; wipes her hands on her dress.

BEATRICE

This girl never finishes a thing…. It's gonna rain… *(She picks up two plates with forks.)*…probably clear off in the morning… *(pause)*

Well, would you two like some of my applesauce cake? *(She presses it on them; they accept; begin to eat.)*

ROENA

This good, Beatrice. Thank you.

NAJEAN

Thank you, Aunt Bea.

ROENA

I've been swaying from the lingering smell ever since…

BEATRICE

It's strange washing the windows of an old room… sometimes. *(pause)* There's snot-filled finger prints on the window pane – along with other things that got started in other windows and come'd pressed here…

NAJEAN

Why are you going on so about the window, Aunt Bea?

BEATRICE

There's still dirt on it and it's your job, get it done.

NAJEAN

But it's night! 9 o'clock… I can't even see to wash the window clean, Aunt Bea.

BEATRICE

In the morning you can wash it again when you can see what you missed.

NAJEAN

(to ROENA) Mama?

ROENA

You're bearing down, Beatrice.

BEATRICE

No. I'm bearing up. *(pause)* You got your daughter, Roena. *(pregnant pause)* You want some more cake?

The lights fade on the trio.

The end.

yagayah
two.womyn.black.griots

debbie young
&
naila belvett

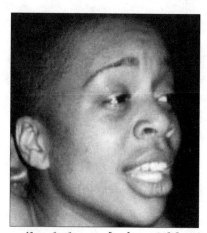

naila belvett [nah-ee-lah] lawd gawd. sometimes yuh jus haffi try a ting. her ting is poetry. writing for more than a decade, her poetry has manifested into spoken word and dub pieces, plays, published articles, as well as songs. she is a spoken word artist who has graced stages in canada, the united states as well as south africa. performances include; native yard, parlez inn, brown girls in da ring, cowansville institute, nuyorican cafe, organix and kirstenbosch gardens. her plays include; *yagayah* (1999), *stuck* (2001) and *(muted tongue)* (2003). nah-ee-lah is also a recording artist. she released "nah-ee-lah: free dome" – her debut spoken word cd through the canada council for the arts. "free dome" later went on to receive the 2002 urban music association of canada's award for best spoken word recording. she received her ba from concordia university and upon graduation (june 2000), opened her own company yah ga yah that produces any project she believes in – including her own. (smile)
she continues to write
to keep sane.
most days it works.

debbie young is a bald-headed. broad-nosed. thick-lipped. dark-skinned. blackbushoomaan. jamaican born and raised. dub-poet. actor. playwright. she appeared in *'da kink in my hair* (toronto, halifax, new york 2001-2003), zakes mda's *and the girls in their sunday dresses* (2001) and *stuck* (2003). she was recently invited by leda serene films to play a lead in the new canadian-caribbean sitcom "lawd have mercy." she has performed at numerous poetry shows and concerts throughout north america, europe and cuba and has opened for such griots as lorraine klaasen and antibalas afrobeat band. she performed on def poetry jam 3 hbo in new york recently. she is a member of rAisin' the sun, at b current and is founding artistic director of fiwibloodrun inc. an artist-activist resource company. she released her debut dub poetry album "when the love is not enough" in april 2000. her fourth album "dubbin revolushun: blood" is a political, musical and cultural exchange with some of havana's top musicians. debbie believes that storytelling is the ultimate revolutionary form. "there is no revolushun widout pashun."

Mirroring Duality
a dialogue about *yagayah*

by ahdri zhina mandiela and Rachael Van Fossen

— • — — • — — • —

Rachael Van Fossen (RVF): *yagayah* is a highly theatrical play, at once poetic and populist. The play's "singular" success as a work of theatre art is largely due to a skillful rendering of dualities: duality of place (Jamaica and Canada); duality of difference between the protagonists as best friends (imogene, who is the more privileged, middle-class Jamaican, raised by her father following the death of her mother, and mary, born to a working class single mother); dualities of characterization, wherein each of the two actors portrays other characters in the drama; and of course the duality of having two writers, naila belvett and debbie young, creating together. The tensions in the space *between* what is in the "singular"—I am reminded especially of mary's "singularity" speech—and the "twos" that make up a "duality," provide the central metaphor around which the play (and the two b current productions I have seen) are structured. A beautiful intermingling and transformation come when imogene and mary engage in a simultaneous mirror-dialogue, the character(s) speaking at once with and to the self and with and to each other.

ahdri zhina mandiela (azm): singularity of course is just a part of duality... or is it the opposite? maybe it is a progressive state of being; definitely a fluid interchangeable one, inasmuch as the tendency in people is to vacillate between aloneness and joining with others.

RVF: Was this sense of duality important to the development and rehearsal processes undertaken at b current?

azm: absolutely! i deliberately let the playwrights' own artist process mirror the development, by essentially, honouring their approach... two young Black women, personal politics/world view solidly intersecting; sharing cultural and artistic dualities; both living in canada with immediate jamaican roots, and both just starting out as writer/performers – begin generating text by thematically collating pieces from two distinct voices in their poetry works. when they found that the poetry didn't fully encompass their desires, they began generating dialogue. after two independent performances they looked to formalizing the theatrical structure; not too successfully at first, then they approached b current.

in the first workshop phase in 2001, i worked with dramaturge diane roberts and the writer/performers to shape a showcase for the SummerWorks Festival, being very attentive to the theme of duality and really trying to ensure that the playwrights were confident with their intent in content &

structure. the fine-tuning and second workshop would be in pre-production for the rock.paper.sistahz festival in may 2002. this time i took a huge leap of faith and rested the development and production mount in the hands of debbie & naila and emerging director, weyni mengesha. weyni's injection emphasized another duality... that of diasporic african identity. the result was a script and performance which very accurately animated the playwrights' vision.

RVF: When I first met naila belvett in the summer of 2001, over cups of tea at a sidewalk café on Ste. Catherine Street in Montreal, the purpose of our meeting was in fact to discuss development for a different piece of hers. I mentioned that I thought ahdri zhina mandiela from Toronto would be an ideal director with whom to collaborate, based not on knowing you, but on having read your play *dark diaspora... in dub* in the first volume of *Testifyin'*. Just the day before, naila had learned you were to be directing the first workshop production of *yagayah*.

azm: twelve years ago when i worked *dark diaspora... in dub* i was hoping for more exploration of "dub theatre." there has been a proliferation of incorporating rhythms and poetry and choreography in different ways in theatre, but no "dub theatre" piece. not surprising, being that dub poetry has spawned quite a bit of exploration and innovation in music, and both written and performance poetry, yet itself never made huge waves in any "mainstreams."

RVF: From what I understand the first dramaturgical process for *yagayah* was not entirely successful. In your opinion, was this because a white director from a mostly Western theatre background was dramaturge? The piece is written largely in Jamaican patois, and the rhythms of the very particular, precise and poetic language in the play seem so important to its success in theatrical terms.

azm: indeed the first structured workshop of *yagayah*—involving just dramaturgy—took the writers to a place of wanting/needing to start over... probably due to attempts to squeeze the rhythms, the language, the poetry and assiduous attentiveness to the theme of duality into a more common, dramatic narrative mold. dramaturgical sessions can oftentimes yield disaster even for well-experienced folks. in this case, i think a lack of familiarity with the form [probably on both sides] may have sounded demise.

seeing the potential with form and style of the script, i immediately sensed what I could offer these first time playwrights; thru b current and my own experience.

RVF: Another striking thing about the play in production is the way its episodic structure effects an interweaving rather than an unfolding, so that individuals and life events—past present and future—are shown to be interrelated and interdependent. But interrelation is quite different from the causal connections generally associated with a more conventional play. It seems to me this is part of the "invocation" you've spoken about. A more feminist approach?

azm: i think overt invocation is mainly a woman's tool; very much like pots and pans and wombs. the duo of naila & debbie use it well in *yagayah*. within the poetic form, situations and times and places seem more "invoked" rather than created or recreated. it's like cocooning an audience in atmosphere and presenting a progression of images thru which the story unravels. and this would be my definition of "dub theatre." the intricacies are not necessarily revealed in the text... which brings me to the question of the published work and its usefulness in academic/educational situations? how do you see *yagayah* being used in these arenas?

RVF: I think publication is really important, especially because in academic circles the written word is dominant. I think the potential for envisioning and making change—for seeing new possibilities and perspectives—will be extremely limited if students can only read plays that conform to a more "familiar" (read: "Western World") map.

Certainly the experience of seeing a production is very different from the experience of reading the same play. As an audience member for *yagayah*— and I am speaking here from the perspective of a white North American woman—I did not "understand" everything in a literal sense. But then the most powerful theatre experiences resonate in me, as opposed to telling me or even showing me everything – like the difference between pantomime and other, more evocative forms of physical theatre. If relating the plot of a play can sum up the experience, it is probably not—at least not for me—an inherently *theatrical* script.

At the same time I do think examining the written text reveals details that are different from those evoked and provoked in a production. Reading a text allows me time to stop, re-read, reflect, re-read, pose questions, and re-read again. For example, taking the play's parallel story of yemoja and ogun: in performance, these characters are not familiar to me personally, at least not in precise terms. I did however "get" their sensuality, and that this theme of the sensual transcends mere romance, weaving in love of self, love for another, love of self in another – taking us back to the mirror scene. But it's in reading the text and asking questions that I can learn more...

azm: yemoja and ogun: yoruba deities... a fully spiritual way of invoking ideas of good and bad, and love of self and romance, and rejection and redemption. the conjured romantic encounter of these deities in *yagayah* mirrors the women's yearning for a bold sensual/tactile confirmation of their existence and identity. they want to/need to/have to say yes! i am! me! Black woman... as seen in each other's/mirror. then! they can feel free to fully love themselves.

RVF: And the children's' game Emmanuel Road…

azm: emmanuel road is an old children's game which had all but disappeared when i was a youngster, growing up in jamaica. down in the country – at my grandmother's – my cousins and i would try to simulate as much as we knew. there it was, near the beginning of *yagayah!* i was intrigued as the song [embedded in what was originally a poem written by debbie] invoked childhood lost and revisited. it invoked danger and warnings, and within the context of the first workshop, it embodied the journey of the young women… down some rocky emotional tracts. i wanted the music of the piece to fully emerge from an environment of rhythms on rocks. turns out the production used drums… close enough.

RVF: And "bushooman…"

azm: bushooman is my invocation of self in this modern urban jungle; some images of this explored on the cd, "step in to my head." it's my living/breathing Black/woman/mother/child/artist space, and the young women…

RVF: mary/imogene, imogene/mary, debbie/naila, naila/debbie, mary/debbie, imogene/naila…

azm: yes, all of them… embody this admirably.

ahdri zhina mandiela. dubb aatist, founder/artistic director of b current, writer, maker of film and video works, mother, and a lazily ambitious world being. current passions include development of a radio series, two film projects, and passing the baton thru rAisin' the sun. check her work samples at: www.bcurrent.ca/inthebush

Rachael Van Fossen *is Artistic Director of Black Theatre Workshop in Montreal, and teaches in the Theatre and Development Program at Concordia University.*

yagayah: two.womyn.black.griots was first produced by b current at SummerWorks Festival, Toronto, in August 2001 with the following company:

mary   debbie young
imogene   naila belvett

Directed by ahdri zhina mandiela
Setting by Robin Akimbo
Lighting by Andy Moro
Costumes by Raven Dauda

this published version was produced as part of b current's rock.paper.sistahz festival at Theatre Passe Muraille, in May 2002.

—•— —•— —•—

CHARACTERS:
mary: a seven-year-old, a sixteen-year-old, a twenty-one-year-old woman. jamaican. she is from a working class family. she lives with her mother, younger brother, grandmother, aunts, and cousins in maxfield, kingston thirteen.
imogene: an eight-year-old, a seventeen-year-old, a twenty-two-year-old woman. jamaican. she is from a middle class family. she lives with her uncle in jamaica in waltham, an affluent neighbourhood near maxfield. in canada she lives in st. henri with her father.
mary and imogene are best friends from a very young age. mary's mother is imogene's housekeeper. as a result mary practically lives with imogene throughout their childhood.

these other characters are played by the two actors: yemoja, ogun, tyrone, mary's baby, derek.

SETTING:
kingston jamaica – summer 1984, summer 1985, summer 1993, december 1998
montreal canada – winter 1993, winter 1998

l to r: naila belvett & debbie young
Photo by Sandra Alland.

yagayah
two.womyn.black.griots

by debbie young & naila belvett

— • — — • — — • —

ACT I
Scene One
blouse an skirt

kingston, jamaica, summertime 1985. mary is on stage playing, waiting for imogene to come home. imogene is at the back of the theatre behind the audience.

mary
imogene, imogene yuh deh deh?
imogene? imogene?

imogene
mary is dat you?

mary
yuh wan come outside and play wid me?
eeh imogene?

imogene
mi ah come mary.

mary
alright mi ago wait fi yuh.
yuh ready yet?

imogene
mi sey, mi aguh come!

mary
alright.

imogene walks down aisle onto stage walking slowly & modelling a new scarf.

imogene
yuh like it mary?

mary
is pretty imogene. it remind me a di likkle girl pon tv weh she name again imogene? and she have tall tall hair. tall dung to di grung. an she

live inna one high up building big suh. and she fling har hair dung pon
di grung. an memba imogene, di likkle bwoy did climb up pon har hair.
yuh memba weh she name imogene? di likkle girl wid di tall hair dung
pon di grung like yuhrs? yuh look like a cristal gale princess.

imogene
mi know – mi go a halfway tree plaza wit suzette and har madda dis
morning.

mary
mi like it imogene.

imogene
yuh want to try it on?

mary
hummmum. *(she nods her head yes.)*

imogene
but yuh haffi bi careful.

mary
mi ago careful imogene.

she tries the scarf. imogene fusses over her and the scarf.

mi madda ago buy mi one fi mi tomorrow. mi ago ask har fi buy one…

imogene
cum mek wi play tag mary. mi aguh hide.

mary
which one you wan play imogene – tag or hide and seek?

imogene
you count. *(she pushes mary down to count.)*

mary
umm hmm. gwaan go hide. 1-2-3-4

imogene
slow down mary. ya count too fast.

mary
5-6-7-8-9-10. ready or not here i come. *(mary finds imogene right away.)* mi
find yuh!!

imogene
that's why mi neva wan play wid yuh. cause you love cheat.

mary
untrut mary. mi neva did a look.

imogene
me a go play hopscotch by myself. *(she begins to draw the hopscotch while mary stands and watches.)*

mary
ah no so imogene. *(she shows her how.)* ah so. *(imogene gives her the chalk and watches impatiently.)*

imogene
yuh finish yet? *(imogene hops over and around mary while she's working.)* mary – ah no so yuh fi write the four. ah so. *(mary continues to work and imogene continues to play.)*

mary
imogene yuh cyan do dis? *(she jumps and spins in a circle on the hopscotch – imogene tries and falls.)*

imogene
mi naw waan play anymore. mi aguh a mi yawd.

mary
so wah yuh waan play imogene?

imogene
emmanuel road mary.

mary
so yuh cyan mash mi finga? di las time wi play emmanuel road yuh did a play too fast and yuh use di rock stone and mek mi finga bleed.

imogene
dis time mi aguh play slow. mi nah guh mash yuh finga, mi promise.

they play emmanuel road.

mary & imogene
guh dung emmanuel road gyal an bwoy fi guh bruk rock stone
guh dung emmanuel road gyal an bwoy fi guh bruk rock stone
bruk dem one by one gyal an bwoy
bruk dem two by two gyal an bwoy
bruk dem tree by tree gyal an bwoy
bruk dem four by four gyal an bwoy
bruk dem five by five gyal an bwoy
finga mash no cry gyal an bwoy
memba a play we a play gyal an bwoy.
(they repeat.)

mary
> imogene mi hear yuh uncle john a call yuh. *(imogene ignores her.)*
> imogene yuh nuh hear uncle john a call yuh? stay deh gwaan like
> yuh a big ooman, an watch if yuh nah go get a beating.

imogene
> mary yuh too fraidy fraidy.

> *imogene gets up and reluctantly leaves.*

mary
> mi a go wait until yuh come back.

> *mary sits and plays emmanuel road by herself.*

imogene
> yuh know mi nuh understand
> why my uncle john
> insist fi hol up mi han
> when mi a sleep
> an if mi open up mi eye
> an look inna him face
> him tell mi fi shshshs/close yuh eye/don't be shy
> don't mek no noise/cause we nuh waan yuh madda fi wake inna di
> place
>
> don't tell nobody what a gwaan
> mi have a special love fi yuh
> yuh madda cannot understand
> so keep dis between me an you
>
> las week him tek him time
> an climb pan top a mi
> den him open up him pants
> an hol down mi hands
>
> an all mi feel is pain again an again
> an all mi feel is pain again an again
>
> mi granny used to say dat in di olden day
> dey used to put hot peppa in yuh punny
> if yuh do it wid a man an yuh was a likkle gyal
> yuh was in di wrong yuh mek it happen
>
> an all mi feel is pain again an again
> yes all mi feel is pain again an again
>
> uncle john mi nuh like when yuh touch mi right dere
> mama say i shouldn't let nobody touch mi right dere

uncle john dis is wrong please let guh a mi han
uncle john dis is wrong please put on back yuh pants
an now it hurt between mi leg when mi a walk
mi haffi spread mi leg apart when mi a walk
mi haffi sit dung pon di side when mi at school
because di benches feel too hard

di pickney dem at school laugh after mi
dem point an jeer all day long
mi bes frien mary tell mi fi look pon mi skirt
when mi turn it around mi get a big alert
mi did a bleed an bleed pon mi uniform
red blood red blood pon mi uniform

mi bleed an bleed all day long
mi bleed an bleed all day long

uncle john mi nuh like when yuh touch mi right dere
mama say i shouldn't let nobody touch mi right dere
uncle john dis is wrong please let guh a mi han
uncle john dis is wrong please put on back yuh pants

tonight mi aguh sleep wid a knife
mary tell mi uncle john at night
should only touch his wife
mi tell him i don't want his special love
but him still insist fi tek mi from above

tonight uncle john tek him time
an climb pon top a mi
mi sink di knife into him spine

him neva hol mi hands
him neva tek off him pants

an all him feel is pain
again and again
an all him feel is pain
again and again

uncle john mi nuh like when yuh touch mi right dere
uncle john dis is wrong yuh nuh heed weh yuh hear
an so mi pull di knife an lodge it in yuh spine
yes mi pull di knife an lodge it in yuh spine

   imogene exits.

mary
   memba a play we a play *(repeat)*

Scene Two
yemoja and ogun

kingston, jamaica, summertime 1993. mary is at home cleaning, waiting for imogene to come do her hair. imogene enters.

the story parallels the movement of their relationship. imogene plays the character of yemoja and mary plays the character of ogun.

imogene
yuh ready?

mary
of course. look how long mi a wait pon yuh. yuh naw guh believe weh mi do dis marning.

imogene
yuh guh a foreign and come back.

mary
no gene. mi guh someweh betta dan foreign. mi guh a afrika.

imogene
afrika again. lawd gawd mary yuh mean seh yuh go back a bobo dread mikey yawd?

mary
today him tell mi bout afrika gawd people named orisha. yuh did know imogene dat if yuh waan anyting fi happen yuh pray to di gawd a di moon, or di gawd a di sun or di gawd a di...

imogene
...a di obeah blackheart business?

mary
sisterin imogene – yuh need fi ovastand babylon plan. i and i haffi ready fi repatriation.

imogene
fi wha?

mary
afrika a fi we lan. *(mary breaks into an african dance.)* di gawd people dem cyan mek wi dreams cum tru.

imogene
mary yuh wan mi fi comb yuh nappy head or what?

mary
> yuh nuh waan see di magic cowrie shell weh bobbo dread mikey gimme. him seh two a di afrika gawd people dem weh name yemoja an ogun use it fi do magic. an fi talk to dem one anedah. it have magi story inside a it.

imogene
> yuh nuh have no magic shell.

mary
> wha dis? *(imogene looks away.)* alright mi alone will have di magic. *(mary looks away.)* cause all yuh haffi do is put yuh han pon it… fi a likkle bit.

> *imogene reluctantly places her hands on top of mary's. mary chants.*

imogene
> a lie mary. no magic nuh inna it.

> *they transform into yemoja and ogun.*

yemoja (imogene)
> dear ogun
> was it oludunmare who
> wrote our distance on the clouds
> this morning the sun
> flirted with me
> in your absence
> though
> her embrace was merely routine
> not a spontaneous caress
> wind stroked my ear
> whispered your name
> all day
> i worked in the fields
> noon-day sweat damped my lower lip
> and
> i inhaled you across a thousand
> and one nights
> ogun
> can destiny
> carved
> on
> vanishing sky
> be rewritten

ogun (mary)
> dear yemoja
> do not be anxious

our tribulation is
short-lived
fate
an unusual friend of mine
promised our eventual
hereafter
i believe him
you visited the zimbezi
high sun river bathing
on a saturday morn
you didn't see
me
when you went behind the macka tree
i watched
you removed your
lappa
then stroked black hairs crowning breasts
and belly button
river waata lay them flat
i watched
your fingers fell lazily against the dark patch
grass at centre
you began to braid them
yemoja
if only i could have touched you
then
my tongue
your personal hair bush comb
to tidy pearl black nipples
zimbezi river deep belly button
thick bush at the centre
yemoja i thought you
in a dream

    they revert back to their child selves.

mary
    yuh feel dat?

imogene
    maybe.

mary
    a di magic shell do it. *(she begins to do an african dance.)*

imogene
    gimme it mary.

mary
    not until yuh learn di afrikan dance.

    she takes imogene by the hands and shows her the dance.

Scene Three
separation

    kingston, jamaica, summertime 1993. mary and imogene are sixteen and seventeen years old. they are in imogene's kitchen dancing.

mary
    yuh finally get good wid yuh two left foot. mi tell yuh man, when yuh guh a foreign everyting aguh nice. trust mi imogene.

imogene
    really mary? cause cho… me don't really know.

mary
    mi would a tell yuh anyting weh nuh good fi yuh? how long now mi know you?

imogene
    long enough fi know seh you cyaan live widout mi.

mary
    cho. mi cyaan live widout you or you cyaan live widout mi?

imogene
    but serious enuh mary. foreign far yuh know. far like… well far like… well far. we cyaan just talk anytime yuh know. foreign a long distance yuh know. a international call dat. nuff dollars haffi run.

mary
    den nuh foreign yuh aguh? of course nuff dollars haffi run. nuff dollars an nuff oppartunity. suh imogene yuh aguh foreign guh big movie star like angela bassett and denzel washington?

imogene
    me? a nuh mi yah chat bout. is figet you figet seh who… you a miss juliet. romeo romeo, wherefort art dow romeo?

mary
    wait wait, me tek di pyzen yet. romeo, romeo, romeo *(she falls to the ground and pretends to take poison. she dies melodramatically.)*

imogene
juliet, juliet. mi deh yah juliet. a you mi love juliet.

she flops on the ground, pretends to stab herself and falls on top of mary.
they both laugh hysterically.

mary
a suh mi know seh me was di best hactor inna dat play man.

imogene
member di look pon ms bernice's face? mary, cho me nearly pepe up mi
self. mi nearly wet up miself a suh mi was trying not to laugh.

mary
mi madda beat dat night yuh see man – she beat me. "mary ann eunice
gladys simit yuh neva embarass mi suh inna mi life. yuh granny a turn
inna har grave, bout yuh han dat deh likkle tegereg bwoy tyrone a form
fool inna de school play." lawd god gene, she beat me bad dat night
yuh know. but it did wurt it.

imogene
no more st. jago high school theatre productions.

mary
and no more shakespeare wid ms bernice who swear seh she cum from
england.

mary & imogene
welcome class to shakespeare 101.

imogene
but serious enuh mary. if mi guh a foreign dat really mean seh… well
mi just a seh dat mi nuh really sure mi waan guh – no more jamaica?

mary
how yuh mean yuh nuh sure? gene yuh nuh membra seh anuh every
and everybody get to go a foreign every day. yuh haffi to tek de chance
when yuh get it. yuh tink she if my fadda did live a foreign an him send
fi mi, you tink seh mi would a talk bout mi nuh sure.

imogene
hmm. yuh know mary mi really waan guh fi trut enuh. it's just dat, well
certain tings here mi aguh miss.

mary
well whatever yuh aguh miss will be right here when you come back.

imogene
hmm. is just… well…

mary
> lawd god imogene *(mary gets up and walks away.)* stop screw screw up yuh face man. yuh a gwaan like anuh foreign yuh aguh. cho. *(mary pulls out the magic cowrie shell.)* an plus memba seh we aguh write each odda everyday.

imogene
> a true. *(imogene gets up to joke with mary.)* a true yuh talk ms juliet. a true.

> *mary hugs imogene then gives her the shell.*

mary
> hol on pon dis... seen.

> *mary leaves imogene. as she exits she sings a part of the jamaican national anthem.*

> eternal father bless our land. guide us with thy mighty hand... justice truth be ours forever, jamaica land we love. jamaica. jamaica. jamaica land we love.

Scene Four
letters

> *mary is in kingston, jamaica, summertime 1993. imogene is in montreal, canada, winter 1993.*

mary
> mi friend imogene deh a foreign fi di last 2 weeks, one place call montreal. everytime mi ask har if dat mean seh she deh close to brooklyn, new york she tell me seh she nuh know. well foreign a foreign an who cyaan guh foreign a bat. me dun know seh mi have one whole heap a family a foreign. mi have family a florida, a atlanta, even a new york. mi have family inna a brooklyn, new york city represent. well di one imogene she a mi best friend, we been bes friend fi, mek mi si, bout 13 years, since wi a 3 years old. we used to give each odda everyting, from ice-cream to blouse and skirt to book an pencil. wi did even go a di same basic school togedda. imogene tell mi dat when she get pon top har feet a foreign she a sen mi new shoes an clothes an nuff panty an brief. well di brief dem a fi mi bredda jacob, him a 7 now, just turn 7 last week. mi hear seh foreign nice enuh. tings free. di street dem pave wid gole. an money grow pon tree basically. yuh tink inna foreign people live inna zinc house, a brick dem live inna like inna di story book dem like hansel and grekkle. people nuh live inna poverty and degradation like we do. all di cussing an fighting, looting an murdering nuh gwaan a foreign. inna jam dung life hard an people wi do anyting fi back bite yuh. inna foreign everybody live inna one white pickett fence, wid

house, an lan, an cyar, an dog and 2.3 pickney. dem even have washing machine and dryer. dem even have machine fi wash up cup an plate. a laziness dat if yuh ask me. but nobody neva ask.

mi soon gawn a foreign but imogene guh quicker dan mi.

> *we hear oh canada from the back of the house, then see imogene coming down the stairs with her luggage and interacting with the audience (canadians). she goes to her apartment and unloads her books and starts cleaning.*

> *6 months later, imogene in montreal begins to open up a letter that mary wrote.*

how cum di one imogene nuh write mi back yet. after she dun tell me bout seh she a mi bes friend. yuh know weh dem seh bout people like dat. dem get rich an switch. yes imogene gawn a foreign an get rich an switch.

imogene
rich an switch!!! after mi wuk overtime an sen di likkle $20 di odda day.

> *she begins to write mary a letter angrily.*

imogene
dear mary, i am sorry that i took so long to write you but i have been having some very very hard times. foreign is not what it is cracked up to be. and i know you think i forgot about you but i sent you $20 wid miss bernice couple months ago.

mary
which $20 she a talk bout. *(mary continues to respond to imogene's letter as she writes it.)*

imogene
canada…

why is your accent so thick? how come you can't speak proper english? you don't speak french… where do you come from? here i am an immigrant inna foreign land. in jamaica i was imogene, mass edwards dawta… here i am just black, black and struggling… an they hate jamaicans. every crime weh commit is a jamaican get blame fi it. every black person is a jamaican as far as dese people are concerned. african, trinidadian, vincencian, guyanese, all of us are "jamaican" here. first they say we come an take away their jobs, then they say that we are all on welfare. mi sey – di white people don't want us in dem land. and it's not even their land cause dem tief it from the indian people dem.

basically my father and i are struggling here mary. he – well, he just lost
his job and they are telling him that he has to go back to school even
though he studied mechanical engineering in jamaica for so many
years. they told me that i have to redo a couple of years of high school
cause dem have one different school system here. as a result i decided
to take some time off from school so that i could work. but i am going
to night school instead. right now i have a telemarketing job cause work
over here is hard to get. if i don't work we won't be able to pay the rent,
if you can't pay rent then you're "ass out" as they say here.

mi seh mary, please don't believe them when they say that there are no
poor people in foreign. people sleep pon di streets here just like they
do inna jamdown. but at least inna jamaica there is an excuse for the
poverty, mi wan know a wha kind of excuse they have here – first
world country mi ras.

ah telling yuh mary, dese people don't mix with black people much.
they have their own neighbourhoods wid big house and car and plenty
lan. one rich neighbourhood name westmount is right beside one poor
neighbourhood name st. henri.

mary foreign is not easy. i know that jamaica is hard but when you
come here is a new set of battles. i will try to send you a pair of shoes
and a brief fi jacob as soon as i work some money.

your friend, imogene

mary
new set a battles mi… (*chupse her teeth*) wha imogene a talk bout. a
gawn imogene gawn a foreign guh skylark. yuh si from marning she
neva know wha hard work was. likkle hard work must eh tek har an
she get fraidy fraidy. come to mention it, dis one letta she a write me
inna how much months. but gene, yuh really bright yuh know.

imogene
mary mi neva write yuh back cause i have been working very hard. mi
wake up from 5 o'clock inna di marning hours. go to work, come home,
go to night school, tek care of mi fadda an den study. mi seh, mary –
dese days i'm always tired.

mary
as if everybody inna jamaica nuh haffi work. an which part a foreign
imogene deh anyways, bout she a talk bout she si poor people a sleep
pon street. yuh mus work imogene. yes work, because no matter which
part of foreign yuh go if yo work yuh cyan mek it big big. gene if i was
in foreign i would definitely like to be dere. cum to tink of it yuh know.
a lie imogene a tell bout mi wouldn't like it dere, is cause she know i
would do betta dan har.

imogene

then you come to montreal mary-ann eunice gladys simit. please. i wouldn't be here in the first place if it wasn't for you and your fake dreams dem... as if you knew anything about being here. "foreign" is not just one place mary. i am in canada, in montreal, living in st. henri and trust me, you can work very hard and still have nothing here.

mary

cause mi know bout hard work. mi a tek care a jacob from mi eye deh mi knee and now jacob a big man an mi still a tek care of him. a lazy she lazy. from morning she born wid gold spoon in har mout, live right pon top a di hill an mi modda haffi slave an work fi har people dem. yuh si how mi modda raise me, fi learn fi cook an clean an tek care a pickney.

imogene

that's why i can't take you on sometimes yuh know mary. cause you too dyam small minded. this is not jamaica. mi fadda nuh have no job and tings are not free.

and yes i am hard working mary, but that is not all it's about here. dese people don't acknowledge black people, dey don't acknowledge me, it's like i don't exist.

mary

but imogene a big oomaan now she supposed fi know how fi do hard work. hmm hmm a true people seh sometimes certain kind a people guh a foreign an get lazy. yuh si me – mi nuh waan guh a foreign like imogene an get lazy. mi will stay inna jamaica an si if mi cyaan mek someting of myself. born wid gold spoon in har mout anna complain complain. she luckier dan mi.

imogene

lucky mary. who lucky?

mary

p.s. jamaica is fine.

imogene

suh who dead now?

mary

mek mi si – johnny dead, harry dead, clive an barry dead. police kill two a dem, gunman kill di odda two. dem kill horrett cause him wouldn't tell dem where one a di twin dem live. dem tek juney frock from off di clothes line, wrap it roun' him head suh dat nobody woulda hear and shot him dead two time – rain di fall di morning. jamaica is quite fine, tek care of yuhself an write me back.

imogene
> p.s. mary, jamaica hard but in foreign there is a new set of battles. hold it down and keep tight.

> *imogene goes and opens her books and freezes in studying.*

Scene Five
singularity

> *jamaica december 1998. mary is at home cleaning.*

debbie
> singularity no clarity
> run mary run
> singularity no clarity
> run mary run
>
> tell me why is it dat
> at a party
> everybody jolly an hearty
> i'm sitting on a stool
> denying dis loneliness
>
> girl you's an only child
> you's a fortunate child
> you's a privilege child
> you's an intelligent child
> so why don't you smile for a while
> an give your face a rest
>
> yes i will smile for many whiles
> and pledge a prayer of pretense
> so i could exist in the present
> live my pseudo experience
> reconfirm existence
>
> yes i will smile
> no i will laugh
> ha ha
> laughter is the weapon of fools
>
> i will laugh
> find humour
> in any sorta blunder
> humour in pride
> humour in genocide
> humour in suicide

laugh for many whiles
though under black blubber skin
blood boils and bleeds
for a break of monotony

suicide/singularity
suicide/singularity
suicide/singularity

is eating me from the insides
is eating me from the outsides
is eating me from all sides

run mary run
run from dem white walls
stiff as stone
a try trap yuh inna dem cell
dem institution
run from machine pave foundation
dat a alienate you from di rest of dem

run from discomfort pain loneliness want want of sex want of food
run from people who want acceptance
run from di ting
wid two han
two leg
head
an no name
run from you

mama yuh had mi
mama yuh didn't plan
to start yuh family dis early
but yuh had mi
1 month 2 month 3 month to 9
mama yuh mek mi invade yuh space an force yuh outta shape
physical and emotional pain.
she 15 and she breeding
nutting will come of dat girl
shame on di family but yuh had mi
going and coming from school wid a expanding belly
mama yuh couldn't hide naussia sickness self hate
but yuh had mi

mama yuh neva plan fi start yuh family dis early
but yuh tell mi
sometimes yuh get a blessing from di skies
mama yuh wise

mama had mi
mama hol mi fi di first time
mama had mi mama hold mi fi di first time

run mary run

Scene Six
ain't i a oomaan

*montreal, canada, wintertime, 1998. imogene is at home. mary is in
jamaica at home.*

imogene
i wonder how much longer my foreign dream will last, two more
minutes, two more hours, two more days? no money pon tree, no
prosperity, no opportunity, jus hard livity and struggle inna dis ya cold
place. what a disgrace... mary this reality is shitty and lonely.

mi guh inna class
feminism 101
hear di teacha seh we'll elaborate on betty friedan
gloria steinem
an discuss di liberation of the white middle class woman
from oppression in society

mary
di solution of which is to go out there into di workforce an work
an darkness,

imogene
di absence of light skin,
widout white skin

darkness

mary
i have been force working since i was brought here

imogene
"women got the vote in 1918"
me tell di teacha mi nuh undastan weh yuh mean
when you say "women" could you be more specific
if my recollection serves me correct
1918 i wasn't voting yet
an darkness,

mary
    di absence of white skin,
    widout light skin

    darkness

imogene
    i have been work forcing
    since i was brought here

mary
    "georgy-you-best-go-gets-cleaning-ups-now yuh here
    aunt-jemima-gowna-make-you-some-real-nice-pancakes"

imogene
    cum mek wi look pon disya shituation
    dis feminism 101 where we elaborate pon betty friedan
    glora steinem
    cannot have room for i

mary
    it forces di exclusion a di black oomaan
    black black
    black bush oomaan
    a di black oomaan
    black black
    black bush oomaan

imogene
    an ahdri said "step into my head
    come on and step step step into my head
    black bush oomaan"

    step into my head
    where fear and loathing
    stalk single strands of my kinky hair

mary
    beauty looks warp as you exotify me
    a-sexualized
    demonized

mary & imogene
    but we both agree
    dat mammy raise black an white pickney
    dat tanty raise black an white pickney
    dat auntie raise black and white pickney
    yuh nanny raise black an white pickney

mary
> mi nose a likkle broada

imogene
> mi lips a likkle ticka

mary
> mi ass a likkle higha

imogene
> mi skin a likkle darka

mary
> yuh lips a likkle fatta

imogene
> yuh nose a likkle rounda

mary
> yuh ass a likkle higha

imogene
> yuh skin a likkle darka

mary
> yuh ass a likkle bigga

imogene
> yuh nose a likkle a rounda

mary
> yuh skin a likkle darka

imogene
> mi hips a likkle wida

mary
> yuh skin a likkle darka

imogene
> makes you an outsidah

mary
> you an outsidah

mary & imogene
> me an outsidah?

mary & imogene
> an darkness is di embrace a di absence of light
> di beginning
> darkness is black womb
> weh we all come from
> black womb
> weh we all come from
> black oomaan

mary
> ain't i a oomaan?

imogene
> ain't i a oomaan?

> *mary and imogene stare at each other as in a mirror and reach for each other. mary breaks away early and walks stage right.*

Scene Seven
cho tyrone

> *kingston, jamaica, summertime 1998. mary walks by tyrone her admirer.*

tyrone
> pssst. pssst. pssst.

mary
> watch yah, mussi tire a let off air. *(tyrone holds mary by the hand.)* cho tyrone, stop it nuh man.

tyrone
> yuh nuh see big man a talk to yuh. cho a long time wi nuh reason enuh mary.

mary
> stop it man. stop hole on pon mi han suh tight. mi nah tell yuh again. everybody aguh si mi.

tyrone
> a who yuh a worry bout? chattabox bernice cross di street. yow, jus mek har know seh, who a big man a talk to yuh.

mary
> she an mi madda a bes friend now. every likkle man mi try talk to she run back an guh inform.

tyrone

nuh badda worry bout dat zeen. jus mek har know seh, who, a big man a talk to yuh.

mary

mi seh leggo offa mi han tyrone. mi cyaan tek how oonu man stay suh enuh. jus cyaan hear when people a chat to oonu.

tyrone

nuh badda screw screw up yuh face pon mi mary. mi jus a tell yuh seh mi a watch yuh an yuh a grow into a sweet young ting.

mary

cho tyrone

tyrone

a suh yuh belly fat an round mary. an yuh bumpa jus nice suh. yuh jus look so fatabulous an buffalous suh. mi ouldn't mind get a piece offa yuh.

mary

get a piece offa who. yuh tink mi madda raise nuh tegereg gyal. a nuh miss bernice stupid school play dis, enuh romeo bwoy. yuh try leave mi alone. leave mi alone tyrone.

tyrone

ay mary. mi is numba one pon di look good chart enuh. an me need a oomaan who is *(he begins singing the song.) numba one pon di look good chart, whole up yuh han girl a you me a talk. numba one pon…*

mary

mi don't want to be in anyting wid yuh. yuh really tink yuh turn big man now. mi memba when yuh nose used to run an yuh madda beat yuh fi wipe it. an plus mi dun have my man already, lebert leford wilfred junior smith.

tyrone

a who yuh a talk bout? scellion. *(he kisses his teeth.)* yuh mi nuh see nuh ring deh pon yuh ring finga. if yuh did deh wid me, one cris ring oulda deh pon yuh ring finga.

yow, mi jus waan tek dis oppartunity fi big up all di man dem from east side, wes side, nort side, all sides. yuh know. an all di man dem deh pon di corner yuh know – big up who yuh fi big up an small up who yuh fi small up seen. yeah yeah. yuh nuh si it mary – a big man a talk to yuh enuh.

mary kisses her teeth, breaks his hold and begins to walk away.

tyrone

suh which part yuh nice brown skin friend deh? weh she name imogene wid di pretty hair?.

mary

(*she snaps at him.*) look how long now imogene gawn a foreign.

tyrone

gawn a foreign?

mary

yuh neva know dat... dyam hediot. mi have tings fi duh.

tyrone

(*he begins to sing.*) ...mi love mi browning cuz she is a nice sistren. mi love mi browning cuz she have really nice skin. mi love mi browning...

Scene Eight
yemoja

yemoja (mary)

dear ogun
i had a dream
you kissed me with
chalk on your lips
my tongue searched
powder thick hoping
to find home in
familiar
you covered white across
my face into and
under my eyes. they burnt
you smiled
i dreamt
you tasted disgust and hate
denied me holding you
three times over
you turned your back
smiled as my eyes
burnt. i could not feel you
ogun
i dreamt
you turned your black
you turned your black
you turned
you're black ogun
my eyes still burn from chalk

Scene Nine
pop songs

kingston, jamaica, summertime 1993 at imogene's house.

imogene
mary mary, mi get a tape from foreign wid all di latest tune an mi know
di words to all a dem. listen to dah one yah... gimme a riddim.
i feel horny. i feel horny. i feel horny. i want some sex-y
i feel horny. i feel horny. i feel horny. i want some boot-y...

mary
well me know all a di tune dem weh a mash dung jamaica.
yuh know da one yah
mi love black oomaan cuz dem have nice complexion.
mi love black oomaan cuz have wholeheap a plan.
mi love black oomaan...

imogene
well yuh know da one yah.
mi want a gyal whe know how fi ride har man.
mi want a gyal who stan pon it long.
mi want a gyal...

mary
well gene a bet yuh nuh tell wha a di numba one chune a mash dung
jamaica right now.

imogene
which chune dat? mi jus tell yuh di numba one chune dem.

mary
a suh you tink. hear di numba one chune yah, a mash dung jamaica.
mek mi ride it like a stallion.
ride it like a horse.
ride it real long widout a pause.

imogene
don't need fi stop becuz a me have di stamina.
ghetto girl mi naw watch nuh gyal enah.

mary
irish mosh or cabbage wata.
gimme it cuz it put di oil inna yuh back dawta.

mary & imogene
mek mi ride it like a stallion
ride it like a horse.
ride it real long widout a pause

Scene Ten
mary's pregnancy

jamaica, december 1998. mary is throwing up, she then turns around and finds the audience.

him sweet me up wid him lyrics
den him pyzen mi wid him seed
tell mi big man nuh fi wear latex
end a month cum an mi still neva bleed

mi cyaan tell mi madda
mi granny a tun inna har grave
each generation 'spose fi get betta
a dat mi granny would seh

mi did waan fi be a teacha
mi did waan fi move to town
mi did waan fi rent one one room
18 mi's a big oomaan now

nuff oomaan a duh it
raise dem pickney all alone
mi did wrong
taught i could be different
which part gene deh now

yuh si deep deep inna mi closet
right near di back
dere's a white metal hanga
a sit down pon di rack

slowly mi could untwist it
tek mi time an stretch it out
mek di hook a likkle smaller
and den well – jus tek it out

money fi guh a clinic
tell mi, which part mi aguh find it
use di hanga inna mi closet
an dem well, jus tek it out

him sweet mi up wid him lyrics
dem him pyzen mi wid him seed
tell me big man nuh fi wear latex
end a month an mi still neva bleed

mary starts to sing miss lou and imogene joins in.

miss lou. miss lou. miss lou from alabama
she's sitting in a rocker eating betty crocker
watching the clock go tick tock. tick tick…

Scene Eleven
birtrite

jamaica, december 1998.

mary's baby (imogene)
    claims of miseducation bear no weight in the court of conception
    you both knew sex with no protection
    would bring forth the manifestation
    of this life
    my life
    earthly form i yearn to adorn
    fresh air though in these days spare i yearn to inhale
    all the firsts i yearn to reveal
    first smile, first laugh, i have steps to take
    but some doctor's hands could ripe out my fate
    cold metal prying, wrapped around my unformed skull
    faint heart once beating, to be reduced to an ever lasting lull

    i can feel each breath you take
    i live off the air you intake
    on your emotional rollercoaster entitled disillusioned
    i sit in the front seat, almost living proof of your confusion
    awaiting the end of the three month stretch,
    when the doctors will tell you it's too late to alter my fate
    and all you can do is start planning for my birth date
    but you hesitate again

    with two weeks to go – you second guess again
    you want to stop the natural flow
    that is my life again
    it's like you don't want to reach the peak,
    give me a chance to speak
    your name
    mommy
    my life is not a game

    mommy – can you hear me?
    i'm you and my pappy ready to manifest in flesh
    but with each beat of our heart i feel your hesitation
    i worry all i could bring you is stress and confusion
    it is my birth right to come into this world with love
    no desire to be a burden on you resides in me
    mommy – can you hear me?

if you can't raise me right
if you know you will deny me my birth right
though you had not the forsight to plan me
have the forsight to not bring me here
while you're laced with uncertainties and fear
no disrespect will be felt by me if you choose not to have me
my spirit will just sit heaven and continue waiting to be born
and it will one day come forth
just with a different earthly form
but at least i'll have a fair chance,
to live a life where i never see that closed glance
the one that will tell me in so many ways
that you regret me
that you didn't want me
mommy can you hear me?

Scene Twelve
shame shame shame

kingston jamaica, 1985. mary and imogene are seven and eight years old.

imogene
mary which game yuh waan play now shame shame shame?

mary
alright.

mary & imogene
shame shame shame
i don't want to go to foreign
no more more more
dere's a big fat policeman
at di door door door
if yuh hol him by him colla
lawd him oulda holla
if yuh hol him by him head
laws him ould dead
so i don't want to go to foreign
no more more more
beeeeeeep… (becomes imogene's answering machine)

Scene Thirteen
love rationed

canada winter 1998. the answering machine of imogene's boyfriend in canada plays.

derek (mary)

hey imogene. it's derek. yeah. i had a great time too. i got all your messages today. remember i said i was gonna be real busy soon? well yeah. we should get together some time though. take it easy my caribbean queen.

imogene

if if if if – if you do this i'll give you this
if if if if – if you do this i'll give you this

love rationed
portioned like grams of fat
two seconds on my lips
twenty years on my psyche
bloating my mind

a little reward for conformity
do you love me?
love rationed
served in bite size bits
never enough to quench hunger
always wanting more
always wanting more
more

more

love rationed
from lover to lover
partner to partner
treat me well
i'll reward you with intimacy

love rationed
mislabelled as passion
love rationed

the cup is empty
and there's no love potion
the flask is empty
and there's no love solution

i'm a producer
problem
options
pick one
solution
problem

solved
then i entered a relationship
demoted from producer to lay worker
addicted to love
pumping others' desires into my veins
inhaling others' wants
exhaling them as my own

pawning self-respect
selling identity and beliefs
just to get a fix
thinking a little dick can heal a loveless heart
addicted to love
i want to rap myself in your skin
'cause mine hurts

lonely bed
cold bed
warm it for me
be my security blanket
so i might blanket myself in insecurities
please let me rap myself in your skin

cause mine is tired of trying
scaled, cracked, thinning, veins exposed

wanting for, searching for me

for nothing is the emptiness felt inside

Scene Fourteen
dolly house

kingston, jamaica, summertime 1985. mary and imogene are playing dolly house.

imogene
dolly house. dolly house.

mary
imogene mi too big fi play dolly house.

imogene
yuh will get fi be suzette.

mary
alright. alright. alright. so who yuh waan play? di madda?

imogene

no mary. mi a play paulette.

mary

look here, me naw play di madda yuh know. cause mi nuh waan no pickney fi just look afta an do all di work wid one husband weh just deh deh a duh nuting. cause yuh know when mi turn big oomaan mi aguh…

imogene

well mi a play paulette an she nah guh have nuh man inna di house an nuh uncle. paulette is going to be one big oomaan yuh know mary. big an strong di man dem fraid of har.

mary

no man naw guh fraid of suzette yuh know. mi aguh jus tell dem seh, yuh si di cooking an di cleaning, an di looking afta di whole heap a pickney dem, dem mus duh all a dat while mi free fi duh what mi want fi duh. suzette nah go let nobady tie har down, neither pickney, nor man.

imogene

paulette too. as a madda of fact mi will look afta di pickney myself. any girl child mi have, mi nah lef har wid nobady. trust mi paulette aguh be responsible till she live to see many a years old.

mary

suzette aguh live till she old too. as a madda a fact suzette an paulette aguh be best best best friend til di two a dem dead.

imogene

an an an dem aguh talk every single day. all di time.

mary

an eat whole heap a ice cream too.

imogene

vanilla.

mary and imogene leap together, their heads touching. they walk towards their mirrors.

Scene Fifteen
mirror

mary is in kingston, jamaica. imogene is in montreal, canada, 1998. both women are looking in the mirror, at themselves and at each other.

imogene
    i miss you mary.

mary
    no you're lying to me.

imogene
    i miss you mary.

mary
    no you're lying to me.

mary & imogene
    how could you love me and treat me this way
    old habits die hard at the end of the day.

mary
    i woke up this morning

    i saw you staring at me
    in the mirror and you didn't greet me
    didn't say hi,

imogene
    tell me why
    you turned your head and started to cry

    mary why can't you look me in the eye

mary
    you don't love me.
    you don't love me.

imogene
    tell me mary what have you been told

    what have they sold you mary
    what have you been told
    they are lying mary don't believe what they say

mary
    how could you love me and treat me this way?

    dis country don't give a damn about my calloused hands

imogene
    dis country don't give a damn about my aching back

mary
    it don't give a damn about my tired feet

imogene
    it don't give a damn about my breaking heart

mary
    tell me gene, what have you been told
    what have they sold you gene
    what have you been told
    they are lying gene don't believe what they say

imogene
    old habits die hard at the end of the day

    whenever i go by the friendly corner store
    i can't deny the urge of wanting magazines galore
    white images of beauty are haunting taunting me

mary & imogene
    white images of beauty like sailing shipwrecked off at sea

mary
    white images of beauty i know they cannot set me free
    these nurtured insecurities as they commodify me
    robes are riding on my back as they build this economy

imogene
    dark and lovely hair straightener

mary
    ambi skin fader

imogene
    wax hair remover

mary
    and don't forget max factor

imogene
    to cover your face cause you come from an ugly race

mary
    why don't you cover you face cause you come from an ugly race
    and like a festering sore
    keep wanting more and more
    they just help to cultivate my internal self-hate
    vultures flying in the sky waiting to prey on i and i

imogene & mary
vultures flying in the sky waiting to prey on i and i.

Scene Sixteen
phone call

jamaica and canada, winter 1998. mary calls imogene in canada.

mary
hello i would like to make a collect call to montreal. 514-656-8932.
imogene lucreatia edwards. tell har a mary-ann simit.

imogene
yes, i accept the charges.

mary
whappen imogene – foreigner.

imogene
mary is really you?

mary
lawd gawd is who else you expect? ah me man.

imogene
everyting alright?

mary
(*pause*) yes. everyting alright. you?

imogene
yeah.

mary
well mi just did a call fe mek sure yuh alright. is a collect call suh mi
naw go too tarry.

imogene
seen.

mary
alright me gawn.

imogene
mary. i (*pause*)… mi will write yuh back dis time.

mary
> hold tight.

> *they hang up the phone.*

mary & imogene
> five hundred years
> five hundred years
> old habits die hard at the end of the day
> old habits die hard at the end of the day
> old habits die hard at the end of the day
> these old habits must die!!! at the end of the day.

> *the end.*

playwrights' notes on *yagayah*

di first mount a *yagayah* was pon a saturday. april 10, 1999. pon a $25 budget. we were two artists from toronto. a live. a study. anna work inna montreal. we'd seen one anedah work. felt a good vibe from it. an we decide fi duh a likkle ting. *yagayah* is an old jamaican expression we grow up wid. it mean anyting from "howdy doo" to "mi gawn." we use *yagayah* cuz it diverse like we subject matter. originally we jus put we poetry togedda. within di process wi decide fi perform one anedah work and build pon dee's two letters weh introduce imogene and mary. late late di night before di show when we was rehearsing and planning, dee seh – "we should write one script." nai nai kiss har teet an dee begin fi type. nai nai drop asleep. den dee wake har up fi start har typing shift. suh she work an dee sleep. we decide di night of di show dat yagayah mus get publish an get a professional run by a black theatre company. over 100 people siddung pon di hard hardwood grung dat faithful night of april 10, 1999. dem pay $5 fi cum si di show inna dee loft pon avenue des pins. some people even decide fi leave cause di subject matta did too heavy. bwoy. den wi workshop di piece wid btw where it was dramaturged by kate bligh. at di end a di session we did a reading at infinitheatre (2000). we try carry di script a btw dat year but it neva work out. imagine… so den we present di script inna montreal again (2001) tru yah ga yah productions. dee tell ahdri bout di script an ahdri get it inna di summerworks theatre festival inna toronto (2001). during dat process di piece was dramaturged by diane roberts who patiently help we fi put di scenes dem in order an develop di character dem. from dere it was inna di rock.paper.sistahz. festival inna toronto (2002). director weyni mengesha refuse fi let we get way wid anyting. she diligently and brilliantly brought *yagayah* to new heights where imogene and mary's friendship became the focal point of di whole piece. an here we are, back inna montreal inna 2003. ah rehearse fi wi run. anna wait fi di pressing a dis anthology. *yagayah: two.womyn.black.griots* has come full circle. thank you nai nai. thank you dee. for deciding to cum when you did. thank you *yagayah*. tru dis piece we learn how fi let guh a we work. an how fi hol on pon it. cuz people will use an abuse yuh. if yuh don't careful. we a learn fi ask for weh we deserve. an we learn seh life is indeed a cycle. from beginning/birth/middle/mother/crone/death an back again. weh yuh put inna har is mos definitely weh yuh aguh get in return. our friendship is interwoven wid di journey of *yagayah*. dis process of learning to love ourselves tru each other as black oomaan is beautiful. painful. and necessary. we live fi si di ending/beginning a dis cycle. ase. walk good.

Consecrated
Ground

George Elroy Boyd

A former host of the CBC Morning News, respected broadcaster and journalist **George Elroy Boyd** was born in the north end of Halifax. An award-winning playwright, his work has appeared on stage and television. His play *Shine Boy*, about the life of Halifax native George Dixon, the first Black man to win a world boxing title, made Mr. Boyd the first African-Nova-Scotian to have a play professionally produced on Neptune Theatre's Mainstage. *Consecrated Ground* had its world premiere at Halifax's Eastern Front Theatre in January 1999. George Boyd is working on a new play and his first novel. Mr. Boyd lives in Montreal and is currently Playwright Associate at Black Theatre Workshop. *Consecrated Ground* was nominated for a Governor General's Award in 2000.

Making the "Damn" Nation the Race's "Salvation": The Politics of George Elroy Boyd's *Consecrated Ground.*

by George Elliott Clarke

— • — — • — — • —

George Elroy Boyd's play, *Consecrated Ground* (1999), lays bare the raw wound of the only Canuck, anti-Black racism most Canadians know about: the slow razing, between 1964 and 1970, of the historical Black village of Africville, a rural, harbour-side enclave of the City of Halifax. In the decades since the completion of the Africville Relocation, as the bulldozing *cum* social engineering of the 400-resident community was labelled, ashamed liberals have had reason to rue the liberalism that insisted, in the cause of "progress," that the so-called ghetto be eliminated. Indeed, part of the tragedy of the crucifixion of Africville—a polity that had existed for approximately 150 years—is that, in the early 1960s, it didn't sound racist and it didn't seem wrong to demand its destruction. Many—Black and white—thought it was all for the best that Africville be broken into rubble and its people dispersed to public housing, where they would have access to city services and, gradually, "integrate," if only with the white poor. However, the refusal of the former Africville residents and their descendants to forget this lost "oasis" has engineered its almost continuous resurrection in political spirit – if not in architectural flesh. Certainly, Africville is, now, merely a little used park and a memorial site, and no one "lives" there anymore. But the community persists as an act of memory and an act of witness, one that deems the Africville Relocation an act of injustice – and of racism.

Boyd's play participates viscerally in this radical revision of the Africville "news" story. No longer a narrative of social progress, where rural, Black outcasts are forcibly introduced to the benefits of the urban, welfare state, and where untutored Black preachers meet their match in white social workers, the history Boyd attends to is one of an epochal clash between Black religion and "white" modernity. In *Consecrated Ground*, the struggle over the fate of Africville and its citizens is viewed as a political-philosophical contest between conservatism—i.e. the conservation of the "race" (to refer to an 1897 essay by the great African-American sociologist W.E.B. Du Bois)—and liberalism, or the reduction of community to an assembly of individual "consumers." When Willem Lyle signs over his wife's property to the City of Halifax, and does so on the coffin of his son, Tully (slain by rats drawn to the neighbourhood by the garbage dump that the city deliberately placed nearby), he concedes, dramatically, that a conservative regard for heritage must give way to the liberal ideal of individual, socio-economic advancement. If the life of his son means little to the City of Halifax, the life of Africville means little to Willem. In I.v, he comments, with aptly selfish individualism, "I wanna job. I wanna home. I want *the hell out of Africville!*" His attitude disregards utterly the beauties of a Black realm built by hard work and centred on the spiritual life of the Seaview (United) Baptist Church, then one of the two-dozen-plus churches in the Black-created, African United Baptist Association of Nova Scotia (established in 1854). (Importantly, these churches constitute the archipelago that is the African-Nova Scotian "nation." To lose a church—as Africville lost Seaview—is to lose a constitutive element of the community.)

By suggesting that the conservative/conservationist vision may be superior to the liberal/individualist option, Boyd sets his play in dialogue with larger, African Diasporic concerns, especially as articulated in African-American drama. Introducing *Colored Contradictions: An Anthology of Contemporary African-American Plays* (1996), co-editor Harry J. Elam, Jr., notes the plays "struggle with definitions of family and with notions of what is community." Here, says Elam, "external and internal forces threaten the security and the values"—that is, identities—of the families portrayed. For Elam, *family* is the site of identity and of crisis. Clearly, Boyd's play, with its dramatization of the implosion and exile of the Tully family—because of Willem's lack of faith in the worth of his heritage—re-enacts the dynamics Elam discusses. But, while Willem becomes the spokesperson for—and the symbol of—Black defeat, his wife, Clarise (Leasey), emerges as the heroically obstinate articulator of Black worth and faith. With her sassy interventions and take-no-guff actions, Clarise projects the Black nationalist alternative to an effete integrationism. It is she who insists, over the objections of her traitorous husband and the good-intentioned but ultimately Machiavellian city official, Clancy, that Africville is not an impoverished hell, but rather, "consecrated ground." Significantly, it is a woman who maintains "the faith of the fathers" – not Tully and not Reverend Miner (whose name suggests he is "minor"). Unlike Willem, Clarise refuses to "sell out" to the blandishments of liberal modernity. She succeeds—though in a perfectly Pyrrhic victory—in honouring her dead infant son in Black "nation" space despite the objections of a powerful, white-controlled city. She remembers who she is and where she is from: "My great-granddaddy built this [house] outta his own hands, Willem. It was just him and the dirt, Willem…. And he farmed that ol' acid-ee, rocky dirt out there so he could feed his family" (I.v). These blood-and-soil sentiments are, for Clarice, far more vital and virtuous than Willem's yearnings to enter, over the body of his dead son, a rich, white society that scorns Black people.

If, as *Black Atlantic* theorist Paul Gilroy claims, in African-American discourse, "the integrity of the race is… made interchangeable with the integrity of Black masculinity" and "the contemporary political and economic crises of Blacks are [portrayed as] crises of self-belief and self-identity," these truths apply to the African-Canadian drama of George Boyd as well. Willem is an abject example of the "failed" Black male (Clarice calls him a "Black bastard" in II.ix); the death of the male Tully symbolizes the looming death of Africville itself; only Clarise holds fast to the principles of her culture, thus emerging as a "masculine" character, given her pluck, her determination to see Tully properly buried, and, in II.ix, her command that Willem leave their home. The sadness of the loss of Africville is figured here partly as the emasculation of Black males and the "masculinization" of Black females, within the inclement context of a white male-dominated society. Thus, in I.v, Clarice tells Willem, "It ain't the [Africville] men that got the power. It's just we women let them *think* they got the power." If, to cite Gilroy again, "the symbolic reconstruction of [Black] community is projected onto an image of the ideal heterosexual couple," here, in this case, the actual destruction of Africville is symbolized by the "withering away" of the marriage between Clarise and Tully and the death of its only "fruit." By telling Willem to leave, Clarise ejects her husband from their marital bed – and from the land she has inherited, but that he has liquidated over the body of their heir apparent.

In the last scene of the play, II.x, the Lyle family is reconstituted—perhaps ephemerally—in the instance of Clarice's triumphant consecration of her son's casket with Africville soil. Still, this "triumph"- is empty, given that both the scion of the Lyle household and of Clarice's inheritance is lost. Thus, the once-Promised Land of Africville becomes a graveyard and a ghost town. Moreover, if Willem and Clarise remain married, the play itself becomes a truly *black* comedy, with these parents reduced to ghouls picking over the remains of their infant and the memories of their patrimony.

Arguably, in *Consecrated Ground*, Boyd posits conservative nationalism as the best guarantor of cultural survival, thus rejecting the communal dissolution threatened by liberal individualism. Indeed, in most of his dramas to date, including *Consecrated Ground: The Teleplay* (1992, 1996) and *Gideon's Blues* (1996), Boyd dramatizes a pitiless excoriation of Black male "failure" and the compensating necessity for Black matriarchal assertion so as to preserve—or conserve—the race.

Perhaps Boyd was fated to write such dramas. Born in Halifax, Nova Scotia, in 1952, he grew up as a member of the two-century-old Black community, and would have been only ten when Halifax City Council voted the destruction of Africville, then twelve, when the first homes fell. He lived his teen years while Africville was dissolving before wrecking balls and urban renewal propaganda. He also came of age when a new insurgency began to animate African-Nova Scotia – or *Africadia*, partly in reaction to the evisceration of Africville. (One must note that Africville was only one of forty-three—43!—Black settlements in Nova Scotia in the 1960s; hence, the same recriminations lodged against it—its status as a segregated space, its "poor" housing, its lack of sewer and water services—could have justified the removal of *every* Black territory in the province.) True: the only good produced by the disappearance of Africville was the appearance of a *conscious* Black cultural nationalism.... In this regard, *Consecrated Ground* is the heir of fierce, vengeful, and epic activism that produced the Black United Front of Nova Scotia, the Society for the Protection and Preservation of Black Culture in Nova Scotia, and the Africville Genealogical Society.

George Elliott Clarke *teaches African-Canadian literature at the University of Toronto.*

Consecrated Ground was first produced at the Sir James Dunn Theatre by Eastern Front Theatre, Halifax, Nova Scotia, in January, 1999 with the following company:

CLARICE LYLE	Jackie Richardson
WILLEM LYLE	Jeremiah Sparks
SARAH LIED	Murleta Williams
JIMMY WILLIS	Lucky Campbell
GROOVEY PETERS	Anne-Marie Woods
TOM CLANCY	Chris Shore
REVEREND MINER	David Woods

Directed by Richard Donat   Set Design by Stephen Osler
Lighting Design by Leigh Ann Vardy   Stage Managed by Christine Oakey

— • — — • — — • —

CHARACTERS:
Clarice Lyle: A lifelong resident of Africville and the wife of Willem. She's just had a baby, probably her last, as she's an older woman, older than her husband in fact.
Willem Lyle: Husband of Clarice; younger than she. He's from Annapolis Royal, Nova Scotia, and moved to Africville—into her home—when he married Clarice.
Sarah Lied: A matriarch of Africville.
Jimmy "Double Speak" Willis: An Africville resident. He stutters, thus the nickname.
Groovey Peters: The "loose" woman in Africville. Originally from Jamaica via Montreal.
Tom Clancy: White and fresh out of social work school, he has been assigned to the Africville relocation project.
Reverend Miner: The minister of the Seaview Baptist Church. This Africville church is one of the many he serves.

SETTING:
The community of Africville, 1965. Our set is comprised of several hanging cutouts in the background. These are individually lit, painted and formed to represent the various houses, Victorian and Georgian, that populated the site. These hang at different levels, providing a sense of depth. The light on the cutouts switches to indicate the location of various scenes, i.e., for scenes inside the church, the church cutout is appropriately lit. For outdoor scenes, all the cutouts are lit. The uppermost cutout is of the church. At the end of the play, of course, this is the last piece to go black. Stage right contains Willem and Clarice's house. Here we have a stove, a fridge, an old vinyl 1960s kitchen table, chairs, as well as a pull-down couch. All are cramped stage right, as these people live in one room. To the extreme right is a doorway with a curtain for a door which leads to what they refer to as the "back room." Stage left is the interior of the church. A pulpit, of course, and about three pews. It's arranged diagonally for sight-line purposes, with the pulpit facing directly and squarely to the audience. In "the pit" stands the well. A sign, authentic to Africville, reads: "Please boil this water before drinking and cooking." During intermission, the well is removed to make way for the final scene.

l to r: Lucky Campbell, Jeremiah Sparks.
Photo by Ken Kam.

Consecrated Ground

by George Boyd

—•— —•— —•—

ACT I
Scene One

The house lights dim to the a cappella sound of "Poem #1" from Joe Sealy's Africville Suite. The sound fades into Aunt SARAH humming a lullaby. She sits in an chair rocking Tully. It's mid to late dusk as CLARICE enters.

CLARICE
Oh, he's gone now, Aunt Sarah, I better take 'em–

SARAH
No-no, Clarice, I enjoys it! *(beat)* Why look, he be sleepin', Leasey. Sleepin' like a... like a–

CLARICE
Like a *(beat)* baby? ...Aunt Sarah?

SARAH
Yeah! Like a baby!

CLARICE
(chuckling) Aunt Sarah, the chile is a baby!

SARAH
Well you know-what-I-mean! *(She chuckles. Beat.)* Where'd you say Willem be's? I hear he's the new choirmaster.

CLARICE
Ain't that somethin'? That's where he is now, rehearsin'.

SARAH
Oh...

CLARICE
Well they can rehearse all they want if you ask me.

SARAH
I was always wonderin' how come you never join the choir.

CLARICE
'Cause I can read me my music, Aunt Sarah, that's why.

SARAH
What?

CLARICE
Aunt Sarah I can read me my notes. Music notes. Sharps. Sharps and stuff. Sharps I tell ya. 'Cause every nigger know that choir put the flat in the pancake.

SARAH
(laughing) Girl you better stop!

CLARICE
And don'tcha be caught bakin' no bread when they sings. Why every woman in Africville tippy-toein' round here and askin', "Leasey? The choir rehearsin' today?" Now Aunt Sarah why they be askin' me that?

SARAH
Why?

CLARICE
'Cause they...

CLARICE & SARAH
(in unison) Flattt!!

SARAH
Now you better not tell Willem that! The choir sound fine to me.

CLARICE
It is a fine choir, Aunt Sarah. Just I... I love teasin' Willem about it that's all.

SARAH
I think you wanna tell that man right about he's-self.

CLARICE
Why? (She chuckles.) More fun like this, Aunt Sarah.

SARAH
Oh the love-birds!

CLARICE
And Willem gonna be singin' a couple of solos soon he tells me.

SARAH
Now see what I tell ya about coloured women? They push the men down, just to pull 'em up. Throw 'em in that corner to pull 'em into the other – no wonder our men be so confused!

CLARICE
Aunt Sarah I don't do that!

SARAH
You guilty as charged. Poor Willem prob'ly think you think he can't sing, the way you go on about that choir. Well he the best thing that ever happened to the Africville choir I tells us. They been soundin' real good since he come to Africville, and I'm gonna tell 'em some-such. Now git me some tea.

CLARICE
Oh, all right. (*She goes about her business, then halts.*) Aunt Sarah why I always feel I'm your little girl. "Go git me some tea" – what I do? Git right up and run for your tea.

SARAH
S'pose to give me my propers, Leasey. I'm old.

CLARICE
Old?! Aunt Sarah you be older than the Hills-a-Rome! In fact, you been old ever since I met ya. I think your momma made history: first woman to give birth to a senior citizen! *Old!!*

They laugh.

SARAH
Ain't tired though. Say? You sign them papers you was goin' on about? (*CLARICE hesitates.*) Leasey?

CLARICE
(*vacantly*) Uh-hunh?

SARAH
I say – those papers?

CLARICE
I signed 'em. I'm puttin' everythin' in Willem's name. See, if anything ever happen to me, him and Tully be taken care of.

SARAH
Little-girl, now I know what you doin', don't need to be repeatin' it. It just foolish-ins if you ask me. This land always been in your–

CLARICE
Well this my family now, Aunt Sarah. I'm older than Willem. And if somethin' ever happen to me – I know Willem take care of himself – but I got a baby now. I got a son.

SARAH

He'd take care a Tully. Ya know that.

CLARICE

I know he would, that's why I trust 'em. I signed all the land— everythin'—over to 'em, and please don't start.

SARAH

Now have I said a word? *(She chuckles.)*

CLARICE

But Aunt Sarah I know what you're thinkin' and I know I'm doin' what's right. The lawyer downtown that I clean for say he do all the legal stuff *pro bono*. That means for free.

SARAH

Little-girl? *(beat)* You a Smith, Willem be a Lyle.

CLARICE

I'm a Lyle too, Aunt Sarah. So's Tully. This all for Tully.

SARAH

Little-girl...

CLARICE

Aunt Sarah – you know when you mad at me you always call me "little-girl." Why you mad at me now?

SARAH

'Cause this is not *necessarily*!! *(She whispers.)* And Little-girl?

CLARICE

Whaa?

SARAH

(blurting) I don't care what lawyer wanna do a Sonny Bono!

CLARICE

Pro bono!!

SARAH

That too!

They laugh.

CLARICE

Well it's done now. Everything in Willem's name. 'Ventually, Tully's.

SARAH
Suit yourself.

CLARICE starts humming "The Storm is Passing Over."

Why you hummin' that hymn?"

CLARICE
What hymn?

SARAH
"The Storm is Passing Over."

CLARICE
Oh... I always hum that, it's my favourite.

CLARICE continues humming.

SARAH
Well if the storm ain't come yet, how can it be passing over?!

CLARICE
Aunt Sarah?! You sumpin' else. *(beat)* Maybe I put Tully in his basket now.

SARAH
Just a little longer, 'kay? Leasey?

CLARICE
Oh, all right.... Lord, Sarah, you shoulda been his momma. You always holdin' 'em.

SARAH
'Cause this child's been blessed. Look how late in life you had 'em. Tully be you and Willem's gift from God, I tells us.

CLARICE
I know, but Momma had me late in life, maybe... I take after Momma.

SARAH
Ain't no takin' after her a-tall! I mean ya met Willem so late in life. That's why ya had Tully so late. *(pause)* You and Willem all the times up here in this house wif the door closed. A " Do not disturb" sign on the door too, thank-you-very-much! I mean, whatcha all thinks?! You in the Ritz Carl-a-ton or sumpin?! This be Africville, girl! Africville! *(She laughs.)*

CLARICE
Now Aunt Sarah don't be–

SARAH
And don't be blushin' and goin' on over there, Leasey. Everyone knowed you weren't makin' no dinner with that sign on yer door!

They laugh.

CLARICE
Oh, Aunt Sarah...

SARAH
But why y'all had to be so oblivious about it–

CLARICE chuckles.

What now?

CLARICE
"Obvious," Aunt Sarah. Why we had to be so "obvious about it."

SARAH
That too!

They laugh again.

CLARICE
Aunt Sarah, like... like don't you wish you would've had babies?

SARAH
Girl I've had all you babies. I been all your mommas. I raised you when your momma was in-service. You was there.

CLARICE
Yeah – I guess you was in-service too, right? To all of us.

SARAH
Uh-hunh.

CLARICE
And made me eat my carrots.

SARAH
And your turnip greens.

CLARICE
And to this day Aunt Sarah, I can't stomach me no turnip greens and no carrots!

SARAH
That so?

CLARICE
Uh-hunh. Willem say they sumpin' the mice nibble on!

SARAH
(laughing) Good! 'Cause we ain't got no mice in Africville – we got rats!! Ever since that damn dump…

CLARICE
Yeah…

SARAH
Blame that one on me too, baby?

CLARICE
'Course!

CLARICE
And come to think of it Aunt Sarah – you was old back then.

SARAH
Can't study it! *(pause)* The choir sounds. I wonder what they rehearsin' for Sundee?

CLARICE
Willem never said. Aunt Sarah you boilin' your water?

SARAH
Hump!

Offstage, WILLEM, solo, sings "My Lord What a Morning."

That Willem now.

CLARICE
Don't he sound precious, Aunt Sarah? Like a angel. Tully gonna have a voice just like him. You wait and see.

SARAH
And look-it y'all a blushin' and bloomin' over there. Course he sound precious. I already tol' ya: the best thin' that ever happen to the Africville choir.

There is a pause.

CLARICE

Now what was we talkin' about? *(beat)* Oh-yeah, the government say "boil before drinkin'" so I boil.

SARAH

Girl I been drinkin' out that well since I was Tully's size and ain't poisoned me yet. The gov'ment? The gov'ment also put that dump out there. Give us all rats. You truss the gov'ment?

CLARICE

Aunt Sarah I got nothin' to say 'bout no governments. They mind their own business, I mind mine. And you were drinking that well water long before there was a dump. The dump *old-ddd* too! *(She laughs.)*

SARAH

Can't study it!

GROOVEY *enters carrying a pail.*

GROOVEY

(lifting the pail) Hi everybody!!

SARAH

Groovey, the baby!

GROOVEY

Lobster, Leasey, lobster! They're runnin' and the men be down there throwin' 'em ashore!

SARAH

Humph! Lobster ol' poor people's food!

CLARICE

Well it sound good to me. Aunt Sarah do you mind watchin' Tully a bit and I'll go get us some lobster!

SARAH

Take all the time you want, Leasey. Groovey, you remember the "Do Not Disturb" sign?

GROOVEY

Uh-hunh... sure do!

CLARICE

Aunt Sarah!

SARAH

(laughing) And Leasey... Leasey up here runnin' and tellin' everybody: "Willem be a carpenter. Willem be a carpenter. Willem be a carpenter."

Well, Little-girl, we all knows Willem be a carpenter, but we also knows
your cupboards is fixed!!

They burst out laughing.

GROOVEY
Fixed?! Fixed 'er like a dog they did!!

CLARICE
Fixed? Girl, I just had Tully ya know!

GROOVEY
Well Groovey Peters ain't doin' that for nobody. Ya hear? Nobody. Sides,
I got me my, ah "special friend." And he don't want no babies!

SARAH
Oh… and who that be now, Groovey?

CLARICE
Yeah, tell us.

GROOVEY
Oh… I… dunno… ah, one of yer, ah… "higher-ups."

CLARICE
Really?

SARAH
Go-on.

GROOVEY
Got me an account at Klines he did!

CLARICE
You got an account at Klines?! Well baby they must be givin' 'em away
is all I can tell ya. I mean… who you give as you references? *(They
chuckle.)* Then ag'in, with all them fellas comin and goin' in yer place–
(She chuckles.) –guess that ain't no problem is it?

SARAH
No, but Groovey… well where ya tell 'em ya work girl?

GROOVEY
Whaa…? Oh you two think I'm payin'?! Uh-unh. Groovey Peters got…
friends.

SARAH
Rich friends I'm thinkin'.

GROOVEY
Uh-hunh. Say? Who's dat white man down at de well with Jimmy?
I mean, he kinda young for Groovey... but... Groovey, ah, gotta keep
the books open like.

CLARICE
I seen 'em too. Jimmy look real excited-like.

GROOVEY
Groovey didn't get dat close, girl! Why, look at de way Groovey
dressed!!

SARAH
Yeah... you is a sight all right.

GROOVEY
(laughing) Aunt Sarah! *(beat)* Leasey? Do Groovey look dat bad?!

CLARICE
Groovey-girl we're goin' catchin' lobsters ain't we? Ya want high-heels
and lipstick or sumpin'?

SARAH
Don't be temptin' that ol'fashion-plate, Leasey. She be down on the
beach in gowns and tiaras and some-such.

CLARICE
Well let's git. *(beat)* Aunt Sarah you sure you gonna be all right?

SARAH
I'll be fine.

GROOVEY
Bye, Aunt Sarah.

SARAH
Bye.

CLARICE
See ya in a bit.

As they exit they shuffle and sing-song, ad libbing.

CLARICE & GROOVEY
(in unison) Lobster! Lobster Aunt Sarah!! We gonna git lobster... *(etc.)*

They exit.

Scene Two

The next night, WILLEM approaches the well carrying a bucket. JIMMY sits there on the ground. He seems to have been under some stress and is preoccupied.

WILLEM
Double-speak? That you over there? *(beat)* Whatcha doin' sittin' out there in the dark?

JIMMY doesn't reply.

Double-speak?

JIMMY
What?

WILLEM
How can ya tell a man stutters by his sneeze?

JIMMY
H-h-how?

WILLEM
(chuckling) He goes "Ah-chew! *(beat)* Ah-chew!"

He laughs. JIMMY doesn't respond.

Now Double-speak we all know you eat so much lobster – you stutter. You know? – Two-claws?! *(He laughs.)*

JIMMY
S-s-shouldn't make no f-f-f-fun of a man's G-g-god-given c-c-complaints.

WILLEM
Hey, Double-speak, man – lighten up. The world ain't comin' to an end.

JIMMY
(softly) Is for me.

WILLEM
What? Where's yer bucket?

JIMMY
A-a-ain't got a b-b-bucket.

WILLEM

Well whatcha doin' sittin' down here then? You fixin' to rob somebody or somethin'?

JIMMY

(excitedly jumping to his feet) No! No! No! No! ...I-I-I-I don't s-s-steal, Willem!!

WILLEM

I ain't sayin' ya do!! *(beat)* Just strange to be sittin' here by yourself this late at night. Man!! You're one of the only brothers in Africville that got a full-time job. You shouldn't be mopin' around here unless you... *(pause)* Oh that it? You got laid off?

JIMMY

No-no, I-I-I still... da-da-da-drivin' my truck.

WILLEM

Well then, you should be on top of the world. I mean you got a job. And what else ya tell me? When ya joined the choir you tol' me it was the first time a word came outta your mouth without–

JIMMY

S-s-stutterin'...

WILLEM

Yeah, so why'd ya quit?

JIMMY

C-c-cause I ain't g-g-gonna be here no m-m-more.

WILLEM

You mean at the church?

JIMMY

No-no-no-no-no... I-I-I mean h-h-here.

WILLEM

Here?! *(He lowers his voice.)* You mean in Africville? You ain't gonna be here in Africville no more? *(JIMMY nods affirmatively.)* Well where ya goin'?

JIMMY

A-a-aways...

WILLEM

I mean... where you *gonna* be?

There's a long pause.

JIMMY
Y-y-ya gotta k-k-keep my this a s-s-s-secret…

WILLEM
Yeah…

JIMMY
K-k-keep this a s-s-secret – you hear?!

WILLEM
All right – it's a secret! It's a secret!

Pause.

JIMMY
Ya g-g-gotta p-p-promise.

WILLEM
I promise, I promise. *(under his breath)* Man-oh-man.

JIMMY sits down and stares off. WILLEM consults his watch.

JIMMY
I-I-I sole my p-p-place.

WILLEM
(incredulously) You whaa?! You sole yer–

JIMMY
I-I-I dun t-t-tol'ya I–

WILLEM
You sole yer place? *(He chuckles.)* That's a good one! Like somebody's gonna buy a place in Africville? Jimmy there's some miracles even Jesus can't make happen. *(He starts lifting his bucket.)* Unless you gonna be serious, I gotta get me goin'.

JIMMY
I-I-I is s-s-serious, Willem. I-I-I… is!

WILLEM
Well who bought it?

JIMMY
(blurting) The city!!

WILLEM halts abruptly.

WILLEM
The city!?

JIMMY
Uh-hunh...

WILLEM
Halifax?... City?

JIMMY
Uh-hunh... y-y-yeah.

WILLEM
Man, how big a fool you think I am? You expect me to believe–

JIMMY
It-it-it t-t-t-true. I-I-I got me, five thousand d-d-dollars.

WILLEM
Five thousand dollars?! Now what's the city want with this ol' piece a land?

JIMMY
T-t-they says w-w-we don't live w-w-well enough.

WILLEM
Don't live well enough?! Well why don't they help us fix it up then?! *(beat)* Here I am livin' in the middle of Halifax in 1965 – and I'm lugging water from a well?! *Don't live well enough?!* I mean if rats was money – man I'd be livin' me on some ol' tree-lined boulevard. And no dump would be my next door neighbour either. And, and, the rats would have ta pay room and board! *(He chuckles.)*

JIMMY
T-t-t-this my h-h-home, Willem. Born and raised here on t-t-t-this ground.

WILLEM
Oh, you sound like Leasey.

JIMMY
But... but... t-t-the white man s-s-say, we all g-g-gotta move.

WILLEM
We all gotta move? *(He chuckles.)* He obviously ain't met Leasey yet. So where *we* all movin' to?

JIMMY
P-p-place called U-u-uniacke S-s-square.

WILLEM
That in Halifax?

JIMMY
T-t-they call it t-t-the p-p-projects. On Gott-Gott-Gott–

WILLEM
Gottingen Street. I seen the place. I never thought nothin' of it. I thought it was for city folk.

JIMMY
It-it-it for us. They th-the projects, I-I-I tells ya.

WILLEM
Well yer lucky if you ask me. You're gonna have what I ain't. Now who ya say this white man was?

JIMMY
Mister C-c-clancy. Ya-ya-ya gots ta k-k-keep this a secret, Willem ya gots to keep this a–

WILLEM
Yeah-yeah. *(beat)* Well I just hope this Clancy comes to see Leasey and me. When ya gotta leave?

JIMMY
Next week.

WILLEM
Next week?! *(chuckles; slyly)* Man! If you need a hand movin' and all–

JIMMY
I-I-I ain't g-g-gonna g-g-go!

WILLEM
So you mean you really ain't sold nuthin'. You ain't signed nuthin'?

JIMMY
I signed…

WILLEM
Well the man own the property now, Double-speak. You gotta move.

JIMMY
C-c-c-can't force me o-o-o-out.

WILLEM
If you signed the papers there's nuthin' you can do about it now, Jimmy. It's too late.

JIMMY
I-I-I ain't m-m-m-movin'.

WILLEM
Suit yourself. *(He stands, lifting the buckets.)* Look, if you want me to help you move or anythin' like that, I will. But now I gotta get me goin'. See ya later.

WILLEM eyes him for a few moments.

You gonna stay here all night, Double-speak?

JIMMY
Just a little b-bit.

WILLEM moves on. Lights dim on the well as he approaches the house.

Scene Three

WILLEM notices someone or something crawling. It is GROOVEY crawling towards the house. He drops his bucket and runs directly to her.

WILLEM
Groovey! Ohmegawd... Groovey!

She slumps into his arms.

GROOVEY
(stirring; delirious) Please... no mo'... no... don't hit me... no mo'...

WILLEM
What happened?!

GROOVEY
I... I... I was...

WILLEM
(calling) Leasey?! Leasey?! *(to GROOVEY)* Here... let's git to the porch.

He guides her to the porch where they sit down. GROOVEY stands and starts swinging wildly, attacking him.

It's me!! Willem! Calm down, now! Sit...

GROOVEY sits and openly weeps as CLARICE enters the porch.

CLARICE
What is going on out – *OhmyGod, Groovey?!* Groovey what happened?! *(She glances at WILLEM.)* She's cut! Git some water!

CLARICE starts wiping GROOVEY's face with the end of her apron.

Boilin' on the stove! Hurry!

WILLEM hurries off.

And some cloths!!

GROOVEY
My... shoppin'... bags...

CLARICE
Shopping bags?!

GROOVEY
Dey in de road.

CLARICE
Willem will get the bags. What happened girl?! What happened to ya?

GROOVEY
...walkin'...

CLARICE
Walkin?! Walkin' where?

GROOVEY
...dey come...

CLARICE
Who come?... *(calling off)* The water Willem!! Hurry up!!

CLARICE
(aghast) My God, girl.... You're a mess.

GROOVEY resists.

Just let me wipe your face now Groovey! Blood all over the place here.

GROOVEY
...dey slap... dey hits Groovey...

WILLEM enters with a basin and a cloth. CLARICE dabs and wipes GROOVEY's face.

CLARICE
What ya s'pose happened to her?

WILLEM
Ya gotta ask, Leasey?

CLARICE
Broom the coon, right?

GROOVEY
(blurting) Dey broom and dey kick and dey spit–!

CLARICE
Now take it easy child.

WILLEM
Well that's what I thinkin', look at 'er. I mean we know what she do, *they* know what she do.

CLARICE
Well I heard a broom the coon before, but usually ain't no women be involved.

WILLEM
Oh yes! *(beat)* Maybe not in Africville, but they are.

CLARICE
She say somethin' 'bout shopping bags in the road.

WILLEM
I'll get them.

He exits.

CLARICE
They hurt you, girl? You know? In that way?

GROOVEY
...naw dey don'ts, girl... dey just punch, and kick, and spit, and yell nigger whore, and... and... dey kicks some mores...

CLARICE
Where this happen?

GROOVEY
On de road... dis car come behind me...

WILLEM
(entering) Were you by yourself?

GROOVEY
(blurting) Yes I be by me-self!

CLARICE embraces her.

CLARICE
You gonna be all right, honey... all right...

GROOVEY
When de car swoosh by, sumpin' hit me in de head. I looks and den dey get come out de car, throwin' rocks, yelling, hittin and kickin'... I crawls... Groovey crawls here...

GROOVEY stands, yelling defiantly.

Dey don't know who Groovey Peters is!! Dey don't know...

WILLEM
Oh yes they does.

CLARICE
Sit down now, rest. Rest...

GROOVEY
Wait till I tells de man!!

WILLEM
What man?

CLARICE
Some white big-wig, some man buyin' 'er gifts and 'spense accounts.

WILLEM
So what?

CLARICE
She thinks it real.

WILLEM
(in total disbelief) Jee-sus. Only thing real is one thing.

GROOVEY
(*yelling*) My friend be different!! He gonna marry me!! And he gonna git dem dat do dis to Groovey!! He gonna git dem!!

CLARICE
Shush, now – Willem you gittin' her all upset.

WILLEM
Well somebody gotta talk that girl into some sense. (*beat*) Groovey – ya can't trust them. Any of them. They're good with words to yer face, but don'tcha turn yer back. They talk about this at work and laughs and grins, I hear 'em Leasey. And when they know you heard 'em, they all pleads none of them ever did it. Oh-no. Not them. Maybe not. But they laughs and slaps the ones on the back that do. And... and... see? Somehow that free 'em of the guilt. Ain't no fertile ground in their minds, just old fallow fields. And when it comes to niggers, that's just how they prefers it. Groovey?! You listenin' to me?!

CLARICE, hands rolling into fists, defiantly stands and looks WILLEM in the eye.

CLARICE
Is now the time, Willem? This the 'propriate time?!

WILLEM
When's the 'propriate time, Leasey?! When?! When she in a box?! She believe some white knight gonna ride into Africville and marry her?! Protect her?! He gonna laugh and say, "Stupid whor-r-r-e!!" just like the ones that broomed her!!

They regard one another for a few moments.

I'm so tired of this!! (*beat*) 'Cause a what they do... we... suffer!!

He storms off and exits. CLARICE returns to GROOVEY.

CLARICE
Come on, baby. Come on inside.

They exit into the house and shut the door.

Scene Four

It is Monday morning. The abrupt and rude noise of bulldozers sounds as SARAH silently goes to the well. She carries two buckets and starts pumping water. Momentarily CLANCY approaches, carrying an attache case.

CLANCY
Howdy.

SARAH
(*reluctantly*) Oh… hell-low.

CLANCY
They sure start early in these parts, don't they?

SARAH
You come for some water, Sonny?

CLANCY
No-no, just passin' through, but I–

SARAH
Oh.

CLANCY
I was thinkin' how do they sleep with that bulldozer raging and going-on like that?

SARAH
You know that dump just a recent fixture to Africville and I for one hates it. All that noise drive the rats into our houses.

CLANCY
Shame.

SARAH
Wasn't no dump here afore, just a recent fixture I tells us. They need a dump, so why not put it right next to where coloured peoples lives? That make sense to you, Sonny?

CLANCY
Ah, I think, ah they–

SARAH
Me neither! It got to be seen that the white man then, don't think the coloured is human, right?

CLANCY
I, ah, saw, ah, the–

SARAH
That too! Don't gotta be no Philadelphia lawyer to figure that one out. 'Cause little ol' me with my grade-three schoolin' – I been readin'.

CLANCY
Really?

SARAH
Been readin' all about it. 'Bout South Africa.

CLANCY
Oh, I thought you were referring to–

SARAH
That too! I gits Jimmy's Sonny to go to the lie-berry for me. All kinds a books 'bout South Africa in the lie-berry. You read about South Africa, Sonny?

CLANCY
No, I, ah…

SARAH
Didn't think so! See ya don't need learnin' to put this picture all together, Sonny. Age is all the learnin' I got, and this place be just like South Africa.

CLANCY
But this is Canada, Mrs.…?

SARAH
Miss Lied. But most around here call me Aunt Sarah.

CLANCY
Aunt Sarah.

SARAH
"Miss Lied" to you!

CLANCY
Oh… oh, I'm sorry, Aunt Miss Lied.

SARAH
That's better.

> CLANCY consults his attache case as SARAH puts on her spectacles, approaches and peers into his case.

My!! You sure got a lotta important papers in that-there bag.

CLANCY
Yes, I, ah, guess I do.

SARAH
And just 'cause it's Canada don't mean it ain't racist.

CLANCY
Excuse me? Oh, ah, I'm by no means am sayin' that Aunt–

SARAH
Now the Lawd never did bless you people with long memories, did he?

CLANCY
Ex… excuse me?

SARAH
Miss Lied to you! *(pause)* Now, ya know what I figures?

CLANCY
What, ah, Miss Aunt Lied?

SARAH
I figures Africville be just another name for township – you heard of the townships in South Africa, ain't ya?

CLANCY
Of course, the–

SARAH
Well Africville be just like that! They put all the coloureds in one place, close to the white city so they got a ready stock of labour, like maids, butlers, and gardeners and cleaners and the like.

CLANCY
I don't think I'd go that far.

He finds the document he's looking for and closes his attache case.

SARAH
I would. 'Cept in Canada, we just use different words for township. We calls it a "community" or a "village" or some-such. To me, it just be a township. Plain and simple. No runnin' water like the townships. No plumbin' like the townships. Everything like the townships 'cept what it be called.

She continues filling the pail.

CLANCY
Can I give you a hand with that?

SARAH
My, you a polite Sonny, ain't ya? Well Sonny, I been fetchin' my water here for almost nigh eighty years. What's gonna stop me now?

CLANCY
(pointing) That sign for one thing.

SARAH
(contemptuously) It a gov'ment sign.

CLANCY
Yes. It is.

SARAH
Uh-hunh.

CLANCY
Well Aunt – Miss Lied. *(pause)* You should–

SARAH
See that dump, Sonny?

CLANCY
Yes.

SARAH
It a gov'ment dump. See that abattoir?

CLANCY
Yeah…

SARAH
Gov'ment give 'em a license. The gov'ment don't put no plumbin' in here. Why the gov'ment put all the coloureds here in the first place. No jobs 'cause the gov'ment. *(beat)* Now you think Sarah Lied truss the gov'ment? You think any coloured person in he's right senses truss the gov'ment and they signs?

CLANCY
Well I never thought–

SARAH
Didn't think so! And ya see, people don't usually be sleepin' here in the mornings, Sonny. You must a come up the road and seen everybody headin' out, didn't ya? *(beat)* Well where'd you think they was all goin'?

CLANCY
It hadn't crossed my mind and–

SARAH
To work! Most the womens be going to the south end to clean and scrub on their knees to make a few cents. The mens goin' almost all to pier nine. They waits in lines almost never to be picked for work. While the new white man who just showed up gets hired. So "Sleepin'?" Sonny? "Sleepin'?" We ain't got no time to be sleepin' in Africville. We too busy pickin' up the droppin's behind those white asses and too busy livin' to put food in our chile's mouths.

CLANCY
(consulting his file) You're Sarah Lied, right?

SARAH
Now I done tol' you that! *(beat)* Hand me that pail.

CLANCY
(handing her the pail) You use a lot o' water for an–

SARAH
Old woman? *(She chuckles.)* I always drops off a pail at Leasey's house. She got small Tully now to tend to in the mornin'.

CLANCY
"Leasey?" Would that mean Clarice Lyle?

SARAH
Why that her name proper. Yes.

CLANCY
She's married to Willem?

SARAH
My, all these big questions comin' outta such a little Sonny. But if ya must know, yes.

CLANCY
I don't mean to pry, it's just that I have some business with him. *(beat)* Do you know if he's home?

SARAH
He's at work! Down waitin' on the pier like the rest ol 'em! Waitin' and waitin' and waitin'. Might git one day's work this month if he's lucky. Anyways I gots to be going.

SARAH starts off.

CLANCY
(calling) Would you mind if I stopped by your place a little later, Mrs. Lied?

SARAH
MISS! *(halts)* Now whatever for!?

CLANCY
Maybe, ah some tea? Gets cold out here you know? And I'd like to hear more of what you have to say about South Africa.

SARAH
Well! *(long beat)* Guess everybody entitled to a little warmth... AND SOME SCHOOLIN'!!

CLANCY
The yellow place?

SARAH
(slowly) Why that's right. That's right. The yellow place on the knoll. Say what you doin' here in the first place Sonny?

CLANCY
I'm here for the same reasons everybody else comes to Africville.

SARAH
And just what might that be, Sonny?

CLANCY
I'm a walker, Miss Lied. That's how I think. I enjoy the fresh air. The north end of the city is the best end of the city, I always say.

SARAH
That so?

CLANCY
Yes it is.

SARAH
Well don't let the secret out because we'll have all them white people 'sendin' on us with their poopin' dogs and stuff.

CLANCY
(chuckles) Well I was just thinking, in fact. This place would make a good place for a park.

SARAH
NO IT WOULDN'T!!

CLANCY
Why, ah, why not, Miss Lied?

SARAH
Can't ya see!? *(beat)* Cause people lives here, Sonny! Ain't not a soul livin' in the Point Predential Park!

CLANCY
(laughs) Caught me again, right?

SARAH
Right! Well I best be gitten. You walk careful round here now, Sonny. Right careful, you hear?

CLANCY
Oh I will. Bye.

SARAH
And good, day, to, ya.

> *She turns and exits. CLANCY kneels, opens his attache case and rummages through his files.*

Scene Five

> *CLARICE and WILLEM's place. WILLEM peruses the newspaper. CLARICE is off in the back room.*

CLARICE
(off) Willem?

WILLEM
Uh-hunh?

CLARICE
Whatcha doin'?

WILLEM
Hunh?

CLARICE
I said, "Whatcha doin'?"

WILLEM
Readin' the newspaper, baby.

CLARICE
(off) Can you pass me Tully's blanket? It's on the table.

> *WILLEM obliges, handing it through the curtained doorway, then returning to his newspaper preoccupied.*

Thanks. *(pause)* The choir was sounded real nice the other night.

WILLEM
Yeah...

CLARICE
And you sounded like a angel when ya sang, "My Lord What a Mornin'." *(beat)* All by yourself too.

WILLEM
A cappella.

CLARICE
Hunh?

WILLEM
Yeah...

CLARICE
'Course ya need more tenors if ya asks me. Always been a problem with the men-folk in Africville: all scared to go sing the Lord's praises.

WILLEM
I hear.

> *WILLEM flips pages. CLARICE enters carrying Tully in his basket.*

CLARICE
My God though, Bethy Williams can sing! She like 'Retha Franklin. She hit them high notes – she straighten your hair. *(She pauses, staring at Tully.)* I best be keepin' quiet before I wake this baby up, though that be impossible with Tully.

WILLEM
Yeah...

CLARICE
You want some tea? A sandwich or somethin'? *(There's no reply. CLARICE halts and regards him.)* How about a nice, warm glass a poison?

WILLEM
(preoccupied) Okay.

CLARICE
Aunt Sarah got raped.

WILLEM
(turning pages) Cool.

CLARICE
Yep! By a Martian.

WILLEM
I heard, yeah. Too bad hunh?

CLARICE
Now she got an Albino baby with three heads.

WILLEM
That so...

CLARICE
Willem, you ain't even listenin' to me!

WILLEM
What?! Yeah! I'm listenin'...

CLARICE
And Aunt Sarah got a Albino baby with three heads, does she?

WILLEM
Whaa?

CLARICE starts the kettle.

CLARICE
Lately your mind been a million miles away, Willem. *(There's no reply.)*
Willem?!

WILLEM
(vexed) What, Leasey?! What is it? I'm tryin' to read the newspaper.
Can't a man read a newspaper in this house?!

CLARICE
You been readin' the newspaper a lot lately. Every day since last week.
Why alla sudden this big interest in the news?

WILLEM
Woman, I think you're struck.

CLARICE
Well, ya never took such a notice of the newspaper before is all I'm
sayin'.

WILLEM
Well I guess I never had to.

CLARICE
And ya got to now? What's that s'pose to mean?

WILLEM
Milk and sugar in my tea, Lease.

CLARICE
I know what ya take in your tea! I'm your wife!

WILLEM
Are ya?! You got a husband? You got a *real* husband?

There's a pause.

CLARICE
(chuckling) Ya know, Aunt Sarah said to 'spect this.

WILLEM
'Spect what?

CLARICE
You know, husbands be sorta put out when their first chile arrives. The woman give the chile all the attention. *(beat)* I said, "And what about the wife? The man don't give her no attention a-tall." Now Willem, *(She giggles mischievously.)* you *knows* I luv-me *my* attention. *(WILLEM chuckles.)* I mean, how you think Tully got here? *(beat)* By he's-self?

They laugh.

WILLEM
Well baby, I know the postman been by quite a bit.

CLARICE
Ain't no postman ever set foot in Clarice Lyle's house, so there!

WILLEM
But I was just starin'. Babies don't come from no starin'!

CLARICE
(tapping him playfully) Doin' more than starin'!

WILLEM laughs.

And where ya ever git that "Do Not Disturb" sign ta put on the door? Aunt Sarah ain't never let me live that one down yet. *(mocking)* "Oh-the-love-birds, oh-the-love-birds, oh-the-love-birds!" You know how she does.

WILLEM
Tell 'er I was just fixin' up a few things round the place.

CLARICE
(Standing; mockingly putting her hands on her hips.) "Fixin' up a few things?!" And what I look like, a jigsaw drill?! 'Cause honey, you was workin' on me!!

They laugh loud and hard.

Sssshhh!! You'll wake Tully!

WILLEM
Me? You laughin' just as hard. *(pause)* Look, your water's boilin'.

CLARICE
Was in them days, baby! *(more softly)* Was in them days…

CLARICE chuckles and goes to make tea. WILLEM returns to his newspaper.

Can't get your nose outta that paper, can ya?

WILLEM
Just lookin', Leasey.

CLARICE
For what?

WILLEM
A job! A house!

CLARICE
What do ya mean a house? We got a house right here.

WILLEM
Tully's gonna git older.

CLARICE
'Course, he just a baby.

WILLEM
I mean, he gonna need his own room. Why we ain't even got a bedroom Leasey, just that ol' pull-down couch.

CLARICE
And I been workin' on that.

WILLEM
Oh, you have, have ya?

CLARICE
Yep. All the *men* are gonna help ya build a add-on.

WILLEM
That so?

CLARICE
Yep, I been talkin' to all the *women*.

WILLEM
Oh, you talked to the women – you ain't talked to the men.

CLARICE
Willem... and you a married man. It ain't the men that got the power. It's just we women let them *think* they got the power. A bedroom can be a mighty cold place when yer partner got a headache. *Allll the time-ee!!* *(She chuckles.)* You know what I'm sayin'?

WILLEM
Well... it just goes beyond a bedroom, Leasey. *(earnestly)* I mean, it goes beyond any room—living room, bathroom, playroom—it goes beyond rooms and add-ons.

CLARICE
What?

WILLEM
Well what about schools, Leasey?! What about a job? Honey we gotta face it – Africville is the problem.

CLARICE
Oh it is, is it?

WILLEM
Yes, it is.

Pause.

CLARICE
Now ain't that juss like some nigger from the Valley?

WILLEM
Whaa?

CLARICE
In fact, it just like some nigger from anyplace in Nova Scotia other than Africville.

WILLEM
Leasey–

CLARICE
Walkin' round with yer noses in the air–

WILLEM
Leasey I never meant–

CLARICE
–like, like there be a stench here. Oh, I knows we got the dump and the abattoir and the prison and the little white racists tauntin' us. But 'member Willem, the white man put all that here. Not us. It was pushed in our faces. It a white stench. The stench ain't Black.

WILLEM
Clarice all I'm sayin' is that I'm tired of hearin' how the white man did this and the white man did that. I'm tired of it, 'cause this Black man wants to do somethin' too. I wanna work, I want my chile to go to a decent school and I wanna live in a decent house – not some scraggily ol' shack.

CLARICE
Oh, so this all this is to ya, hunh? A "scraggily ol' shack"?!

WILLEM
I'm not sayin'–

CLARICE
My great-great-granddaddy built this outta his own hands, Willem. It was just him and the dirt, Willem. This land was given to us by Queen Victoria. Queen Victoria! And he farmed that ol' acid-ee, rocky dirt out there so he could feed his family. He fished in the Bedford Basin. He did whatever was necessary, and he made and gave love out here, raisin' his children. And he was proud. So don't you dare—ever!—come and say to me–

WILLEM
Clarice all I'm sayin' is that times change. I just want the best I kin provide for my family.

CLARICE
This is the best, Willem!! This is the best!!

WILLEM
What, Leasey? What's the best?! *(He stands angrily, slamming his fist.)* A drafty house?! Dirt roads?! No running water?! You can't even have a shower here!! What's the best, Leasey?! What?! This?! *(He regains his composure and sits down.)* I wanna job. I wanna home. I want the hell outta Africville!! *(lowering his voice)* And I'll have all those things, too. Just watch me.

CLARICE
Over my dead body... over my dead body Willem Lyle!! Tully's gonna be raised here – just like me!! Just like me!! Where he's loved... where he's loved Willem!!

WILLEM
Leasey, all I meant was–

CLARICE
No!! *(pause)* See, I better go for a walk now, 'cause if I don't? It'll be the first time I lay my hands on my husband without love behind it...

Calmly, yet angrily, CLARICE walks out the door.

WILLEM
Leasey?! *(He slams his fist on the table.)* Goddamnit!!

Scene Six

CLANCY sits alone in the church staring at the pulpit as REVEREND MINER comes brushing into the room, removing his overcoat.

REVEREND MINER
Either you're early, or I'm late, boy.

CLANCY
I'm early, sir. Tom Clancy.

REVEREND MINER
Say... we got some coloured Clancys here in Africville – any relation?

CLANCY
No... but, ah...

REVEREND MINER
Cool in here. Maybe I'll start the furnace.

CLANCY
Can it wait, sir? I'm rushed for time.

REVEREND MINER
You're rushed for time?

CLANCY
Yes I have some people to see and–

REVEREND MINER
So you're the one they "sacrificed." *(He chuckles.)* Lord, listen to me. I'm still thinking yesterday's sermon. I mean, you're the one they "picked."

CLANCY
Yes. Is there something wrong?

REVEREND MINER
No, no. It was just I was expecting someone a little older that's all. I thought you sounded young on the phone – but not this young. I mean, you're a kid. Just a boy, really. Relatively speaking.

CLANCY
Relative to what?

REVEREND MINER
Relative to what you're charged to do.

CLANCY
I'm twenty-four, a graduate of Dalhousie University and the Nova Scotia School of Social Work. I have two degrees.

REVEREND MINER
That's mighty impressive. When did you graduate?

CLANCY
Last spring.

REVEREND MINER
Oh… master of the world!

CLANCY
Sir, I–

REVEREND MINER
Call me "Reverend" like everybody else.

CLANCY
Life experience wasn't a prerequisite when the city posted this job. I simply applied. I got the job and you're the first one to mention–

REVEREND MINER
I see. Well, "boy"—I'm sorry—"Mister Clancy."

CLANCY
Call me what you want, Reverend. I've been called everything since I got on-site: "Sonny," "kid," "little boy," "man" – everything since I got on the site.

REVEREND MINER
Boy—and don'tcha forget this—this job is gonna require a lot of life experience from you. A lot of soul searching and not a little grief. I mean, what are they doing down there thrusting a job like this on a kid?

CLANCY
I guess you'll have to ask them. Anyway, as I mentioned, I'm really strapped for time, Reverend. Can we get down to business?

REVEREND MINER
By all means.

> *CLANCY opens his attache case.*

CLANCY
Here's your envelope sir, hand delivered. It's the agenda for the Mayor's Africville Committee meeting.

REVEREND MINER
I see. Our friends at city hall are very efficient – aren't they?

> *He opens and peruses it.*

CLANCY
The committee will meet twice a month.

REVEREND MINER
Yes, I already know.

CLANCY
Sir?

REVEREND MINER
I know you have an agenda and you probably have your speech ready. So let's not beat around the bush and get down to brass tacks. There's nothing you can tell me on behalf of the city that I haven't already discussed with the city. Nothing you can tell me that I already don't know about.

CLANCY
Reverend?

REVEREND MINER
It rather seems that the city was of the opinion that the performance of your duties left something to be desired. And at a little meeting they asked me to attend, they thought your presence wasn't particularly needed. It was agreed that I would help you bring your task to a swift and successful conclusion.

CLANCY
(*nervously*) Yes, well… yes, ah, that was brought to my attention—the need for expediency and all—and well, as you apparently already know, unless we can get everyone to agree to our offer, the city is prepared to expropriate this land. That's not public knowledge yet, but we don't have much time. With your help, I believe we can convince everyone to sell and avoid expropriation.

There's a long pause.

Reverend?

REVEREND MINER
Do you really know—do you really understand—what you're getting yourself into?

CLANCY loudly snaps the attache case closed.

CLANCY
It's not often a kid my age gets an opportunity like this, Reverend. I mean, I can write a book, maybe a master's thesis. Build a career based on what happens on this site.

REVEREND MINER
Good, because Africville is more than anyone's "site." It's more than a headline or a paper for a master's thesis; a so-called "career-builder." It's a way of life. Now you keep asking me to keep quiet. Well I'm asking you about my concerns for the church.

CLANCY
The church stays, Reverend. That's done, but without our agreement we'll have a circus on our hands.

REVEREND MINER
No "we" won't. You boy, you and the city will have a circus on your hands. I mean what's the problem here – the real problem here? (*beat*) They say they can't provide water and basic amenities to the people here? Well in the years to come—and you mark my words—when they build a park or a shipping terminal or whatever they decide to build here – just see if those establishments don't have paved roads, sewage and running water, okay? Just observe… observe… and mark my words.

CLANCY
Are you saying the city's lying, Reverend Miner?

REVEREND MINER
I'm saying they're not telling all the truth. I'll tell the whole truth... at the appropriate time.

CLANCY
All I want, Reverend, is a full and fair hearing, that's all. I mean before the onslaught of opinions and editorials and–

REVEREND MINER
Just because I listen to the city's plans, doesn't mean I condone them. I realize the inevitable–

CLANCY
All I'm asking for is a chance. I can make this a smooth transition.

REVEREND MINER
For who? A smooth transition for who? You and the city?

A long pause.

All I need to know is does the church stay?

CLANCY
It does. That's correct.

REVEREND MINER
Then good-day to you sir. I've got to get some warmth in God's house.

REVEREND MINER exits.

Scene Seven

All save the REVEREND and CLANCY have gathered at the church.

JIMMY
W-W-What you think the-the-the–

GROOVEY
"The Reverend wants?!" Spit it out, fool, 'cause Groovey Peters got her no patience today.

SARAH
(admonishing) Groovey! Now what I tell you?

CLARICE
Whatcha think, Aunt Sarah?

SARAH
Well, the last time Sarah been at a "family meeting"–

WILLEM
I ain't from Africville. What do that mean, Leasey? "Family meetin'?"

JIMMY
It-it-it–

SARAH
Yes we is. We all family, son, and we all in God's Church.

CLARICE
It means all of us folk here gets together, honey. And just us folks. We ah… *(She chuckles.)* manage to avoid invitin' the whites.

SARAH
And it mean somethin' import be up. We don't call a family meetin' to talk foolishin's. *(beat)* Hear that Groovey?

GROOVEY
Now Groovey Peters be sittin' right here, Aunt Sarah.

REVEREND MINER enters, removing his coat, and goes to the pulpit.

REVEREND MINER
Now I'm not gonna preach to y'all– *(He gets down and stands on the floor, looking at them.)* –I'm not going to pontificate, I'm gonna elucidate…

GROOVEY
Hell-oh!

SARAH
Groovey! Now what I tell ya?!

CLARICE
Go ahead, Reverend.

REVEREND MINER
Now I know ya all seen that white man around here a lot.

JIMMY
Oh Lawd.

REVEREND MINER
We all seen him, we know that. Well he's not here 'cause he likes the view–

JIMMY
He's here on ba-ba-ba-ba-ba-ba-ba-ba–

GROOVEY
Now the damned fool sound like a sheep!

SARAH
Groovey!

JIMMY
–business!

SARAH
What kind of business, Reverend?

REVEREND MINER
City business. He's here because he's been instructed by his bosses—the city—to buy your land.

CLARICE
Well we ain't sellin'!

WILLEM
Leasey will you listen to Reverend Miner?

CLARICE, holding Tully, stands and gathers her purse.

CLARICE
No, let's go home, Willem. 'Cause we ain't sellin' so this ain't none of our business.

REVEREND MINER
I think you should stay, Leasey. Really.

WILLEM
I wanna hear what the Reverend's gotta say. If it affects Africville – I wanna hear.

Reluctantly CLARICE sits.

REVEREND MINER
Like I was saying, this man—this Clancy—he's here on official city business. Now they're going to develop this land and they're making financial offers. Offering those with families a place in Uniacke Square.

JIMMY
The-the-the projects!

CLARICE
Then they gotta pay us.

REVEREND MINER
Yes. A fair price – the city assures me. Now think of this: you all be close by. You'll have all the amenities the white folks have – water and plumbing. You'll be closer to grocery stores, hospitals and schools. And – we'll have the church right here in Africville.

SARAH
Hallelujah!

CLARICE
(*standing*) Now when the city gonna be fair to niggers? Never have, never will be, I say. (*to WILLEM*) I tol' ya this ain't got nothing to do with us, Willem. We ain't sellin'. Now c'mon.

CLARICE *exits with Tully. WILLEM stays.*

GROOVEY
Rev'rund Miner?

REVEREND MINER
Yes, Groovey?

GROOVEY
You been talkin' to de city?

REVEREND MINER
I have.

GROOVEY
And you never told us?

REVEREND MINER
The meetings were confidential. And I was forced to keep my mouth shut or I probably would not have been invited. We wouldn't even possess this much information. Now keeping the church was a struggle – but that's the great thing. We all know what the church means to coloured folk: it's our monument to those who died on the middle passage – every spirit that lies on the bottom of the Atlantic.

ALL
(*variously*) Amen…. That's right…. Uh huh… (*etcetera*)

REVEREND MINER
The church embodies all that we do: it's where we baptize our young, and not-so-young. Where we get hope, when hope doesn't appear to be on the horizon. Where we mourn and get strength for the loss of a loved one. The church, as you all know, is a living monument. A testament to a race of Black people; a proud, hard-working and loving people. Our divine power and spirituality – all of our mothers. It is the very cement which our community was founded upon. Our sustenance when we're weak–

SARAH
Yes, Lord.

REVEREND MINER
Our warmth when we are cold. Our very essence itself.

SARAH
Praise God.

REVEREND MINER
So just because we live down the street—a little way from here—Africville will never die. In this church, our soul shall live.

GROOVEY
You said you wasn't gonna preach!!

SARAH
(*standing up*) That was a great sermon and such, Reverend. Fancy words and all. But lemme tell you this: it's well known that if you lay down with dogs, you come up with fleas. (*She sits.*)

ALL
(*variously*) Go on Aunt Sarah! I hear ya! (*etcetera*)

REVEREND MINER
Africville will not be lost – you'll all be neighbours in the city.

JIMMY
G-g-g-good! Then we can all m-m-m-move together!

REVEREND MINER
Where there will be no bulldozers. No dumps. No abattoir stench and above all – no rats.

JIMMY
They-they-they gittin' bigger than the c-c-c-cats, Reverend.

GROOVEY
So what do we do now, mun?

REVEREND MINER
Go home–

> *All save REVEREND MINER start to exit.*

Wait for this white man, this Mister Clancy, to approach you with an offer. If you decide to move, he assures me everything will be handled in an orderly fashion.

GROOVEY
Good! *(standing)* What he look like, honey?

SARAH
Groovey, git your mind out the– *(She grabs her arm.)* –C'mon, girl.

> *All exit, REVEREND MINER stands alone. Blackout.*

Scene Eight

> *CLARICE and WILLEM's place. A bulldozer sounds. CLARICE is off in the back room; we hear something thumping on the floor.*

CLARICE
Damn rats!!

> *As CLARICE enters, we hear the bulldozers start.*

Oh Lord, please have mercy on me!! *(She goes to the crib and looks in on Tully.)* My son, I don't know how you can sleep through all of this? I just dunno.

> *SARAH enters.*

SARAH
Leasey! – the rats! My kitties scamperin' this mornin'.

CLARICE
You ain't kiddin'!

SARAH
It's that racket from the bulldozer I tells us.

CLARICE
All that bulldozer is doing is pushing trash from one side ta the other. And every time they do it, I gotta deal with these damn rats.

A rat hurries across the floor.

SARAH
(startled; pointing) Oh!!

CLARICE
Looked it scamper!! Looked it!!

> *CLARICE grabs a broom, smashing and stabbing the floor as she runs haphazardly around the place, lifting or pushing whatever is in her path. SARAH surveys the madness.*

SARAH
Why you like you playin' hockey, girl! *(She laughs.)*

CLARICE
Git out my way, git out my way! *(stabbing)* Damn! Git outta my way!

> *SARAH laughs initially, but screams in horror, eyes blanching, as she spies a rat nearing her.*

SARAH
Oh me Lawd Jesus!

> *She hops on top of a chair, lifting her skirts and running on the spot.*

Git it Leasey, git it!! Git it 'fore it–

CLARICE
Don't be screaming-jumpin' round me! white womens screams and jumps! We niggers fights!!

SARAH
Git it git it git it!! *(She laughs.)*

> *CLARICE stops suddenly, breathlessly slumping into a chair.*

CLARICE
I's... I'm, I'm too tired to git it!

SARAH
Uh-hunh... *(She laughs.)* Leasey, how I git up this chair, girl? *(laughs)* Help me down.

> *CLARICE, laughing, obliges as Tully suddenly erupts, crying. SARAH goes to the crib. The bulldozers stop.*

CLARICE
(to the ceiling) Thank... you... Jesus!!

SARAH
Aw, Tully don't like rats, either. *(She picks him up.)* You the best gift ever.

WILLEM enters.

WILLEM
Hi Leasey.

CLARICE
Hi baby. No work?

SARAH
Again?

CLARICE surreptitiously signals for SARAH to "shush."

WILLEM
(angrily) What the hell can I do about it?! The man don't hire us – he hires the new white guys!

CLARICE
We was just sayin' is all, Willem. No need to be nasty.

WILLEM
But you-all act like I don't wanna work or somethin'. *(beat)* Why you all outta breath, Leasey? And where's the paper? Jesus. *(gestures to Tully)* And what's he yellin' about?

CLARICE
Only you and Walter Cronkite ask so many questions, Willem.

SARAH
Leasey, *(She chuckles.)* Leasey was chasing rats.

WILLEM
Oh.

SARAH
Like a bull in a china shop, she was!

She laughs. WILLEM goes to SARAH and takes Tully.

WILLEM
(to the baby) How's my big boy, hunh? Yeah, it's all right now, Daddy's here... Daddy's here now.

CLARICE
(sharply) He was all right before his daddy got here, thank-you-very-much.

WILLEM
Leasey, please. Don't start. The paper ain't here yet?

CLARICE
Aunt Sarah hand that man the paper, please, before I have to get up and knock him out.

SARAH obliges and WILLEM takes the paper and Tully into the back room.

SARAH
Leasey? Weren't I fetchin' water and guess who was down by the well?

CLARICE
Who?

SARAH
That white man – a boy really.

CLARICE
A white man? Another one?

SARAH
Uh-hunh...

Pause.

CLARICE
Welll?!

SARAH
Well whaa?

CLARICE
Did you ask this white man what he was doin' here, Aunt Sarah?

SARAH
Now I just tol' ya what I saw. I think he the one the Rev'rend was talkin' 'bout. But, Leasey, if I ask every white man that come to Africville what he was doin' here, Groovey be after me for edgin' her business.

CLARICE
And we all knows you does pose a threat to Groovey, Aunt Sarah! *(She chuckles.)*

SARAH
Humph! *(pause)* Still plenty a mileage on this ol' Cadillac!

CLARICE
(laughing) Aunt Sarah you better stop!

SARAH
No no. You always teasin' me bout my age, Leasey – well look-it you. You're whatcha call, "older." Well, your sun ain't quite set girl, but it's headin' for the Rockies!

CLARICE
Aunt Sarah! *(She laughs.)*

SARAH
And before I forget, you can tell that man of yours that if his actions ain't the be-all-and-end-all I don't know what is! He never say how-ya-do or kiss-yer-ass to me. He just grunt and grab Tully.

CLARICE
(whispering) Aunt Sarah, I hope, I pray, work comes soon. He so ornery I tells ya. He bangin' this pot and slammin' that door and then he be so quiet-like. He just read the papers.

SARAH
Umph-umph-umph – men! They so confused. Oh well. I best be goin' I tells us.

CLARICE
Here. I'll walk ya to the door. Bye, Aunt Sarah. See ya later. *(returning)* Willem? I might be goin' into Halifax sometime this week. I need material.

WILLEM
Suit yourself.

A great noise and hullabaloo comes from outside.

GROOVEY
(off crying) Leasey?!... Leasey?!

CLARICE
What... the... hell...

GROOVEY, noisily, and out of breath, bursts into the room. She is hysterical and crying. Tully cries again.

GROOVEY
Groovey dun know what dey doin'! I dun know!

CLARICE
What is it?! What is it?!

WILLEM
(*entering with a crying Tully*) Jesus Groovey we got a baby ya know!

GROOVEY
They gone, Leasey! Gone!

CLARICE
Who? Whatcha talkin' about?!

WILLEM
This racket better calm down!

GROOVEY
Go and look, Leasey! Go and look!

CLARICE
Go and look at what, baby?! What–

GROOVEY slumps her head into her hands and cries.

GROOVEY
Jimmy! Da Willises move out.... Dey move out...

CLARICE
People move in and outta Africville everyday, Groovey.

GROOVEY
(*sobbing*) But not like dis... not like dis...

CLARICE
Hunh?

GROOVEY
In a garbage truck?! Dey move 'em in a garbage truck!!

CLARICE
Now, Groovey, ain't nobody moving in garbage trucks. What's wrong
with you, girl?

GROOVEY
There's nothing wrong with me I know what I saw! I know what I saw!!
Dem... white... bastards!! Dem mens – wif dere overalls and gloves on,
like dey was gonna be contaminated – contaminated!! Dey just threw
Bonita's and Jimmy's furniture on dey truck. Dey broke stuff.... Dey
joked among themsell... it was... was... and poor Bonita. She cry and
beat on Jimmy's chest.... Now da dozers be dere... dey knockin' it
down!!

CLARICE looks about, hands quivering, eyes wondering, then she and GROOVEY bolt out the door, as WILLEM exits to the back room with Tully.

Scene Nine

WILLEM enters the room, sips his beer, and peruses a newspaper that's sprawled on the floor. A knock comes from the door. He looks to it, then goes and opens the door.

WILLEM
Yes?

CLANCY
Mister Lyle? *(pause)* Hi, my name's Clancy. *(He extends his hand.)* Tom–

WILLEM
I know who you is.

CLANCY
Yes, ah… I'm Clancy. *(He drops his hand.)* I was wondering if I might speak with you for a few seconds.

WILLEM
Okay.

Both awkwardly stand there for a few seconds.

CLANCY
(clearing his throat) Might I come in?

Pause.

WILLEM
Okay.

CLANCY enters, looking about.

CLANCY
Your wife's not home I take it.

WILLEM
That's right.

They stand awkwardly.

Have a seat. *(beat)* Like a beer?

CLANCY
No thanks. *(He sits.)* Mind if I smoke?

WILLEM
No.

> *He lights up, leaving his Zippo on the table, and coughs violently.*

CLANCY
I... just started... to... to... smo... smoke!

WILLEM
(chuckling) Oh.

CLANCY
Now, *(He coughs.)* as I was saying, I represent the City of Halifax, I'm a social worker—here's my card—and I've been asked to speak to the families here and–

WILLEM
I know, I know.

CLANCY
Uh-hunh yes. Well you're not from here are you, Mister Lyle? "Willem," if I may.

WILLEM
No.

CLANCY
Where are you from?

WILLEM
Annapolis Royal. I'm a carpenter. Visited here and met Leasey and got married. Look Mister Clancy–

CLANCY
Tom. Call me Tom.

WILLEM
Tom. You're wasting your time. My wife ain't givin' this place up. If it were up to me – I would've been outta here yesterday – but you know women.

CLANCY
(smiling) That I do. But *(beat)* why would you leave?

WILLEM

I may be coloured, Mister, ah, Tom, but I don't like slums. White people believe coloureds like slums. Well we don't.

CLANCY

I'm certainly not saying that, Willem.

WILLEM

I'm sure you ain't. Not in this house anyway. See? I was brought up in the country – on a farm. Good, solid houses; proud people. We all worked and produced. We never had no outside jobs, we made our own jobs. Here – if the white man don't wantcha – you outta luck. And we're down on our luck in Africville I tell ya.

CLANCY

I understand. So what are you going to do?

WILLEM

(shrugging his shoulders) Don't rightly know, but I tell ya, things gotta change. I got me a little mouth to feed now.

CLANCY

Yes, I noticed the crib. Boy or a girl?

WILLEM

Boy.

CLANCY

Congratulations.

WILLEM

Thanks. *(pause)* Mister Clancy–

CLANCY

"Tom," okay? Call me "Tom." Might I have a coffee?

WILLEM

Just put a pot on. Milk? Sugar?

CLANCY

Both, thanks. Now you said you wanted to leave, right?

WILLEM

Damn right. Somethin' gotta happen round here.

CLANCY

Well what would you say *if* – if I said I could help you out?

WILLEM shrugs. CLANCY opens his attache case and withdraws a file.

You now possess the deed to this place, Willem. Mrs. Lyle – according to this, Mrs. Lyle has just–

WILLEM
Clarice.

CLANCY
Yes, Clarice. She just signed it over to you – just recently in fact. *(pause)* Look, Willem, I guess the best way to talk about this is to be frank. I'm sure you're aware of Africville's reputation. I mean people call it the "slum by the dump" among other things right?

WILLEM nods affirmatively.

Well the city wants to rectify this problem, correct it if you will. You see we realize there's no running water here, no plumbing, and well—you know—the dump's next door. The abattoir and, well, I could go on. Despite all of this – you live here. Now it's no longer acceptable to the City of Halifax that Negroes live in one place, Willem, and white people another. You follow me?

WILLEM
Uh-hunh.

CLANCY
You know, a place where the kids don't get a proper education – I guess what I'm trying to say *(beat)* is all the benefits that white citizens get and take for granted. So, I'm rather happy to inform you that the city has decided to deal with the site.

WILLEM
"The site"?

CLANCY
Yes. You know… Africville. We want to buy all the families out. Everything. Every door, board, lamppost and window. Everything.

WILLEM
Everything?

CLANCY
Everything.

WILLEM
Just like that?

CLANCY
Just like that.

WILLEM
Even the church?

CLANCY
No, not the church. The city's not in the habit of desecratin' sanctified ground – but everything else you see here. Everything. The city wants to buy it fair and square.

WILLEM
I see.

CLANCY
Now we're offering fair price for the properties. We're even giving five hundred dollars to those people who don't possess a deed as a sign of good faith. Now lemme see… *(He consults his file.)* you possess the deed. The deed's in your name.

WILLEM
This land been in Leasey's family for years – well over a century.

CLANCY
Well, we'd be prepared to offer you five thousand dollars. In fact I have the cheque right here, Willem.

He produces an envelope containing a cheque and a large envelope and places them on the table.

You look suspicious.

WILLEM
You wanna give us five thousand dollars *(looking about)* for this?

CLANCY
Yes. See Willem, the city realizes it's been, well let me put it this way, less than an ideal administration to the people of Africville. We want you people—all our people in fact—to live and walk and drive on paved roads. We want all our people to have street lights. We want you to live in a place where the police and the ambulances aren't afraid to come, and are nearby. We want you to live close to services, like grocery and drug stores, and we want your kids to have proper schools. I mean, you've got a young one to think about now, Willem.

WILLEM
But where would we go?

CLANCY

Well, we're building a new housing development in town. You know, on Gottingen Street?

WILLEM

Yeah, walked by it once or twice.

CLANCY

See? The houses there have running water and plumbing. Furnaces. No more gathering wood or dealing with coal – these work off oil. The schools are down the street and there's a grocery store just a block away. And we're prepared, the city that is, to give you the first year's rent free. Of course, you're free to seek your own residence, but a place in Uniacke Square is reserved for you and your family.

WILLEM

Uniacke Square... yeah, Double-speak was talkin' about that place.

CLANCY

"Double-speak"?

WILLEM

A friend.

CLANCY

Oh. Anyway, what I have here is a simple contract. All you have to do is sign it and all that I just described is yours. I mean, your family's and yours.

> *WILLEM makes coffee. CLANCY walks to the window.*

My God it's beautiful out here though isn't it, Willem? Especially at night. I always say it's like you're in the middle of the universe. I mean with all the city lights twinkling around you, it looks like you're surrounded by stars. *(Beat; he chuckles.)* Sorry, I wax poetic.

WILLEM

No, everybody says that.

CLANCY

Well it's time.

WILLEM

You talk to many other people out here Mister Clancy? I mean, besides Double-speak?

CLANCY

Who's this "Double-speak," Willem?

WILLEM
Jimmy Willis. *(suddenly angry)* And ain't no garbage trucks moving us!!

CLANCY's face goes limp.

CLANCY
Now that was very unfortunate, but all the moving trucks were booked. And you don't know how the city works downtown. There's clerks that've never been to Africville and they probably thought they were moving some office furniture from a city warehouse and they sent that garbage truck. I know it wasn't intentional and I've been assured by the city this will not happen again. I was very distressed. So what's it to be, Willem? I mean, you've made no secret that you're not happy here. Don't you want a good school for your son?

WILLEM
Who – Tully? Yes.

CLANCY
Good *(pause)* I, ah, just think you should have a lawyer look over this document. Take it to a lawyer, okay? *(He's packing up.)* Because it's gotten back to the city some moving issues have been noted, and we want people to be assured that this is all above table. So now the city wants me to tell everybody to take the documents to a lawyer. I leave it with you.

WILLEM
I gotta talk with Leasey.

CLANCY
(taking back the envelope) Yes, of course, speak with your wife. I'm sure she'll agree it's the right thing to do. It's the only thing to do. I'll be out of your hair then.

He stands and extends his hand. WILLEM shakes it.

WILLEM
You're forgettin' your lighter.

CLANCY
No no, you keep it. There's plenty where that came from. It's a Zippo. Has the city's coat of arms on it.

WILLEM
Well I… I don't smoke.

CLANCY
Maybe someone you know does. Listen, Willem, I'll drop by again. If you have any questions you've got my card. See you later.

CLANCY exits, as WILLEM sits at the table. Fondling the lighter, he glances over the contract.

Scene Ten

Pandemonium in the Lyle household. CLARICE enters preparing a thermos and filling a sandwich bag. WILLEM is hurriedly grabbing his tools, coat, gloves etcetera.

WILLEM
Hurry, baby, hurry. I was s'pose to be there a minute ago.

CLARICE
I'm rushin'. OhmyGod, Willem, work? I mean, real work?!

WILLEM
For a few days straight anyways. White men don't wanna work over the holidays, so they–

CLARICE
–*call us.* When you gonna be home?

WILLEM
Aunt Sarah took the call. The man say long shifts, so I don't know. You ready?

CLARICE
Almost.

WILLEM
Oh… I forgot to get water from the well.

CLARICE
I kin manage. Willem calm down, honey you're so excited.

WILLEM
Okay… I'll try.

CLARICE
(handing him a sandwich bag) Here ya go. Didn't put no turnip greens in there, either.

WILLEM
(laughing) What would I do without ya, Lease?

CLARICE
Baby you'd starve, 'cause ya can't even boil water without burnin' it!

They laugh again. She goes and picks up Tully.

WILLEM
Now listen to me Leasey. Look like a storm comin', but there's plenty a wood out there. If ya need anythin' call me on Aunt Sarah's phone. Okay?

CLARICE
Okay.

WILLEM
But don't call me unless it's important, 'cause it's hard to reach me down the pier.

CLARICE
Okay, baby.

He kisses her quickly. He starts off, but returns and kisses his son.

WILLEM
See ya, baby-boy.

As he exits, CLARICE follows him to door.

CLARICE
(calling) We luv you too, Willem. Bye!

Scene Eleven

CLANCY is in the church sitting in a pew with his attache case open beside him. He's distracted and preoccupied. He walks behind the pew and opens the big Bible, perusing with his finger. He looks closer and absently whispers.

CLANCY
My God... there's deaths and births and weddings in here dating from the eighteen-hundreds!

After flipping a few more pages he steps down and sits in a pew, lights a cigarette, and of course, coughs. We hear a door slam behind him, yet we see nobody. CLANCY, stubbing his cigarette, stares straight ahead.

That you, Reverend? *(There is no reply.)* You know, Reverend, here I am sittin' in a church in Africville. I mean, my friends would call it a "nigger" church. Here I am sittin' in this "nigger" church in Africville. I should be at the Boat Club, sipping whiskey with my buddies and laughing about the dirty niggers in Africville. But ya know, Reverend? *(swigs)* I don't feel like laughing. I don't feel that way... I mean, most of

the places I been to out here, you can eat off their floors they're so
waxed and polished.... Look, I believed... I believe what I was told.
I think what I'm doing is right. I'm doing the right thing.

JIMMY
(entering) M-m-m-mister Clancy?

CLANCY is startled and turns towards the voice.

CLANCY
Jimmy?! What the hell are you doing here? I thought you were
Reverend Miner.

JIMMY
Ma-ma-ma-mister Clancy? I need a c-c-c-c-come back to Af-af-af–

CLANCY
Africville.

JIMMY
I still have the money you gave me. Most of it. I can buy back my land,
rebuild my house.

CLANCY
That's impossible!

JIMMY
But my kids... they-they-they run the streets, wild... and... and-and-
and... we have no... we-we-we–

CLANCY
You signed, you got–

JIMMY
I-I-I... but... I-I-I... don't know my fa-fa-fa-family no mores. Kids don't
listen to me. They runs the streets, all hours of the nights. I-I-I-I can't
com-com-com-plain to the neighbours, cause I-I-I-I don't knows who
they be's. Please, Mister Ca-Ca-Ca-Clancy, I needs to–

*Glaring at JIMMY, CLANCY slams the attache case shut and walks past
him.*

CLANCY
I'm sorry, but you signed. There's nothing I can do!

JIMMY
But Mister Clancy?!

CLANCY exits.

Scene Twelve

There comes a humongous sound: a storm at the well. CLARICE enters, dressed only in a billowing housecoat and slippers. She gets to her knees, trying to clear the pump spout of ice. Very low, we hear Tully crying; and in the far background, the choir rehearsing a hymn.

CLARICE
Momma's comin', Tully. Momma's comin'. I just need some water...

She gets to her feet again and pumps. Water drools slightly. She bends again, trying to clear the spout. Still quite low, we hear Tully crying. CLARICE now cocks an ear towards the sound.

(muttering) Tully... that you, baby? Momma be right there... just gittin' water for your formula...

Tully's wailing intensifies, then abruptly stops as does CLARICE. She cocks an ear to the wind.

Tully?

She gets to her feet, looking in the direction of the house.

(louder; concerned) Tully?

She runs towards the house.

Tully?!... Baby?!

She enters the house, dropping her pail on the table and enters the back room. We hear screeches and shrieks. Finally she emerges. And as the stage darkens she's lit in a pin-spot, and lifts the dead baby in her arms and screams.

Tull-eee-ee!!

Blackout.

ACT TWO

Scene One

CLARICE sits in a chair, the very archetype of pain and extremity. WILLEM stands next to her, holding her hand.

WILLEM
I love ya, Leasey... and it hurts to see ya hurtin' like this...

CLARICE remains mute. The light broadens; we see SARAH sitting at the table.

SARAH
Well I guess I best be goin'.

WILLEM
No no, Sarah, you stay. Leasey wants you here, ain't that right Leasey?

CLARICE makes no response.

SARAH
I'll make you some tea, Leasey. Don't worry now, the pain gotta come out. Grievin's only natural. It helps take the pain away.

She walks by WILLEM, whispering.

She don't need me here. She needs you, son, she needs your strength. Be strong, strong enough for the both of ya.

SARAH exits. There's silence.

CLARICE
Where's Tully?

WILLEM
He'll be at the church, soon, Leasey. They gonna bring 'em to the church.

CLARICE
Did you tell Reverend Miner what I tol' ya to tell 'em?

WILLEM looks away.

Look it me, Willem. *(pause)* I'm talkin' to you. Why I gotta pull teeth?

WILLEM
I tol' 'em, Leasey, okay? I tol' 'em.

CLARICE
What he say?

WILLEM
He said he wants to hold a little memorial service for Tully the day
tomorrow.

CLARICE
(angrily) Now that ain't what I'm talkin' about! That ain't what I asked
ya to tell 'em! *(beat)* Oh! *(She starts to break down.)* I can't take this I can't
take this! *(beat)* Why I gotta be the one to undertake alla this? Why?...
None of this my fault... none of it I don't understand... my baby...

WILLEM
Leasey.

CLARICE
...my baby.

WILLEM
Leasey please don't cry. Don't cry, I tried–

CLARICE
(yelling) Why not?! Why not cry, Willem?! No one else 'round here
appears to be mournin'!!

> There's a very pregnant pause. CLARICE's demeanour changes.

Oh, Willem, I'm sorry... I'm so sorry...

WILLEM
It's okay. Leasey, it's–

CLARICE
I was just–

WILLEM
You know the Reverend wants to help us Leasey, but... but his hands
are tied. And Mister Clancy say there are strict laws about–

CLARICE
Mister Clancy?! *(beat)* Why?... What he got to do with this? He don't
know nuthin' 'bout nuthin'!

WILLEM
Do it matter, Leasey?! *(He slams his hand down angrily.)* He's from the
city!! Now how many times I gotta tell ya?!

CLARICE
Well why you askin' *him* about Tully? He dunno nothing about Tully. He don't know about… about… *us*. He ain't got no business… you shoulda asked Reverend Miner!

WILLEM
But it *is* his business. That's what I'm tryin' to tell ya, Leasey. Mister Clancy say it *is* his business.

CLARICE
Oh, he do?

WILLEM
He say the city got strict laws against what we're askin' and–

CLARICE
Laws?! What laws? What kinda laws say a mother can't bury her baby? *(beat)* What? What kinda laws?

WILLEM
He say he got city ordinances-like, ah… whatcha calls by-laws, and he got the police behind him.

CLARICE
And where was the police when I was cryin' with Tully dyin' in my arms? Where was they when I needed them? Where was the ambulance?

WILLEM
Leasey, I think you should lay down.

CLARICE
I CAN'T LAY DOWN NO MORE!! *(pause)* We been layin' down for those white bastards all our lives!! All, our, goddamn, tired-ol' lives!! Well no more!! I'm sick!! I'm sick and tired of them games they been playin'!!

WILLEM
Leasey, please.

CLARICE
Games I tell ya!! *(beat)* They play games and experiment with people's lives. They think they're God he's-self!! Live here! Bury them over there!! Well screw those white bastards and the train they rode in on!! And the train run right through Africville, Willem. Has it stopped? It ain't stopped!!

WILLEM

Leasey, they say ya have to have a special permit for this. People just can't go round diggin' holes and–

CLARICE

Permits?! Then we apply.

WILLEM

Ain't no use they tells me. Just be throwin' good money after bad.

CLARICE stands.

CLARICE

I don't see no permits for them tractors. And them destroyin' creatures – them life-sucking rats – they got permits?! And them trucks – and yes, Groovey was right. They move the Willises in a garbage truck. They got permits for that? Permits to be movin' people's belongin's in garbage trucks? Don't tell me, Willem, I know! The city uses permits only when it suits the city. And the city don't permit no *niggers!!*

WILLEM

Leasey the man say you gotta have consecrated ground to bury someone. And there ain't no consecrated ground in Africville.

CLARICE

(in disbelief) No… consecrated… ground? *(beat)* No *consecrated ground?!* What is Africville if it ain't consecrated ground, Willem? *(beat)* This land been in my family for years, *hundreds a years…*. My ancestors, they consecrated this ground… the kids laughing and playin' in Kildare Field consecrated it! The funerals, the hymns at the church, consecrated it… All the baptisms down at the beach, Willem, they consecrated this ground. This is where they lived and died… where… where they cried… where they loved, Willem… *loved. (pause)* Surely… *(She starts to cry.)* Surely no one, ain't nobody on this-here earth tellin' me Africville ain't no consecrated ground!! Ain't no Mister-Clancy-city-white-man tellin' me. I saw it… I lived it… I loved it… Africville is consecrated ground!!

She collapses, breathlessly, to the chair.

Now… you go. You hear me? You go run, and… and tell… tell Mister Clancy what I say. Tell him he got it all wrong, cause there ain't a single lick a land in Africville that ain't consecrated. You tell 'em that.

WILLEM

Leasey we gonna bury Tully. Bury him in a city cemetery.

CLARICE
You listen here!! *(beat)* They took my chile away from me once, Willem... once!! They ain't takin' 'em away again – ya hear?! Ya hear me?! They ain't layin' a finger on my baby. Ya hear, Willem?

WILLEM
Leasey they gonna do what they wanna do and that is that.

CLARICE
Well they got it all wrong. They ain't layin' a finger on my baby. You go tell Mister Clancy that. You tell 'em Tully's gonna be buried in Africville where he belongs and–

WILLEM
Leasey—I tol'ya, baby—it's too late. It's too late for all that now. All ya gotta do is look around ya and see that they made up their minds what they're gonna do with us. They're demolishin Africville Leasey–

CLARICE
No they ain't!! We ain't sellin'!

As WILLEM picks up his gloves to exit, a bulldozer suddenly starts. Both look to the sound, then WILLEM exits in silence.

Scene Two

CLANCY, smoking and waiting, stands next to the well as Aunt SARAH approaches. She doesn't appear to recognize or notice him and keeps walking.

CLANCY
Hi!

SARAH
Mister.

She keeps walking.

CLANCY
Miss Aunt Lied? *(beat)* It's me, Sonny.

SARAH halts.

SARAH
Oh my. Sonny... you look diff'ren'. Like you changed or growed or some-such. How ya been doin'?

CLANCY
Could be better.

SARAH
Always can be. You look cold. Ya never did come by for that tea.

CLANCY
I know... but I'll be by shortly.

SARAH
Maybe yes, maybe no... but let me tell you somethin', Sonny. Ya know, all God's chillin' got a role ta play. Just like in them movies. Some plays bad roles, some plays good roles. Then there's thems in them movies that don't know what kinda role they's playin'. Ever see them movies like that-there, Sonny?

CLANCY shrugs; he chuckles.

CLANCY
Guess.

SARAH
Now ain't that sumpin'. *(pause)* Well I... I gotta git I tells us. Bye, Sonny.

She starts off.

CLANCY
See ya.

SARAH
(halting) Say, Sonny?

CLANCY
Yeah?

SARAH
Did ya ever git them books from the lie-berry I was tellin' ya about? You know? *(beat)* The ones 'bout South Africa?

CLANCY
No, Miss Aunt Lied. I just didn't have the time.

SARAH
Too bad. *(starting off)* Whole world a knowledge in that there lie-berry. Whole lotta understandin'.

She exits. CLANCY butts out his cigarette and exits.

Scene Three

CLARICE lies apparently napping in a chair. WILLEM stands nearby.

WILLEM
(*whispering*) Leasey? (*She doesn't answer.*) Leasey? (*pause*) I just stand here and look up through the window into the stars, ya know, Leasey? (*pause*) I kin see... I kin see before all those twinkling stars that the Big Dipper and Venus be as bright... as bright as the Star of David, baby... (*pause*) Leasey, I–

CLARICE shifts, her eyes open wide.

It like... it like the whole universe out there, just waitin' for us to... step out into it.... Like, baby, I been thinkin'... maybe it's time we got outta Africville... and... and, well, there ain't hardly no one left here anyways. Everybody's gonna go. I'm thinkin' yeah... maybe we should take the city's offer and sell. People always movin', Leasey. White folks move all the time. Mister Clancy say we can relocate to a good, warm place in, ah, Uniacke Square.

CLARICE doesn't stir, but stays perfectly still.

I'm thinkin'... maybe now's the time to leave. See, the city ain't too happy with all the publicity it's gittin' in the papers and stuff and so... well, they wanna make a deal with us. They got big plans for this land. They talkin' like a park and maybe some industry and stuff. (*pause*) Yeah... Mister Clancy mentioned a park or sumpin'... Leasey, I dunno... don'tcha see what this means for us? Now's our chance to get out – get a good price for our land, 'cause the city wants it bad and it don't want no trouble. Know what I mean?

CLARICE doesn't answer.

There ain't nothin' we kin do, Leasey. Can't you see that? If the city wants our land, they're gonna take it and it don't matter what the nigger wants. Never has, never will... Leasey, you listenin' to me? Are you listenin', baby?

CLARICE suddenly turns to him, sound asleep.

Scene Four

REVEREND MINER is doing some some business behind the pulpit as a dishevelled and drunken CLANCY enters. He takes a swig from a flask.

REVEREND MINER
Oh, Mister Clancy.

CLANCY
Hello, Reverend…

REVEREND MINER
I see you've had your taste of the flask again today, Mister Clancy. You shouldn't fret yourself. You should simply ask God why He won't give you license.

CLANCY
I have my problems, Reverend, but why are you talking to me like this? I mean, like in circles?… What license? What are you talking about?

REVEREND MINER
A license to barter, boy, to buy and sell these people's souls. 'Cause that's what you're trying to do. But see, only God possesses that phenomenal currency. *(pause)* Now lock the door when ya leave, will ya? *(He starts off.)*

CLANCY
Reverend?

REVEREND MINER
(halting) Yeah?

CLANCY
I have to talk to you, Reverend.

REVEREND MINER
I don't want to talk right now! *(He lowers his voice.)* Yes, even ministers get tired of talking sometimes.

CLANCY
But I have – I mean, I just need somebody to talk to.

REVEREND MINER
I want nothing more to do with this business, Mister Clancy. Now you sober up, and try and make your peace with God.

CLANCY
No, Reverend it's not about that, or, *(lifting his flask)* even this. It's about me. I mean, the Lyle boy. Dead… he's dead. Circumstances beyond my control. But I thought when I got in here, I'd be the hero – I mean save the people from these living conditions. Just look at how they live? Next to a dump for Godsakes.

REVEREND MINER

The people were here first, boy, then they moved in their new tenant; the dump. Then there's the abattoir. Naturally, along with abattoirs and dumps—right along with them—comes rats. I mean, don't you understand what's going on here?

CLANCY

You know Reverend? I did everything a good boy—a good little white boy from the affluent end of town—is supposed to do. I… I went to the right schools, the right church. I… I cultivated the right friends. My folks have money – guess you never guessed that, hunh? *(He chuckles; contemplates.)* But I realize now that I never got this job because they saw some brilliance in me, or any special aptitude. I got this job because I'm William Clancy's boy – and you better believe it. The party that sits on the government side owes my father some favours. Big, political favours and I'm my father's payback. None of the other bastards downtown would dirty their hands with this, you know. By hiring me they killed two birds with one stone, didn't they? I mean they paid off what they owed my father and got rid of the Negroes at the same time.

> *CLANCY stands.*

I just want you to know, Reverend, I want you to know, for the record: I never had anything to do with people being moved in garbage trucks! I didn't make that decision. In fact I tried my best to make sure every-one here would be treated with respect… dignity. And that baby? My God, Reverend, that should have never happened. I… when I took this job I thought I could do good. I thought the city was on the up-and-up. But… Reverend, I'm so sorry. So sorry.

REVEREND MINER

Tully's death wasn't your fault.

CLANCY

And I'm sorry about the church…

> *REVEREND MINER is taken aback for a few moments.*

REVEREND MINER

What?! They're going to tear down the church?!

CLANCY

It was after your request to bury the baby. Some members were against the burial. They felt it would encourage–

REVEREND MINER

Raze my church?!

CLANCY

–it would encourage an attachment to this place long after the people were gone. Then, an alderman said if we allow one there would be many more. He felt that allowing the burials in Africville would cause some problems – now, and in the future. Then the next thing I know, someone asks why they should keep the church in Africville. I reminded them of our commitment to you. Some supported me... but the majority voted to get rid of the church too. I thought you–

REVEREND MINER

Tear down the church?! What—in God's name—are those imbeciles thinking?! Do they not know, that this church is the very badge of identification for my people?! Do they not know that this is the very cement that holds my people together?! Do they not know that this church is the very soul of... of Africville itself?!

CLANCY

Reverend Min–

REVEREND MINER

Of course they know! *(beat)* And that's the very reason why they're tearing, it, down! *(beat)* Because if you divide – you conquer. Those e-vil... gen-it-tal-cutting, bastards!!

There's a long pause.

CLANCY

(deliberate and even) They need Africville 'cause they need more harbour frontage! They need Africville so they can build a new bridge – approach ramps. Reverend, if they allow people to be buried on the site, I mean around the church, it would create problems. I mean, it's just not this baby so much. It would be all the people of Africville and the generations to come. They don't want people seeing a grave site.

REVEREND MINER

Then if they don't want those graves, and if they don't want this so-called shantytown, why don't they fix up Africville like they did every other community?! Surely it's costing them more money to build that Uniacke Square than it would cost to fix up Africville!! My people have been asking for their help for centuries!! *(beat)* For centuries!!

CLANCY

Reverend Miner, I–

REVEREND MINER

Damn them!! And damn you Mister Clancy!!

There's an eerie silence as REVEREND MINER walks to the pulpit.

CLANCY

I don't like this any more than you do, Reverend. But what choice do we have? Unless both me and you do what the city says, they'll expropriate all the land and give everybody five hundred dollars as was the initial plan. And there would be no church here or anywhere else. Listen, Reverend, as hard as it is, we must complete this plan before the city's deadline. They promised me they will rebuild your church at a new site. You will have your church.

REVEREND MINER

Do you really think they would desecrate a church just to build it up again?! This is not part of their, brilliant and evilly, executed plan.

CLANCY

(*angrily*) Reverend Miner I'm so sick of this!! All this subterfuge!! All this lying – this explaining and re-explaining. All this deal-making!! Look what it's turning me into!! Look what it's doing to you!!

REVEREND MINER

Don't pity me, Mister Clancy. My heart goes out to you and your city. Now! (*beat*) You've had your first taste of power – your first taste of the inhumanity and insensitivity of your system. And you're wondering if it's really you, you're wondering if this is what you wanna be for the rest of your life. You're looking at yourself and you don't like what you see, do you? That's why you drink.

CLANCY

Let's just get these last people signed. Get your new church. At least with me and you here, there's still a chance.

REVEREND MINER

A chance for what?

CLANCY

A chance for the church. A chance for human dignity.

REVEREND MINER

(*thoughtfully*) There's no chance for anything now, Mister Clancy. Can't you see? There's no chance for anything now.

> *There's a very pregnant pause between them, then CLANCY collects his things and exits. REVEREND MINER simply stands there.*

My God... Why?... Why have You forsaken me?... Why?... Why have You let me down in my time of trouble?... Why?... why have You chosen me to be strong when everywhere I turn I gaze into the omnipotent eye of adversity?!... Why have You failed me?!

With Bible in hand, he slumps defeatedly into a pew as the bulldozers start again.

In the face of this You give me words?! In the face of metal and bristling machine?!... *(pause)* ...You, give, me, words... *(He stands.)* I cannot stand before the gluttonous mouth of a bulldozer and fight with... with words!! *(pause)* And my people... my flock... they line up behind me... seeking solace and, and... wisdom and strength... and yet I fail... I fail... I may as well lead them to your abattoir over there and prepare them for Your forthcoming slaughter!!... Why?!... Why have You forsaken me in my time of need?! *(Long pause; he lowers his voice.)* Upon this Earth I have served Thee. I have served Thee faithfully. Truthfully. My mouth has sung nothing but Your praises. What is my reward?... A displaced people, a dead baby and a church to be bulldozed. And when I call on You, You give me impotent words?!

He flings the Bible to the floor.

I, need, a, miracle!! *(pause)* I... need... a... miracle...

Slowly he re-approaches the pulpit.

"Fret not thyself because of evildoers, neither be thou envious against workers of iniquity... " those are Your words. "For they shall be cut down like the grass, and wither as the green herb..." those are Your words and I have been nothing, nothing but Your mouthpiece. I... do... not... need... Your... words!!

He glances to the Bible, retrieves it from the floor and kisses it.

"Thou wilt keep him in perfect peace, whose mind is stayed on Thee... because he trusteth in me... "those are Your words.... And my God... my heavenly Father... I trust... I trust...

Blackout.

Scene Five

CLARICE is dressing in black, gathering her clothes.

CLARICE
I ain't worn these clothes since Momma died. Still fits though, don't it?

SARAH
Oh sure it do. Sure it do. *(pause)* Leasey, you sure you don't want me to come with you?

CLARICE

No, it's somethin'... somethin' I gotta do...

SARAH

Okay. I just...

> *CLARICE starts to break down. SARAH embraces her.*

Oh, Leasey.... It be okay. I promise. It be okay...

CLARICE

But how? *(pause)* How? *(crying)* Tully-Tully-Tully-Tully...

SARAH

You got to be strong, girl. We the ones that gotta be strong. Oh yes, we bring 'em into the worl', but we gotta be strong enough to take 'em out of the worl' too. Strong... strong.

CLARICE

But... but... *(breaking down)* I'm tryin'... I'm tryin' so hard, so hard, Aunt Sarah... but it's so hard!

SARAH

I knows. I knows, but... but this what yer granddaddy and yer grandmomma done for you, and yer momma and poppa, too. You gotta be strong. They taught ya how to be strong.

> *Silently, CLARICE puts on her veil and goes towards the door, where she pauses.*

CLARICE

I'll be back later.

SARAH

Yes. You gotta have some of that blueberry pie I made for ya. It good ya know.

CLARICE

(smiling through her tears) Yeah, I know. *(She embraces SARAH.)* Lease it ain't no turnip greens!

> *They laugh awkwardly, then CLARICE leaves as the kettle boils. SARAH goes about the business of making her tea for a few moments, when GROOVEY appears in the door; suitcase in hand. Unseen by SARAH, she drops the suitcase, and simply stands there. SARAH finishes her tea, and as she turns, sees GROOVEY.*

SARAH
Jesus!! Groovey ya plumb up and startled me! Whatcha doin' just standing there?!

With a rag she's now wiping up tea.

GROOVEY
Now I raised a lotta babies and I gotta revert to a momma's old standby: "In or out! In or out!" *(She chuckles.)*

SARAH becomes concerned as GROOVEY continues to stand.

Groovey, you all right, baby? You okay? Come in. Sit down. Come on, honey...

GROOVEY
No, Aunt Sarah-girl, Groovey not comin' in, Groovey goin' de udder way.

SARAH
What? My Gawd, what be wrong wif you, Groovey? I mean–

GROOVEY
Groovey's leavin, Aunt Sarah. Goin'.

SARAH
On a vacation?! Never thought I'd see the day when Groovey Peters got tired of her men-friends! *(She chuckles.)*

GROOVEY
No vacations, no day-trips, I'm tellin' ya girl, Groovey Peters is leavin' Africville.

SARAH
Whatever for?

GROOVEY
"Whatever for"?! Aunt Sarah 'ave you been watching da goings-on 'round dis place lately?! You ain't seen?! *(Pause; she lowers her voice.)* Groovey Peters been told. Groovey Peters knows when Groovey Peters ain't wanted.

SARAH
You been told? Told what?

GROOVEY
I got my notice, Aunt Sarah. Groovey Peters is gone, ya hear?

SARAH

Gone where? What notice? Girl, what are ya talkin' about?

GROOVEY

Da man done tol' me: "Groovey Peters you must vacate said properties by…" –all dat white bullshit, you know? *(She chuckles.)* Only ones dat don't know it is dem! I appeal to de man. I dun tings. I mean, for… "my friend." Me beg – me plead. Groovey plead for all of Africville, but he drop me like Groovey fulla polio. Like Groovey don't have no never-minds. *(pause)* Me t'ought… *(She starts to cry.)* Groovey t'ought dis time it be different for Groovey. He gonna git a divorce and marry I. *(beat)* Groovey actually believed, Aunt Sarah!! *(She cries, but regains her composure.)* Well!! *(beat)* Groovey ain't no believer no mores. Groovey goin' back to Montreal where da people are real and where ya know ya ain't no, "Neg-ro." Where yer a just plain, "nig-ger." Where dey take advantage of ya *(pause)* but dey kiss ya first, Aunt Sarah!! Lease dey kiss ya first…

SARAH

Now Groovey.

GROOVEY

Here? *(beat)* Here Aunt Sarah?! *(beat)* Groovey just don't want to see anymore carnage, 'cause that what it be – carnage!!

SARAH

Don't say that.

GROOVEY

Why not? It be the truth! I see people move in garbage trucks! Why you yoursel' say it be like South Africa!

SARAH

You thought he was gonna marry ya? You really thought that he was gonna marry ya? Girlll…

GROOVEY

Groovey let her guard down. Me t'ought… me t'ought me politician was real. But Groovey knows now – Aunt Sarah: dere ain't nuthin' in dis worl' dat's white and real. Ya gotta spread de dark gravy over de white rice before it palatable.

SARAH

Groovey!

GROOVEY

Groovey is tired. Nuthin' but lies lies lies lies lies and more of dem lies.

Offstage, we hear a car horn.

My cab!

SARAH
Let 'em wait! They make us wait, don't they? I'm surprised it even come to Africville.

The car toots.

GROOVEY
You know Aunt Sarah, *(She chuckles.)* when de cabs do come to Africville dey always so very anxious to get out! *(chuckles)*

SARAH
Well I'm goin' too, honey. I'm movin' too. Mister Clancy and all his friends dun seen to dat.

GROOVEY
Whatcha you tink Clarice might do wid all dis, Aunt Sarah?

SARAH
Clarice gotta realize that Africville's over. Over, baby.

The bulldozers start, then, we hear another "beep-beep."

GROOVEY
Groovey got to git her train, Aunt Sarah. My Groovey-train dun come in.

They embrace.

SARAH
You write or call now.

GROOVEY
I will.

SARAH
'Cause you know wherever Sarah Lied be, she gotta phone.

GROOVEY
All right, Aunt Sarah. Groovey Peters gonna miss ya.

SARAH
Oh, go on now. Ya gotta run to yer destiny, Groovey. I think that's what they calls it… yeah… destiny…

GROOVEY
You tink dis is Groovey's destiny, Aunt Sarah? Oh no, dis just be *dere* rendition of Groovey's destiny. And dey all strummin' da wrong tune.

GROOVEY exits to porch, picks up her bag, waves then exits.

Scene Six

WILLEM sits alone in a pew of the church. We hear a door shut, and silently CLANCY appears and sits behind him.

CLANCY
Willem? (He still doesn't stir.) Willem Lyle?

WILLEM wipes his eyes and glances behind.

Maybe this is the wrong time. I can come back.

WILLEM
No, no, come in, Mister Clancy. God's house is open to all.

CLANCY
You're the deacon here, right?

WILLEM
Nope. The choirmaster.

CLANCY
I see. Well... I brought along that agreement we were talking about the other day, remember?

WILLEM nods affirmatively.

This won't take long.

WILLEM
Sure. *(pause)* You see Mister Clancy, this place took our baby and we just wanna... I just wanna git out as quick as possible.

CLANCY
Was Tully your only child, Willem?

WILLEM
Uh-hunh. Yeah.

CLANCY
Oh...

WILLEM
There's no problem is there, Mister Clancy? No problem...

CLANCY
No... it's just... well... I mean... you do realize the city can't find you a place in Uniacke Square. I mean... according to their criteria... it's a–

WILLEM
Why, Mister Clancy?

CLANCY
Because the complex was made for families.

WILLEM
But we is a family – me and Leasey.

CLANCY
No no no. Not according to this, I mean, our, criteria. You see you and your wife are now a childless couple. The city will, however, work to find you a place outside Uniacke Square. Okay? You understand?

WILLEM nods affirmatively.

You're happy with your assessment? You're sure you understand what I'm saying?

WILLEM
Yes. I do.

CLANCY hands WILLEM his pen and the Quit Claim Deed. WILLEM doesn't take it and CLANCY retreats. Then he re-offers it. WILLEM takes it and CLANCY leans his attache case forward so WILLEM can sign on it. CLANCY takes the deed, gives WILLEM a copy and silently leaves. WILLEM also exits. He walks to another part of the stage, where CLARICE stands.

Scene Seven

CLARICE is standing in the middle of field. She's deep in thought and vacantly staring off. WILLEM enters.

WILLEM
(Softly) Leasey!

CLARICE
(gesturing) Look, Willem...

WILLEM
What?

CLARICE
I kin feel 'em, Willem. Just like it was yesterday, I kin feel 'em.

WILLEM
Baby? It's cold out here, too cold to be doin' this. Why don't we–

CLARICE
This be right where my grandmomma and granddaddy on Momma's side lived. Right near this spot, well... just over there. We had the closest house to the well.

WILLEM
(*weakly*) Leasey?

CLARICE
Why you practically standin' in the middle a their living room. And Granddaddy built their place with his bare hands... and home-made tools. And... and... ya know? I kin feel his spirit, his pride, his love of his land...

WILLEM
What happened to the house, baby?

CLARICE
It... it burned down... and Granddaddy died in that field tryin' to save it.... Once again (*pause*) 'cause once again the fire trucks came late to Africville. They was always late, real late, and I guess Granddaddy breathed in too much smoke. He died right in Momma's arms he did. Right there in that-there field much like... much like... much like my Tully did in mine.

WILLEM
Baby, I never knew–

CLARICE
All the men folk pitched in and built Momma a new house. The house we livin' in now, and Willem?

WILLEM
What, baby?

CLARICE
This is where Tully's gonna be buried. There ain't no one gonna–

WILLEM
Leasey–

CLARICE
No I tell you! Tully's gonna be buried right here near to us... where he ain't never gonna be alone...

She throws off WILLEM's arm and bolts. She heads towards the church.

WILLEM
Leasey!!

Scene Eight

CLANCY is sitting in a pew in the church. CLARICE enters. He stands.

CLANCY
May I help you?

CLARICE ignores him.

Haven't we already–

CLARICE
I've come to talk to Reverend Miner.

CLANCY
He'll be back in a moment. Are you sure there isn't something I–

CLARICE
I want to speak to Reverend Miner I said!

They retreat to pews, CLANCY in front, CLARICE angrily eyeing his back. Momentarily REVEREND MINER enters.

REVEREND MINER
Clarice! Why I didn't expect–

CLARICE
In the church, Reverend?! You lettin' this man conduct his business in the Church?

REVEREND MINER
God's house is open to all, sister, you know that.

CLARICE
Even to the ones that wanna destroy it?!

REVEREND MINER
(clearing his voice) Clarice. This is Mister Clancy. Why don't we sit down?

She takes REVEREND MINER aside.

CLARICE
Tully got to be buried in Africville, Reverend.

CLANCY
Excuse me for interrupting–

CLARICE
No excuse! I ain't here to talk to you. *(pause, to REVEREND MINER)* Now Tully's gonna be buried here, Reverend. In Africville where he belong.

REVEREND MINER
Clarice, do you know why we–

CLANCY
Excuse me Reverend, but Mrs. Lyle–

CLARICE
Save it!! Just save it!! *(beat)* You desecratin' everything you touch!

CLANCY
I'm sorry. I'm very, very sorry, Ma'am. Look Mrs. Lyle, I do empathize with your situation, but the facts are clear–

CLARICE
You should be sorry!! *(beat, emotionally)* 'Cause you took my baby away from me, Mister Clancy!! I ain't got no baby no more, 'cause you killed 'em!!

CLANCY
We did not kill your child, Mrs. Lyle, we–

CLARICE
Oh yes you did! Killed 'em the day you built that dump on our doorstep. Black, proud people, living right here, and your city comes along and builds a home for rats. But you ain't happy yet, are ya? You ain't happy till ya feed the helpless Black babies to 'em!!

Again CLANCY pauses.

CLANCY

Mrs. Lyle... look, I'm sorry. I truly am sorry about the loss of your child and the living conditions you endured. But I must remind you, the city, under no circumstances, will agree to consecrate any land in Africville. Do you understand me? Under no circumstances.

CLARICE chuckles, actually chuckles.

CLARICE

You know Mister Clancy, I like you.

CLANCY

Thank you.

CLARICE

But you so young for this job.

CLANCY

I've heard that so many times, Mrs Lyle.

CLARICE

But lemme ask you somethin'.

CLANCY

What might that be?

CLARICE

Why they send a boy to do a man's job?! 'Cause I ain't acceptin' no apologies for Tully from a boy! Send me a white man! You hear me?! You Goddamn well send me a white man! Make him apologize! *(pause)* Good day to you Reverend.

CLARICE starts off.

CLANCY

Mrs. Lyle, may I please ask you one last question?

CLARICE

No. I got no more to say to you!

CLANCY

Just one more question?... Please?

She halts.

CLARICE

What is it?!

CLANCY
If you feel so strongly about this place, why'd you agree to sell your land?

She turns to him.

CLARICE
Whaa–? *(to REVEREND MINER)* What... is... he... is... he... crazy?

CLANCY lifts a piece of paper, and hands it to her.

CLANCY
You do recognize your husband's signature? Don't you? On this Quit Claim Deed?

CLARICE gasps in shock and runs off.

Scene Nine

WILLEM sits at table. Peacefully, sipping coffee and reading the newspapers. We hear a door slam and CLARICE appears. She's holding the Quit Claim Deed.

WILLEM
Leasey! Groovey's back for the funeral!

CLARICE
You!... You Black bastard!! You ungrateful sonofabitch!!

WILLEM
It... *(standing)* it was the best thing. The best thing for us, Leasey. We kin get a place of our own, start a new life – just you and me. Leasey... we... we been working. Workin' hard baby, and – and we deserve better than this. There's nothing wrong with wanting something better. What's wrong with wanting something better? Why can't we have the same things as the white man?

CLARICE
'Cause they're lyin'!! *(beat)* They don't let niggers have them things, Willem!! Mister Clancy – all of 'em! They're lyin' to us!! Can't you understand that?! *(beat)* Why can't you understand that?!

WILLEM
This place killed our son!! It killed Tully – you want us to die, too? What is it Leasey, what is it about this place?! This is nothin' but a tired ol' shack with rats about the doors!!

CLARICE
Did you sign it on his casket?

WILLEM
What?

CLARICE
These papers?! You sign 'em on Tully's casket?!

WILLEM
I'd have signed them on his grave, and so woulda you! But you ain't thinkin' right, Leasey. I would sign anything to get out of here!

He goes to hug her and she responds; lifeless.

I did it for us... I wanted the best... for us... Leasey *(pause)* I love you. Leasey... I love you so much...

CLARICE
(weakly) Willem? *(no reply)* Willem?

WILLEM
What baby?

CLARICE
Willem... I... I don't want you here, no more. I... Willem... I–

WILLEM
Leasey – what're ya sayin'?

CLARICE
I want you to leave... to go...

WILLEM leaves as CLARICE slumps onto the couch in a mass of tears. The lights fade, then come up on the church.

Scene Ten

The church. JIMMY enters carrying the coffin and places it in front of the pulpit. He pays his respects and sits in a pew.

SARAH and GROOVEY enter next. They pay their respects, SARAH sitting in the front pew, GROOVEY behind. Next comes CLARICE, who breaks down horribly in front of the coffin. SARAH goes and consoles her, and helps her into the pew as REVEREND MINER takes the pulpit.

REVEREND MINER
Now let us pray...

> *CLARICE glances behind occasionally, looking for WILLEM.*

Our Heavenly Father, we ask that You give us Your blessing, Lord. Now let us pray. Lord this child unable to speak, was known and loved by all who ever held him. Lord please grant him a place at Your side, in Your Eternal Kingdom. He was born of Your flesh, dear Lord. He was delivered of Your blood. He was foreseen to grow into a man who would do good and great things in Your name. But the longevity of his life was not in Your will, and You called him home. Oh, God, there are many who do not understand. Many who grieve at this close, but Your will is omnipotent and Your reasons are always sound. The Lord works in mysterious ways for His wonders to unfold. He guideth us through the valley of our fears into the place of Eternal peace. He has brought us out of a horrible pit, out of the mirey clay, and set our feet upon a rock, and established our commission. Oh, Lord, Your truth will deliver us.

> *WILLEM enters and starts towards CLARICE, but stops. He stands in the aisle.*

Blessed is the man that make the Lord his trust, and respect not the proud, nor such as turn the lies of the malicious. For even though we walk through the valley of death, we shall fear no evil... and he shall judge the world in righteousness... and he shall minister judgement in righteousness, oh, Lord. Amen.

JIMMY, SARAH, GROOVEY, CLARICE & WILLEM
(together) Amen!!

REVEREND MINER
Let us now turn to–

> *WILLEM interrupts, singing a hymn a cappella. He walks to the casket and lifts it. Still singing, he exits and places it on the soil of Africville. All follow him as he exits. CLANCY stands off in the distance as CLARICE and WILLEM bend over the casket, lifting the soil and pouring it over the coffin. Finally, REVEREND MINER lifts soil and pours it over the coffin, while saying the following.*

Out of the mouths of babes and sucklings hast Thou ordained strength, oh Lord, because of thine enemies. When mine enemies are turned back, they shall fall and perish at Thy presence. And he shall judge the world in righteousness, he shall minister judgement to the people in righteousness, oh Lord. Tully Lyle. The firstborn of Clarice Lyle nee Smith and Willem Lyle. A descendant of Africville was born on August 5, 1965, and passed away on October 1st, 1965. His short life received the blessing of the Lord. I do consecrate this holy *(CLANCY crosses himself.)* and sacred ground and do bless the small soul that lives herein to eternal and everlasting life in the name of Jesus Christ Our Lord, amen.

The cast is now back-lit, in silhouette, by the cutout houses. One by one the light on each of the houses dies. One final light pauses on the church, then it too is extinguished.

Blackout.

The end.

The Adventures of a Black Girl in Search of God

Djanet Sears

Djanet Sears is an award-winning playwright and director and has several acting nominations to her credit for both stage and screen. She has been honoured with a Governor General's Award, a Martin Luther King Jr. Achievement Award, a Chalmers Canadian Play Award, a Harry Jerome Award, and Dora Mavor Moore Award. She is artistic director of the AfriCanadian Playwrights' Festival, and the editor of *Testifyin': Contemporary African Canadian Drama: Vols. I & II*. Plays include *Harlem Duet, Afrika Solo, Who Killed Katie Ross, Double Trouble*, and most recently *The Adventures of a Black Girl in Search of God*. Djanet is currently an adjunct professor at University College, University of Toronto.

History at Negro Creek; Djanet Sears'
The Adventures of a Black Girl in Search of God

by Leslie Sanders

— • — — • — — • —

Djanet Sears' *The Adventures of a Black Girl in Search of God* is a delicate weave of history, sorrow, resolve and faith. It is also an act of reclamation. Set in Holland Township, Ontario, an area approximately 140 kilometres north of Toronto, *Adventures of a Black Girl* centres on Rainey, a woman still in mourning three years after losing her young daughter and about to divorce her minister husband. A doctor, she blames herself for not diagnosing her daughter's meningitis, and has taken up post-graduate studies in Religion and Science in an effort to grasp intellectually what her heart cannot bear to consider. Counterpoint to the narrative of Rainey's journey of loss and healing is that of her father Abendigo, a retired judge, who, with his cronies, has dedicated his later years to the liberation of all stereotypic representation of Blackness: "enslaved lawn ornaments, cookie jars, piggy banks, plaques, figurines, visual images and ephemera." These they methodically steal from all over the neighbourhood, and then refashion the artefacts' minstrel grins into human smiles, and consign them to Abendigo's basement until they figure out what to do with them. These racially demeaning artefacts are not the only objects of their reclamation, however. In their final escapade, they liberate from the local museum the army uniform worn by Abendigo's grandfather when he fought for the British in the War of 1812 – for which service he was deeded land by Negro Creek, as were other early Black settlers in Grey County.

Sears' inspiration for *Adventures of a Black Girl* was the battle in Holland Township over the Township's decision to rename Negro Creek Road, ostensibly because the word Negro had become problematic.[1] They renamed it Moggie Road after a nineteenth century white settler, effectively eradicating any trace of the almost two centuries of Black habitation of the area, and reversed their decision only after the intervention of the Ontario Human Rights Commission. This incident, of course, speaks to the much larger issue of the invisibility of Black Canada in the national narrative and the national imaginary. In *Adventures of a Black Girl* both that history and its invisibility are brought to light. The play lays eloquent and insistent claim to the soil of Grey County and to the place of African Canadians in the making of the nation.

Adventures is rife with gestures of reclamation in all its meanings.[2] When liberating artefacts, for example, retired judge Abendigo and his friends acquire invisibility by donning the uniforms of janitors, delivery men, chauffeurs and domestics. Their donning and removing the uniforms of stereotypical Black roles has its analogue in the "human" smiles they paint when re/figuring and re/fashioning their booty. What one character decorously calls "unconscious classification" cloaks the vibrant humanity of this elderly group of rebels. Many details of the final theft are evocative of African Canadian history, remote and recent. The jacket, not surprisingly, is in storage, along with a set of photographs and captions clearly based on the 1989 controversial exhibit "Into the Heart of Africa" at Toronto's Royal Ontario Museum. The group *rendezvous* at a totem pole. Pretending to dust, Darlene rewrites the caption of a portrait of John A. MacDonald's wife, indicting her Jamaican ancestry. Bert insists on the code name of Olivier Le Jeune for the mission.

The reclamation of the jacket, couched in comedy, literally is Abendigo's final gesture. However, his heart problems, too, are symbolic. As his name suggests, Abendigo has been tested. Unable to find work as a lawyer, for many years he worked as a porter, and cleaned toilets, before being able to commence a career that led to the bench. After twenty years of what Abendigo thought was a friendship with a white man, the man tells him he is "different" from other Blacks, crushing his faith in genuine change. Personal sorrow also haunts him, an impetuous first marriage to Rainey's mother, and a second to the sister of the woman he truly loves. Abendigo's anguished rage at the attempted erasure of his community's and his own family's roots in Negro Creek erupts before his first collapse. His rage continues to smoulder, deepening the comedy of what are otherwise hilarious scenes.

The theme of reclamation recurs in other ways. Throughout *Adventures*, Rainey eats dirt, a practice frequent especially among pregnant women in central Africa and the southern United States. She longs for "soft, sugary earth by Negro creek," Rainey tells the audience early in the play, but since the death of her daughter Janie, she eats chalk, aspirin, and cigarette ashes. The conflation of an action suggestive of pregnancy, mourning, loss and land resonates eloquently. At the end, her husband Michael, too, eats the dirt from Negro Creek, signalling their rootedness and their reconciliation.

The play's title, however, promises a concern with theology, not history, a theology that turns out to be both complex and ambivalent. The Book of Job echoes through the text, speaking to Rainey's losses, not only of her daughter, but also her many miscarriages, and the deaths of her mother and stepmother, and finally, her father. Land and history are also stripped from the community of Negro Creek, for the play takes place just before the name is restored. Job triumphs because he trusts in God; like Job, Rainey asks why God did not heed her prayers, like Job, she does not renounce faith, and in some senses, all is restored to her. Michael, however, has renounced his faith, despite the eloquence of his preaching. Thus, although church service, sermon and hymn punctuate the action of *Adventures*, certain traditional correspondences are disrupted. The faith that sustained the slaves and their descendants, and the church that provided strength during the Civil Rights Movement, retain meaning and place, nurturing the community. Neither faith nor church, however, provide resolution to the individual or collective struggles in the play.

Yet, despite its ambivalent theology, *The Adventures of a Black Girl in Search of God* is a deeply spiritual play, its spirituality perhaps more palpable in performance than on the page. In the play's premier production at DuMaurier Theatre in Toronto, February 2002, directed by the playwright, the chorus flowed like water; a visual human evocation of Negro Creek, extending the characters' deepest emotions, performing the pantheism that expresses itself in Rainey's desire to be a willow, the wildflowers on Janie's grave, the profound relation to land that goes beyond even two centuries and more of being planted in Canadian soil. Their singing, too, seemed constant, almost as though the action interrupted their sounding, rather than the reverse. Three huge blue silk scarves shimmered from the ceiling as the play opened, dropping gracefully to the floor before the action began. As theme, emblem and subject, water was everywhere in the production, extending the geography of Negro Creek, to the Atlantic itself and to Africa, the source. When the chorus, moving as Negro Creek, beckons to Rainey; when she promises to consign her daughter's dolls to the water; in these moments, a palpable Negro Creek reaches beyond the particular history and struggles that the play addresses. It evokes the river-crossings that saved escaping slaves and the Middle Passage that brought them into slavery, the waters of baptism and the waters of birth. Through voice, dance and spectacle, as well as in story, *The Adventures of a Black Girl in Search of God* situates the struggles of African Canadians within a national narrative, indeed, but also within the history and space of the African Diaspora, a larger imaginary and a deeper root.

Leslie Sanders currently teaches at York University and specializes in African American and African Canadian studies. She has published articles on writers such as Dionne Brand, Claire Harris, Nourbese Philip, Austin Clarke, and written extensively on the plays of African American writer Langston Hughes. She is co-editor of *The Collected Works of Langston Hughes*, (University of Missouri Press, 2001).

[1] Breon, Robin. 2002. Interview With Djanet Sears: A Black Girl In Search Of God. Aislesay Toronto. www.aislesay.com/ONT-SEARS.html
[2] 1: the act of making a claim or protest <reclamations of disappointed investors – R.E.Cameron>; 2: the act or process of reforming or rehabilitating <an agency devoted to the reclamation of delinquents> <its ministry of reclamation to down-and-out men – Sidney Lovett>; 3: the act or process of restoring to cultivation or use <land reclamation> <a large-scale reclamation project> *Unabridged.Merriam-Webster.com*

The Adventures of a Black Girl in Search of God was first produced at the du Maurier Theatre by Obsidian Theatre Company and Nightwood Theatre, Toronto, in February, 2002 with the following company:

RAINEY	Alison Sealy-Smith
MICHAEL	David Collins
ABENDIGO	Walter Borden
IVY	Lili Francks
BERT	Herbert Johnson
DARESE	Jackie Richardson
GIRLENE	Barbara Barnes-Hopkins
PARAMEDIC	Michael Spencer Davis
DOCTOR RADCLIFFE	Michael Spencer Davis
DELIVERY MAN	Michael Spencer Davis
GUARD	Michael Spencer Davis
CHORUS	Ingrid Abbott, John Campbell, Jennifer Dahl, Xuan Fraser, Sharon Harvey, Monique Mojica, Carlos Morgan, Alejandra Nunez, Vivine Scarlett, Lincoln Shand, Shameema Soni, Saidah Baba Talibah, Tricia Williams

Directed by Djanet Sears
Production Designed by Astrid Janson
Lighting Designed by Paul Mathiesen
Composers: Alejandra Nunez & Djanet Sears
Choreographed by Vivine Scarlett
Additional Choreography by Fleurette S. Fernando & Ingrid Abbott
Musical Director: Alejandra Nunez
Dramaturge: Kate Lushington
Ensemble & Vocal Consultant: Michele George
Movement Consultant: Mark Christmann
Props by Anne Webster
Wardrobe by Joanne Lamberton
Marketing Director: John Karastamatis
Assistant Director: Weyni Mengesha
Design Apprentice: Raven Dauda
Production Manager: Martin Zwicker
Stage Managed by Michael Sinclair
Assistant Stage Manager: Trina Sookhai
Apprentice Stage Manager: Andrea Schurman

—•— —•— —•—

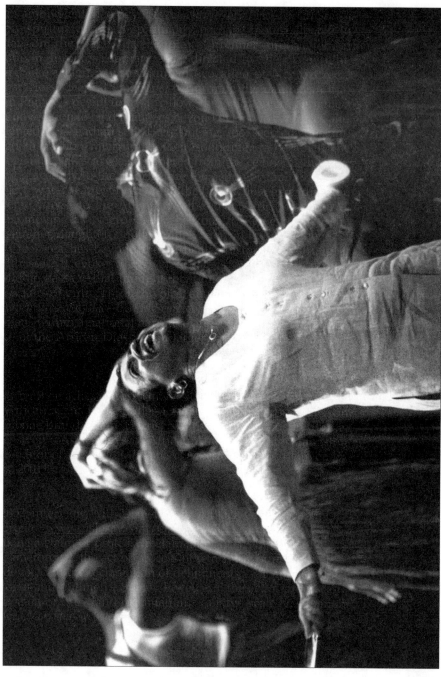

Alison
Sealy-
Smith.

Photo by
Cylla Von
Tiedemann.

The Adventures of a Black Girl in Search of God

by Djanet Sears

— • — — • — — • —

We, Africans in America, come from a people tied to the Earth,
people of the drums which echo the Earth's heartbeat.... People tied
to soil and wind and rain as to each other...
—Aned Kgositsile; *Part Of Each Other, Part Of The Earth*

He destroys both the blameless and the wicked.
—Job 9:22

If this Being is omnipotent, then every occurrence, including every
human action, every human thought, and every human feeling and
aspiration is also His work; how is it possible to think of holding
men responsible for their deeds and thoughts before such an
almighty Being? In giving out punishment and rewards He would
to a certain extent be passing judgement on Himself. How can this
be combined with the goodness and righteousness ascribed to Him?
—Albert Einstein; *Out of My Later Years*

ACT I

Prologue

From a deep darkness, a dissonant CHORUS of naked voices rises up out
of the morass of earth and water. As the lights come up, Lorraine
(RAINEY) Baldwin Johnson stands alone. Her face is wet with sweat,
tears and rain, masking her tarnished gold beauty. Her feet are bare. She
stares at the heavens.

A CHORUS of souls approaches the stage from all corners of the space.
The CHORUS slowly sings the sound of heavy rain pounding on the dark
and deserted country road. The CHORUS forms the surrounding woods
and lush farmland and almost devour RAINEY and the two lanes of
asphalt road. Flashes of lightning turn night to day and the thunder roars
loudly.

RAINEY begins to run down the empty roadway towards us. She is
running as fast as she can down the centre line. She is holding a bundle
in her arms.

RAINEY
Oh God! Please, please, please God! Oh Jesus. Please. Oh God. Oh God.
Oh God.

RAINEY's bruised and bloody feet begin to tire. She stops to catch her breath.

Pastor MICHAEL, a tall, auburn-coloured man in his early 40s, is dressed in a church robe, and stands to one side of the stage as if at a pulpit. The remaining CHORUS members sit in rows in front of him like a congregation.

MICHAEL
(reading from the Bible) "He saved others; himself he cannot save. If he be the king of Israel, let him now come down from the cross, and we will believe him. He trusted in God; let him deliver him now…"

The CHORUS (as congregation) signifies sadly.

RAINEY places the bundle higher up, almost at her shoulders. The leg of a child involuntarily kicks free from the bundle, then relaxes. The sound of a siren can be heard in the distance.

RAINEY
(almost under her breath) Our Father, who art in heaven. Please. I beg you. Beg you. Hallowed be thy name. Thy kingdom come. Thy will be done…

Choral voices become sirens as headlights appear before her. RAINEY and her bundle are soaked to the skin. RAINEY catches a second wind and begins to run again. She clutches the bundle with one arm, using her free hand to wave frantically at the approaching headlights. The centre line remains constant under RAINEY's feet.

The church is rife with "shouts" and "praises."

MICHAEL
(reading) "Now from the sixth hour there was darkness over all the land unto the ninth hour. And about the ninth hour Jesus cried with a loud voice saying, *Eli, Eli, lama sabachthani*? that is to say, My God, my God, why hast thou forsaken me?"

RAINEY
And lead us not into temptation. But deliver us from evil. And I will do anything. Take me. Please. Take me instead.

A paramedic enters. He rushes to RAINEY and tries to take the bundle of child from her. RAINEY resists at first.

MICHAEL & CHORUS
For thine is the kingdom. The power and the glory. Forever and ever. Amen.

RAINEY finally relinquishes the contents of her arms.

MICHAEL
God so loved the world that he gave his only begotten son. Jesus
suffered. Jesus could have taken himself down from that cross. But
he had a deep and abiding faith. The Lord calls on all of us, each and
every one of his children to have abiding faith. He asks us to put our
trust in him, especially at those times when faced with things we
cannot understand. He is with us. He is by our side.

> *She unwraps the bundle revealing a beautiful little girl, no more than five
> or six, her eyes closed. There is no movement. Her limp body remains a
> still life to dead weight. The paramedic takes the child and exits. RAINEY
> lingers in place, arms outstretched as if they remain still full with child.*

"What a Friend We Have In Jesus. All our sins and griefs to bear. What
a priv – Privilege to carry. Everything to God in prayer." Janie, I know
how you love that song. So – So we're – Your mother and I – We will –
We will miss–

> *He struggles to continue. A member of the congregation stands.*

DARESE
(singing) What a friend we have in Jesus.
All our sins and grief to bear.

> *The CHORUS instinctively joins her in the song.*

CHORUS
(as congregation) What a privilege to carry,
Everything to God in Pray'r.

> *RAINEY begins to walk slowly and what was once the road, is now the
> aisle of the church. She makes her way to a seat in the front row. She sits
> almost frozen.*

Have we trials and temptations?
Is there trouble anywhere?
We should never be discouraged.
Take it to the Lord in Prayer.

> *The CHORUS continues to sing as RAINEY suddenly rises from her seat
> and begins to exit the church alone. MICHAEL goes after her. He tries to
> stop her. He tries to take her in his arms, but she struggles with him.*

RAINEY
(overlapping) I begged. I begged him. I begged him, Michael. Michael,
I begged God. I begged you. I begged you. I begged you.

RAINEY exits leaving MICHAEL alone as the congregation looks on.

The voices crescendo singing the stage lights up on another part of the stage. The Church, MICHAEL and the CHORUS disappear and the soundscape transforms into a quiet rhythmic melody of curiosity.

Scene One

The CHORUS forms the edge of the woods by the porch. The lights shrink to a horizontal beam, revealing five figures who span the stage. We see their faces and upper torsos. Above and below the beam of light, their images are indistinguishable and blur into darkness. They are two men and three women. They all put on dark sunglasses simultaneously. The women wear darkly coloured church hats. They are all dressed in dark clothing. They themselves are dark in complexion. They are firmly in their darker years – septuagenarians all. They stare out at us from beyond their dark lenses like an army of Black 70-year-old 007s.

ABENDIGO
Ivy.

IVY
Uh huh!

ABENDIGO
Darese.

DARESE
Yeah!

ABENDIGO
Bert.

BERT
Here Judge.

ABENDIGO
Girlene.

GIRLENE
(taking off her dark glasses) Yes.

ABENDIGO
(glaring at GIRLENE) Not yet.

GIRLENE
(putting her dark glasses back on) Oh, oh, oh…. Yes, I'm here!

ABENDIGO
Now!

ABENDIGO, IVY, BERT, GIRLENE and DARESE remove their dark glasses in unison. (Well not exactly in unison but they're working on it.)

(checking his watch) Synchronizing watches…. Fifteen minutes to in 5, 4, 3, 2, set! Okay? Okay. Let's recap the game plan.

ABENDIGO unfolds a large map and lays it out onto the ground.

Darese, Bert and Girlene will take the Lotsa Soap Cleaning Company Van, and Ivy and me, we'll follow in Darese's Mercedes. We'll take Negro Creek Road all–

BERT
You mean Moggie Road.

ABENDIGO
It's been Negro Creek Road since way before I can remember and no new by-law is going to change that fact.

BERT
You're the Judge.

ABENDIGO
So, we'll take Negro Creek Road all the way to the highway, and from the highway–

BERT
(clearing his throat) I believe that Darese will have to make a pit stop at the gas station.

They all turn to DARESE.

IVY
Oh Darese, not again. You've taken this price comparison thing too far.

ABENDIGO
How much was it this time?

DARESE
Three cents a gallon adds up. You know how much I could've saved if I add up all the cents I've wasted.

GIRLENE
Yeah, you could've been an Einstein with all the sense you've wasted.

IVY

What's the point in having a Mercedes if you're gonna be worried about an extra three cents a gallon?

BERT

We're gonna be late again.

ABENDIGO

So, Darese, where are you going to fill up this time?

DARESE

The Petro Can on Highway 6. I did a quick drive by this morning and–

ABENDIGO

Ivy and I will meet you, Bert and Girlene at the Petro Can on Highway 6. And from the highway we'll take the Collingwood exit all the way to Balmoral. Number 153.

GIRLENE

Number 153.

BERT

153.

ABENDIGO

It's the same route we took when we were just observing the location. We'll rendezvous at the top of the street. Darese, you and Girlene will exit the vehicle and enter on foot. Ivy will join Bert in the Lotsa Soap Van. Bert, you will park it right outside said location. I'll park the Mercedes a little further up and put on my cap. *(to IVY)* Where's the cap?

IVY

(to GIRLENE) Where's the cap?

GIRLENE

You gave it to Darese.

IVY

No, I specifically recall giving it to you last time.

GIRLENE

Darese, where's Abendigo's hat?

DARESE

In your bag. You put it there for safekeeping when Ivy gave it to you to hold, dear.

GIRLENE reaches into her bag.

GIRLENE
I'm sure she gave it to you Darese. No…. Wait…. No. Yes, yes, praise the Lord. Here it is.

GIRLENE takes out a chauffeur's cap.

IVY
And I won't say I told you so.

GIRLENE
Good 'cause I hate it when you do that.

DARESE
And she really does. She really hates it.

ABENDIGO
Anyway… I'm in the Mercedes with my cap on, then?

GIRLENE passes it to IVY.

DARESE
Then we approach the nosey neighbour at 151.

GIRLENE
Number 151.

BERT
Number 151.

ABENDIGO
The target is 153. The nosey neighbour is at 151. You've prepared the introduction?

DARESE
"My name is Mrs. Jordan and this is Mrs. Mays, and we were wondering if you have any idea where you'll be going when you die?"

GIRLENE
We give her the *Watchtower*, and engage her for as long as we can with fire and brimstone.

DARESE
The Bible tells us in Revelations 19, verse 11, that the–

GIRLENE
Etcetera, etcetera, etcetera…

ABENDIGO
Good. Very nice. Then Ivy and Bert–

BERT
We'll take the portable garbage can and roll up the driveway of 151–

ABENDIGO
No, no, 153.

BERT
Yes, 153. And we'll roll the garbage can up the driveway of 153 and into the back yard.

IVY
Just don't forget your broom.

BERT
I didn't forget it last time. I just didn't have time to go back and retrieve it.

IVY
I'm not saying you forgot it. I'm saying you shouldn't forget it this time.

BERT
Why would I–

ABENDIGO
Anyway.... Then phase two begins. At which time we'll have an estimated 7 minutes and–

IVY
What if the postman's late again?

ABENDIGO
If the postman gets there between a quarter after and half past, we'll still have plenty of time.

BERT
And if the postman's early?

IVY
Bert, he's never been early.

BERT
Once he was early.

IVY
> Okay, once.

ABENDIGO
> Do we need to go over plan "B" in case of trouble?

DARESE
> In case of trouble we'll begin scrubbing, sweeping and cleaning anything in sight then start in with that old faithful:

IVY, BERT, DARESE & GIRLENE
> (*singing*) Abide with me.
> Fast falls the e'ven tide…

ABENDIGO
> Good. Very, very good.

BERT
> Judge, I'm using the code name Chaka for the duration of this operation.

> *ABENDIGO's eyes roll skyward.*

IVY
> Oh no, not again.

GIRLENE
> Who?

BERT
> Chaka, the Zulu warrior.

ABENDIGO
> Okay Bert – I mean Chaka…. And as phase two begins, you will have 7 minutes, and–

> *ABENDIGO's legs appear to give out on him.*

IVY, BERT, DARESE & GIRLENE
> Abendigo. Judge, you all right? Oh no! Ben, what's wrong.

> *ABENDIGO almost collapses to the ground, but the CHORUS of trees seem to catch him and hold him upright, even though they are some distance away.*

ABENDIGO
> I'm all right. I'm all right. I'm fine. Don't break formation, please. I'm okay.

IVY

Why don't you sit down awhile?

ABENDIGO

No, no, I'm fine. Now.... Now, where were we? Ah, yes. As phase two begins, you will have an estimated 7 minutes, and thirty five seconds.

IVY

(to ABENDIGO) And if you feel an attack coming on, your pills–

ABENDIGO

–are in the inside pocket of my jacket.

IVY

–are in the inside pocket of your jacket.

ABENDIGO

(to IVY) I know where my pills are, Ivy. I do believe we've been through this already. Okay. So we'll meet in 8 minutes at the Petro Can. Everyone ready?

IVY

Set.

ABENDIGO

Go!

BERT

And we're off!

> *DARESE, BERT and GIRLENE head off in the direction of the Lotsa Soap Van. ABENDIGO hesitates a moment. IVY hands him the chauffeur's cap.*

IVY

You don't look so good, Ben. You sure you're all right?

ABENDIGO

Ivy.

IVY

Just making sure.

> *IVY removes her coat, revealing a housekeeper's uniform.*

I always feel like Superman. Take off my coat and suddenly no-one can see me.

ABENDIGO
You mean the Invisible Man.

IVY
No, Superman.

ABENDIGO
Superman flies through the air like a speeding bullet. The Invisible Man takes off his coat, his dark glasses and his bandages.

IVY
Oh, yes, yes, that's right.

ABENDIGO places the chauffeur's cap on his head, transforming in front of our very eyes into a livery driver.

ABENDIGO
Just a little unconscious classification on their part and voila!

IVY
And we could walk right into the premier's office–

ABENDIGO
And empty his garbage pail in the middle of a cabinet meeting–

IVY
And they just kept right on talking. I was so terrified they'd look up and see we weren't the regulars.

ABENDIGO
They'd swear we weren't even there. Ready?

IVY
Here, let me just fix your lapel. What did Lorraine say about a second opinion?

ABENDIGO
Well I, I'm, I–

IVY
You haven't told her?

ABENDIGO
I'm just waiting for the right time.

IVY
You said she was doing well.

ABENDIGO

Sometimes I think she's getting better. Sometimes she seems worse. She still doesn't like to come up here. She hasn't set foot in a hospital in three years.

IVY

Can you blame her? The sky fell on top of her, Ben.

ABENDIGO

Giving up her medical practice was supposed to be a temporary thing, but she's practically buried herself in that Masters program. The thesis took up all of her time. Now she's got this PhD thing in her head.

IVY

You still need to tell her.

ABENDIGO

She still hasn't seen Janie's grave.

IVY

Ben...

ABENDIGO

I don't want her to hurt anymore.

IVY

I know. I know. Kids.... Sometimes I'm glad I didn't have any.

ABENDIGO

With all those children you taught over the years.

IVY

Sent them home at half past three – it's not the same.

ABENDIGO

You didn't want any.

> *IVY turns to ABENDIGO.*

IVY

Is that what you think?

ABENDIGO

Well, that's what you said.

IVY

I never said I didn't want any.

ABENDIGO
But I asked you.

IVY
Let sleeping dogs lie, Ben.

ABENDIGO
But I asked.

IVY
For Lorraine, not for me.

ABENDIGO
My child needed a mother.

IVY
You weren't asking for a wife.

ABENDIGO
I always – You know – I asked you.

IVY
Yes. Yes, you did. A very long time ago.

IVY looks at her watch.

Are you ready?

Pause.

ABENDIGO
Yes. Yes, I'm ready.

ABENDIGO follows IVY to the car.

Scene Two

A capella voices moan the lights up at the front of the stage. The CHORUS moves and dances into existence the water that makes up the living creek.

RAINEY enters from the porch.

RAINEY
Pa! Pa!

She looks at her watch, then makes her way down to the creek.

"What do you eat?"

She looks out at the audience.

What do you eat. Asking me like she's my God damn mother or
something – I hate it when they do that. See, she doesn't know that
I know she's some second rate, just finished her residency, walk-in
clinic, witch-cum-doctor.

"Why, whadda you eat?" That's what I was gonna tell her right to her
big ass face. But then she wouldn't write me a prescription and that's
why I'd stopped there in the first place seeing as how I couldn't drive
anymore – retching cinders and cotton balls all onto my lap and all over
the God damn steering wheel. And I'm supposed to meet Michael –
and I can do Toronto to Negro Creek in just over an hour if no one's
looking – but there I am at Avenue Road and Bloor, getting the third
degree just to get some meds, and trying to figure out how I'm going to
stay over at Pa's when I can't use his toilet. He used to wash toilets,
was a sleeping car porter on Canadian Pacific, for years before anyone
would hire him as a lawyer. Says he could wash a toilet bowl so clean
you could lick the rim, the thought of which really makes me feel
like retching all over again, 'cause I can't hardly look at a toilet bowl
anymore, even if it's on TV – 'cause of Janie. I can't use any other toilet
but my own.

*She begins to form small mounds of dirt. She takes a Ziploc bag out of her
pocket and carefully places the earth in the bag. She is methodical.*

"I haven't been eating too well. Chronic lesser curve peptic gastritis,"
falls quickly out of my mouth. Medicalese for stomach ulcers. 'Cause
I've been to med school too and I know, I want her to know that. And
I know she hears it 'cause while she's looking down her nose at me, her
big ass eyes nearly fall out of her big ass head.

*RAINEY takes a morsel of earth and places it delicately on her tongue,
savouring it.*

I should have told her to prescribe Omeprazole or a prostaglandin.
Better yet, 2g of Sucralfate a half hour before I eat. Instead I say, "I
don't eat well."

I don't, eat well, I know that. What am I gonna tell her, for Christ's
sake? I'm an obstetrician? Haven't practiced in three years? That it
started when Janie was still inside me. Me, secretly binging on freezer
frost from the old fridge we'd bought in Fergus before Martha, my
mother who raised me, before Martha passed – I hate that word –
"passed." Gone on. Like there's something to go on to.

I could tell her the truth, tell her I've been trying to get out here all my life and now, now I just hunger for the soft sugary earth by Negro creek. My Pa's family's lived and died on this bush land – been ours since the war of 1812. Maybe that's why it tastes so sweet. My great grandmother gave her life to this water trying to save a soldier's uniform. Lorraine Johnson. I was named for her.

Her grandfather Juma, Juma Moore was granted this Ojibway territory for fighting against the Americans in the Coloured Militia. Once a year his uniform would get a ritual cleaning.

> *A soldier's jacket appears and floats above the bodies that make up the water.*

They'd go in the water with it, hold it under, and let the creek purify it. Lorraine had done it for years, but this time…. Well, she was in the water when it happened. The uniform slipped down, out of her hands and she went after it.

> *The jacket begins to float along the creek and a woman rises out of the water in pursuit of it. Both the jacket and the woman are enveloped by the flood of bodies.*

They found her downstream when the creek thawed that spring, her hands still gripping that jacket. The authorities returned her body but kept the uniform – said it was the property of Her Majesty's army. They can be like that sometimes up here in God's country. Christ, they can be like that in the city.

I should have told her, I should have just told her, told her now since Janie, I yearn for chalk to dry the flood inside me and that's why I pop aspirins, only 35 on good days, not just any, it's got to be Bayer, original, not extra strength or that Life Brand shit, just Bayer acetylsalicylic acid, and, that's why I've got me a hole in my belly – it's white willow bark. Aspirin, it's willow bark. So I've got a tree growing inside me. And I can't take the iron pills I need. Any doctor worth her salt knows that the intentional and compulsive consumption of non-food substances is eradicated with a forceful regimen of iron. But I can't hold something that heavy inside me – falls through the holes in my belly when I swallow and when it stays down, it bungs me up so bad I have to sit on a toilet for days, and I don't like to sit down on toilets, since Janie. Could you just see her face if I told her I was now eating ashes from cigarettes, not that I smoke them or anything, it's just, well, I don't know why, and it's got to be Export A, and I don't know why Export A. I'm just praying…. Funny, I'm praying a lot lately. I don't know why I do that either. I don't even know that I'm praying. Praying for one more aspirin before my guts fold into my spine, or I'm praying to reach the toilet, in my house, before I weep all over the floor.

I'm not praying to God though. God, the Father. No father of mine would allow Janie…

RAINEY searches out a new section of earth and begins to discard the top layer of dirt with her hands.

I can still feel her…. Wrapped around me. She would hug me round my waist so tight sometimes like she was trying to get back inside me, like I was her fingers and toes and she'd missed having them around her all day, like I was her everything. She was…

Janie on the toilet – that's all I remember sometimes – that's my only image of her. Janie on the toilet holding my hands. Five and frail with a fever and I can fix her, there's a doctor in the house, Pa's house. And it's late. We'd been running through the woods all afternoon, she loved the woods so much, laughing and yelling for me, and she's got a fever and her neck hurts, but we've been running. And I send Pa with my car to get some Tylenol, Children's Tylenol, and she's on the toilet, so clean she could lick the rim and I'm holding her, holding her on the toilet and, and she, she, she, she…. She falls, falls… on me. And I can't find the keys to Pa's car and I'm running…. Running with her through the middle of Holland Township, wishing I had wings, feeling her slip away from me, going somewhere without me – she always, always, always wanted me to come along with her before.

She's gone. They tell you she's gone. She's in my arms, I'm looking at her and and where's she gone. She's in my arms. I see her little copper feet, I see her tiny brazened fingers, her gilded neck, her coral lips… I know I'm looking at her. And I know… I know she's not there. And I'm, I'm, I'm… I'm wondering where she went. And you feel… I feel…

RAINEY looks up at the sky, trying to dam a stream of tears flooding up inside her.

Ten billion trillion stars in the universe. Ten billion trillion stars. That's not even counting the planets revolving around them. But it's mostly dark matter. It's 99% empty. One huge vast realm of nothingness.

MICHAEL enters casually dressed. He stops for a moment and stands at a distance. RAINEY appears to see something out of the corner of her eye.

Janie… Janie…

A choral moaning surges then fades. MICHAEL makes his way toward RAINEY. RAINEY does not see him. She closes the Ziploc bag full of earth and places the excess earth on her tongue.

MICHAEL
I didn't think you were coming.

RAINEY
Sorry I'm late.

MICHAEL
What is that?

RAINEY
It's a long story. I, I had to–

MICHAEL
No, no. You have a little something – on the corner of your mouth.

RAINEY
Excuse me?

MICHAEL
Dirt on your mouth.

RAINEY
Oh. Oh.

> *RAINEY wipes her face and collects the various Ziploc bags piled around her.*

MICHAEL
How are you doing?

RAINEY
I'm good.

MICHAEL
Summa Cum Laude?

RAINEY
The Masters wasn't that hard. Just a lot of work…. Drowning in a sea of textbooks and paper.

MICHAEL
Exactly what you were looking for. When's the PhD start?

RAINEY
They haven't even accepted me yet. I do the oral petition a week Saturday.

MICHAEL
That's what, another 4, 5 years?

RAINEY
If I'm lucky. How's the flock?

MICHAEL
The congregation's thriving.

RAINEY
Good. Good.

MICHAEL
I told you about the "Save Negro Creek" committee.

RAINEY
You're going to save the three remaining souls in town who don't attend?

MICHAEL
We've taken the township council to court.

RAINEY
Oh yes.

MICHAEL
They've changed the name of Negro Creek Road. This bunch of white folks on the town council are saying they're not comfortable using the word Negro. The Human Rights Commission took the case.

RAINEY
Yes, Pa told me.

MICHAEL
We're expecting a ruling any day now.

RAINEY
You're turning them into a bunch of activists, Michael. Whatever happened to "the meek shall inherit the earth?"

MICHAEL
God helps those who help themselves.

RAINEY
Yes. Yes, of course.

RAINEY makes her way towards the porch. MICHAEL follows.

MICHAEL
What's your area of study this time.

RAINEY
It's the same department.

MICHAEL
Theological science?

RAINEY
Science and Religion. It's a new faculty.

MICHAEL
So? What's the title? You do have a preliminary thesis title?

RAINEY
I've changed the title so many times.

MICHAEL
It's early days yet. I had the hardest time settling on a thesis title. 300 pages, two departmental extensions – no sleep. It was hell.

RAINEY
"Deliverance."

MICHAEL
"Deliverance: The church as a fundamental vehicle for covert resistance from slavery to the civil rights movement." I'm surprised you remember.

RAINEY
Most men would have brought me flowers or chocolates or something. You presented me with your damned thesis.

As they approach the farmhouse, RAINEY climbs the stairs.

MICHAEL
I'm a senior at seminary college. You're a sophomore. I wanted to impress you.

RAINEY
I was impressed. I loved the chapter on Santeria, Vodun, Obeah, and the Black Baptist Church.

MICHAEL
Systems of African cultural self-assertion and preservation.

RAINEY
There's something about those African religions. Something about an understanding of the extraordinary forces of nature. She giveth and she taketh away.

MICHAEL
"The Lord giveth and the Lord taketh away."

RAINEY
But with him it's personal.

MICHAEL
God is personal.

RAINEY
And that's why I transferred to medical school.

MICHAEL
You didn't want to be a preacher.

RAINEY
A doctor could, could really do something.... Could really save souls.

MICHAEL
Could play God?

RAINEY
Tea, coffee?

MICHAEL
Just water.

RAINEY
Sure. Cold, no ice.

MICHAEL
Yes.

RAINEY
Sure.

> *RAINEY places her Ziploc bag on one of the porch tables, beside a stack of enamel paints and art brushes. She enters the house. MICHAEL rises the steps to the porch and goes over to the bag of earth.*

MICHAEL
Does your father really paint? I've only ever seen brushes and tubes of pigment. I've never seen any of his masterpieces.

He holds several of the bags up to the light.

RAINEY

(*off-stage*) I think he hides them somewhere.

> *He tries to resist the urge to open the bag. As he is about to unzip it he hears RAINEY approaching. He quickly closes the bag and replaces it on the chair, just as RAINEY enters with the water. She hands him the glass.*

MICHAEL

Yes. Thank you.

RAINEY

You're welcome.

> *Pause.*

So...

MICHAEL

It's nice to see you.

RAINEY

Yes.... Well.... I guess we should.... You know.... As I told you on the phone.... I spoke with Dad and.... Well, once we've agreed on the actual division of the marital property, the rest should be simple. All we have to do is sign.

MICHAEL

Okay.

RAINEY

We both have equity in the home and you can either sell it or buy me out.

MICHAEL

You're sure you want to do this?

RAINEY

Please don't ask me that.

MICHAEL

If you're not sure, I–

RAINEY

Michael, don't...

MICHAEL
What should I do with all of Janie's things?

RAINEY
Yes… I know.

MICHAEL
I keep thinking I'll get someone to box everything and cart it away. But I, I didn't know what you'd want.

RAINEY
I don't feel… I can't think of anything.

MICHAEL
You'll want the dolls, those Black dolls.

RAINEY
No.

MICHAEL
You loved those dolls more than she did.

RAINEY
Yes.

MICHAEL
I just can't seem to throw anything away.

RAINEY
She'd be eight now.

MICHAEL
And tall…

RAINEY
And…

MICHAEL
Yeah.

RAINEY
Pa said there were wildflowers growing all around her. I filled the pockets of her long white pinafore with wildflower seeds. Now there are wildflowers all around her.

MICHAEL
They're beautiful.

RAINEY
Yes, that's what he said.

MICHAEL
You should see them.

RAINEY
Yeah. Yes.

Pause.

MICHAEL
Do you have a lawyer?

RAINEY
That's the next step.

MICHAEL
I can get my lawyer to draw up the papers if you'd like?

RAINEY
That'd be, that'd be great.

MICHAEL
All right. I'll try to get her to turn it around quickly.

RAINEY
Thank you.

Pause.

You seeing someone?

MICHAEL
Not exactly.

RAINEY
Oh.

MICHAEL
I wasn't sure you, that we…

RAINEY
No, yes, of course.

MICHAEL
That's all.

RAINEY
No. No.

MICHAEL
Er…. Good.

RAINEY
All right.

Pause.

MICHAEL
So is it a secret?

RAINEY
No, I'm not seeing anyone, I just–

MICHAEL
No, your thesis title?

RAINEY
Oh. Yes, well it's, er, "The Death of God and Angels." It's a quantum theoretical challenge to contemporary monotheism.

MICHAEL
A challenge to God?

RAINEY
A challenge to the supposition of a Judeo-Christian God.

MICHAEL
Oh!

RAINEY
Well, that's what it's about.

MICHAEL
Oh. I see.

RAINEY
Please don't patronize me.

MICHAEL
I didn't say anything.

RAINEY
You said, "Oh."

MICHAEL
"Oh?"

RAINEY
I know your "Ohs."

MICHAEL
All right. All right.

RAINEY
All right what?

MICHAEL
Congratulations on becoming an atheist.

RAINEY
I never said I was an atheist.

MICHAEL
No. No, you didn't.

RAINEY
Well, now that that's clear.

MICHAEL
It's just so easy, Rainey.

RAINEY
Sorry?

MICHAEL
Tragedy strikes and suddenly all your faith dissolves.

RAINEY
And your faith grows stronger.

MICHAEL
We only grow through our suffering. He has a plan.

RAINEY
And Janie was all a part of God's plan?

MICHAEL
I'm in sales, not management.

RAINEY
Spoken like a true broker for God.

MICHAEL
Let's not do this.

MICHAEL gets up to leave.

RAINEY
Okay, if he has a plan, what's the point of praying?

MICHAEL
Rainey...

RAINEY
I'm just trying to understand.

MICHAEL
Prayer is a means of communicating with God. If you pray and have sufficient faith, the Bible tells us that anything is possible.

RAINEY
So we can influence God's plan?

MICHAEL
Of course. Black people would be nowhere without the church. Reverend Martin Luther King used the church in the tradition of African resistance in the Americas going all the way back to slavery.

RAINEY
But if God created the possibility for resistance in the slave, he is also responsible for the oppressive behaviour of the slave masters.

MICHAEL
If you don't believe in God, you can hardly be expected to believe in the devil.

RAINEY
And all I have to do is believe?

MICHAEL
Ask and you shall receive. Seek and it shall be given unto you.

RAINEY gets down on her knees, closes her eyes and clasps her hands together.

RAINEY
Dear Lord in heaven.

MICHAEL
What are you doing?

RAINEY
(*sincerely*) Lord, my daughter Janie lies resting in the church cemetery just beyond the field. Bring her back to me, Lord. Raise her as you did your only son, Jesus. Let me hold her in my arms again. And I will, I will with all my heart and soul believe. Amen.

MICHAEL
Stop it, Rainey.

RAINEY opens one eye.

RAINEY
Anything happening?

MICHAEL
Stop it. Just, just stop it.

RAINEY
You think I didn't pray hard enough?

MICHAEL
He knows it wasn't your fault.

RAINEY
Who said anything about fault.

MICHAEL
Have I ever blamed you?

RAINEY
You could hardly touch me.

MICHAEL
You didn't want me to touch you.

RAINEY
I could see it in you.

MICHAEL
I'm sorry. I'm not doing this.

MICHAEL hands RAINEY the glass, descends the steps and turns towards the field.

Tell your father I'll be by to check on him.

RAINEY
Michael…

MICHAEL heads across the field.

MICHAEL
(shouting back) He's been to see some doctor.

RAINEY
(shouting) What doctor?

MICHAEL
(shouting) What?

RAINEY
What doctor?

MICHAEL
Speak to your father.

RAINEY watches him leave. Her gaze hangs on him for just a moment longer than it should.

RAINEY
(to the audience) He's always had an extraordinary back. Grade six – he was in the eighth grade – the way it bore his shoulders, his head, everything. So upright. So firm. So sure. And his faith. Like the vertebrae in his spine. It holds him up.

RAINEY takes a small bottle of aspirins from her pocket. She takes an aspirin tablet and bites into half of it, savouring the taste. She nibbles at the pill until there is only aspirin powder left on her fingers. She licks off the powder.

I used to be just like him. Believe, like him. Think about it. God has allowed the most vicious atrocities…. When that man, Byrd, James Byrd, was dragged by a chain from the back of a pick-up truck, conscious to the last, feeling his limbs crumble, separate from his body, one by one – WHAT DO YOU SUSPECT GOD WAS THINKING? "Well, this is all part of my plan. I sure hope they learn something from this down there." What do you suspect the man learned as his arms fell away behind him. What were You thinking?

RAINEY glances at the creek. Her gaze floats upward towards the sky for a moment, as if she sees something. She then takes MICHAEL's glass and enters the house. The CHORUS emits a thick and tangible drone.

Scene Three

The choral tones lighten. We hear cars pull up onto gravel. Engines stop. Doors open, doors close. ABENDIGO, IVY, BERT, GIRLENE and DARESE enter dragging an enormous and heavy garbage pail on wheels. They still have their dark glasses on. They form a line across the stage once more.

ABENDIGO
Ivy.

IVY
(peeking above her lenses) Uh huh!

ABENDIGO
Darese.

DARESE
(peeking over her sunglasses too) Yeah!

ABENDIGO
Bert.

> *Silence.*

Bert!

> *Silence. They all look at BERT.*

Chaka.

BERT
(flipping up his clip-on shades) Yes, Judge.

ABENDIGO
Girlene.

GIRLENE
(taking off her dark glasses) Well, I didn't think I was gonna make it but I–

ABENDIGO
Girlene!

GIRLENE
Oh. Oh. Yes sir! Girlene Mays, present and accounted for.

ABENDIGO

(*checking his watch*) All present. Liberation successful. Mission complete.

Like a choreographed movement all shades are simultaneously removed, all except GIRLENE who unceremoniously removed them before she should have.

That was our slowest incursion, folks. We'll have no more of that. There'll be plenty of time for tardiness once we're in our graves, and if we're going to hit the museum, we'll need to be a lot more exact.

BERT

I told you the postman was going to be late.

IVY

We'd have been on time if you'd have come when I called you.

BERT

You weren't calling me by my code name.

IVY

Stick to one code name for all the operations. Chaka, Martin Luther King; Josiah; Pushkin; Alexander Dumas. Stick to one name!

BERT

Olivier Le Jeune.

IVY

What!

BERT

Olivier Le Jeune. He was the first known Black resident of Canada: 1628.

IVY

Abendigo?

ABENDIGO

Bert. Stick to one name.

BERT

Fine.

IVY

Fine.

IVY, DARESE and GIRLENE open the pail and with the tenderness of midwives, they take out the little Black garden gnome wrapped in swaddling.

ABENDIGO
How's our little man dealing with his new-found freedom?

IVY
Here he is. Look at him.

GIRLENE
He's beautiful.

DARESE
Praise the Lord.

BERT
A little worse for wear.

DARESE
There's a strange hole that goes straight through the centre of him.

ABENDIGO
Wound from a pellet gun.

BERT
An innocent bystander in a game of cowboys and Indians, no doubt.

IVY
He'll need a little help from our paint brush, Ben.

ABENDIGO
That's right my little man, a few scoops of stucco, a drop or two of enamel and you'll never have to smile like that again.

RAINEY
(*off-stage*) Pa? Pa?

ABENDIGO
Lorraine?

RAINEY
(*off-stage*) I'm coming.

ABENDIGO
Lorraine! Oh shit. Quickly, quickly, Lorraine's here.

BERT
That's whose car that was.

ABENDIGO
You saw her car and didn't say anything.

BERT
It's up by the shed. I couldn't remember if it was there before we left for Collingwood, or not.

ABENDIGO
(indicating the garden gnome) Put him back in the garbage pail.

GIRLENE
(to the garden gnome) Don't worry, little fella, not for long.

IVY
(to the group) We won't make it.

> RAINEY enters, approaches ABENDIGO and pecks him on the cheek.

ABENDIGO
Lorraine! I didn't know you were coming. Lorraine.

RAINEY
I had to see Michael.

DARESE
You saw Michael?

RAINEY
Hey Darese, Aunt Ivy, Auntie Girlie. Bert.

> Rainey notices the Black lawn jockey.

What is this, number three?

ABENDIGO
Yes, about three.

RAINEY
It's becoming a real obsession, with you guys.

IVY
It's a calling.

RAINEY
Where'd you get it?

BERT
The flea market.

GIRLENE & DARESE
The antique shop.

IVY
There's an antique flea market in Collingwood we like to go to.

RAINEY
(*to ABENDIGO*) The one you go to after church on Sundays.

ABENDIGO
No, no.

IVY
YES.

ABENDIGO
It's very close to that one.

GIRLENE
It's just so nice to take little outings during the week and after church and such, you know.

DARESE
And we're always at church. Michael's such a good preacher, Rainey. You should have heard the sermon he gave last week, eh Girlie?

GIRLENE
On Sunday? But we – Oh yes. Yes. Marvellous, marvellous sermon.

RAINEY
What're you going to do with all of them?

GIRLENE
Well, we... er...

IVY
We're trying to.... Um...

DARESE
(*waving*) Oh-oh, Pastor Michael's crossing the field.

ABENDIGO
Michael's coming over, Rainey?

IVY
(*eyeing DARESE disapprovingly*) And we haven't seen Michael since MORNING SERVICE LAST SUNDAY, have we?

IVY sets the Black garden jockey down on a small table.

BERT
He's trying to save Negro Creek. He's gone all liberational on us.

IVY
Liberation theology.

BERT
That's what I said.

DARESE
He's looking so good these days, isn't he Rainey?

GIRLENE
Any chance the two of you, you know?

IVY
Girlene!

GIRLENE
Ain't no harm in asking, is there Rainey?

RAINEY
No. We're getting divorced.

ABENDIGO
You're going through with it.

RAINEY
Yeah.

GIRLENE
My Earl and me, we divorced three times.

DARESE
And Lord, it would have been four, 'cept he died.

GIRLENE
It would have worked out this time!

DARESE
That's what you said the previous three.

GIRLENE
It's the only reason I'm not officially a widow. See, he was in the house and everything. We'd even set a date. Then he died. Me a single woman.

DARESE
Ahhhh.

RAINEY
What's this about a doctor?

ABENDIGO
Who said anything about a doctor?

RAINEY
Michael told me to ask you about a doctor. What's up, Pa?

ABENDIGO
Yes, well, I've, I, I'll tell you later, when…. You know…. Later, before you go. Anyone for a few drops of homemade sherry?

BERT
We like a little sherry after our, our, our excursions, don't we Judge?

ABENDIGO is about to get up.

RAINEY
(to ABENDIGO) It's all right. You sit. I'll get it.

RAINEY enters the house.

ABENDIGO
(shouting after her) It's in the pantry.

RAINEY
(off-stage) I remember.

BERT
Boy, that was close.

GIRLENE
(fanning herself) My blood pressure just hit an all-time high.

BERT
You all need to keep your stories straight.

IVY
Well if that ain't the pot telling the kettle.

DARESE
Lord knows I hate to lie like that.

IVY
We'll have to reschedule the strategy session for the museum heist.

ABENDIGO
Let me find out how long she's staying.

IVY
Or we could have it at my place.

RAINEY
(*off-stage*) Pa, do you have any more sherry?

ABENDIGO
Lorraine, it's in the pantry.

RAINEY
(*off-stage*) There's none left.

ABENDIGO
On the top shelf.

RAINEY
(*off-stage*) I'll look in the cellar.

    Pause.

ABENDIGO, IVY, BERT, DARESE & GIRLENE
No!!!

    *ABENDIGO rushes for the back door, when MICHAEL steps onto the
    porch.*

MICHAEL
Hey everyone. Dad.

ABENDIGO
Michael!

GIRLENE
So you're getting divorced, huh?

IVY
Girlene! Something to drink, Michael? (*trying to get ABENDIGO to stop
RAINEY from reaching the cellar*) Abendigo, why don't you GO GET
MICHAEL SOMETHING TO DRINK FROM THE CELLAR.

ABENDIGO
Yes, good idea. I'll just go and get Michael something to drink from the
cellar.

    *As ABENDIGO opens the door a loud scream comes from inside the
    house. ABENDIGO slams the door shut again. MICHAEL rushes to the
    door. The others stay motionless. ABENDIGO prevents MICHAEL from
    entering.*

(holding the door shut) She'll be all right.

RAINEY
(off-stage) Oh my God!!

MICHAEL
Shouldn't someone go and find out what's wrong?

ABENDIGO
Oh no. She'll be fine.

> *RAINEY tries to exit the house but ABENDIGO is still holding the door shut.*

RAINEY
(off-stage) Pa? Pa? What's going on.

> *ABENDIGO steps away from the door and RAINEY bolts through it.*

MICHAEL
Are you okay?

RAINEY
What's going on!!

ABENDIGO
Look Lorraine, it's Michael. Michael, Lorraine.

MICHAEL
(to ABENDIGO, trying to redirect the conversation) Yes, well… I just came by to check on you, Dad, since I hadn't seen you at Sunday services in a few weeks.

RAINEY
But you just said you went to church last–

IVY
No, no. We were saying–

GIRLENE
We just said that the sermon was marvellous.

DARESE
Yes Lord, that's what my neighbour told me.

BERT
I didn't say anything about Sunday services at all. They said it.

ABENDIGO

Now Lorraine, this isn't exactly the way it looks.

RAINEY

Just stop, okay, just stop it. What are all those God damn things doing in the cellar? What the hell is going on around here?

Scene Four

A sharp ray of light breaks the darkness as the CHORUS makes an eerie tone, turning the lights onto a virtual gallery of 357 little Black garden gnomes; Aunt Jemimas, little Black Sambos, Black watermelon eaters and other such artifacts. They give off the eerie appearance of being living souls trapped in clay or wooden sarcophaguses.

RAINEY, ABENDIGO, IVY, DARESE and BERT are gathered in the centre of the room. GIRLENE and MICHAEL stand by the door. The 357 Black objects stare at them like an attentive audience.

ABENDIGO

The golf course.

RAINEY

What?!

ABENDIGO

The Owen Sound Golf and Country Club.

GIRLENE

We dressed up as kitchen staff and liberated him from the courtyard.

RAINEY

And this one here?

DARESE

That was one of the easiest. Heavenly Father, I wish they were all like that.

IVY

A night-time heist. We all got decked out in cleaner's blues and went straight to the CEO's executive patio.

RAINEY

And no-one said anything to you?

BERT

Well, as we were leaving, they gave us free pancake mix.

RAINEY
Is it just me, or is anyone else even slightly afraid you're going to wind up in the penitentiary?

MICHAEL
Covert resistance.

RAINEY
Don't start, please.

MICHAEL
What?

RAINEY
They're going to end up in jail.

ABENDIGO
I for one am proud of our little collection. In all, we have liberated 357 enslaved lawn ornaments, cookie jars, piggy banks, plaques, figurines, visual images and ephemera.

RAINEY
Pa, you're a provincial court judge, for God's sake.

ABENDIGO
A retired Provincial court judge.

RAINEY
You're 71 years old!

ABENDIGO
I know how old I am, Rainey.

RAINEY
So what were you thinking?

DARESE
We want to change the world.

RAINEY
You, you what?

BERT
We want to change the world, and we've started with our neighbourhood.

RAINEY
They're all stolen from around here?

ABENDIGO
Liberated...

MICHAEL
What are you going to do with them?

RAINEY
Exactly! What are you going to do with them?

IVY
Well, we're currently working on a plan.

RAINEY
Yes?

ABENDIGO
We just don't know what it is as yet.

MICHAEL
This is extraordinary.

RAINEY
Michael! You may not recall it yourself, but I believe there is a commandment about stealing.

ABENDIGO, IVY, BERT, DARESE & GIRLENE
Liberating!

RAINEY
But you are, er, "liberating" property that is not your own. You understand that don't you?

MICHAEL
They believe in something, Rainey.

RAINEY
(to MICHAEL) And you're there preaching all this covert resistance, liberation theology. Did you know about this?

MICHAEL
No. No, I didn't.

ABENDIGO
Lorraine, it's got nothing to do with him.

RAINEY
So what's going to happen when you get caught? And you will get caught. What you're doing is, is, commendable, honourable even. But it's illegal, Pa. That's all.

ABENDIGO
When Harriet Tubman forged the underground railroad, was that legal? When Miss Rosa Parks refused to give her seat to a white patron, was that legal?

RAINEY
So you're the Black Panthers of western Ontario now?

ABENDIGO
The Lotsa Soap Cleaning Company.

RAINEY
Excuse me?

IVY
The Lotsa Soap Cleaning Company. It's an acronym.

RAINEY
This I can't wait to hear.

ABENDIGO
For the...

ABENDIGO, IVY, BERT, DARESE & GIRLENE
Liberation Of Thoroughly Seditious Artifacts Symbolizing (the) Oppression (of) African People.

ABENDIGO
See? Lotsa Soap.

RAINEY
Pa, how is this going to change the world? This is not Detroit. We're not in the sixties anymore. The struggle is over. What you fought for back then worked, I'm a doctor, was a doctor. I have choices. Things have changed. This is Canada. This is Canaan Land.

ABENDIGO
One flower does not a garden make.

IVY, BERT, DARESE & GIRLENE
Amen! That's right! Yeah! Preach!

ABENDIGO
(like a lawyer making a closing argument) I have worked in the legal system all my life, you know that. When I was a lawyer I took special care to defend the rights of any Black person who came to me. And you didn't have to be poor. Right there in Ontario, in Dresden, Black tourists making pilgrimages to Josiah Henson's grave, you know Uncle Tom, Black tourists would not be served in the restaurants there.

RAINEY
I understand, Pa. And I've told you about the times other doctors or patients assumed I was the nurse. Some patients didn't even want me to treat them. But that's changing too.

ABENDIGO
There's no use cutting down the weed and leaving the root.

RAINEY
But us just being there changes that.

ABENDIGO
We're tokens.

RAINEY
Now you're being ridiculous.

ABENDIGO
There was a clerk, John Sheppard. When I was still practising, we had a deal that if a Black defendant came into the custody of the court, he would call me in to do *pro bono* work, instead of dumping him into the lap of the already overburdened legal aid system. I became a Judge. Twenty years, Rainey, twenty years. John Sheppard and I had become good friends. We ate together, drank together, and my last day on the bench, on my last day, he says to me, we'll miss you, he says, the legal system will really miss you. You're not like other Blacks. You're a very special Black. This is what he tells me. And I realized…. My friend John Sheppard helped me to realize that after all those years of trying, of setting an example, of trying to make them understand that we are as good and as bad as everyone else, I realized that all of it was for nothing. I was an anomaly to him. A freak. A talking monkey. A Black man, different from the rest. I am no different from the rest. Just my circumstances.

RAINEY
I understand that, but–

ABENDIGO
NO, NO. YOU DON'T UNDERSTAND. TO TOLERATE AND TO ACCEPT ARE TWO COMPLETELY DIFFERENT THINGS. They want to take away this place. Just like they did Juma Moore's soldier's jacket. And I won't let them. Our blood is in this soil. Two years ago there was a rally here. Fifty of us, marching down Negro Creek Road, protesting the town council's bid to change the name to Moggie Road. They wanted to name it after some white settler who hadn't lived in this community but a few years. Something about the word "Negro" being politically incorrect. When in truth most white folks call this Nigger Creek. But the council didn't ask us. We pleaded with them nicely. Then

we told them how our forebears were granted this land by Sir Peregrine Maitland, Lieutenant-Governor of Upper Canada, after fighting with Canada against the Americans. This is Ojibway territory. But the Holland Township council were firm – Moggie Road they'd decided, Moggie Road it would be – regardless.

ABENDIGO stumbles slightly.

RAINEY
Pa? Papa!

ABENDIGO
I'm just, I'm just…. It's been a long day. My legs are just a little tired, that's all.

RAINEY helps ABENDIGO locate a seat amongst the objects.

RAINEY
Pa, this is why you can't be doing this kind of stuff anymore.

RAINEY stays close to him.

ABENDIGO
That day we marched. Nearly all of Negro Creek. We marched from the water, right up to the highway. And it was there, at that march that we decided to take them to court. They can't just erase us from nearly 200 years of history. It's wrong. And for the first time in my life we were taking our own destiny in our own hands. Even if we don't win the case, we're not going to just sit back and take it anymore. You get so, so, so tired of asking, cajoling, convincing, you get so, so tired of begging for–

ABENDIGO collapses onto the floor. They all rush to his side.

RAINEY
Pa? Pa!? Someone give me a hand.

IVY & BERT
Oh my God! Ben? Judge? Judge!

MICHAEL
Oh no! Quickly!

DARESE & GIRLENE
Oh Lord! Is he hurt?

RAINEY checks ABENDIGO's pulse and after opening ABENDIGO's mouth to make sure nothing is blocking his airway, she begins CPR.

RAINEY
Call an ambulance!

MICHAEL
Is he breathing?

Everyone is in shock.

RAINEY
Call 9-1-1! Please!!

MICHAEL rushes out of the room and up the stairs. RAINEY continues CPR.

Oh God! Please, please, please God! Oh Jesus. Please. Oh God. Oh God. Oh God.

Scene Five

The CHORUS have transformed into the living set of a hospital. ABENDIGO is lying in the hospital bed, hooked up to all manner of tubes and devices. RAINEY and MICHAEL stand in the waiting room.

MICHAEL
You're cold.

RAINEY
I'm fine.

MICHAEL
You're trembling.

RAINEY
Hospitals. I, I, don't seem to be able–

DOCTOR RADCLIFFE enters.

DOCTOR RADCLIFFE
Dr. Johnson?

RAINEY and MICHAEL approach him.

(to MICHAEL) Dr. Johnson, I'm Dr. Radcliffe.

MICHAEL
Pastor Michael Baldwin, this is Dr. Lorraine Baldwin Johnson.

DOCTOR RADCLIFFE
I'm sorry, I thought Baldwin was the first name. I'm sorry. Mrs., Dr. Baldwin Johnson, Phillip Radcliffe.

RAINEY
What's the diagnosis?

DOCTOR RADCLIFFE
Acute congestive heart failure. The prognosis is not very good.

RAINEY
(involuntarily) Nooo!

DOCTOR RADCLIFFE
His condition had gone undetected for God knows how long. We decided against treatment–

RAINEY
When? When? Why?

DOCTOR RADCLIFFE
His age makes him ineligible for a transplant.

RAINEY
What about mechanical devices?

DOCTOR RADCLIFFE
The pericarditis was already well into its second stage. We didn't give him more than a few months at best. And he's out-lived even our most optimistic prognosis.

RAINEY
Can I see his medical file?

DOCTOR RADCLIFFE
I'm afraid it's not hospital policy–

RAINEY
Is Jeffers still the head of cardiology?

DOCTOR RADCLIFFE
Yes, but–

RAINEY
I used to practice here.

DOCTOR RADCLIFFE
Oh, well then, here, take a look.

DOCTOR RADCLIFFE hands RAINEY a large file, full to bursting with papers.

MICHAEL
So what now?

DOCTOR RADCLIFFE
Well, once he's stabilized, I'd suggest that you and your – Dr. Baldwin Johnson consider a full care nursing home. There are two wonderful facilities in the area. Meadowbrook and–

RAINEY
How long…. How much time has he got?

DOCTOR RADCLIFFE
Not long. A few days, maybe. A week. Two weeks at the most. It's hard to say. He's got a great constitution. And with these types of cases, he could be up and about one minute and…. Well, I don't have to tell you.

RAINEY
What about, what about, what about alternative treatments, Dr. Radcliffe?

DOCTOR RADCLIFFE
Of course that's not where my expertise lies. Besides, I believe it might be a bit late for that. I can prescribe medication for the pain, and the edema and try to make him as comfortable as possible.

MICHAEL
Have you told him any of this?

DOCTOR RADCLIFFE
Yes. He's been expecting this for quite some time, now. Well, if there's nothing else…?

RAINEY looks up from the medical file.

I can come back for the file later if you'd like?

RAINEY
No, no. No, it's okay.

RAINEY hands the file back to DOCTOR RADCLIFFE.

DOCTOR RADCLIFFE
I'll be back to check on him later.

MICHAEL
Thank you, doctor.

DOCTOR RADCLIFFE exits. RAINEY takes a deep breath, and with MICHAEL in tow, she approaches ABENDIGO's bed.

RAINEY
Papa.

ABENDIGO opens his eyes.

ABENDIGO
(speaking with difficulty) Bad news, huh, Rain?

RAINEY takes ABENDIGO's hand.

RAINEY
Yep. Not looking so good right now.

RAINEY squeezes his hand.

ABENDIGO
I didn't want to worry you.

RAINEY
I could have done something.

ABENDIGO
I just didn't want you to worry.

RAINEY
It's no worry, Pa.

ABENDIGO
I want to go home, Rain.

RAINEY
If anything happens, they can get to you faster if you're here or at a full care facility.

ABENDIGO
I want to go home. I'm ready. I've been preparing for this for a long time. I want to be in my own home, in my own bed. I want to be gazing out onto Negro Creek.

RAINEY
I don't…. I don't think…. Pa, you need a lot of care right now. And…. And I, I…. I–

MICHAEL
You'll have lots of help if you need it.

RAINEY
I, I…. Thank you, but I don't think this is a very good idea.

ABENDIGO
I have to go home. I'm not afraid. I'm not afraid of dying, Rain.

RAINEY
You're not going to. I won't let you, Pa.

ABENDIGO
Lorraine, take me home. I just have to go home now.

RAINEY looks at MICHAEL. She's on her own here.

RAINEY
Okay. Okay. Okay, Pa. Okay. Okay. Let's go home.

ABENDIGO squeezes RAINEY's hand. A familiar choral moan fills the air.

Scene Six

The CHORUS dances and forms the woods just beyond the farmhouse. RAINEY makes her way through these living trees and sits, her back against a trunk, a trowel and a roll of toilet paper beside her. She lights a cigarette. Then covers her face with her hands. Slowly she removes her hands from her face and places the cigarette ashes in the palm of her one hand as the cigarette burns.

RAINEY
I want to be a tree when I grow up. A willow, an aspirin tree set deep in the earth with great big tobacco-shaped leaves draping over the edge of the creek. Me…. I'm a tree in progress. Okay. Okay. Okay, tell me. Tell me what I need to do. Just…. Just…. Talk to me. Burn the bush. Do something! Say something! Please!!

It's okay. It's okay. It's okay. It's going to be fine. Everything's going to be all right. All right? All right. There must be cardiac trials going on in the city. You know that. Just get him into one of them. Call in the morning. I'll call in the morning. It's okay. See. It'll be okay. Just have faith that…. Faith – that's a good one. You've really got a good thing going, I tell you.

She addresses the audience.

You'd think I'd be used to this by now. I was two when mama…. Pa says she could sing the sweet into honey and the blue into a midnight sky. We were living in Toronto and Pa was in front of a judge in a criminal case when he got word. The judge adjourned the case and gave Pa ten days to bury his wife and see to his infant daughter. He buried Ma in Chatham, with her people, then drove up here to Negro Creek – me in tow. He set himself a task did my Pa. He had one week to find a mother for his daughter.

Folks around here say that Pa had loved Ivy since they were in high school. That he'd promised he'd come back for her after university, then law school, then once he'd got a job. Since no one would hire him, Bert got him a job working on the trains. And he met my mother, a singer in a blues club, on a run to Montreal and they got married and had me and the next time Ivy saw him he'd come home, looking for a mother for his child. But he didn't marry Ivy. He married her sister, Martha.

Martha raised me like a vain woman tends her best feature. She couldn't have children. When Martha got sick, and I prayed and I prayed and when she died – I thought I'd lost the earth below me. Pa thought he'd lost the sky.

I just get stuck in all those dead places. Why do people have to die? It's such a strange feature of existence. I mean, what is that? People just up and disappear into some invisible black hole, worm hole, never to be seen again. And you're sitting there on the event horizon, watching them fall in. Gone forever. And, and the worst of it…. You can't see them, hold them. But you feel…. You still feel…. You can still feel them.

> *She is silent for a few moments. Then she looks up at branches. She outs the cigarette on the ground, takes the ashes in her hand and mashes them lightly with her fingers. She takes the handful of ashes and brings it to her lips. She opens her mouth and licks the ashes from her palm, like it was candy.*

Scene Seven

ABENDIGO sits almost upright in his own bed. RAINEY enters with a fresh glass of water.

ABENDIGO
Rainey?

RAINEY
Yes.

ABENDIGO
I need to get up.

RAINEY
Not today, Pa. If you're feeling up to it, we can get you up tomorrow, okay?

ABENDIGO
Okay. Rainey?

RAINEY
Yes Pa, what is it?

ABENDIGO
Nothing. Nothing.

RAINEY
It's time for your medication.

ABENDIGO
No, no.

> *Pause.*

Rainey?

RAINEY
What's wrong?

ABENDIGO
Rainey, I really need to urinate right now. I can't hold it any longer.

RAINEY
Here, I've got the bedpan.

> *RAINEY approaches the bed and is about to lift the bed clothes.*

ABENDIGO
It's all right. I can do it.

RAINEY
Pa. All right.

> *RAINEY hands him the bedpan and he slips it under the covers. After a few moments of silence we hear the trickling of water into a bowl. RAINEY begins to hum a tune to drown out the sound.*

ABENDIGO
You still have a beautiful voice, just like your mother. She could sing the sweet into honey and the blue into a midnight sky.

RAINEY
Finished?

ABENDIGO hands RAINEY the bedpan.

ABENDIGO
I don't know, this will sure take some getting used to.

RAINEY
It's just for now. We'll get someone in. Until then I can do it. I can clean you. I can wash you. I seen private bits before, Pa.

ABENDIGO
Well, you've never seen my private bits before.

RAINEY
You used to wash me.

ABENDIGO
When you were five.

RAINEY
We'll get a nurse.

ABENDIGO
As long as I can get to the bathroom to do, you know. To do the do.

RAINEY
We're getting a nurse. I won't be able to be here all the time–

ABENDIGO
Where are you going?

RAINEY
I have to do some research. I'll tell you all about it when I get back. Besides, I have to make an oral petition to enter the PhD program, Pa, I told you. I have to prepare. I'll organize everything before I go.

ABENDIGO
You can prepare out here.

RAINEY
We'll see.

RAINEY exits with the bedpan. ABENDIGO reaches for the telephone and dials.

ABENDIGO

(into the phone) Yes, hello. I made an order several months ago. Yes. Yes. Last August. Johnson. Judge Abendigo Johnson. That's right. I would like it delivered to my home. Yes, my home. Yes. Tomorrow would be good.

RAINEY returns with the empty bedpan.

(still on the phone) No, no, I need it tomorrow. Well, if I'm anywhere at all, I'll be here. Yes. Tomorrow then. Thank you.

ABENDIGO replaces the receiver.

(to RAINEY) What time did Ivy and them say they'd be over?

RAINEY

They didn't say exactly. Who was that?

ABENDIGO winces in pain.

It's okay, it's okay. Let's take your medication.

RAINEY gives him some water and several pills to take.

Now, I can up the dose at any time.

ABENDIGO

Rainey, I want to be buried facing the creek.

RAINEY

Take your pills.

ABENDIGO

Janie took my spot. Seven generations of Johnsons are buried in that church ground. I want to be buried facing the creek.

RAINEY

I want to be cremated.

ABENDIGO

Well, you can do what you like, I'm just glad I won't be there to see you go up in flames.

RAINEY

I don't believe I'll be there either, Pa. Drink up.

ABENDIGO

I've got my dead suit picked out. The navy one at the back of the closet.

RAINEY
Oh Pa.

ABENDIGO
My dead shirt, my dead tie and my dead underwear are in the bottom drawer.

RAINEY
Okay, Okay.

ABENDIGO
My dead shoes are in a box on the floor of the closet. I don't care about the socks. Just make sure they match.

RAINEY
I don't think I want to do this right now.

ABENDIGO
I've had this worked out a while now.

RAINEY
Clearly, but I'm not, I'm not…

ABENDIGO
(firmly) Lorraine, whether you're ready or not, I will not be here for much longer. I've already made all the plans and you just need to know what they are.

RAINEY
Fine.

ABENDIGO
Fine.

RAINEY
Fine.

ABENDIGO
I will not be sent to a funeral home.

RAINEY
So, you want me to just pitch you into the creek? I think that's illegal and not being a member of the Lotsa Soap gang–

ABENDIGO
Just look in the top drawer.

RAINEY
Pa!

ABENDIGO
The top drawer!

> *RAINEY takes the glass of water from ABENDIGO and places it on the night table. She goes over to the dresser and opens the drawer.*

RAINEY
I don't see anything in here.

ABENDIGO
Underneath the socks. On the right.

> *RAINEY pulls out a large paperback book.*

RAINEY
This?

ABENDIGO
I've made lots of notes with numbers to call.

RAINEY
(reading) "Honouring Death Naturally. Detailed instructions for carrying out a home or family-directed funeral." You have got to be kidding?

ABENDIGO
Lorraine!

RAINEY
No. No way, Pa!

ABENDIGO
I've had this all worked out for a long time.

RAINEY
I don't care.

ABENDIGO
I swear I'll come back and haunt you, child.

RAINEY
Pa, I, I couldn't...

ABENDIGO
I know. I know. Just open it.

RAINEY opens the book to the index.

RAINEY
(reading) "Deathing Midwifery Manual." Oh my God.

ABENDIGO
Read it first, Rainey.

RAINEY
(reading) "Eyes and Mouth. Fluids. Turning a Person. Bathing the Body."
I was an obstetrician, not a mortician. I don't know anything about that
kind of thing.

ABENDIGO
Please, Rainey, just read it.

RAINEY
But I–

IVY
(off-stage, shouting) Hello! Anybody home!

RAINEY
(shouting back) We're in the bedroom!

ABENDIGO
(to RAINEY) Read it for me, Rain.

IVY
(off-stage) Hello!

> *IVY, BERT, DARESE and GIRLENE enter the bedroom. IVY has a small
> bunch of flowers in her hand, and BERT carries a dark plastic shopping
> bag.*

(trying to be upbeat) I found these along Negro Creek Road. There's
Chicory, and Bachelor Buttons, Queen Anne's Lace, Black Eyed Susans
and Daisies.

ABENDIGO
You know how I love those wildflowers and creeping vines.

RAINEY
I'll go get a vase.

> *RAINEY exits with the home funeral book.*

BERT
Hey judge, what d'you think you're doing?

ABENDIGO
All trains come to the end of the track, old chap.

BERT
I thought I'd go before you.

ABENDIGO
I'd be more than willing to trade places.

BERT
If I could, you know I would, judge.

> BERT unpacks his shopping bag, revealing a large bottle of scotch and a dark-coloured bottle of carbonated mineral water.

Single malt, just the way you like it.

ABENDIGO
Just the thing to chase this medication.

IVY
It might kill you.

BERT
Can't think of a better way to go, myself.

> BERT returns the scotch to the shopping bag and uncaps the carbonated water.

DARESE
Abendigo Johnson.

ABENDIGO
Darese Jordon.

DARESE
As God is my witness, Abendigo, I'm, I'm...

ABENDIGO
I know Darese, I know.

GIRLENE
Abendigo, where're you going when we still have so much work to do!

ABENDIGO
And I've never been one to leave things unfinished.

IVY
We're not doing it without you, so we're not doing it at all.

ABENDIGO
Don't count me out 'cause I'm not dead yet. I'm gonna live my last days, not die my last days.

DARESE
Heaven's above! You're not saying what I think you're saying?

GIRLENE
You right Darese. That's a man with a plan if I ever heard one.

IVY
There's absolutely no way!

BERT
Come on, let's at least hear the judge out.

RAINEY enters with the vase full of wildflowers.

RAINEY
Here we go. Can I get anyone anything?

BERT
Just some glasses, we brought some carbonated water.

RAINEY
Oh, okay.

DARESE
We love carbonated water, you know.

RAINEY
I did not know. No problem. I'll be right back.

RAINEY exits.

GIRLENE
Carbonated water just gives me gas.

ABENDIGO
Then you'll just have to join us in some single malted scotch, my dear.

GIRLENE
Now you talking.

BERT empties the contents of the mineral water into the vase on the night stand.

IVY
Bert, you better not kill my wildflowers.

BERT
It's good for them, Ivy. All that air and minerals. It's good for them.

BERT pours some of the contents of the scotch into the empty mineral water bottle.

That should keep us going for now.

He places the mineral water on the night stand beside the medicine and hides the scotch bottle in the shopping bag once more.

ABENDIGO
Once a subversive, always a–

RAINEY enters with a tray of glasses.

RAINEY
Here we are.

RAINEY sets the tray of glasses down on the chest of drawers. She looks around, spots the bottled water on the night stand, and heads for it.

IVY
Don't bother yourself, Rainey, we can do it.

RAINEY
That's all right.

BERT grabs the bottle before RAINEY can get to it.

BERT
No, no. I've got it.

RAINEY sits on the bed. They all stare at her. After a few moments of silence, she senses that the group would rather talk in private.

RAINEY
Well, all right then. Call me if you need anything.

ABENDIGO
Thanks Rain.

RAINEY exits. BERT uncaps the water bottle and pours a capful of scotch onto the floor.

BERT
For the ancestors.

The CHORUS of ancestors responds to the call. BERT proceeds to pour scotch into the glasses.

DARESE
So out with it, man, what's the plan?

ABENDIGO
Day after tomorrow. That's my idea. We do the whole thing the day after tomorrow.

Scene Eight

RAINEY sits on the porch reading the book her father gave her.

RAINEY
Oh God.... Please.... Oh please.... Oh.... No ,no, no, no, no.

Faint traces of laughter can be heard coming from inside the house. MICHAEL approaches the porch steps.

MICHAEL
Is everyone else inside?

RAINEY
Um.... In the bedroom.

MICHAEL approaches the door.

MICHAEL
The lawyer said she can have something drawn up by tomorrow. I'll drop it by as soon as she's done.

RAINEY
Oh. Good. Good.

MICHAEL
Okay.

RAINEY holds up the book.

RAINEY
Do you know anything about this?

MICHAEL
Er, yes. A bit.

RAINEY
How long have you known?

MICHAEL
He swore me to secrecy, Rainey.

RAINEY
I should have been told.

MICHAEL
That's what I told him.

RAINEY
(referring to the book) So what about this?

MICHAEL
Have you read it?

RAINEY
I've skimmed it.

MICHAEL
Just read it, Rainey.

RAINEY
He's not going to…

MICHAEL
All of us are going to die.

RAINEY
Then it's not as if he'll be alive to know the difference.

MICHAEL
Then tell him you don't want to do it.

RAINEY
Maybe I will.

MICHAEL
Well, I told him you couldn't do it.

RAINEY
Of course I can do it. Of course I can do it. I just don't want to do it.

MICHAEL
That's what he wants, Rainey. It's what he wants. He didn't tell you because he's so busy protecting you. We're all so busy protecting you. You can't do it. You couldn't even look at your own daughter. You didn't see Janie in that casket. You didn't see her looking like she'd looked when we tucked her in nights. You couldn't even go to the grave. Have you even seen her grave? Have you? You had the affair. You wanted to give up medicine. You wanted to go back to school. You want the divorce. It's always what you want, Rainey. Do something for someone else for God's sake. You're eating dirt, Rainey, I've seen you eating dirt. Janie's gone and your father's dying. And yes, yes I am seeing someone. And yes she's nice. She very nice. But she's not you. But every day I think of you a little less and a little less. And I pray there'll come a day when I won't think of you at all. I'm going inside to see your Dad now.

MICHAEL opens the screen door.

RAINEY
He held me. He held me in his arms. That's all.

MICHAEL stands with his back to her.

MICHAEL
You wouldn't come home.

RAINEY
I couldn't come home. The way you looked at me. I guess I might feel the same way if she'd have died and you were supposed to be looking after her. I don't know. I just wanted someone to make the earth stop shaking.

MICHAEL
I see.

RAINEY
He, we never made love. It is too raw and sour and full of blood in there. I lose my all blood from there. An ocean of blood pours from me. My blood is dying. My line. My lineage. All those times we tried. All those dead babies we lay to rest in the creek. Tiny beings no bigger than my finger. I haven't let another man touch me there. Janie came from there. It's Janie's home.

Pause.

Michael?

MICHAEL
Yes?

RAINEY
Was I a good mother?

MICHAEL
Yes, Rainey. Yes, you were a wonderful mother.

RAINEY
Michael?

MICHAEL
Yes.

RAINEY
Was I a good pastor's wife?

He does not answer for a moment.

MICHAEL
Yes Rain. You were a great pastor's wife.

MICHAEL approaches RAINEY. He kneels down beside her. He rests his head in her lap. She does not move. He kisses her belly. He kisses the tender space below her belly.

RAINEY
No. Don't, don't, don't.

MICHAEL gets up and returns to the door. He looks at her for a moment, then enters the house.

RAINEY sits silently for a few moments, trying to calm her breathing. She rises suddenly and runs down the porch steps towards the creek. She stands alone at the very edge of the water.

Scene Nine

Back in ABENDIGO's bedroom, IVY, BERT, DARESE, GIRLENE and MICHAEL sit gathered around him. Everyone except MICHAEL has a glass of scotch in their hand.

ABENDIGO
Go on, go get yourself a glass, son.

MICHAEL
No, no, I'm fine.

GIRLENE
Just a tip in your glass, Pastor Michael.

DARESE
It sure ain't a sin, praise God.

MICHAEL
Okay… okay. Sure, why not.

MICHAEL leaves the room in search of a drinking glass.

ABENDIGO
I think we should ask him.

IVY
Don't try that, the answer's still no.

DARESE
(to ABENDIGO) I don't know, either. If he says yes, no way Rainey's gonna let you out of her sight.

ABENDIGO
You're being rather quiet, old man, what you thinking?

BERT
I don't know. I don't know. The museum is by far our biggest project ever. Even if you were in tip top shape, it'd be a mighty undertaking.

GIRLENE
I'm with Abendigo. I believe we should hit the museum. He could stay in the car and play lookout. I'd rather spend my final days in jail for what I believe than puttering around my home, waiting to die.

IVY
Well, I am not of that opinion. And unless we all do it, no one does it.

ABENDIGO
Then here's what we do–

IVY
No, Ben.

ABENDIGO
Hear me out, Ivy.

IVY
You were just in intensive care with tubes coming out of every orifice of your body. None of us can handle heavy objects any longer. Darese's arthritis is so bad, she's like the tin man in a rain storm. The only reason Bert remembers his head is it's the one thing in life he takes great care not to forget. Girlene holds the Guinness world record for the highest blood pressure ever registered in human history and I am–

ABENDIGO
If Michael says yes, we could buy Giuseppe and his cleaners out for the night, and the uniform could be placed in a cleaning cart. It's no more intricate than the time we liberated the template of Aunt Jemima from the pancake company. It'd be easy.

MICHAEL enters with an empty glass.

BERT
Pass your glass, Pastor Michael, let's get a little of this tonic inside you.

MICHAEL
Just a drop, mind you.

BERT pours MICHAEL a hefty dose.

Whoa, whoa! That's good, that's good. Cheers!

MICHAEL uncharacteristically downs much of the glass. The others look at each other.

GIRLENE
Looks like you needed that drink, Pastor Michael.

MICHAEL
Yes, seems I did.

ABENDIGO
Michael?

MICHAEL
Yes sir?

ABENDIGO
I need a favour.

MICHAEL
Anything.

ABENDIGO
It's a big favour, son.

MICHAEL
You know I'd do anything for you, sir.

A choral rap rhapsody emanates from beyond the stage.

Scene Ten

RAINEY stands on the porch by ABENDIGO who is sitting sipping tea. She hovers over him as he finishes his drink.

RAINEY
You okay? You still look tired.

ABENDIGO
I'm fine. What a beautiful morning.

RAINEY
You sure you want to try this?

ABENDIGO
I feel fine, Rain.

ABENDIGO slowly rises from the chair.

RAINEY
Don't move too fast now.

ABENDIGO has only a little difficulty making himself upright.

ABENDIGO
Good. Good.

He takes several steps.

It feels good.

RAINEY
Don't over exert yourself.

ABENDIGO
I'm fine.

ABENDIGO swings his body very slightly as if dancing.

See. I'm fine, really.

RAINEY
I'll go put on some breakfast. While you wash up. Remember, I'll be going to the city today. I'll get someone to watch you.

ABENDIGO
You running away?

RAINEY
Pa... I'll be back tonight.

ABENDIGO walks slowly to the door.

Oh, I looked through the book.

ABENDIGO
Good girl.

RAINEY
I, I can't, Pa. I can't do it.

ABENDIGO
You mean you won't do it?

RAINEY
While you seem to have accepted the idea that you're going to disappear right off the face of this planet, I'm certainly not ready, qualified or interested in the idea of preparing your dead body do-it-yourself style.

ABENDIGO
I know it's a lot to ask, but Michael can help.

RAINEY
Then ask him to do it.

ABENDIGO
Okay. Okay. I think I will.

ABENDIGO exits into the house.

RAINEY
Pa.... Pa, I, I...

RAINEY follows behind him.

MICHAEL, dressed in church robes, appears to one side of the stage. The congregation fan themselves with their hymn books.

MICHAEL
(*reading*) "And the lord said unto Satan, Hast thou considered my servant Job, that there is none like him in the earth, a perfect and an upright man, one that feareth God, and eschewth evil? And still he holdeth fast his integrity, although thou movedst me against him, to destroy him without cause."

There's a knock at the farmhouse door. RAINEY goes to the door and opens it. A DELIVERY MAN stands in the doorway with a clipboard and a pen.

DELIVERY MAN
I have a shipment for a Judge Johnson. Sign here please.

RAINEY
There?

DELIVERY MAN
Yes, ma'am.

RAINEY signs the ledger. The DELIVERY MAN exits to his vehicle.

RAINEY
(*shouting*) Pa! There's a package for you. You need help Pa?

ABENDIGO
(*off-stage*) No, no, I'm coming. I'm coming.

MICHAEL continues to read from the book of Job.

MICHAEL
(*reading*) "And Satan answered the Lord, and said, Skin for skin, yea, all that a man hath will he give for his life. But put forth thine hand now and touch his bone and his flesh and he will curse thee to thy face. And the lord said unto Satan, Behold, he is in thine hand;"

RAINEY stands beside ABENDIGO as the DELIVERY MAN wheels a simple wooden coffin into the house.

DELIVERY MAN
Where d'you want it?

A somewhat speechless RAINEY turns to ABENDIGO.

ABENDIGO
Anywhere. Right there's as good a place as any.

The delivery man sets the coffin right in the centre of the living room, locking the wheels of the stand below it. The DELIVERY MAN hands ABENDIGO his card.

DELIVERY MAN
Call me when you're done with the stand?

ABENDIGO nods and passes the card to RAINEY. The DELIVERY MAN exits. RAINEY stares at the pine box incredulously.

The CHORUS (congregation) continues to signify. MICHAEL reads as if he himself were Job.

MICHAEL
"So went Satan forth from the presence of the Lord, and smote Job with sore boils from the sole of his foot unto his crown." And still this good man, this pious man, this man who served God faithfully all his life. Still, with all these trials, Job did not turn away from the Lord.

The CHORUS signifies joyfully. MICHAEL raises his arms as if to conduct. The CHORUS begins to sing.

CHORUS
Stand still Jordan. Jordan,
Stand still. Stand still
Stand still Jordan.
I can't stand still.

After a few moments the CHORUS exchanges words for melodic sounds.

ABENDIGO places a hand on top of the wooden casket. He caresses it gently. RAINEY walks down to the creek.

RAINEY
(to the audience) It's not about dice. It's not about whether God plays dice. The underpinning of most monotheistic religions is the belief in an omnipotent and loving paternal figure who, as the saying goes, will not allow a person to experience more suffering than he or she can bear. This belief, however, begs the question, why the need for suffering at all. And if indeed God can take credit for creating the world, why does he not also take credit for being the author of that suffering?

RAINEY picks up a morsel and places it on her tongue.

"The Lord giveth and the Lord taketh away."

MICHAEL has crossed the field towards the house. He spots RAINEY, hesitates for a moment, then makes his way down to her. He has a piece of paper and a legal-sized envelope in his hand.

MICHAEL
Job? You're quoting from the book of Job?

RAINEY
Two years of seminary school – it's hard to erase.

MICHAEL hands RAINEY a piece of paper.

MICHAEL
Here are the names and numbers of members of the congregation who've agreed to come by and help you, help your Dad.

RAINEY
Thanks. Thank you, but I think we'll be fine.

MICHAEL
I'll be by every day.

RAINEY
You don't have to.

MICHAEL
I know. I want to.

RAINEY
You've been so much more of a son to him than I've been a daughter, these last few years.

MICHAEL
I'd do anything for him.

RAINEY
Yes, I know.

MICHAEL
Well, you've been…. I saw the lawyer.

MICHAEL hands RAINEY a large envelope.

I've already signed it. Take your time. There's no hurry. No hurry. Call me when you're ready. I'll come, come by, you know, pick it up.

RAINEY
All right.

MICHAEL
All right.

RAINEY
All right.

> *MICHAEL exits. RAINEY stands alone by the creek with the envelope and piece of paper in her hand. She looks out into the audience.*

Don't get me wrong. It's not that I don't believe in God. The problem is... I do.

CHORUS
Stand still Jordan. Jordan,
Stand still. Stand still.
Stand still Jordan.
I can't stand still.

ACT II

Scene One

A choral vocalese fills Negro Creek. ABENDIGO and IVY stand in the living room staring at the large pine casket. RAINEY rushes by, still quite unnerved by the presence of the coffin.

RAINEY
Aunt Ivy, you're sure you can manage?

IVY
We'll be just fine. Michael's just across the field if anything – you know, if anything.

RAINEY
All right. All right. I'll, I'll, I'll be doing some research at the medical, I mean university library this afternoon. I'll work on my speech, my presentation for the interview a bit, then I'm, I'm, I'll be back. All right. Be good Pa. Don't, you know, don't…

ABENDIGO
Believe me, I'm not going anywhere just yet.

RAINEY
No, yeah…. Yeah. All right.

RAINEY exits. ABENDIGO and IVY continue to stare at the casket.

IVY
Sure is ugly.

ABENDIGO
Better learn to acquire a taste for it. We're all ending up in one of those.

IVY
You could have chosen a nicer style.

ABENDIGO
This one will let the worms in faster. I'll be part of the creek before you know it.

IVY leads ABENDIGO out to the porch.

IVY
You can't find a better place to put it?

ABENDIGO

It can't fit down in the cellar, the stairs are too narrow. Rainey's got the spare room. Martha's room is full of all Rainey's worldly possessions. And it's not going in my room. I'm not dead yet.

IVY sets ABENDIGO sitting facing the creek. She sits across from him with a small newspaper-covered table in front of her. On the table there are several bottles of different coloured enamel paint. She puts an old towel on her lap and with a small paint brush she puts the finishing touches on the new smile of one of the little Black lawn ornaments. ABENDIGO puts polyfiller into the chest of another little Black man. He looks out at the view in front of him, trying to take in as much of it as he can.

IVY

I just don't see how Lorraine won't find out about the liberation operation at the museum.

ABENDIGO

I'm still working on that one.

IVY

No way she's going to help us. Anyway, I'm not sure you should be doing this right now.

ABENDIGO

If not right now, then when? You all have most of the work to do.

IVY

We can't do it without Michael, and he didn't exactly say yes.

ABENDIGO

He didn't exactly say no either. The court's handing down its ruling on Negro Creek that day, and since the museum closes early, all we have to do is get Michael back in time for the march.

He closes his eyes for a moment.

IVY

Ben? You all right?

ABENDIGO

I'm fine, Ivy, just fine.

IVY

You want your pills?

ABENDIGO

No, no. It's the sun. The feeling of the sun on my skin. The warm of it. The tingle. The brilliant yellow, white, orange of it. Close your eyes, Ivy.

IVY closes her eyes.

What do you feel?

IVY
I see blue spots on my eyelids.

ABENDIGO
What do you feel?

IVY
I feel like – I don't know what I feel. What do you feel?

ABENDIGO
I feel… I feel alive.

With a sigh, he places the little man on the newspaper-covered side table beside him.

There you go old fella'. You know, I'd have made a good heart surgeon had I put my mind to it.

IVY
And hundreds of innocent Black men would have gone to jail without you to defend them.

ABENDIGO
I would have made more than enough money to send you through law school though.

IVY
I would have had to fight for the right to breastfeed during cross examination, and day-care facilities in the court house.

ABENDIGO
You'd have had the judges in day-care and the babies presiding.

IVY
A much fairer justice system for all, I'm sure. Though Martha wouldn't have approved of you sending me off to study law.

ABENDIGO
Martha thought you hated her for marrying me.

IVY
Well… I did – for a while.

ABENDIGO
> She was there when I needed her.

IVY
> She always loved Lorraine, raised her like her own.

ABENDIGO
> And I loved her for it.

IVY
> Yes.

ABENDIGO
> But she knew about you.

IVY
> There was nothing to know.

ABENDIGO
> She knew how I felt about you and she knew that I cared for her so much that I wouldn't do anything about it.

IVY
> Anyhow.... Is your man ready for a new smile?

ABENDIGO
> Ivy?

IVY
> Yes Ben?

ABENDIGO
> Give me your hand. I want to stand a while.

> > *IVY helps him up onto his feet. He rests a hand on her shoulder, as if to steady himself.*

> In all these years, I've never told you about Rainey's mother.

IVY
> And I don't need to hear it now.

ABENDIGO
> Steady, or I'll fall.

IVY
> Okay? Better?

ABENDIGO

Better. You've always been a strong woman.

IVY

Still, I don't need to hear.

ABENDIGO

You're the prettiest girl I ever met.

IVY

Ben!

ABENDIGO

With Rainey's mother – I was working on the trains – we met, were married by the end of the week.

IVY

Don't Ben!!

ABENDIGO

It was a whirlwind, Ivy, and–

IVY

I'm going to drop you if you don't stop, Ben, probably kill you in the process.

ABENDIGO

Go ahead. You more than anyone deserve that opportunity. You're the only person I really hurt in all my life that I can think of. So go ahead.

IVY

I'm going to place you down on the chair.

ABENDIGO

I don't want to sit down, Ivy.

IVY

I'm going to set you down now.

ABENDIGO

Well, you're gonna have to drop me, 'cause I'm not going to stop tellin' the truth, since it's my last chance and I get the feeling I've got to set things straight with you–

IVY moves and ABENDIGO falls to the floor. He does not move.

IVY

Oh Ben. Ben? Oh my God!

IVY leans over him to check his pulse. ABENDIGO opens one eye and raises his head slightly.

ABENDIGO
Feel better?

IVY
You all right?

ABENDIGO
Never felt better, myself.

IVY
Abendigo Johnson, don't you ever do that to me again.

ABENDIGO
It's difficult to be certain, who's doing the doing right now.

IVY
Here, let me help you up.

IVY helps ABENDIGO sit up on the floor.

ABENDIGO
Yes, there, that's better. I prefer the world this way up.

IVY
Let's get you on your feet.

ABENDIGO
I'd like to kiss you, Miss Ivy.

IVY
Old man, stop your foolishness and let me help you get on your feet.

ABENDIGO
The last time I kissed you was over forty years ago, on the steps of that church over there, and saying I'd be back for you.

IVY
You're losing your mind along with every thing else, you know that.

ABENDIGO
I wonder if your lips still taste of blackberries in maple wine.

IVY
Come on. Up you get.

IVY tries to pull him up by herself. ABENDIGO kisses her lightly as she leans over him. IVY stumbles back and falls. She shakes her head.

ABENDIGO

That was nice. Blackberries and summer apples in maple wine. Wasn't that nice?

IVY

Well frankly, I don't know, I can't rightly tell, it happened so fast.

ABENDIGO

Here, let me try again.

IVY

I've hated you more than I loved you, Ben. I hated you when I heard you'd married Rainey's mother. I hated you even more when you asked me to raise another woman's child. And I hated you worse when you married my own sister. But I hate you more than ever, wanting to kiss me now. My hate kept me together. I could do something with that hate. I could spend my time caught up in my own evil thoughts. Hate has been my companion. Please don't take it away from me. Don't leave me longing for you just as you're leaving me for the last time.

ABENDIGO

I love you Ivy Moore.

IVY

Stop your ravings.

ABENDIGO

I've always loved you, and you've always loved me. Now you can either kiss me or leave things be. But as it stands, I'd rather have just one last day of kissing you, because there might be no more days to come.

IVY and ABENDIGO sit silently for a moment. IVY goes over to ABENDIGO.

IVY

Here, let me help you to your feet.

IVY helps ABENDIGO to stand.

ABENDIGO

Sure, I understand. And don't worry, it won't happen again.

IVY

Don't be sorry. I want you standing on your own two feet when you kiss me this time.

ABENDIGO is upright. With one hand on her shoulder, he steadies himself. He caresses the side of her face with the other. He kisses her softly.

ABENDIGO
Blackberries, summer apples and peaches in a sweet maple wine.

MICHAEL comes running up the field, yelling.

MICHAEL
Dad! Dad!

As MICHAEL approaches the porch, ABENDIGO and IVY quickly part.

Dad! Ivy. They've desecrated the church – on the walls – on the outside…. They've scrawled "Nigger" and "Niggers Go Home" all over it, everywhere.

Scene Two

MICHAEL stands in front of the CHORUS (congregation) without his church robes. The small church is packed. ABENDIGO, IVY, GIRLENE, BERT and DARESE are seated in the front row. RAINEY is also in attendance, seated at the back.

MICHAEL
"This kind of thing never happens here." That's what they think. That's what we think. "Everything is fine here in this country." We've grown so comfortable that we believe racism, no, white supremacy is a phenomenon that only happens south of the border. Well folks, we live in the south of the north. That they could do this to God's house…. And we will not take those hideous and repugnant words down. We will not whitewash the truth of our situation. We will leave this desecration in place as a reminder. Because this is all about our attempts to upturn the Holland Township council decision to change the name of Negro Creek Road, you know that. This is our home. And these threats…. This racial intimidation will not deter us in the least from our cause. We are a steadfast people. It is this characteristic in us that has helped us survive the most severe and vicious of atrocities. Our forbears survived so that we may breathe the air we breathe at this very moment. They can try to put fear in us. They can even burn us down. But we will continue to fight for our right to take up space on this earth. See you at the march tomorrow.

MICHAEL descends the pulpit. A single voice begins to sing.

CHORUS MEMBER
Singing with a sword in my hand.
Singing with a sword in my hand.

Other voices soon join her, clapping and singing as they exit the church.

CHORUS
Singing with a sword in my hand.
And the Angels are singing too.

Singing with a sword in my hand.
Singing with a sword in my hand.
Singing with a sword in my hand.
And the Angels are singing too.

RAINEY alone remains behind. MICHAEL approaches her.

RAINEY
It's a good thing you're doing, Michael. I know…. I don't usually….
You're, you're doing a good thing.

MICHAEL
I'm glad you were here.

RAINEY
I swore I'd never set foot back in this…

MICHAEL
I'm glad you were here.

RAINEY
It felt like old times.

MICHAEL
Yeah.

RAINEY
I'm so sorry.

MICHAEL does not respond. He only looks at RAINEY.

Let's pick a time – to sort out Janie, Janie's things – give them to charity.

MICHAEL
(almost disbelieving) Okay.

RAINEY
How's your morning? Tomorrow?

MICHAEL
It's fine. Yes. I mean no, no. I'm taking your Dad to the museum.

RAINEY
The museum?

MICHAEL
He said he'd like to go.

RAINEY
No.

MICHAEL
He's got a wheelchair. We'll, I'll just shove it in the trunk in case he gets tired.

RAINEY
No, he just has to rest. I was speaking to – I've been trying to get him in on a clinical trial at a teaching hospital in the city. It's already full, but there's another one in Buffalo coming up, and there's a good chance, and if he can just make it, make it 'till then...

MICHAEL
He didn't say anything–

RAINEY
I haven't told him. I wasn't even sure about it until this afternoon.

MICHAEL
Buffalo? Rainey–

RAINEY
I know it's a long shot but I can't just let him, let him–

MICHAEL
Die? You can't just let him die?

RAINEY
Die, die, die. I can't, I can't just let him die.

MICHAEL
I don't believe it's up to you, Rain.

RAINEY
I know it's not up to me, but while he's still alive I can do something.

MICHAEL
So you'll keep him in bed for six months, only to have him tied up to tubes and pumps?

RAINEY
You don't understand.

MICHAEL
Oh, I understand. He still has life in him yet, Rainey. Let him live it. And help him prepare to let it go.

RAINEY
You see I don't believe that death is a good thing.

MICHAEL
And that's why you haven't been to Janie's grave.

RAINEY
I should get going.

RAINEY gets up to leave.

MICHAEL
Come. I'll go with you.

RAINEY
No thank you.

MICHAEL gets up, takes RAINEY's hand and begins to exit the church.

MICHAEL
Come with me.

RAINEY
I start to go – I can't, Michael. I can't! Not yet.

RAINEY pulls her hand away.

MICHAEL
Janie died almost three years ago, Rain. It's time. We'll do it together.

RAINEY
I can't. She's there.... It's because.... I can't, it's–

MICHAEL
It wasn't your fault. Meningitis. She had Meningitis.

RAINEY
And I am a doctor, Michael. She had all the symptoms. It was textbook. It was textbook. It's why, it's why.... It's why I.... When Martha got sick... I prayed. I really prayed, Michael. I told him. I told God, bring her out of this please, and I'll do anything. Anything! And when she....

When she died, I thought.... I thought, fine.... Fine.... You're just going to have to do it yourself. I left the seminary. I had to learn how to help, really help people, heal people.... Cheat.... Cheat death. And when I saw my first birth.... I'd studied, I mean, I'd seen the films. When I saw life come into being, come into the room. When I caught the miraculous fruit of life with my own two hands. I knew that's what I wanted to do. Bring life. Help bring as many lives into the world.... Catch as many new souls. That was cheating death. It makes no sense, but that's what I thought. I mean, meningitis is.... If I couldn't catch meningitis in my only child, to save her, save me, and truly do battle with death.... You know.... You know how much I wanted babies, our babies. And when we kept losing.... I kept losing.... Then Janie.... She stayed. She grew. She was.... She would hug me round my waist so tight sometimes like she was trying to get back inside me, like I was her fingers and toes and she'd missed having them around her all day, like I was her everything. She was mine.

MICHAEL
Rain...

RAINEY
I'm still there, Michael. I'm always there. She's on the toilet. I'm on my knees, holding her hands, and she falls, she falls on my breast. I feel her heart. She's playing. I think she's playing. And she won't wake up, Michael. I'm trying, I'm trying to wake her up. She's in my arms. I'm calling 9-1-1. And then it stops. Her heart stops. Time stops. And I get it started again. It's going to be okay. She's going to be alright. And I run. I start to run. I'm running because it comes to me. If I can run fast enough, faster than time, time will slow down and go backwards. And I can't. I can't run fast enough, Michael. I can't run fast enough.

MICHAEL
Come. Come with me.

RAINEY
I... I just.... If, if I start to feel.... If it starts, it's, it's.... If I cross the event – If I cross the horizon, I'll never come back, it's never ever going to stop. I'll drown, I'll drown in it.

MICHAEL
Just come.

MICHAEL takes RAINEY in his arms and carries her out of the church.

Scene Three

RAINEY runs from the cemetery to the creek. She stands at the edge of the creek for a moment trying to hold herself together. MICHAEL appears from the direction of the cemetery as if following behind her. RAINEY jumps into the living water.

MICHAEL
Rainey! Rain!

The CHORUS of souls envelopes her and she disappears into the creek. By the time MICHAEL reaches the water's edge, RAINEY re-emerges, buoyed by the movement of the water.

RAINEY
I just want to die. Why can't I die?

MICHAEL leans over the water's edge and strokes the side of her face.

MICHAEL
You did good, Rain. You did good.

RAINEY
It's so easy for you.

MICHAEL
Let me help you out of there.

RAINEY
You have your God. He has His plan. I don't understand your plan.

MICHAEL
Give me your hand.

RAINEY
I hate it. I hate your faith. Even when you see that God's house can't protect you, you, you–

MICHAEL
No. No. I'm a fraud. I'm a fraud, Rainey. I'm a faithless preacher. If there is a God I'm surprised he hasn't struck me down by now. I simply, I just believe that the church, it helps people. It helps me. That's why I do things the way I do there. It's a comfort. The church is…. It's the people. When you left. They brought me food. Girlene would just show up and clean my house and do the laundry. She didn't ask if she could come. People just showed up. They made me feel like I had to show up on Sunday morning. Since I'd been there for them. They'd be there for me. 'Cause when you left…. After Janie…. And

you're right I blamed you – but just for a minute. If you'd just have waited a, a, minute longer. And I'm sorry for that. Come out of the water, Rain. Let me help you out.

> *RAINEY doesn't move. MICHAEL takes a handful of water and pours it over her forehead. He does this several times. His action is almost baptismal. Finally RAINEY gives him her hands. MICHAEL helps her out of the water, which almost seems to help deliver her onto the land. He takes off his jacket and tries to dry her with it.*

RAINEY
(almost shivering) I'm sorry about what they did to the church, did to you.

MICHAEL
The church isn't those four walls. They'd have to kill all of us niggers down here to really hurt me.

> *MICHAEL drapes his jacket around her.*

RAINEY
And I'm sorry you've lost your God.

MICHAEL
Maybe God is in the people. In those tiny miracles of human kindness.

RAINEY
Maybe.

> *RAINEY moves even closer to MICHAEL.*

Why do people have to die, Michael?

MICHAEL
I don't know why people die, Rainey.

RAINEY
It's, it's…

MICHAEL
I know. I know. *(pause)* You all right?

RAINEY
Yes. I'm, I'll be fine. And, er, thank you.

MICHAEL
Aaahh…. I, I should go.

RAINEY
Yes.

> *RAINEY hands MICHAEL his jacket. He takes it and exits to the house.*

Scene Four

> *Inside the living room, ABENDIGO, IVY, GIRLENE, BERT and DARESE are gathered around the casket, looking at a large detailed blueprint of the museum, laid out on top of it. MICHAEL enters quietly and stands at a distance, unnoticed at first.*

GIRLENE
Then we make our way to the museum storage room, find the soldier's uniform with the Black militia insignia on it, and get out of there.

ABENDIGO
It's really a simple operation at a complex location.

IVY
The real difficulty will be avoiding the suspicion of the guards.

ABENDIGO
Guiseppe has told them that another cleaning company will be subbing in for the evening. We should be all set.

BERT
I just want to make it official. My code name will be Olivier Le Jeune for the duration of the operation.

IVY
Just, just stick to that name.

BERT
Olivier for short.

IVY
I swear.... I swear I'm going to–

> *MICHAEL approaches the group.*

DARESE
Pastor Michael!

MICHAEL
I told her. I told her we were going to the museum. But I don't think she's going to let you go.

ABENDIGO
You just let me see about that.

MICHAEL
I feel kind of badly about lying, though.

ABENDIGO
Well, you weren't lying. We are going to the museum.

MICHAEL
The sin of omission.

ABENDIGO
Only if we're Catholic, and only if we're caught. And we won't get caught.

MICHAEL
This is crazy.

DARESE
And Lord knows, it's not as if we're even stealing anything this time.

MICHAEL
Liberating.

DARESE
Yes, yes, liberating.

GIRLENE
No, no, reclaiming something that is rightfully ours.

ABENDIGO
Come on son, let's review the plans. Okay…. You'll be with me on the…

Scene Five

RAINEY takes some pills from the medicine bottles on the night stand and gives them to ABENDIGO. She hands him a glass of water.

ABENDIGO
You went for a swim? At this time of night?

RAINEY
It's the best time, Pa. I'm upping your dose. You don't need to be in such pain.

> *ABENDIGO takes the pills and drinks the water. RAINEY feels his forehead with the back of her hand.*

You've got a slight fever.

ABENDIGO
I'm still going with Michael tomorrow.

RAINEY
We'll see in the morning.

ABENDIGO
Fever or no fever. But I need you to pick up some socks for me in town tomorrow morning.

RAINEY
You've got plenty of socks, Pa.

ABENDIGO
I want a new pair of socks to go with my suit.

RAINEY
I'll go in the afternoon on my way to the interview.

ABENDIGO
So you'll have to leave a little earlier then.

RAINEY
You trying to get rid of me?

ABENDIGO
No. It's, if, if you miss the store, you won't get another chance 'till, 'till, 'till Monday.

RAINEY
I'll pick up some socks, okay?

ABENDIGO
Okay. Don't worry. Michael can look after me.

RAINEY
Okay. Just stay still. I want you to keep the medicine down this time. And I picked up a stronger dose of nitroglycerin for you. I want you to keep it with you at all times.

ABENDIGO
Remind me to put it in my jacket pocket in the morning.

RAINEY
Remind me to remind you.

ABENDIGO wants to lie down, but tries to keep upright.

Pa?

ABENDIGO
I'm still here.

RAINEY
Pa, I went to the teaching hospital this afternoon.

ABENDIGO
You're going back?

RAINEY
Not exactly.

ABENDIGO
You were a good doctor.

RAINEY
They're doing some trials.

ABENDIGO
They've got a court house in the hospital?

RAINEY
No, Pa, clinical trials. There's a brand new mechanical heart device that–

ABENDIGO
Absolutely not.

RAINEY
Pa, I–

ABENDIGO
I won't be hooked up to some plastic pump for the rest of my days.

RAINEY
What about me?

ABENDIGO
Well I don't think you're in need of a heart just yet. Least not that kind.

RAINEY

I'm being serious.

ABENDIGO

So am I.

RAINEY

Look Pa, I'll make a deal with you. If you promise me you'll register for the trial, I will do all I can to make sure that you're buried you the way you want.

Pause.

ABENDIGO

A plastic heart, huh?

RAINEY

They've had great success with it so far. Patients have extended their life by, by, I don't know, almost–

ABENDIGO

I'm still going to die, Rain.

RAINEY strokes his forehead.

RAINEY

Just not so soon.

RAINEY kisses him on the forehead.

I miss you already.

ABENDIGO

I'll always be with you, Rain.

RAINEY

You think so?

ABENDIGO

I've no doubts about it.

RAINEY

You think there's a heaven, Pa?

ABENDIGO

Yes I do. Heaven is Negro Creek. My grandmother left her life in that water. My body will rot in the earth and nurture the land, enriching the soil and more grass will grow and flowers and shrubs. And a cow might eat the grass and a part of me will be in the cow and in the cow's milk. And maybe someone on Negro Creek will drink that milk or eat that cow. And the circle will just keep going, and going and going.

RAINEY kisses ABENDIGO again. The CHORUS sings lightly their wordless melody, filling the space left by RAINEY and ABENDIGO.

Scene Six

The lights shrink to a horizontal beam, revealing six figures who span the stage. The women wear blue cleaner's uniforms and the men, blue cleaner's shirts. They all put on dark sunglasses simultaneously (except for MICHAEL, who's having a hard time keeping up).

ABENDIGO
Ivy.

IVY
Uh huh!

ABENDIGO
Darese.

DARESE
Yeah!

ABENDIGO
Bert. I mean Olivier Le Jeune.

BERT
Here Judge.

ABENDIGO
Girlene.

GIRLENE
Yes.

ABENDIGO
Michael.

MICHAEL
What? Oh. Oh! Yes, present and ready.

ABENDIGO
(looking at his watch) Synchronizing watches… five minutes to in 7, 6, 5, 4, 3, 2, set! Okay. I'm going with Michael and Ivy in the Lotsa Soap Van

and Bert, you, Girlene and Darese will take the Mercedes. We'll park out by the back entrance of the museum and do a final review of the plans when we get there.

RAINEY appears as if out of nowhere with some wildflowers in her hands.

RAINEY
What plans, Pa?

ABENDIGO
What are you – I asked you to go to town. What about my socks?

RAINEY
I had to plant some wildflower seeds in the cemetery. I was just on my way to town. I didn't know you were all going to the museum. What's your plan?

ABENDIGO
Ah, well, we've, we just agreed on a route through the exhibit, that's all.

RAINEY
Why are you all dressed like that.

IVY
Dressed like what, Rainey?

RAINEY
You're – Don't do this. Michael, I can't believe that you'd–

MICHAEL
I'd what?

RAINEY
(sarcastically) "I want to take your father to the museum."

MICHAEL
That's where we're going, Rainey.

RAINEY
You're not going, Pa. Look you guys, you know he's not well enough to do…. Do that anymore.

ABENDIGO
You're right, Lorraine. You're right. But I'm going. Keeping me here will make my life a little longer, but it certainly won't make it any better. You're not my parent. You are my child and you can't stop me.

RAINEY
Please! Have you all lost your senses. Michael, please. Do something.

MICHAEL
I am doing something. I believe in what he's doing. I can't stop him – short of calling the police. So I'm going along to make sure he'll be all right.

RAINEY
Okay… I'll call the police.

ABENDIGO
No. No you won't.

RAINEY
Just watch me.

> *ABENDIGO looks around at the gang.*

ABENDIGO
I've never forced any of you into this, so if you want out, now's the time.

> *No one moves.*

Ready?

RAINEY
Why?

ABENDIGO
Set.

RAINEY
Why is this more important than living?

ABENDIGO
We pretend we're alive. But we spend most of our lives living in spaces that no longer exist. I am here now. And I have to live as I believe.

> *ABENDIGO looks around.*

And go!

> *The gang of six begin to exit the stage.*

RAINEY
No. Don't.

The gang slowly makes its way off stage.

Please!

ABENDIGO turns back toward her for a moment.

NO! DON'T. Please Pa!

ABENDIGO exits.

Scene Seven

*The museum is huge, classical and daunting. The CHORUS segués from formal 18*th *century sounds to a kind of non vocal rap rhapsody. IVY pushes a large rolling cleaner's cart across the foyer. DARESE appears from the other side of the stage with her own cleaning cart. A security GUARD enters doing his rounds.*

IVY
   (quietly) All set, Darese?

DARESE
   All set, Ivy.

IVY
   By the totem pole in one minute and thirty seconds.

DARESE
   That way or this way?

IVY
   That way! Where's Girlene?

DARESE
   Still dusting out Canadian history.

   The security GUARD's inspection routine brings him very close to where the two women are standing. He comes within hearing distance of them.

IVY
   You go on. I'll get her – Her, her office floor should get a good wash.

GUARD
   Good evening.

IVY & DARESE
   Good evening.

The GUARD moves on without incident.

IVY
You go to the totem. I'll get Girlene.

The two women go in opposite directions.

On another part of the stage, MICHAEL and BERT are standing by the back end of a replica of a dinosaur skeleton on display. ABENDIGO sits on an upturned trash can on the edge of another cleaning cart, using it almost like a wheelchair.

MICHAEL
Well that takes care of that.

BERT
No thanks to you.

MICHAEL
Without me, you'd never have been able to put those dinosaur bones back together.

BERT
Without you, there would have been no one to ram the floor polisher into the damn thing either.

BERT notices something – a large dinosaur vertebrae on the ground.

ABENDIGO
Uh-oh! What's this?

MICHAEL
The missing link? It's part of the dinosaur's tail.

ABENDIGO
But where does it go?

BERT
(*sadistically*) Well, this should be easy, shouldn't it.

ABENDIGO
We've got to be at the totem pole in one minute and fifteen seconds and counting...

MICHAEL, ABENDIGO and BERT looks up at the huge monstrosity. They are overwhelmed.

MICHAEL
Let me see...

BERT drags a step ladder to the dinosaur.

Pass me the vertebrae – and the Crazy Glue there, Bert. Hurry!

At yet another corner of the stage, GIRLENE is standing on a small step-ladder rewriting the wording on a caption under a large portrait of John A. MacDonald's wife.

GIRLENE
(*reading*) Our first prime minister's second wife Josephine...

GIRLENE revises the caption, adding the appropriate corrections.

(*writing*) Born in Jamaica, comma.... (*reading*) Lived with the Prime minister in their Kingston, Ontario home.... (*writing*) And is of both European and African descent.

IVY enters.

IVY
Girlene Mays, come down off that thing this minute before you hurt yourself!

GIRLENE proceeds to lower herself off of the step ladder.

GIRLENE
When my Earl was alive. He would say, "Girlie," that's what he'd call me. "Girlie," he'd say, "there's another one of those obscene articles dehumanizing African people in this month's *National Geographic*." And we'd get on our coats and go to town and buy up all the *National Geographic*s on the newsstands, and in the tobacco shops. Then we'd make a huge bonfire and sometimes we'd invite the neighbours over for roast corn and marshmallows. Yeah, those were the good old days.

IVY leads GIRLENE to the totem pole near centre stage, where they find DARESE, ABENDIGO, MICHAEL and BERT huddled together in the corner.

ABENDIGO
All accounted for. Okay, let's just do what we came here to do and get out of here!

MICHAEL
According to the blueprint, Storage Room B should be down the stairs, somewhere in that direction.

The group takes off in the direction of the storage room.

Scene Eight

The jumbled collection of artifacts in Storage Room B are spectacular. An exquisite collection of sculptures, carving, cloth and jewellry. DARESE, BERT and GIRLENE wander around in search of the object they came to rescue.

GIRLENE's expression turns from one of awe to utter shock. She reads the caption below an enlarged photograph of a white woman and several semi-clad Black women.

GIRLENE
(reading) The missionaries taught the members of this primitive tribe how to wash their clothes and stop disease by using basic hygiene techniques.

BERT
Here's another one. This one suggests that we knew nothing of even the simplest kind of furniture-making before the missionaries came and taught us.

DARESE
Look, Chris Columbus discovered America, even though he met people living here.... He probably takes credit for discovering the Indians too, or do you think he gave them credit for realizing they already existed?

GIRLENE
I constantly have to remind myself what century this is, with all of society's technological know-how, it amazes me the rubbish they still hold dear...

IVY, ABENDIGO, and MICHAEL pass by in the background, searching through the jumble of objects. IVY stops at an impressive wooden Yoruba Goddess figure.

IVY
Oh my.

ABENDIGO
What is it?

IVY
She doesn't belong here.

MICHAEL
She's beautiful.

IVY
Can't we take her with us?

ABENDIGO
I don't think so.

MICHAEL
We could put her in a trash bag on the cart.

ABENDIGO
It's not what we came for.

MICHAEL
He's right, it's not what we came for.

IVY
(to the wooden goddess) Maybe we can come back and get you.

ABENDIGO
Wheel me to the door so that I can keep a lookout.

> *MICHAEL pushes the cart over to the door. ABENDIGO opens the door a sliver and peeks out.*

GIRLENE
I think we've found something.

> *The others gather around GIRLENE. ABENDIGO remains at the door to stand watch.*

BERT
There's a whole trunk full of soldier's uniforms in here.

ABENDIGO
Okay folks, there's a couple of guards approaching. Yes, I think they're coming straight at me. Emergency plan A goes into effect right now.

> *With some difficulty, ABENDIGO descends the cleaning cart and props himself up against the wall.*

ALL
Abide with me, fast falls the even tide–

> *A GUARD enters.*

GUARD
The subjects have been located. They're in there. *(to ABENDIGO)* I believe you forgot something.

While the GUARD stands at the door, RAINEY enters the storage room.

RAINEY
Pa, you forgot your pills. (*to the GUARD*) Thank you so much.

GUARD
No problem. No problem at all.

The GUARD exits.

ABENDIGO
What on earth are you doing?

RAINEY
You forgot your nitroglycerin! It could save your life, Pa. And though I'm so furious I could kill you myself, I pushed aside the idea of sending it along with the police.

ABENDIGO
What about your interview?

RAINEY
What was I supposed to do, just let you die?

MICHAEL
What did you tell the guard.

RAINEY
The truth, minus the stealing part – excuse me, "liberating."

ABENDIGO
He's coming back, quick, emergency plan "B."

MICHAEL
What's emergency plan "B?"

DARESE
It's the same as emergency plan "A," just a little further up in the song.

ABENDIGO descends the cleaning cart and props himself up against an adjacent wall. Everyone except for RAINEY, begins to clean and scrub and dust the objects around them once more.

ABENDIGO
Clean, Rain.

RAINEY
Don't talk to me. I'm not talking to you.

ABENDIGO
Rainey, get on your knees and–

RAINEY gets on her knees and everyone begins to sing just as the GUARD enters.

ALL
The darkness deepens, Lord with me abide–

GUARD
Working hard, huh?

ABENDIGO
Oh, yes sir, we certainly are.

Everyone nods.

GUARD
I figured I'd go on my break now.

ABENDIGO
Enjoy.

GUARD
Sure.

The GUARD looks at ABENDIGO suspiciously for a moment then exits.

RAINEY
I'm putting an end to this charade right now. Let's go!

ABENDIGO
We've come this far, and we're not turning back.

RAINEY
Come on, Pa. Please. Let's get out of here.

IVY
Ben, come and identify this uniform quickly.

ABENDIGO
Michael?

ABENDIGO sits himself on the cleaner's cart once more, but this time with great difficulty. MICHAEL goes over to him and pushes the cart to the trunk.

RAINEY
Pa, you're sweating.

She places her hand on his forehead.

You're burning up.

ABENDIGO
We're nearly done. We're nearly done.

IVY
This one?

IVY holds up an old woolen army jacket.

ABENDIGO
That's not it.

GIRLENE
What about these.

IVY places them in front of ABENDIGO.

ABENDIGO
(*sorting through them*) No. No. No. It's none of these.

RAINEY
Please! What on earth could be so important.

BERT
Juma Moore's uniform. The records show it ended up right here.

DARESE
Maybe they threw it away.

RAINEY
Juma Moore's jacket?

MICHAEL is searching through another trunk filled with dresses.

MICHAEL
Wait a minute. What about this?

ABENDIGO
Let me see.

MICHAEL brings it over to him.

Look! The insignia. That's it! That's the one!

IVY
Okay, wrap it up and place it in the trash bag on Abendigo's cart.

RAINEY goes over to examine the uniform.

RAINEY
Lorraine Johnson died trying to save this.

MICHAEL
Let's get out of here.

The GUARD enters.

GUARD
I forgot to tell you. I've switched off the alarm at the rear doors just in case you finish before I come back.

ABENDIGO
Good, no problems.

The GUARD has grown even more suspicious since they're all huddled around the trunk.

RAINEY
Er, we're just, er, having a short union meeting.

The GUARD ponders her statement.

GUARD
All right.

The guard looks at ABENDIGO.

You know you look very familiar. Have we met somewhere before?

ABENDIGO
No. I think you're mistaken. I'd remember your face.

GUARD
All right. But you do look familiar.

He exits.

MICHAEL
A union meeting.

RAINEY
It just came out.

ABENDIGO
All clear. He's gone. Let's get out of here before he recognizes me.
I think I may have put him in jail a couple of decades ago.

RAINEY
(*shaking her head*) Oh my God.

IVY
I think we're set. Girlene?

GIRLENE
Set.

IVY
Darese.

DARESE
Yep.

IVY
Bert?

> *BERT does not answer.*

Bert? I MEAN OLIVIER, ARE YOU READY?

BERT
Ready. To the car shall we?

IVY
Yes, Olivier Le Jeune, to the car. Now, you guys are fine getting to the van?

ABENDIGO
We'll be just fine.

MICHAEL
See you at the march.

> *GIRLENE, DARESE, BERT and IVY speed off down the corridor in a most controlled manner.*

ABENDIGO
Okay, let's go. Down the corridor to your left–

> *ABENDIGO shudders and collapses to the floor.*

RAINEY
Oh God. Please. Pa? Pa?

ABENDIGO
I can't seem to move…

RAINEY
It's okay, I've got the nitroglycerin. It's right here.

> *RAINEY reaches into her pocket and retrieves a bottle of pills. She places a tablet under ABENDIGO's tongue.*

MICHAEL
I'm going to call an ambulance.

ABENDIGO
NO! No. It's okay. It's passing. We can manage, son.

RAINEY
Are you sure, Pa?

ABENDIGO
Just help me up. We're nearly there.

> *MICHAEL and RAINEY try to hold him up.*

RAINEY
Okay. Okay. Slowly. Slowly. There. There you go.

> *MICHAEL and RAINEY prop ABENDIGO onto the cleaner's cart. MICHAEL steers while RAINEY holds onto ABENDIGO's shoulders. They exit slowly.*

Scene Nine

> *A large crowd of people have gathered at the creek, the end of the march route. They begin to disperse.*
>
> *BERT, DARESE and GIRLENE say their goodbyes to ABENDIGO, IVY, MICHAEL & RAINEY on the porch. MICHAEL is modelling the soldiers jacket.*

MICHAEL
The war of 1812, huh?

ABENDIGO
Juma Moore served in Captain Runchey's Coloured Militia. The Black Corps they used to call them. He settled this land and he donated the land for the church.

RAINEY
And great grandmother was his granddaughter.

ABENDIGO
That's right. Lorraine Johnson. She gave her life trying to save this piece of cloth.

RAINEY
And you just about gave yours trying to save it too.

IVY
It belongs here, with us.

ABENDIGO
It's part of the foundation of this land. It should be displayed with pride, not hidden away in a museum storage trunk.

MICHAEL
(taking off the jacket) I could put it up in the church.

ABENDIGO
Now you're talking.

MICHAEL
Next to the framed press release the Human Rights Commission issued.

ABENDIGO
Tell me what it said again – just the good part.

MICHAEL removes a piece of folded paper from his pocket.

MICHAEL
All right. Just the good part. Blah, blah, blah…. Yes. Here. "In a good faith settlement with the Commission, Carolynn Wilson, the Ontario Black History Society, the community of Negro Creek and its supporters, Holland Township Council has agreed to voluntarily change the name of the road back to Negro Creek Road, effective immediately." Yes!!

ABENDIGO
Yes!!!

RAINEY
Congratulations.

IVY
We did it. We actually did it.

ABENDIGO
That march…. What an extraordinary celebration.

IVY
It felt like the civil rights days all over again.

ABENDIGO
Exactly. All those people from Collingwood and Toronto, marching down Negro Creek Road. Powerful!

RAINEY
(to ABENDIGO) Come on Pa, it's been a long day. You should go rest.

ABENDIGO
I'm resting now, Rain. Look at the woods. Look at the sky. Just look at the moon shining down on Negro Creek.

RAINEY
I mean in bed.

IVY
And I should be off home.

MICHAEL
I'll help you take him inside.

RAINEY
If I wasn't so relieved to get out of there, boy oh boy, I'd be absolutely furious with you. Both of you.

MICHAEL
Wasn't it exciting though?

RAINEY
Don't push it, Michael.

IVY
Here, let me get the door.

RAINEY
Okay. Pa, up we go. Pa? Papa?

RAINEY tries to locate a pulse. The pulse is faint.

Oh no, no, no. Papa, no.

RAINEY begins to undo his shirt. ABENDIGO breathes heavily. Still his hand rises to grasp RAINEY's hand.

(*almost whispering*) Papa…. Papa…. Papa…

RAINEY takes her free hand to stroke his face.

It's okay Pa. It's okay. It's okay…. It's okay. Okay. Okay…. Kay…

IVY and MICHAEL crowd around. RAINEY rests her head on ABENDIGO's chest. She is still, so very still, until long after no more pulse can be found.

Scene Ten

The CHORUS fills the space, the sounds seem to rise up out of the earth. MICHAEL stands beside ABENDIGO's body. RAINEY looks on at a distance, then turns away. MICHAEL bathes ABENDIGO's body with warm scented soapy water, while IVY holds the basin. IVY sets the basin down and goes to locate ABENDIGO's clothing. MICHAEL dries the body as RAINEY continues to look on.

MICHAEL takes a sash and loops it around ABENDIGO's chin, tying it at the top of his head.

IVY returns with ABENDIGO's clothing and both she and MICHAEL prepare to dress the body. RAINEY sees that they have picked out the wrong shirt. She locates the correct shirt and approaches and hands it to IVY.

RAINEY stays staring at her father. She approaches the body. She takes a cloth from the basin and lightly caresses his lips, his eyes and his cheeks with it. She replaces the cloth, takes ABENDIGO's shirt from IVY and begins to dress her father. The others stay close to her supporting her when she needs assistance moving his limbs and torso.

Finally she places his shoes on his feet and delicately ties the laces. She takes a strip from the soldiers uniform and places it in ABENDIGO's hand. She kisses him. She leaves the room. MICHAEL follows.

IVY approaches the bed. She gazes at ABENDIGO for a few moments then lays herself on the bed beside him, her head on his chest. Her arms around his waist.

Scene Eleven

ABENDIGO lies in honour in the casket in front of the pulpit. The church is filled with mourners. They file by the casket one by one. The mourners often speak with RAINEY briefly. She nods her head and hugs them or shakes their hands. Often, no words need to be said between them. There are no words.

RAINEY makes her way outside where MICHAEL stands alone.

Several young men stream past them carrying little Black lawn ornaments to where ABENDIGO's land meets the cemetery. There is now an enormous gap in the hedge and several men are building a kind of mausoleum with the liberated lawn jockeys, in the space where the hedge once stood.

RAINEY
It was a beautiful service.

MICHAEL
How are you doing?

RAINEY
I'm fine.

MICHAEL
You're sure?

RAINEY
Yes. Yes. And you?

MICHAEL
Yes. Fine.

> *RAINEY takes an envelope from out of her pocket and hands it to MICHAEL.*

RAINEY
I meant to give this to you before.

MICHAEL
Oh. You didn't have to – I mean, right now.

RAINEY
I know. But there's never a right time.

MICHAEL
All these endings.

RAINEY
All these beginnings.

MICHAEL smiles uneasily.

Did you feel that...? When he passed...? When he passed on.... It was so.... Like.... Like when Janie was born. That rush of life. That power that fills the space.

MICHAEL
Yes. Yes. Remember her head came out, and she started to scream, even before she was born, fully born, there she was, her head protruding from between your thighs, just screaming. And I felt so much. The room was so full.... Of her, and you, and me...

RAINEY
Does she come to you?

MICHAEL
Yes. I think so.

RAINEY
I don't believe in angels or anything, but sometimes I get a glimpse, I don't know, out of the corner of my eye. In the air – flying. It doesn't make sense, does it?

MICHAEL
I, I almost smell her. As if she were a perfume all around me. Sometimes only for a few minutes, seconds even.

RAINEY
She'll have company now. Lying between Martha and Papa.

MICHAEL
Willing that piece of land to the church was a brilliant idea.

RAINEY
He always got his own way. He wanted to face the creek and he's facing the creek.

MICHAEL
Though until we complete the land transfer it's not officially consecrated ground.

RAINEY
All of Negro Creek is consecrated ground.

MICHAEL
Not according to section 47 of the Cemeteries Act, it isn't.

RAINEY
I won't tell if you don't.

MICHAEL
The mausoleum of Black lawn jockeys is sure coming along.

RAINEY
What am I going to do with the rest of them?

MICHAEL smiles. RAINEY smiles back.

MICHAEL
What are you going to do with the house?

RAINEY
I don't know.

MICHAEL glances back at the mourners who have just about finished viewing.

MICHAEL
We should get back. Ready?

RAINEY
No, not really. It's been hard, but watching him being lowered into the ground.... All right.

MICHAEL
All right.

RAINEY
And we'll pick a day – to sort out Janie's things before I...

MICHAEL
That would be good.

RAINEY
I know what I'm going to do with those dolls.

MICHAEL looks at her curiously.

Ready?

MICHAEL
Yes.

MICHAEL folds the large envelope and slips it into his jacket pocket. RAINEY and he make their way into the church.

A solo voice sings "Precious Lord, take my hand," as the coffin is closed.

A joyful sadness permeates from Negro Creek A.M.E. Church. MICHAEL opens his Bible and looks at a passage. Sounds and voices become quiet in expectation. He is silent for a moment. He closes the Bible.

Here – at this final hour, in this quiet place, Negro Creek has come to bid farewell to one of its most shining sons, a father, a leader, gone from us forever.... And even in death he leads. He asked that I be brief. He asked that I replace solemn words with joyful ones. He asked me to let you know that he lived a good life. A very good life. And he asked for a joyful hymn. "Abide With Me."

CHORUS
Abide with me: fast falls the even tide,
The darkness deepens: Lord, with me abide.
When other helpers fail, and comforts flee,
Help of the helpless, O abide with me!

Pallbearers take the coffin from the church to the cemetery. RAINEY follows close behind. MICHAEL and the congregation proceed behind RAINEY. They make a joyful noise.

Swift to its close ebbs out life's little day,
Earth's joys grow dim, its glories pass away,
Change and decay in all around I see,
O Thou who changest not, abide with me!

Epilogue

The celebration is over. RAINEY is alone by the creek which swells and moves at her gaze. She holds several beautiful Black dolls in her arms. ABENDIGO appears along one side of the stage and slowly makes his way to the living water. He is greeted by the souls that make up the water. They assist him as he joins them and begins to move as one with them in the creek, as the creek.

One by one RAINEY releases the dolls into the undulating liquid of bodies. The water carries them along the surface for a few moments before they are consumed.

RAINEY is still for several moments. She then searches out a small patch of earth at the water's edge and places a morsel of it into her mouth. MICHAEL appears in time to see her do this. He approaches her. They stand together, alone and separate under the heavens.

MICHAEL
Numinous mysterium tremendum et fascinans.

RAINEY
Numinous mysterium tremendum et fascinans. Don't tell me. God's mystery tremendous and fascinating.

MICHAEL
(impressed) That's good.

RAINEY
The pure unadulterated awe of her.

MICHAEL
Her?

RAINEY
Yes, her.

MICHAEL
Her.

RAINEY
Pa says that heaven is Negro Creek. Sometimes, if you get still, quiet enough, early in the morning or real late at night, you can almost hear her, hear the land singing.

They listen to the silence.

People. That's all we have in this world really, isn't it?

MICHAEL
Don't go.

RAINEY turns to MICHAEL as if she is about to say something, but nothing comes out of her mouth.

Don't go.

Slowly, MICHAEL takes a morsel of earth from the edge of the creek and places it into his own mouth. RAINEY watches him. She approaches him and brushes off the dirt at the corner of his mouth and on his hands. She kisses his hand. He brings her close. They hold each other close for the first time in a very long time. A sudden wave of sobbing is released from her. She kisses him lightly. He kisses her hard.

RAINEY
Oh…. Oh God…. Oh God…

They begin to make love – desperately. And in the process, MICHAEL's jacket, with the envelope containing the signed divorce papers in it, falls into the creek.

The jacket and the divorce papers float along the surface of the water for several moments until they are completely devoured. The choral voices resound as the lights fade to black.

The end.